W9-AWE-164

THE WOMAN WHO PRETENDED TO BE WHO SHE WAS

THE WOMAN WHO PRETENDED TO BE WHO SHE WAS

Myths of Self-Imitation

Wendy Doniger

OXFORD
UNIVERSITY PRESS
2005

OXFORD
UNIVERSITY PRESS

Oxford   New York
Auckland   Bangkok   Buenos Aires   Cape Town   Chennai
Dar es Salaam   Delhi   Hong Kong   Istanbul   Karachi   Kolkata
Kuala Lumpur   Madrid   Melbourne   Mexico City   Mumbai   Nairobi
São Paulo   Shanghai   Taipei   Tokyo   Toronto

Copyright © 2005 by Oxford University Press, Inc.

Published by Oxford University Press, Inc.
198 Madison Avenue, New York, New York 10016

www.oup.com

Oxford is a registered trademark of Oxford University Press

All rights reserved. No part of this publication may be reproduced,
stored in a retrieval system, or transmitted, in any form or by any means,
electronic, mechanical, photocopying, recording, or otherwise,
without the prior permission of Oxford University Press.

Library of Congress Cataloging-in-Publication Data
Doniger, Wendy.
The woman who pretended to be who she was : Myths of self-imitation / Wendy Doniger
p. cm.
Includes bibliographical references and index.
ISBN 0-19-516016-9
1. Impersonation in literature. 2. Self in literature. I. Title.
PN56.I47D66 2004
809'.93353—dc22   2004004039

"Before the World Was Made," by W. B. Yeats, reprinted by permission of A. P. Watt
Ltd. on behalf of Michael B. Yeats and Scribner, an imprint of Simon & Schuster
Adult Publishing Group, from THE COLLECTED WORKS OF W. B. YEATS,
VOLUME I: THE POEMS, REVISED, edited by Richard J. Finneran. Copyright © 1933
by the Macmillan Company; copyright renewed © 1961 by Bertha Georgie Yeats.

1 3 5 7 9 8 6 4 2

Printed in the United States of America
on acid-free paper

For R.D., born on June 9th
Rita Doniger [1911] and Raine Daston [1951]

ACKNOWLEDGMENTS

An early version of this book was presented as an Erbschaft Unserer Zeit Lecture at the Einstein Forum, Berlin, in December 1997, where Lorraine Daston's brilliant response revolutionized my approach to the topic; that lecture, and Daston's response, were published as *Der Mann, der mit seiner eigenen Frau Ehebruch beging; Mit einem Kommentar von Lorraine Daston* (Berlin: Suhrkamp, 1999), and I am grateful to Suhrkamp for permission to reproduce parts of that book here in English. Back in Chicago, William Elison inspired me with ideas about Filmistan, Jim Chandler and Tom Gunning aided and abetted me in our shared addiction to B films, and Sarita Warshawsky brought her deep appreciation of Wagner to bear on my chapter about Siegfried. I am grateful to Annie Dillard for encouraging me to retell several stories that I have told in print before, because, she assured me, none of my readers would remember any of my earlier books.

Some parts of the book, in embryo, have been published as "The Man Who Committed Adultery with His Own Wife," in *The Longing For Home*, edited by Leroy S. Rouner (Notre Dame, Indiana: University of Notre Dame Press, 1997): 128–137; "When a Kiss Is Still a Kiss: Memories of the Mind and the Body in Ancient India and Hollywood," the *Kenyon Review* 19, no. 1 (Winter 1997): 118–133; "The Dreams and Dramas of a Jealous Hindu Queen: Vasavadatta," in *Dream Cultures: Toward a Comparative History of Dreaming*, edited by Guy Stroumsa and David Shulman (New York: Oxford University Press, 1999): 74–84; "The Mythology of the Face-Lift," *Social Research*, "Faces," 67, no. 1 (Spring 2000): 99–126; "The Man Who Committed Adultery with His Own Wife" (Program notes for the Chicago Shakespeare Theatre production of *All's Well That Ends Well*), *Playbill*, April 2000, 24–26; "The Masques of Gods and Demons," in *Behind the Mask: Dance, Healing and Possession in South Indian Ritual*, edited by David Shulman and Deborah Thiagarajan (Ann Arbor, Michigan: University of Michigan Press, 2004): 101-125; "Self-Imitation in Literature," *Kenyon Review* 26, no. 2 (Spring 2004); and "Pretending to Be Who You Think You Are: Identity and Masks," *Union Seminary Quarterly Review* (Spring 2004): 17-31.

I owe an even greater debt than usual to my editor, Cynthia Read, who read and minutely commented on not one but *two* drafts line by line, page by page, and realized, before I did, that I had accidentally written two books rolled up into one. I forgive her for simultaneously urging me to cut and plying me with new examples of books and films ("The stubborn beast flesh kept creeping back," as on the Island of Dr. Moreau). William Elison provided the index and countless useful suggestions. This book is dedicated to Lorraine Daston, who let me talk about self-imitation for hours on end, year after year, and responded in ways that always clarified and often revolutionized my understanding; and when, as usual, I couldn't see the forest for the trees, she told me what the book was about. It is also dedicated to my mother, Rita Roth Doniger, who brought me up on Wagner and *Rosenkavalier*.

Havana, Cuba

CONTENTS

THE WOMAN WHO PRETENDED TO BE WHO SHE WAS

Introduction
The Self-Impersonation of Mythology

When I was a little girl I went to the movies; poor Cary Grant thought his wife was dead, but Irene Dunne, she comes back.

Oh, that just happens in the movies.

> Doris Day (as Ellen) and Polly Bergen (as Bianca),
> in Michael Gordon's *Move Over, Darling* (1963)

Basically, Shakespeare stole everything he ever wrote. . . . Essentially, Shakespeare was a formula writer. Once he found a device that worked, he used it over and over again.

> *The Compleat Works of Wllm Shakspr (Abridged)*

PRE- AND POSTMODERN NARRATIVE RECYCLING

Many cultures tell stories about people who pretend to be other people pretending to be them, thus in effect masquerading as themselves, impersonating themselves, pretending to be precisely what they are. This great theme, in literature and in life, tells us that many people must put on masks to discover who they are under the covert masks they usually wear, so that the overt mask reveals rather than conceals the truth, reveals the self beneath the self; and it tells us that, although such masquerades cannot change people into other people, they may change them into others among their many selves.

The widespread distribution of the theme of self-impersonation argues for both its literary power and its human value. The stories in this book do not range over the whole earth (I do not, for instance, draw upon Native American or African texts[1]) but are drawn largely from the Indo-European world, particularly Sanskrit literature,[2] medieval European courtly literature, Shakespeare, Wagner, Hollywood, and Bollywood. Nevertheless, they cover a pretty wide swath of time and space, from

c. 400 BCE (the *Mahabharata*) through contemporary items in the *New York Times*. Throughout this narrative territory, all the stories cited here are related loosely by historical contact and even more loosely by enduring human nature. Henry Louis Gates Jr. has argued that the feelings involved in passing (black people passing as white—or in some of our stories, white as black as white as black) are "well-nigh universal. The thematic elements of passing—fragmentation, alienation, liminality, self-fashioning—echo the great themes of modernism."[3] But since they are, indeed, "well-nigh universal" (I would prefer to call them cross-cultural[4]), they are also both premodern and postmodern.

The great insight that postmodern writers pride themselves on having discovered—that the copy is more real than the original[5]—is itself nothing but a copy, a reinvented wheel. The reality status of the copy haunts the myth of self-imitation in folk and literary sources throughout recorded human culture. Postmodernism turns out to be premodern, a copy not merely of ancient forms but, sometimes, of itself; it has been called "an idea taken over by its own caricature."[6] Both the postmodern fascination with individuals reinventing themselves and the postcolonial obsession with nations constructing their identities are implicated in this study, though I will seldom address these themes explicitly. Thus this book is postmodern both in its method—its concern for eclecticism and ways of self-imagining and self-construction—and in its subject, its focus upon imitations, copies.

The very form of myth is a kind of self-imitation: the style of a myth immediately identifies its genre to its audience by mimicking the style of another myth. In substance, too, myths tell you what they have told you before and what you already know; they build a potentially infinite number of stories by rearranging a limited number of known mythic themes. Scholars of myth now call the process of recycling these inherited mythic themes *bricolage*, from the French term for the work of the handyman (the *bricoleur*) who makes new things out of broken pieces of the old, a term that the structural anthropologist Claude Lévi-Strauss applied to the work of the mythmaker, whose toolbox consists of fragments of old stories—he called them mythemes[7]— that can be recycled in new stories.[8] Each culture chooses the scraps it wants to keep; some have proved more recyclable than others. But the process of recycling is endemic to the genre; the need to hear the same story over and over again is in part explained by Freud's insight into the repetition compulsion, the mind's tendency to repeat traumatic events (in dreams or storytelling) in order to deal with them,[9] or by Lévi-Strauss's useful insight that certain enduring and insoluble human dilemmas and paradoxes generate a potentially infinite variety of invariably failed answers and solutions that different storytellers have proposed for them.[10] As Terence Cave points out, the sense of cliché that drives the myth "is also the sense of repetition, a compulsive returning to the 'same' place, a place already known, as if one were discovering it for the first time."[11] Mircea Eliade called this essence of myth, after Nietzsche, "the eternal return,"[12] and it is certainly the essence of a masquerade: to present something known in such a way that people mistake it for something unknown (or the reverse).

And this process of self-replication can extend into the future as well as the past. In his essay on Rudyard Kipling, George Orwell offers a definition of a certain type of poetry that functions, I think, like myth (or B movies):

> A good bad poem is a graceful monument to the obvious. . . . However sentimental it may be, its sentiment is "true" sentiment in the sense that you are bound to find yourself thinking the thought it expresses sooner or later, and then, if you happen to know the poem, it will come back into your mind and seem better than it did before.[13]

In the light of Orwell's definition, a myth is a time-released self-imitation, experienced first unconsciously (at the time you hear or read it) and then consciously (when you recollect it on the stimulus of the corresponding event in your life).

Shakespeare lovers may regard the transition from the Bard to the B movie as a bathetic plunge. Certainly the individual genius of the Shakespearean variants illuminates all the others, but so, I would argue, does the individual genius of ancient Indian authors like Harsha and the inspired anonymous authors of many folk variants. Stanley Cavell maintains that "the Shakespearean tradition also survives in film (thus implying that film may provide an access for us to that tradition)"; he views the entire shared corpus as a myth, with variants and inversions.[14] I agree, but I also intend to extend Cavell's paradigm in order to examine the elements Shakespeare and films have in common not only with one another but with other variants of the self-impersonation theme in world literature and folklore. Where Cavell uses Shakespeare and European philosophy (mainly Kant) to provide a context for the remarriage films, I would use a wide range of world mythology, particularly Indian mythology, as the context for both Shakespeare and the films. For since Shakespeare does some inheriting of his own, from the broader narrative tradition of the mythology that films also draw upon, what we have is not so much a family tree as a kind of eternal triangle:

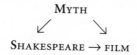

MYTH

SHAKESPEARE → FILM

Films, particularly lowbrow popular movies, B movies (or even B minus movies), provide a rich compost for myths to grow in; they are the reductio ad absurdum of many myths, for Hollywood is as much a myth factory as it is a dream factory. It has even been stated as a kind of law of nature that the worse the film, the better the metaphysics.[15] To make money, filmmakers take what works and copy it, from gross plots and titles right down to names of characters and stunning camera angles; motifs circulate and recirculate in Hollywood much as they do in the medieval cycles or in a Wagnerian opera. What we call mythemes when they occur in myths, we call clichés when they occur in B movies. Whole films recirculate in this way;[16] we might call these retellings of old stories "covers," as popular musicians call their explicit revisions of other musicians' songs.[17] This is Hollywood's version of the repetition compulsion. (In *Move Over, Darling*, the 1963 cover of *My Favorite Wife* [1940], Doris Day explicitly refers to the earlier film as one she saw years ago.) Some people call film plots junk food mythology, but really they're comfort food, mythology like mother used to make.

CHRONOLOGY AND INTERTEXTUALITY

As always, my first concern is to demonstrate the importance and distribution of a mythological theme (in this case, the theme of self-impersonation) and only secondarily to explain what it means and why it recurs so frequently and so widely, let alone how each variant was fashioned by its own time. It would be good to be able to say of a particular story, "This text was written at this moment in history, when the following events were taking place, which are reflected in the text." But in general, it can't be done. From time to time, when we can date a text, we can argue that a particular idea, whatever its history, became useful to a particular author at a particular moment; a knowledge of the historical context, when we can know it, often sheds light on the reasons for the author's choice of that motif at that time, but in the absence of such knowledge we can simply acknowledge that that motif is present in this text and not in another. Some of the ancient Indian sources, such as the plays of Harsha, can be roughly dated, but the *Mahabharata* cannot be dated even within a century. We can date the European materials with far more confidence than the Indian materials, yet even so, the circulation of all of these stories through oral transmission considerably weakens any argument we might make that an idea in a particular text is responding to its moment in history. We have such a small fragment of the variants of any story, with so many holes in the total fabric of ancient, medieval, and even contemporary popular versions, that to arrange what we do have in any sort of chronological order can be misleading, since variants recorded later may actually draw upon earlier, lost variants.

Sometimes we can at least trace a relative chronology, which is sufficient to allow us to argue that an idea in one text might be the source of that same idea when it occurs in another, later text, or to trace a moral development, sometimes up, sometimes down, with occasional doubling back. More important, a relative chronology allows us to observe the workings of intertextuality: one text quotes another, builds on another, often transforming it. Terry Eagleton neatly sorts out the difference between the conventional and postmodern meanings of intertextuality. "Good old-fashioned literary influence," which Harold Bloom had in mind when he said that "the meaning of a poem is another poem," is generally conscious and sporadic; but postmodernist intertextuality is unconscious and so pervasive that, as Eagleton puts it, "it is impossible to open your mouth without quoting."[18] I use intertextuality primarily in the old-fashioned sense of conscious quotation, but its postmodern meanings are also relevant to this study, and the two aspects often overlap. Either variety of intertextuality, conscious or unconscious, or both, may lead to self-imitation, when author A quotes author B quoting author A.

Intertextuality has many uses. It opens many doors that the quixotic search for an absolute chronology slams in our faces. It lets us eavesdrop on the conversations between storytellers centuries and continents apart. It lets us observe the workings of the narrator's art not only within a storytelling tradition but in the transition from one genre to another, as Wagner transforms a medieval source into an opera or Mervyn LeRoy transforms a James Hilton novel into a film. Tracing a theme in this way illuminates the multiple facets of both the theme itself and the genres that adapt it. Thus, for instance, we encounter a different concept of the person in, on the one hand, myths and folktales, which tend to elaborate on generic types who learn but never change, and on the other hand, modern novels, which tend to dwell more on idiosyncratic individuals, who do change.

THE MÖBIUS STRIP AND THE ZEN DIAGRAM

Even in cases where we must abandon our hope for a specific historical context or an absolute chronology or even a relative chronology, we can argue for a more general sort of intertextuality, for a distribution of themes that appear now in one version, now in another, each drawing unconsciously (as any postmodernist would argue) upon an untraceable common source rather than one drawing upon another. These stories overlap like the rings in a Venn diagram, each adding another piece to the great narrative jigsaw puzzle; even if two texts draw upon the same sources or, still more closely linked, are composed simultaneously, even by the same author, one text may choose to use one detail, another text another. The result is a pattern that Wittgenstein described in his theory of "family likenesses" or "family resemblances" in ideas:[19] all the people in the group portrait clearly resemble one another, but there's no one feature they all have in common. This concept is also captured by a term taken from microbiology: polythetic, designating a group of items that share a number of common characteristics, without any one of these being essential for membership in the group or class in question.

Wittgenstein thought almost all classes were of that sort and hence not amenable to the sharp definitions demanded by logicians (including his younger self). Stories, too, are not logical proofs or moral agendas but meditations on the human condition—and Wittgenstein's approach is particularly appropriate to stories in which people make themselves resemble other people, often members of their family.[20] In our day, Carlo Ginzburg adapted Wittgenstein's idea for his studies of history and myth: a basic set of images attract "other elements, whose presence is fluctuating, contingent: they are sometimes absent, sometimes present in an attenuated form. Their superimposition and intersection impart to the figures constitutive of the series . . . a family likeness."[21] Thus there are many resemblances between individual pairs, but no central defining essence.

In the realm of narratives, merely telling the same tale from the standpoint of a different character often produces a new story (as Tom Stoppard demonstrated in *Rosencrantz and Guildenstern Are Dead*). And as the themes overlap, it becomes apparent that there is no actual center to the group, no single indispensable or defining theme, merely a shifting cluster. Often a story has so many of the themes of a particular narrative pattern that the Venn diagram structure can justify including the tale in the corpus. The search for the source, for the urtext, the single text from which all others derive, was a nineteenth-century game that we no longer play, though it is a habit that dies hard; people still tend, when they are not paying attention (or when they are paying attention only to politics), to trace everything back to Homer or to the Vedas. But this is a mug's game: there is no one source, and even if there were, there are more interesting things to look for in the history of a text. Sometimes it might appear that a particularly prominent theme is at the center of a cluster of stories, but then you may encounter a new set of variants in which another theme predominates and the quasi-center shifts. This emptiness in the center, like the still center of a storm, suggests that the figure might better be named a Zen diagram (which is not, as you might think, a Venn diagram with just one ring or one that has an empty ring in the center but one that has no central ring).

The structure of each of the stories also involves rings, not only the rings of the Zen diagram but also a logic that follows the course of the ring of a Möbius strip, a flat tape that joins its ends to form a circle but with a twist that makes the path of the surface change sides infinitely, so that one side leads to the other and back again. The characters in these stories circle back on themselves in a ring with a twist in it—the twist of self-deception or the deception of others, of ambivalence or ambiguity, or of the paradox of married sexual love.

This book is the last in a trilogy, of which the first two are *Splitting the Differ-ence: Gender and Myth in Ancient Greece and India* (1999) and *The Bedtrick: Tales of Sex and Masquerade* (2000).[22] All three books involve confusions of identity in erotic situations fraught with implications for memory, forgetfulness, and inadver-tent self-reference and self-imitation. In all three, women are the protagonists more often than men. But where *Splitting the Difference* was about fragmented identities and *The Bedtrick* about false identifies, this book is about multiple identities, as they overlap within the unconscious and conscious thought of an individual. And where *Splitting the Difference* was about gender and *The Bedtrick* about sex, this book is about love. As the book took shape in my mind, I sometimes felt that I, too, was falling into the trap of self-imitation, that I kept stumbling back upon ideas I had written about before—such as the bedtrick (the secret substitution of one person for another in bed)—and reverting to texts that I had analyzed before—such as the myths of Shiva and Parvati or the film *Shattered*.[23] I keep coming back from the Hindu myths to the Jewish story of the Rabbi from Cracow, which is a story about someone who must return home in order to find the treasures that he learns about in foreign lands; and I keep reverting to the reverting image of the Möbius strip.[24] Mr. Dick, in Charles Dickens's *David Copperfield*, couldn't keep King Charles's head from getting into anything he tried to write, and that Rabbi seems to haunt me in a similar way (as does Dickens's image of King Charles's head, which I have used before to justify reusing things I had used before[25]), though always with that Möbius twist that makes each citation quite different when it comes 'round again. So I hope that if I have in fact picked up some of the same old chestnuts, at least I have cooked them in some new dishes, and I know that I have found new texts that challenge and modify the old ideas. I have also been able to treat some of these seminal texts at greater length than was possible in earlier works to which they were more peripheral. But in many ways, this book is an imitation of a book by Wendy Doniger.[26]

CHAPTER ONE

The Mythology of Self-Impersonation

Everyone wishes to be Cary Grant. Even I wish to be Cary Grant.

Cary Grant

SELF-IMPERSONATION

The people in these stories set out to become other people but, through a kind of triple cross[1] or double back, end up as themselves after all, masquerading as other people who turn out to be masquerading as them. This sort of self-imitation or self-impersonation is a basic human way of negotiating reality, illusion, identity, and authenticity, not to mention memory, amnesia,[2] and the process of aging. Many of the stories involve marriage and adultery, for stories of sexual betrayal cut to the heart of the crisis of identity; as Terence Cave has put it, "Recognition plots are full of epistemophiliacs: the knowledge they seek has the character, whether explicit or implicit, of an impossible or incomprehensible sexual knowledge."[3] A *New Yorker* cartoon in 2003 depicted a man in a bar saying to another man, "My wife ran off with the guy who stole my identity."[4] Some of the rejected wives in these stories win back their forgetful husbands by tricking them into committing adultery with their own wives;[5] other wives (and occasionally husbands) resort to gender masquerades, face-lifts, or reincarnation.

A modern literary classic about a man who unwittingly impersonates himself is Oscar Wilde's play *The Importance of Being Earnest* (1895). When Jack, who has pretended for years to be named not Jack but Ernest, suddenly discovers his name is really Ernest after all, he says to his fiancée, "It is a terrible thing for a man to find out suddenly that all his life he has been speaking nothing but the truth. Can you forgive me?" And she replies, "I can. For I feel that you are sure to change."[6] In the film *The Awful Truth* (Leo McCarey, 1937), when Jerry (Cary Grant) comes home a day early and catches his wife Lucy (Irene Dunne) in the company of a man whom he wrongly assumes she has slept with, she says, "You've come home and caught me in a truth." But inadvertent truth telling is not always a joke; it has tragic results in a Japanese story collected in the twentieth century:

> A mountain ascetic named Kongo-in disturbed a fox's nap. In revenge, the fox allowed himself to be seen changing into the semblance of Kongo-in by a group of the priests' colleagues. When the fox next appeared to them in the form of Kongo-in, they beat him viciously. Only when he was nearly dead did they realize that he was not the fox at all, but the real Kongo-in.[7]

This is a twist on the story of the boy who cried wolf when there was no wolf, so that no one believed him when there really was a wolf. In this tale, there really was *not* a fox in the final scene, but the imagined double disguise (man-as-fox-as-man) made the truth appear to be a double lie. Kongo-in unconsciously became what Winston Churchill accused Clement Attlee of being: a sheep in sheep's clothing. (He also resembled the cartoon sheep who said to another sheep, "Sometimes I worry that I'm a wolf dressed like me."[8])

Whole societies may engage in conscious or unconscious self-imitation. One sort of self-imitation occurs whenever societies first make rules that prove difficult to keep and then devise ways of circumventing their own rules, making them pretend to be where they would have been in the first place had they not made those rules. Laws about pornography inspire this sort of double twist. In the 1960s, when English literature was still heavily censored, Steven Marcus's *The Other Victorians: A Study of Sexuality and Pornography in Mid-Nineteenth-Century England*, a scholarly book *about* pornography, was often read for the citations *of* pornography, which thus became, in effect, instances of pornography masquerading as scholarship masquerading as pornography. Adam Gopnik described a contemporary version of this phenomenon:

> The girls in the Va Va Voom Room are pretending to be live girls, and the audience is pretending to be a burlesque audience. But the performers do all the things that live girls do—taking off their clothes to music while writhing in pasties and thong—and the audience does all the things that burlesque audiences once did, hooting and applauding as the dancers dance, so that in the end it isn't clear how the pretense is different from the actual thing. One has to read the entire book from beginning to end to be reminded that there are inverted commas embossed on both covers.[9]

Many of the characters in the stories of self-imitation seem to enclose significant portions of their lives between inverted commas, knowingly or unknowingly. That's what kitsch and camp are all about: Batman, on television, pretending to be Batman in a comic book, and so forth. As Susan Sontag put it, "Camp sees everything in quotation marks."[10]

Physical objects, as well as people, can be manipulated by a society bent on circumventing its own rules. Alan Dundes has documented the double-back logic that orthodox Jews maintain in order to use, on the Sabbath, machines such as elevators and refrigerators that they would have used had they not made rules forbidding themselves to use them.[11] Kosher food, too, often inspires the left hand to imitate the right hand imitating the left hand: "Occasionally these food subterfuges can backfire. . . . One hundred Orthodox Jews from Baltimore were on a fund-raising cruise in Chesapeake Bay. One of the 'kosher' delicacies served was in the shape of imitation crab cakes. Later, upon inquiry, it turned out that 'the imitation crab cakes were the real McCoy.'"[12] Orthodox Jewish women must shave their heads and wear wigs (to imitate real hair); but some women keep their hair and do it in such a way that it *looks* like a wig (that looks like hair), while others shave their heads but then have their own hair made into the wig they wear.

Other ethnicities indulge in other sorts of self-imitation. The inhabitants of places known for their ethnic charm, where tourism has become a major industry, consciously exaggerate their own stereotypes to please the visitors, the British laying on the ye olde with a shovel, the Irish their blarney, the Parisians their disdain for tourists. The politics of colonialism produced another, more serious sort of self-parody, in this case perhaps unconscious; Edward Said wrote of "the paradox of an Arab regarding himself as an 'Arab' of the sort put out by Hollywood. . . . The modern Orient, in short, participates in its own Orientalizing."[13] Orientalism, like other forms of political domination, has also inspired what James Scott has taught us to recognize as the arts of resistance, the weapons of the weak,[14] which include a kind of apparent self-mockery that actually mocks the mockers.

Self-Impersonation by the Famous and the Literary

Individuals are often driven to self-impersonation through the pressure of public expectations. Hollywood actors under the star system were expected to play the same part over and over, their marketability depending on their predictability.[15] The mannerisms of Cary Grant became the staple of impersonators;[16] one need only recall the running joke of Tony Curtis imitating Cary Grant in Billy Wilder's 1959 film *Some Like It Hot*, capturing Grant's weird upper-class Cockney accent so well that Jack Lemmon mutters (in the Cary Grant accent), "Nobody talks like that." Famously,

Cary Grant (né Archibald Leach) remarked: "Everyone wishes to be Cary Grant. Even I wish to be Cary Grant."[17] He constantly mocked his own self-imitation in his films. In *His Girl Friday* (Howard Hawks, 1940), Grant plays a newspaperman named Walter Burns; when the corrupt mayor threatens him, Grant says, "The last man who said that to me was Archie Leach, just a week before he cut his throat."[18] And when Walter (Grant) sends a prostitute to proposition his ex-wife's fiancé (played by Ralph Bellamy) and she asks what he looks like, he replies, "He looks like that fella in the movies—Ralph Bellamy."

Grant was the best at this but not the only one. Bob Hope's writers said of him, "We took his own characteristics and exaggerated them. . . . He thought he was playing a character. He was playing, really, the real Bob Hope."[19] Katharine Hepburn played Katharine Hepburn for half a century, and when she was young, she was said to be such a bad actress that even when Philip Barry wrote a part for an actress modeled directly upon her (Tracy Lord in *The Philadelphia Story*), she was fired, "suggesting the remarkable fact that she couldn't yet play herself."[20] Nor, apparently, could Roger Moore play himself, according to Anthony Lane: "In *The Man with the Golden Gun*, there was an ill-advised twist in which the real Moore was confronted by a waxwork of himself. Even now, studio insiders like to gossip about precisely which of the two Rogers was put under contract for the remaining films."[21] The ultimate variation on this theme is the casting of an actor in a cameo role "appearing as himself," a very old trick that has become more prevalent than ever in this postmodern age. (In a nice twist, the real mothers of Mia Farrow and Ginger Rogers occasionally played the mothers of their daughters in films.)

Within films, self-imitation is an old gag. In the Marx Brothers' *Animal Crackers* (Victor Heerman, 1930), Groucho says to Chico, who plays Signor Emanuel Ravelli, "You remind me of Emanuel Ravelli." "But I *am* Emanuel Ravelli." "Then no wonder you look like him!" This trick crossed the border from film into both literature and real life. As for literature, a woman (in a story by Annie Dillard) who looked like Ingrid Bergman remarked drily that Ingrid Bergman "at least escaped always hearing she looked like Ingrid Bergman."[22] But perhaps Bergman did not in fact escape such accusations, nor was Hollywood the only locus for this sort of hokey. The hockey player Wayne Gretzky complained, "The hardest part of being Wayne Gretzky is that I get compared to Wayne Gretzky."[23] Hillary Rodham Clinton reported: "Suddenly a woman came up to me. 'You sure look like Hillary Clinton,' she said. 'So I'm told,' I answered."[24] A story was told about a Mick Jagger groupie who said of every man she slept with, "He's great, but he's no Mick Jagger," until she finally got to sleep with Jagger himself and reported, "Great, but no Mick Jagger."[25]

The trap of self-imitation caught many famous writers, beginning with Freud himself, whom Jacques Derrida caught red-handed repeating himself, compulsively, in his discussion of the repetition compulsion (in *Beyond the Pleasure Principle*).[26] But the most infamous repeat offender was Ernest Hemingway. In 1948, Cyril Connolly wrote: "Hemingway's tragedy as an artist is that he has not had the versatility to run away fast enough from his imitators."[27] In 1961, Dwight Macdonald wrote what is still, for my money, the most hilarious of the many Hemingway parodies, demonstrating that it was so easy because Hemingway had already become a self-parody: "Most of the tricks were good tricks and they worked fine for a while especially in the short stories. . . . Later on the tricks did not look so good. They were the same tricks but they were not fresh any more and nothing is worse than a trick that has gone stale. He knew this but he couldn't invent any new tricks."[28] Commenting on Connolly's remark about imitators, Macdonald added: "The list of Hemingwayesque writers includes James J. Cain . . . and Raymond Chandler. It also includes Hemingway."[29] Macdonald felt that "Hemingway had begun to parody himself" in *The Old Man and the Sea* (1952), and he regarded *Across the River and into the Trees* (1950) as "an unconscious self-parody of almost unbelievable fatuity."[30] In short, "[Hemingway] was trapped in his style as a miner might be trapped underground; the oxygen is slowly used up without any new air coming in." Another twist of self-imitation was added when Hemingway in life began to talk like Hemingway on the page (imitating Hemingway in life). In Lillian Ross's devastating critique (in 1961), Hemingway already revealed himself to be, as Christopher Lasch remarked, "acting out, down to the last detail of his private life, the public image of himself. . . . Even his conversation, a mixture of sporting-world slang, assorted unintelligible grunts, and Indian language, had become a parody of the famous Hemingway style."[31]

But another chain of causation may also be at play here: a person parodied by others may take up that mask and only then engage in self-parody. Henry James said that after reading Max Beerbohm's famous parody of him, "he always felt he was parodying himself."[32] The impressionist Will Jordan claimed that Ed Sullivan had stolen his Ed Sullivan impression, "the mannerisms and the phonetics."[33] And Ray Bolger told Al Hirschfield that "he tried to imitate the figure in Mr. Hirschfield's portrait of him, a dancer with amazingly elastic limbs. Mr. Hirschfield conceded that it was one of the phenomena of caricature that often, in a way, the subject began to look more like the drawing than he actually looked like himself."[34] Macdonald realized that Hemingway after a while "had accepted the public personality that had been built up for him by the press—a well-trained lion, he jumped through all the hoops—and even gloried in the grotesque (but virile) Philistine Miss Ross had innocently depicted."[35] We might, therefore, wonder if Lillian Ross (and Dwight Macdonald) fanned the flames of Hemingway's weakness for self-parody.

Macdonald had published, in 1960, an anthology of parodies in which he included a short section on self-parodies, dividing them into unconscious (by Byron, Poe,

Wordsworth, Dickens, Walt Whitman, and Kipling, among others) and conscious (by Coleridge, Swinburne, Max Beerbohm, and William Faulkner), oddly excluding Hemingway. He defines an unconscious self-parody as "a poem or a passage in which the author is both characteristic and unintentionally absurd."[36] A conscious self-parodist might be defined, in contrast, as someone with all the qualities of a person susceptible to parody by others (such as originality, a strong idiosyncratic voice, and a bold style) but with the essential addition of a sense of humor and self-criticism.

Lasch, writing about several authors, including Hemingway and Norman Mailer, analyzed the more general problem faced by a successful writer:

> Success tempts him to become a public "personality," and if he gives in to the temptation, he soon discovers that it is easier to sell his personality than his ideas. . . . The writer has to stay in character, has to play the part that he has made for himself. . . . The writer creates his part for himself and then proceeds not only to act it but, worse, to believe in it. At length he loses his real self and takes on a synthetic self, which he then proceeds to write about as if it were his real one.[37]

The final indignity comes when the imitation eclipses the original, so that the original is regarded as an imitation of the imitation. This process is captured by the old joke about the person who went to see *Hamlet* for the first time and liked it, but complained, "It does have so many quotations in it."

Macdonald accused Hemingway of transforming his best story, "The Undefeated," into a tale (*The Old Man and the Sea*) told in "a slack, fake-biblical style which retains the mannerism and omits the virtues."[38] Hemingway, especially late Hemingway, was imitating a genre in which English literature conventionally presents its myths, a style not so much "fake-biblical" but, more precisely, fake-King-James-version-of-the-biblical—crossed, in Hemingway's case, with Gertrude Stein. And so Hemingway does read very much like a myth; in parodying himself, he was also parodying myth—which is, as we have seen, already its own self-parody. The "fake-biblical" style of Hemingway also signaled an implicit claim to subjects as important as those in the Bible. In this respect, the medium is also the message, or as William Morris put it long before McLuhan, form follows function.

NATURE IMITATING ART IMITATING NATURE

Lasch said of Hemingway: "Nature imitates art; but when the art is the art of public relations, the results, for a serious writer, are likely to be disastrous."[39] The cliché that "Nature imitates art" already conceals an implication of self-imitation, for the punch comes from our assumption that art imitates nature. What the cliché is saying, therefore, is that nature is itself already an imitation of the imitation of nature by art. A good example of this phenomenon is what has been called "the Werther effect."[40] In 1774, Goethe was inspired, by the suicide of K. W. Jerusalem and his own frustrated passion for Charlotte Buff, to write a novel (*The Sorrows of Young Werther*) in which Werther commits suicide because of his frustrated passion for Charlotte. (Art imitating life.) The novel became a sensation; the two figures were portrayed on breadboxes and Meissen porcelain; and "all over Europe large numbers of young people committed suicide with a copy of the book clutched in their hands or buried in their pockets."[41] Public outrage against Goethe grew so strong that he added to later editions a final stanza spoken by Werther's ghost to the reader: "Be a man and do not follow me." (Life imitating art imitating life.) A fictional depiction of the Werther effect occurs in Graham Greene's *Our Man in Havana* (1958), when a vacuum-cleaner salesman pretending to be a British spy fills his fictional reports with tales about secret agents whom he invents—only to discover that they are real people whom enemy agents start assassinating. Another variant was Orson Welles's 1938 radio broadcast of H. G. Wells's *The War of the Worlds*, which pretended to be a radio broadcast of an invasion from Mars and fooled many people into unwittingly acting out the role of the panic-stricken public in the play.

Nature often imitates the plastic arts. M. C. Escher's famous image of the hand (surely Dürer's hand?) drawing the hand that is drawing it is a marvelous visualization of this insight. Artistic forms often produce self-imitating illusions: in Euripides's *Alcestis* and in Shakespeare's *The Winter's Tale*, what is said to be a statue of a woman turns out to be the real woman. These representations of women are replaced by the women they pretend to be representing and thus are self-imitations. But some Greek myths argue that the first human being was a statue that was subsequently brought to life, so that any statue is ultimately a self-imitation—an imitation of a human who is an imitation of the original human, a statue.[42] As Roland Barthes remarks of the statue of an ideal woman, "This relation, in the opposite direction, gives us the Pygmalion myth: a real woman is born from the statue."[43]

In Honoré de Balzac's novella *Sarrasine* (1830–31), a Frenchman named Sarrasine mistakes an Italian castrato, La Zambinella, for a woman. As Balzac tells the story, we first encounter a painting that depicts La Zambinella as a man; we then learn that the painting was not made from life but copied from a sculpture that depicted La Zambinella as a woman. As Balzac says, "But that great painter never saw the original and maybe you'd admire it less if you knew that this daub was copied from the statue of a woman."[44] Commenting upon this passage, Barthes remarks: "The duplication of bodies is linked to the instability of the sexual paradigm, which makes the castrato waver between boy and woman. The picture was copied from a statue, true, but this statue was copied from a false woman. In other words, the statement is true with regard only to the statue and false with regard to the woman." When Sarrasine finally sees the statue of the woman, he cries out, "It's an illusion," and Barthes comments that the statue is an "illusion" not in the banal sense of pretending to be real, material, when it is not, but because the internal hollowness of the statue "reproduces the central deficiency of the castrato: the statue is ironically true."[45] The irony is created by the double masquerade. The painting is illusory in a different sense: since it has a back but no inside, "it cannot provoke the *indiscreet* act by which one might try to find out what there is *behind* the canvas."[46] The chicken/egg pendulum swings from human to art (painting) back to human and then back to art (sculpture), but behind the masks it moves from castrato-as-castrato to castrato-as-woman-as-painting-as-man to castrato-as-woman to castrato-as-woman-as-sculpture-as-woman (more precisely, since the painting is based on the sculpture, to castrato-as-woman-as-sculpture-as-woman-as-painting-as-man). The argument for the authenticity of the statue is that just as two wrongs make a right or two negatives a positive, two unreals make a real canceling out the false middle terms. Statues usually lie (they are not filled with flesh and blood), but since this is a statue of a lie, hollow like the "woman" it portrays, it is a *true* copy, unique among works of art. So, too, since one cannot examine the painting to see if the man is a "full" man, since it is merely two-dimensional like the apparent virility of the man it portrays, the painting, too, is a true copy of that man by virtue of that very two-dimensionality. Art is a lie that tells the truth, as Picasso once remarked.

Slavoj Zizek uses William Tenn's sci-fi story "The Discovery of Morniel Mathaway" (1955) to illuminate the self-imitation implicit in art:

> A distinguished art historian takes a journey in a time machine from the twenty-fifth century to our day to visit and study *in vivo* the immortal Morniel Mathaway, a painter not appreciated in our time but later discovered to have been the greatest painter of the era. When he encounters him, the art historian finds no trace of a genius, just an imposter, a megalomaniac, even a swindler who steals his time machine from him and escapes into the future, so that the poor art historian stays tied to our time. The only action open to him is to assume the identity of the escaped Mathaway and to paint under his name all his masterpieces that he remembers from the future—it is himself who is really the misrecognized genius he was looking for![47]

By imitating the imitator, the author eventually invents him and becomes him.

Even when we attempt to be natural, we are often imitating what we regard as natural, which often amounts to what art has taught us to regard as nature. Unbroken young horses playing freely in a field naturally perform certain extravagant movements, leaping and dancing, which they will not execute under saddle and at command. There is an exception: highly trained dressage horses, particularly the Lippizan horses of the Spanish Riding School of Vienna, after many years of training, learn to transform the horse's natural curvetting (generally horsing around) into the *courbette* (raising the forelegs and leaping on the hind legs before the forelegs touch the ground), while their lethal habit of kicking out in back is imitated by a balletic capriole or "goat's leap" (a high leap in place, the hind legs striking back together at the height of the leap). For people as well as horses, it often takes a great deal of art to look natural.

PLAYING WITHIN THE PLAY

Impersonation is built into the primary processes of the stage and into the many plays within plays that depict actors impersonating real people or real people playing at being actors. At the end of Puccini's opera *Tosca* (1900), Mario is told to pretend to die when he is shot with fake bullets; in fact his executioners use real bullets, and he really dies, but his lover Tosca, watching the execution from her hiding place, thinks he is merely faking and applauds as he falls, a dead man appearing to be a live man pretending to be dead. The poignancy of this scene can take either of two forms. If it's the first time you've seen *Tosca* and you don't know the story, you are shocked when Tosca is shocked and retrospectively disturbed along with her to know that you saw Mario killed and didn't mind it at the time;[48] but if you've seen *Tosca* before, you feel, all through the scene before he is killed, the poignancy of knowing, when Tosca does not, that Mario is really being shot dead right before her delighted eyes.

The outermost frame of the theater, the so-called "fourth wall" that opens onto the audience, onto real people, offers yet another twist to the triple crosses already in place in the inner frame, and often that quadruple cross, too, is incorporated into the play. In films about people who are professional actors, a mere flick of the curtain results in self-impersonation. In *Sullivan's Travels* (Preston Sturges, 1941), a successful film director named John L. Sullivan, disguised as a hobo, meets "the girl" (Veronica Lake), who acts out for him what she would have said to him if he were a successful film director. When he is booked for vagrancy and finally convinces the police that he is who he says he is, the cop says, "How does that girl fit into the picture?" and he replies, "There's always a girl in the picture; haven't you ever been to the movies?" When he finds himself in a tight spot, he remarks, "If ever a plot needed a twist, this one does." In *Miracle on 34th Street* (George Seaton, 1947), Kris Kringle (Edmund Gwenn), who really is Santa Claus, pretends to be a man pretending to be Santa Claus (when the man originally hired to play the part is too drunk to go on). Self-imitations in films-within-a-film have a tendency to chicken-and-egg proliferations. In *Singin' in the Rain* (Stanley Donen, 1952), Debbie Reynolds plays the part of a singer (Kathy Selden) who secretly supplies the voice behind the curtain when the actress played by Jean Hagen (Lina Lamont) lip-synchs in front of the curtain

(Debbie Reynolds playing Kathy Selden dubbing Jean Hagen playing Lina Lamont). But Jean Hagen actually dubbed the voice of Debbie Reynolds (dubbing Jean Hagen) in one of the slow songs: at that moment Jean Hagen was dubbing Debbie Reynolds playing Kathy Selden dubbing Lina Lamont played by—Jean Hagen. The circle closed, and Jean Hagen was imitating herself.

Actors playing actors playing self-imitating vampires have had a long run in Hollywood. In Tod Browning's *London after Midnight* (1927), a disguised Inspector Burke (Lon Chaney) was aided by a double, who played the murdered man in a dramatized reconstruction. When Browning directed *Mark of the Vampire* (1935), a remake of his previous film, Bela Lugosi played Count Mora, suspected of a killing but, in the end, revealed to be an actor playing the part of a vampire. Apparently Bela Lugosi urged Browning to transform the actors into vampires pretending to be actors (pretending to be vampires), but Browning refused.[49] Lugosi's wish finally came true in 1994 in *Interview with the Vampire*, when Neil Jordan presented a real vampire (Antonio Banderas) who infiltrated a play about a vampire and ravished and murdered his prey in the full view of an audience who thought they were just watching a play; when a real vampire watching the show (Brad Pitt) remarked that they were "vampires pretending to be humans pretending to be vampires," the little-girl vampire at his side (Kirsten Dunst) remarked blandly, "How avant-garde." Further avant, in 2000 in E. Elias Merhige's *Shadow of the Vampire*, Murnau (John Malkovich), the director of a film about a vampire, hired a real vampire named Schreck (Willem Dafoe) to play the part. At first, Murnau told his crew that Schreck looked and acted so bizarre because he was a Method actor who had studied with Stanislavski. But later, he admitted that Schreck really was a vampire who had agreed to play the part of an actor playing the part of a vampire.

Theatrical self-imitation was a favorite theme in the romantic films of the '30s and '40s. *Shall We Dance?* (Mark Sandrich, 1937), starring Fred Astaire (as a hoofer named Pete who pretends to be a Russian ballet dancer named Petrov) and Ginger Rogers (as a dancer named Linda Keene), culminates in a Busby-Berkeley-like orgy of self-imitation, appropriately choreographed by the mythologically named Hermes Pan:

Pete and Linda were in love but estranged. Prankster newspapermen borrowed a dummy made to look just like Linda; they snuck into Pete's bedroom at night, put the dummy in his bed, photographed them "together," and printed it in the paper. In the ensuing chaos, Linda walked out on Pete, who didn't know how to reconfigure his act until he remembered the dummy and said, "If I can't dance with one Linda Keene, I'll dance with dozens of her." He then created masks of the face of Linda Keene (that is, Ginger Rogers) for all the women dancers in the chorus line. As they danced, Linda came in and saw them, to her astonishment and amusement; Pete's friend explained to her, "He said if he couldn't dance with you he'd dance with images of you." She then put on one of the masks herself and joined the chorus. Pete heard her voice saying two words in Russian that were a private joke between them ("Ochi chornye," something he used to say to her when he was pretending to be Petrov), a clue that she was masquerading now as he had masqueraded then. And so he knew that one of them was the Real Linda Keene, but he couldn't identify her. Then as he danced he stripped the masks off all the women one by one until he came to her, and they danced together happily ever after.

Dancing is a very thinly veiled metaphor for sex in Fred Astaire movies (as well as for hypnotism, which becomes explicit only in *Carefree* [Mark Sandrich, 1938] but is operative in all the others, too). Therefore, Pete is sleeping with all the other women, all of whom look alike in the dark. Like Fred and Ginger, the Hindu god Krishna and his mistress Radha become separated (the Hindus call this *viraha*, the longing for an otiose god) when Krishna creates multiple doubles of Radha (and the other cowherd women whom he seduced) to dance with him in his erotic circle dance.[50] But Fred, unlike Krishna, is hoist by his own petard: he cannot recognize the real Ginger until he hears the voice of his one true love.

In *L. A. Confidential* (Curtis Hanson, 1998), which imitates the genre of a '40s film, a pimp has a plastic surgeon "cut" his whores to make them look like movie stars. Knowing this, a cop who meets the real Lana Turner mistakes her for an imitation (of some actress playing a prostitute imitating Lana Turner, a triple displacement) and treats her like a slut, whereupon she throws her drink in his face. In *Let's Make Love* (George Cukor, 1960), a famous New York millionaire, Jean-Marc Clement (Yves Montand), who learns that someone is going to impersonate him in a satirical play in Greenwich Village, rushes downtown with his lawyers to stop it. But before he can identity himself, Amanda (Marilyn Monroe), who is playing opposite the millionaire, comments on his uncanny resemblance to Clement and suggests that he audition for the part. He does and gets it and, for a while, her (on camera and off), though she loves him only as the actor, never as the millionaire.

VIRTUAL REALITY

From this consideration of films in which the outer frame of the theater is folded into the story let us move in the other direction, to films that spill out of the frame into the wider world of virtual reality.

Life's bad habit of imitating art is nowhere more apparent than in the long-attested practice of real people offstage imitating actors onstage, the Hollywood version of the so-called Werther effect in literature: mens' underwear manufacturers went bankrupt when Clark Gable appeared shirtless in *It Happened One Night* (Frank

Capra, 1934), the malls of America were invaded in 1999 by kids wearing the black leather coats that were standard issue in *The Matrix* (Andy and Larry Wachowski, 1999), and animal shelters were overrun by Dalmatians after the Disney film and by owls after the first Harry Potter film. But as the frames shift, it can get tricky. It is hardly surprising that a number of actual members of the Mafia began to model their behavior on that of Marlon Brando in *The Godfather* (Francis Ford Coppola, 1972), but then a character on the television program *The Sopranos* began to do imitations of characters from the *Godfather* movies, so there you have an actor playing a mobster imitating an actor playing a mobster. The ultimate result of all of this was the tendency of many Americans to say, when faced with an unimaginable tragedy like September 11, 2001, "It was like a movie."[51]

Some films depict actors who become the characters they impersonate. (This happens in opera, too: in Leoncavallo's *Pagliacci*, Canio and Nedda, a husband and wife, stage a play about an unfaithful wife; but when the actor finds out that his wife is actually deceiving him, he actually kills her in the play in which he usually pretends to kill her.) *Love, Actually* (Richard Curtis, 2003) parodies the notorious tendency of Hollywood stars to fall in love with the people with whom they play love scenes in front of the camera: a man and a woman (Martin Freeman and Joanna Page) who play the body doubles for the stars in a sexy scene—talking about the weather and sports while they do it—fall in love, once removed, as it were. The theme has its dark side, too. In *A Double Life* (George Cukor, 1947[52]), Ronald Colman plays an actor named Anthony John who plays Othello, while John's ex-wife Brita (played by Signe Hasso) plays Desdemona. John goes mad and confuses Othello's jealousy with his own; he almost kills Brita during a performance of the scene in which Othello kills Desdemona. He does kill another woman onto whom he projects the double image of Brita and Desdemona; his victim is a twice removed stand-in for Desdemona who is a stand-in for his real wife.[53] In *The Legend of Lylah Clare* (Robert Aldrich, 1968), an actress becomes possessed by the spirit of the actress whom she is portraying and repeats in her own life the fatal errors of the film character. Someone in the film comments, "Actors don't know who they are until someone writes some lines to tell them who they are," and his companion replies, "But we are all impersonating an identity." Some of us more than others, perhaps.

On the other hand, some film actors imitated offscreen the characters they impersonated onscreen (the "Cary Grant as Cary Grant" scenario), and this often escalated into a triple cross. After Greta Garbo and John Gilbert played lovers in Clarence Brown's *Flesh and the Devil* in 1926, they had a famous love affair offscreen (art to life); then they decided to play lovers in Edmund Goulding's silent film of Tolstoi's *Anna Karenina* in 1927 (life to art), which the studio retitled *Love* so the ads could say, "Garbo and Gilbert in Love," referring simultaneously to the action onstage and off.[54] On a darker note, it is impossible to watch the scenes of Grace Kelly in Alfred Hitchcock's *To Catch a Thief* (1955) driving recklessly around the hairpin turns of the Riviera, laughing as she defies death and Cary Grant, without remembering how she died there in 1982, at what is said to be the same spot where the reckless driving scene was filmed in 1954.[55]

Bollywood, the Bombay branch of the film family, has a complex relationship with reality, particularly religious reality.[56] The actor Vishnupant Pagnis interpreted the part of the Maratha holy man and poet Tukaram in the film *Sant Tukaram* (Vishnupant Govind Damle, 1936) to such effect that in Maharashtra nowadays portraits of Tukaram housed in shrines portray him with Pagnis's face and movie costume, much as many Americans imagine God as Charlton Heston. The fans of some Indian film stars built temples to them.[57] Members of the audience often bring fruit and flowers (standard offerings to deities) and offer them to the screen after showings of such Hindi films as *Jai Santoshi Ma* (Vijay Sharma, 1975), in which a woman established the worship of a goddess (Santoshi Ma) who had had, beginning only in the early 1960s, a small, local cult until the film inspired people all over India to establish shrines of their own.

The very name of the Bollywood studio of Filmistan suggests that a film is a real place—a "-stan" (or "-sthan," from the Sanskrit word for "place")—like "the place of the Afghans" (Afghani-stan) or "the place of the kings" (Raja-sthan). The studio encloses, on its permanent village back-lot set, a settlement of five households, about twenty-five people in two related families of the Warli ethnic group, a disadvantaged "Scheduled Tribe." They live there permanently, and on occasion they act the parts of villagers in films. When William Elison asked them, in 1996, how they had come there in the first place, two of them replied that their houses had been built generations back, when they constituted part of a larger settlement—a "real village"—and that the studio complex had been built around it at around the time of Independence (when the studio was built). The situation is further complicated by the existence of Film City, not far from Filmistan, which is also occupied by Warlis and has an entirely fake village, a set made out of plaster and epoxy and resin, a village that was built to look more like a "real" Warli village than the Warli villages that surround it. Elison notes the difference between coming off a Hollywood set and coming off the village set in Filmistan: "If the Hollywood formula is double take—'real' exposed as 'fake'—my reaction to Filmistan seemed to enact a three-point movement, from real to fake, and back to real again." Or as the case may be, back to fake again. Is Filmistan a village pretending to be a film set or a film set pretending to be a village?

And now that we have reality television, in which real people appear on television acting out their real lives *as if they were on a television show*, the hall of mirrors is truly bottomless. Reality television seems to add the joker to the deck, until we realize that there is nothing but jokers in the deck. Not surprisingly, reality television shows abound in themes of impersonation, including shows in which real people have to "pass" as other people (*Faking It*) or switch identities with other people (*Switched*) or undergo plastic surgery (*Extreme Makeover, Nip/Tuck,* and *The Swan*), in the old tradition of television shows of the 1950s like *To Tell the Truth*, when a panel of celebrities had to separate the sheep from the goats until, "Will the *real* snake charmer please stand up?" But now the fake snake charmer has become the television star.[58] Cross reality television with *Dark City* (Alex Proyas, 1998), *The Matrix* (Andy and Larry Wachowski, 1999), and *The Truman Show* (Peter Weir, 1998), about a person whose life is entirely encased within a television serial that he mistakes for real life, and you get a cartoon show dreamed up by Norman Lear (in 2003), in which, in one episode, "an alien disguised as a giant talking taco [announces] that the Earth is not a planet at all but rather an advanced reality television show."[59]

The twists continue when we note that these programs choose for their subjects people whose lives are like the lives of characters in daytime soap operas. Moreover, many of the "real people" on the reality shows are aspiring actors; one of them "once slipped during a television interview and referred to the women he was dating as 'the cast.'" It gets better. The *New York Times* notes, "As the romance reality shows morph into soap operas, however, soap operas are borrowing from reality shows." According to Brian Scott Frons, president of ABC Daytime and a former producer of European reality shows, "Now we can take some of the authenticity and unpredictability of prime-time reality and put it into soap operas." To which the *Times* merely remarks, "Authenticity and unpredictability are relative, of course."[60]

ACTING OUT IN POLITICS

Long before reality television we had what amounted to reality film, though we did not call it that; we called it politics. Politicians are, like actors and writers and other public figures, great self-imitators, and when an actor actually becomes a politician, the felonies are compounded. India abounds in film stars turned politicians: Vinod Khanna, Raj Babbar, and Shatrughan Sinha, also known as Shotgun Sinha; the Tamil stars J. Jayalalitha and MGR (M. G. Ramachandran); the Telugu star NTR (N. T. Rama Rao); Hema Malini, and many more. NTR founded his own political party in 1980 but was unseated by his son-in-law in 1995. MGR's wife succeeded him as Tamil Nadu's chief minister until his old costar Jayalalitha unseated her.[61] India also has film stars-turned-politicians-turned-film stars: Amitabh Bachchan and his wife, Jaya.

America, too, has its Filmistan—in the White House. When Ronald Reagan auditioned for the part of the president of the United States in the 1960 Broadway production of Gore Vidal's play *The Best Man*, about a presidential election, Vidal turned him down because he didn't think Reagan would be believable as the president. When asked about this in 2002, Vidal said, "Reagan was a first-rate actor as a President."[62] Vidal always referred to Reagan as "our acting President,"[63] which became the title of a book about Reagan, subtitled (on the cover), "Ronald Reagan and the Supporting Players Who Helped Him Create the Illusion That Held America Spellbound." This book recounts the following anecdote: "His entry into politics inspired a famous utterance by his former studio boss Jack Warner. When he was told that Reagan was running for governor of California, Warner, always quick to recognize a casting blunder, protested, 'No, no! Jimmy Stewart for governor, Ronald Reagan for best friend.'"[64] In *Late for Dinner* (W. D. Richter, 1991), a man who was frozen in the early 1960s and awakes in 1991 encounters his wife, who tries to explain to him how much time has passed, how much he has missed. She tells him that Ronald Reagan was shot, and he replies, "Someone shot the guy from *The Cattle Queen of Montana?*"

In *In Like Flint* (Gordon Douglas, 1967), when Derek Flint (James Coburn) discovers that an actor is impersonating the president of the United States, he says, "An actor as President?!?!!" David Thompson's short but rapier-sharp biography of Reagan describes his presidency as a nationwide series in which, after his "West Coast daytime talk show, *Ask The Governor*, from 1966–74, . . . for eight years . . . he played *Mr. President?—That's Me!*, amassing more camera time than anyone else in the Actors' Guild and deftly feeding the lines and situations of Warner Brothers in the 1940s back into world affairs. . . . The rest would be history—and he did seem rested."[65] Lou Cannon, in his aptly named biography *President Reagan: The Role of a Lifetime*, describes an earlier moment when Reagan the film actor played the part of a real actor in history:

> Captain Reagan, an actor who wore his uniform to work in Culver City, played the lead role in *This Is the Army* and participated in a top-secret project used to train U. S. bombing crews for their destructive raids on Tokyo. As Reagan himself told the story, "Our special effects men—Hollywood geniuses in uniform—built a complete miniature of Tokyo"[66] on a sound stage, above which they rigged a crane and camera mount. They then photographed the miniature, showing the targets as they would look from planes flying at different altitudes and speeds under varying weather conditions. Reagan was the narrator, guiding pilots onto their targets.[67]

This war game, the antecedent of children's computer games, enabled pilots—real pilots—to practice their bomb runs on Tokyo—real bomb runs that Hollywood would then reenact in fictionalized films like *Thirty Seconds Over Tokyo* (Mervyn LeRoy, 1944). Thus as Garry Wills argued, Reagan's war service was "based on the principled defense of faking things."[68] When Oliver North was exposed and put on trial, Reagan's comment was, "It's going to make a great movie."[69]

Frank Rich, tracing the appearances of presidents on talk shows on television, starting with Kennedy, argues that the more "authentic" they tried to appear, the more artificial their self-presentation actually was.[70] (This was notoriously the case with Nixon's "Sock it to me!" appearance on *Laugh In* in 1968.) Where others have noted how Reagan acted as president in the White House, Rich argues that he "didn't have to bother with such antics" by appearing on talk shows: "He had been there, done that as a professional before entering politics."[71] That is, because Reagan really *was* an actor, he didn't have to put on an act on television. But something even more invidious was accomplished by Reagan's impersonation of a president. The masking and unmasking went in both directions, finally exposing not just Reagan but the man he pretended to be. As Thompson put it, because of Reagan, "The fraudulence of the Presidency was revealed so that the office could never quite be honored again."[72] In retrospect, we saw that other glamorous presidents, like Kennedy, had also been merely impersonating presidents. And FDR? And Lincoln? Why was the character in *The Truman Show* named after a president—indeed, a president famous for his blunt honesty and lack of pretensions? Rich put it well: "Politics has redefined the word real as fully as reality TV has. Its new definition is fake. . . . For all the lip-service paid to authenticity, many voters have come to prefer a show to the naked truth." He concludes with an adage from George Burns: "If you can fake sincerity, you've got it made."

Arnold Schwarzenegger, governor of California, has been well trained for the part: he starred in three self-imitation movies (*Total Recall*, *True Lies*, *The Sixth Day*) and is said to have committed over five hundred murders—on film. Many have sighed in relief at the knowledge that, born in Austria, he can't be president. But here's an alarming bit of trivia. In the film *Demolition Man* (Marco Brambilla, 1993), John Spartan (Sylvester Stallone), who has been in a coma, frozen in 1996 and thawed out in 2032 (when the movie is set), discovers the Schwarzenegger Presidential Library. He expresses astonishment (perhaps because it is not the Stallone Presidential Library?) that "the actor" could have been president (repeating the gag that *Late for Dinner* had used two years earlier about Ronald Reagan, who *was* president). His colleague Sandra Bullock then explains that, even though Schwarzenegger was not born in this country, he was so popular at the time that people passed a "61st Amendment, which states that . . ." Stallone interrupts her by saying, "I doan wanna know." Out of the mouths of hunks: since Schwarzenegger's election as governor, there has been a movement to ratify an amendment to the Constitution so he can run for president, and Schwarzenegger himself has publicly expressed his belief that immigrants should be allowed to run for president. Moreover, in a move eerily reminiscent of

Reagan's old unsuccessful bid for the role of president in Gore Vidal's play, Schwarzenegger almost failed to be cast in his greatest role, the Terminator, in 1984 because James Cameron had O. J. Simpson in mind for the part; Simpson lost it to Schwarzenegger, however, because, as Cameron told *Esquire*, "People wouldn't have believed a nice guy like O. J. playing the part of a ruthless killer."[73] The implications of this comparative judgment are chilling. So is the further distancing from reality implied in the belief that Schwarzenegger is imitating Reagan (imitating a president); the title of a *New York Times* article about Schwarzenegger's bid for governor was, "An Actor, Yes, but No Reagan."[74] When he was elected, a California woman who voted for him said: "In a fantasy world I'd love to see the Terminator in office. Someone strong and powerful. A superhero. But that's a fantasy, right? The reality is, he's been groping." And Arlie R. Hochschild commented that in a time of economic distress and fear, Schwarzenegger was part of a rescue fantasy.[75]

Bill Clinton's great contributions to this genre, such as making it X-rated, were capped by the film *Wag the Dog* (Barry Levinson, 1997), in which a president embroiled in a sex scandal deflects public attention with a fictitious war film that is sold to the American people as if it were real news footage of a war against Albania. And that film-within-a-film was implicitly cited after September 11, 2001, to undercut President Bush's use of the war and war footage; in Michael Moore's documentary *Fahrenheit 9/11* (2004), *Afghanistan* became the title of a Western movie starring Bush and Cheney. Once faith is shaken, it is hard to keep it out of free fall.

IRONIC TANGOS

Do we, ourselves, always know, consciously, when we are engaging in self-parody? I think not. We often slip carelessly across the permeable boundary between the unselfconscious self-indulgence of our most idiosyncratic mannerisms and the conscious attempt to give the people who know us, personally or publicly, the version of ourselves that they expect. The stories in this book are merely the extreme examples, so enlarged as to be obvious, of what we common folk do, unconsciously, every day in ways that we do not notice, both because our actions are more muted and because we are blinded by self-deception. Terry Eagleton has remarked that "self-parody . . . is the closest we can come to authenticity."[76] And there are situations in which we are particularly prone to self-imitate, such as amateur productions of Gilbert and Sullivan, which often mock both their own amateurishness and the Victorian attitudes that they exhume. Anyone who dances a tango nowadays is willy-nilly imitating someone else doing the tango. Tango dancers move about within a haze of inverted commas, constantly quoting themselves, situating themselves in the midst of some invisible discourse they are playing to an invisible audience, a phenomenon that the tangos in the films *Some Like It Hot* (Billy Wilder, 1959) and *Last Tango in Paris* (Bernardo Bertolucci, 1972) brilliantly exploit. Those invisible commas that plague self-imitators are the sign of irony, compounded, in the case of the tango, by yet another twist, false irony, a form of self-imitation that we all engage in, pretending that we do not mean something when we do. "Scare quotes" are epidemic now, but Proust knew about them in 1913. Writing of his protagonist Swann, he says that often, when discussing an important subject, "he would take care to isolate, to sterilize it by using a special intonation, mechanical and ironic, as though he had put the phrase or word between inverted commas, and was anxious to disclaim any personal responsibility for it; as who should say, 'the "*hierarchy*," don't you know, as silly people call it.' But then, if it was so absurd, why did he use the word?"[77] Why, indeed? The recognition of these shoddy habits of self-deception, these banal posterings, these sad, sometimes tragic, pretenses, is what fuels the constant re-creation of the often happier, sometimes comic, fantasies of self-impersonation.

CHAPTER TWO

The Man Who Mistook
His Wife for His Wife

And so [Tristan] stayed with Isolde for some time, because she
reminded him of Isolde.

Gottfried von Strassburg, *Tristan* (1210)

SELF-IMITATION OFTEN results from the doomed attempt to resolve the circular paradox of marital sexual rejection. That is, the husband desires both an erotic encounter
and a legitimate child, but not always from the same woman, and to close the circle,
his wife must double back to become the person she knows she is, the person he
cannot see until she transforms herself there and back again: his erotic partner (and
often the mother of his children). Wives triple-cross their double-crossing husbands
by substituting for the mistresses who are substituting for the wives, so that the man
commits adultery with his own wife, stumbling home in the dark. When these men
reject their wives for other women, those women turn out to be their wives—who,
by altering themselves so dramatically as to be unrecognizable, prove that they have
not altered as much as their husbands thought they had. The perpetrators of these
double-back bedtricks (secret substitutions of one person for another in bed) are
pretending to be the sexual partners that they secretly know they are but cannot
openly claim to be in any other way. The wife really is the mistress because fantasy
and desire make her so—if for no other reason than because she appears in her erring husband's mind to be so.

The eternal triangle—a married woman, her husband, and the woman he has just fallen in love with—becomes a polyhedron in polygamous India. (More precisely, India was not polygamous but polygynous, for legally there, as extralegally in Europe, the double standard allowed a man, but not a woman, to have multiple sexual partners.) This geometrical figure forms the armature for a cycle of classical Sanskrit texts surrounding the mythical figures of King Udayana, his wife Queen Vasavadatta,[1] and his several co-wives.[2] In two Sanskrit dramas attributed to King Harsha, who ruled much of North India in the seventh century CE,[3] the protagonist employs the erotic equivalent of realpolitik, a cross between Machiavelli and Boccaccio—or, more precisely, between the *Arthashastra* (the ancient Indian political textbook) and the *Kamasutra* (the ancient Indian erotic textbook), which have much in common and were composed a couple of centuries before Harsha. In Harsha's *Ratnavali* (*The Lady of the Jeweled Necklace*), the wife inadvertently masquerades not merely as the mistress but as the mistress masquerading as the wife, while in *Priyadarshika* (*The Woman Who Shows Her Love*), the king advertently masquerades as the king. Here, as so often, merely telling the same tale from the standpoint of a different character produces a new story.

The Lady of the Jeweled Necklace begins in medias res, after several crucial events have already taken place: King Udayana loved Queen Vasavadatta so much that he did not want to take a second wife, but there was a prediction that for the good of the kingdom he should marry the princess Ratnavali ("The [lady of the] Jeweled Necklace"). On her voyage to Udayana's kingdom, Ratnavali was shipwrecked and fished out by a merchant; he brought her to King Udayana's minister, who recognized her and put her in the queen's service as a handmaid named Sagarika ("Ocean Woman"). This is where the play begins:

Ratnavali, The Lady of the Jeweled Necklace

The queen tried to keep the king from seeing Ratnavali-as-Sagarika, who was very beautiful, but Ratnavali-as-Sagarika saw him and fell in love with him and he with her. She then painted a portrait of herself with the king, who found the portrait and declared his passionate love for the unknown maiden who had painted his portrait and hers. Vasavadatta saw the portrait and became suspicious. The king met Ratnavali-as-Sagarika; he took her hand, but when the king's jester remarked, "She is another Queen Vasavadatta," the king hastily dropped her hand, and she ran away. "Where is this Queen Vasavadatta?" asked the king. The clown replied, "She's this one. I just said, 'This is *another* Queen Vasavadatta,' because she was so proud." "You idiot!" snapped the king. The queen gave one of her women some of her own clothes as a bribe to get her to guard Ratnavali-as-Sagarika, but the woman dressed Ratnavali-as-Sagarika in the queen's clothes and arranged for the king to meet Ratnavali-as-Sagarika-as-the queen. The queen learned that Ratnavali-as-Sagarika-as-the queen was going to a rendezvous with the king; she herself went to the place of assignation, dressed in her own clothing. The king mistook the queen for Ratnavali-as-Sagarika-as-the queen and wooed her with words, addressing her as Sagarika. When the king attempted to kiss the queen-as-Ratnavali-as-Sagarika-as-the queen, she threw off her veil in fury and said, "Your majesty, I really am Sagarika. For you have projected Sagarika into your heart, so that you imagine that *everything* seems to be made of Sagarika." The king said, "Oh, no! This really is queen Vasavadatta." Then he cupped his hands in supplication and said to the queen, "My darling Vasavadatta, forgive me, forgive me." But the queen went away with a headache.

Then Ratnavali-as-Sagarika-as-the queen started to hang herself with a vine, in shame that her secret love had been found out. The king, thinking that she was the queen trying to commit suicide because he had made love to another woman, embraced her and addressed her as the queen until her words identified her as Ratnavali-as-Sagarika-as-the queen, and he embraced her again. Just then the queen returned, coming back to forgive her husband and to accept his apologies. She heard his voice and decided to sneak up on him from behind and put her arms around his neck. But then she overheard the king say to Ratnavali-as-Sagarika-as-the queen, "I bow to the queen because she is of naturally noble birth, but the affection that I feel for you has more passion because it comes from overpowering love." As soon as he said that, the queen came forth and said, "Your majesty, this is just like your majesty. Just like you indeed." The king, looking at her in embarrassment and confusion, replied, "My queen! Don't accuse me without cause. I thought that this woman was you; it was a natural mistake, because she was wearing clothes just like yours. So forgive me." She replied, in anger, "Get up, get up, your majesty. Why should you suffer even now by serving a woman who is 'of naturally noble birth'?" The king said to himself, "Did the queen hear that too? Then there is no hope for me to conciliate her."

The queen did not forgive him then, but eventually, when Ratnavali-as-Sagarika was revealed to be Ratnavali, the queen joined Ratnavali's hand with the king's and said, "My lord, accept this woman." The minister asked the king, "Is there anything more that you want me to do for you, your majesty?" and the king replied, "What more could anyone want?"

The queen might want a lot more, but clearly she will not get it.

My summary does the play a disservice by peeling away several subplots in order to highlight the central issue of mis-recognition, but that issue remains complex enough. Both of the king's women are disguised at one time or another. The queen begins the masquerade inadvertently when she gives her own clothes to her rival's friend, but then the reins are taken out of her hands when the clothes are used to deceive her. When the queen unconsciously impersonates Ratnavali-as-Sagarika consciously impersonating the queen, David Shulman remarks, "The queen, in being herself, is playing at being another who is as herself."[4] Through a kind of triple cross, in which the king mistakes his queen for the Other Woman and the Other Woman for the queen, he actually makes love to his queen when she is undisguised, thinking she is someone else pretending to be her. The queen is fragmented both within herself and in her complex relationship with the other woman whom the man she loves loves.

The Other Woman, too, undergoes several layers of disguise. The princess Ratnavali is disguised as a maid, Sagarika, who imaginatively represents herself as the king's lover in the portrait she paints. The princess-as-maid is then disguised as the queen; the queen, not disguised at all, is taken for the princess-as-maid-as-queen; and the princess-as-maid-as-queen is mistaken for the queen. The jester keeps saying that one woman looks like the other, and the king thinks he is saying that one woman *is* the other. As Shulman comments on this, "The clown has inadvertently stumbled upon an important truth. The two women are, on some level, split and replicated images of each other."[5] The king cannot tell his women apart, but from time to time he drops remarks that indicate his deeper knowledge that, in various ways, Ratnavali-as-Sagarika is replacing his wife. For instance, when he casually remarks that his beloved Sagarika "is like a jeweled necklace that I found by chance," his simile suggests his unconscious knowledge that Sagarika is Ratnavali, "The Lady of the Jeweled Necklace." At the end, he calls out for the queen, forgetting that she is beside him, and when she speaks to him he remarks, "How is it that, in my extreme agitation and confusion, I didn't notice that the queen was right here beside me?"—an unconscious comment on his stale marriage. But the queen is even more perceptive than he when she remarks, "I really am Sagarika. You imagine that *everything* seems to be made of Sagarika."[6] The king does not masquerade in this play, but the queen says of him, when he behaves in a characteristically adulterous manner, "Your majesty, this is just like your majesty." The word she uses, *sadrisham*, more specifically refers to something that looks just like something else. She means that he is true to type, but she says that he gives the appearance of being himself.

This idea of the king's self-imitation is taken into new realms of performance in Harsha's other play on this theme, *Priyadarshika*. Now it is the man, not the woman, who is split up and impersonates himself—or in Shulman's words, "undergoes triplication."[7] Here again, a princess (Priyadarshika) is smuggled into the harem under a name with a natural referent: Aranyika ("The Forest Woman"). And again, the king falls in love with her. Then the play begins:

The queen, worried that she had lost the king's affections, decided to stage a play that a woman friend of hers had composed about the queen and king when they first fell in love. Aranyika was to play the queen, while her friend Manorama was to play the king. The queen gave Priyadarshika-as-Aranyika the ornaments from her body, and she gave Manorama the ornaments her father had given the king at their marriage. She said, "Wear them on stage, so you'll look just like the king." But Manorama, without informing Priyadarshika-as-Aranyika, colluded with the king so that he took Manorama's place, taking from her his own costume and ornaments. Manorama said to herself, "Since the queen keeps Aranyika far from the king's gaze, this is how they can meet: let him come and himself play the part of himself."

The play began, and when the king-as-Manorama-as-the king made his first speech the queen said, "Bravo to the king!" rising suddenly to her feet. The king said to himself, "Oh no! The queen has recognized me!" but the playwright said to the queen, "Calm down. It's just a play." And the queen replied, "Oh! It is Manorama! But I thought, 'It's the king.' Bravo, bravo, Manorama! Well acted!" The playwright said, "Your majesty, truly Manorama made you mistake one for another. Look: the form, garments, gait, voice—this clever woman has presented the king to us before our very eyes."

As the play progressed, the king-as-Manorama-as-the king took the hand of Priyadarshika-as-Aranyika-as-the queen, who said (to herself, not knowing that it really was the king), "No, no! The touch of Manorama affects my limbs beyond reason." The queen suddenly stood up again, saying, "I can't bear to see another falsification." The playwright insisted, "But it's just a play, theatre, spectacle. It's not proper to leave the theater at the wrong time and break the mood." The queen, however, walked away and discovered that the king himself had played the part. Eventually, the minister of Priyadarshika's father, who happened to be in the court at that moment, recognized that Priyadarshika-as-Aranyika was Priyadarshika. The queen joined the hands of Princess Priyadarshika and the king, saying, "Her father gave her to you long ago." Then she asked the king, "Is there anything more that you want me to do for you, your majesty?" and the king replied, "What more could anyone want?"

The queen salvages her pride with her final words to her victorious rival, implying that duty, not passion, is what motivates the king to marry Priyadarshika—or so she pretends to think—an inversion of the sentiment the king expressed in *The Lady of the Jeweled Necklace*, to the queen's distress: that it was just duty, not passion, that joined him to the queen herself. But there is surely irony in the queen's last words to the king, in which she asks the king precisely what the Machiavellian minister had asked him at the end of *The Lady of the Jeweled Necklace* and receives precisely the same reply:[8] the king (surely in contrast with both of his women) has gotten everything he wanted. And this time these words have an added bite, for the word for what you want (or love) is *priya*, the first element of the name of the woman who will take the king from the queen.

The queen imaginatively represents herself as the king's lover in a play, just as, in Harsha's other play, Sagarika represents herself in a portrait. In both cases, the projections are the direct cause of their own realizations; they come true. But in this play within the play, the player (Priyadarshika), not the person she plays (Vasavadatta), becomes the actual lover. What did the queen hope to accomplish by having her rival impersonate her? Did she think the king would transfer back to her the love he had apparently transferred from her to the new woman? Did she hope to rekindle his love, fanning an old flame, as it were? How bitter must her humiliation have been when she realized her ruse had backfired in such a way that she herself had made it possible for the king to make love to her rival, right before her eyes. While most women, in Hindu mythology and elsewhere, find it hard enough to watch their men replace them with women who replicate them (often in the form they had when they were young), the queen must literally watch her role usurped by her younger understudy. Priyadarshika's real name is a clue: it tells us that she "reveals" or "displays" or "performs" her love.[9] But the king's duplicity forces her to "perform" that love publicly (and unknowingly) when she had intended to keep it a secret. In this sense, the king "outs" Priyadarshika without her permission or her conscious knowledge, tricking Priyadarshika-as-Aranyika-as-the queen into letting him touch her. Her own body also forces a Cartesian duplicity upon her: her mind thinks she is touching the hand of Manorama, but her body knows she is touching the hand of the king.

For the king, the play within the play is not only a double impersonation but a double change of gender, a double cross-dress, a double drag that cancels itself out; the king pretends to be a woman pretending to be him. The complexities are multiplied when the play is produced by one of those Indian traditions—alluded to in this very play—in which women play the parts of men: at such a moment, one could imagine a woman playing the part of the king playing the part of a woman playing the part of the king.[10] The literalization of the metaphor of the understudy, which makes the king a walking metaphor,[11] makes Priyadarshika-as-Aranyika-as-the queen a walking simile, a walking overlay of two rival women, and the language of the play fully exploits these double entendres. Poetry, then, the linguistic artistry of similes and metaphors, is one of the arts through which an ambiguous truth is revealed, and the theater is another.

As in the tale of Ratnavali, but this time on purpose, the queen begins the masquerade, casting her rival as herself, making her rival impersonate her. But once again, the king refuses to follow the part she has written for him: he takes over the casting, reversing the queen's intention (to bring him close to her) by using her play to stage his own infidelity. The two fantasies intermingle as his fantasy becomes hers, his vision overpowers hers, and she sees not what she wants to see (her straying husband making love to her as she was when he loved her) but what she fears to see, actually sees, and allows herself to be talked out of saying that she sees: her husband making love to her rival. She stages her dream, and the king stages her nightmare. The queen moves, and the king checkmates her.

We may read the two Harsha plays with an eye to the different consequences of the triplication of the queen (in *The Lady of the Jeweled Necklace*) and the king (in *Priyadarshika*). For instance, the fact that (in *Priyadarshika*) the queen immediately recognizes the king when he is disguised, while the king (in *The Lady of the Jeweled Necklace*) wrongly takes the queen for Ratnavali-as-Sagarika-as-the queen, is typical of the literature of sexual masquerade, which generally depicts women as more often tricking, and less often tricked, than men.[12] In both plays, even though the queen fails in her goal of keeping the king's love for herself alone, she is the least deluded character and he the most deluded. In *The Lady of the Jeweled Necklace*, he thinks he is the trickster (disguising his mistress as his wife), but still he is the one who is fooled. In *Priyadarshika*, where he again engineers the trick (disguising himself as himself), the queen sees through it (though Priyadarshika does not). His ignorance and confusion torment him, but her poignant knowledge of what is going on torments her even more.

In both plays, the double disguise frees the self. In *Priyadarshika*, the king-as-Manorama-as-the king is able to make love to his new woman under the eyes of his queen and get away with it, as he fails to do in his own persona, the king-as-the king; as Shulman puts it, "Playing at himself, he is, as it were, becoming more and more like himself, impersonating his own impersonators."[13] And in *The Lady of the Jeweled Necklace*, when the queen inadvertently masquerades as her rival, the queen-as-Ratnavali-as-Sagarika-as-the queen, the truth comes out, first in the king's words and then in her honest expression of her hurt and her anger. In both plays, the Other Woman is disguised as the queen's maid, her false name refers to a natural phenomenon, and her real name appears as the title of the play. The heroine, the woman the king loves, is the one who is disguised; true love thrives under the cover of a mask.

Who is staging the drama? Who is in control? We might make a distinction between active dreams and passive nightmares, conscious and unconscious tricksters. The active masqueraders are the manipulators, while the passive, unconscious masqueraders would include bewitched and possessed characters in myths but also people who discover that, without willing it, they have been masquerading as themselves. Yet even (or especially) the active masqueraders tend to get caught up in their own tricks and discover a frame outside (or inside) the one they themselves construct to impersonate someone else, a frame in which that someone else may be impersonating them or they themselves may unknowingly be impersonating them-selves. This is what happens, in different ways and in different texts, to both Udayana and Vasavadatta.

THE MARRIAGE OF FIGARO

The more widespread variant of the theme of inadvertent adultery, in which the wife simply masquerades as the mistress and the husband, mistaking her for the mistress, takes her to bed, pulls up short before the final convolutions of explicit self-imitation that cap the Harsha plays. But in light of the Vasavadatta cycle, we can see that the final step is implicit in the extant scenario of these simpler plots, too: by masquer-ading as the mistress, the wife is impersonating the woman that she once was and wishes to be again—herself, her husband's wife.

Readers familiar with opera may by now have been reminded of the plot of *The Marriage of Figaro*, both in the play by Pierre-Auguste Caron de Beaumarchais (1783) and in Lorenzo Da Ponte's libretto for Mozart's opera (1786). The Countess Rosina masquerades as her maid Susanna, and the Count Almaviva makes love to Rosina-as-Susanna, mistaking her for Susanna.[14] Figaro—Susanna's fiancé and Almaviva's ser-vant—complicates the plot with several triangles of his own that need not concern us here (Figaro-Almaviva-Susanna and Figaro-Marcellina-Bartolo), and Rosina's intimacy with the young page Cherubino makes Almaviva suspect yet another tri-angle (Almaviva-Rosina-Cherubino). Cherubino imitates himself when the Count, describing to Susanna how he had discovered Cherubino hiding under a cloth on a previous occasion, uses the cloth covering a chair as a substitute for Cherubino and then, taking it off as he comes to the moment of revelation in his tale, sees that the cloth is in fact hiding Cherubino. (In the Beaumarchais play, the Count remarks, "Just like the last time!") But let us, as with the Harsha plays, concentrate on the central triangle:

> In response to Almaviva's insistence that Susanna grant him a rendezvous in the pine grove, Susanna and Rosina decided that Rosina would stand in for Susanna. Rosina formulated this plot in order to humiliate her wayward husband, though she also la-mented the loss of her youth and Almaviva's love, expressing her sorrow that her hus-band did not love her anymore and her hope that she would win him back with this trick. Rosina dictated a letter to Almaviva ostensibly from Susanna, agreeing to meet him in the grove that night.
>
> At the appointed time, Rosina and Susanna entered the grove, each disguised in the other's clothes. Almaviva wooed Rosina-as-Susanna until, as he tried to take her to a secluded place, she fled. Figaro and Susanna-as-Rosina recognized Almaviva's voice and pretended to make love. Almaviva, in search of Rosina-as-Susanna, found them

and believed he had found Figaro and Rosina together. He gathered witnesses, accused Susanna-as-Rosina, and refused to forgive her, but his vengeance was cut short by the arrival of the real Countess Rosina in her own clothes. He humbly apologized to her, and she forgave him.

Rosina's forgiveness is foreshadowed earlier in the opera when, immediately after determining to change clothes with Susanna, she speaks of her humiliation in having to do this and sings the famous aria "Dove Sono":

> Where are those happy moments of sweetness and pleasure? Where have they gone, those vows of a deceiving tongue? Then why, if everything for me is changed to tears and grief, has the memory of that happiness not faded from me? Ah, if only my constancy, in longing for him always in love, could bring the hope of changing his ungrateful heart.[15]

Despite everything, Rosina hopes her faithfulness to her faithless husband will bring him back to her. Thus she implicitly acknowledges her acceptance of the double standard: women, but not men, must be faithful to be loved. Mozart's great aria expands upon a single line in the Beaumarchais play that Rosina remarks not to herself but to Susanna: "He no longer loves me." But then, in response to Susanna's question, she adds: "Ah! I have loved him too dearly. I have wearied him with my solicitude and tired him with my love."[16] Later, in Beaumarchais (though not in Da Ponte), Almaviva tells Rosina-as-Susanna how, though he loves Rosina, he still needs a change. But in both the play and the opera, Rosina-as-Susanna has powers she did not have as Rosina-as-Rosina. Where Rosina-as-Rosina merely hoped her husband would come back to her, Rosina-as-Susanna exposes his infidelity so Rosina-as-Rosina can forgive him.

Northrop Frye wrote of the moment of forgiving and forgetting that often comes at the conclusion of a romantic comedy: "Normally, we can forget in this way only when we wake up from a dream, when we pass from one world into another, and we often have to think of the main action of a comedy as 'the mistakes of a night,' as taking place in a dream or nightmare world that the final scene suddenly removes us from and thereby makes illusory."[17] And so the play within the play, or simply the masquerade within a life, provides that awakening, that forgiveness.

John Corigliano's opera *The Ghosts of Versailles* (with a libretto by William M. Hoffman) contains an opera within an opera. The ghost of Beaumarchais, in love with Marie Antoinette, announces that he has written an opera, a sequel to *The Marriage of Figaro* (itself the sequel to Rossini's *The Barber of Seville*, also based on a play by Beaumarchais), which takes place years later, when both Rosina and Susanna have grown old. Beaumarchais claims he can use the power of his art, his words and music in the opera within the opera, to rescue Marie Antoinette from her death in the French Revolution: "I shall change your past. I shall show you history as it should have been. I'll make you live again." Beaumarchais's opera is intended to work its magic upon the past like a time machine or a sci-fi face-lift, to turn the two-hundred-year-old ghost back into the young woman at the time of the Revolution. But it doesn't work; in the end, the ghosts of Beaumarchais and the queen again watch her execution and then leave the theater together, united for eternity. In the outer frame of the opera, Marie Antoinette is a dead ghost, looking back in history to watch her own live double go again to the guillotine, while the two women within the opera within the opera (Rosina and Susanna) are living ghosts, looking back at their remembered images of themselves as young and beloved women.

THE SELF-REPLICATING WIFE

The classical theme of the self-imitating wife (or husband) survives in modern depictions of husbands who knowingly or unknowingly remarry, or re-bed, their wives in the course of a divorce. Sometimes this circular logic is inspired by the need to forge evidence of adultery when that is the only legal grounds for divorce.[18] In Evelyn Waugh's *A Handful of Dust* (1934), the ever-faithful Tony Last (who lasts and finishes last), the perfect English gentleman, nobly agrees to pretend to commit adultery in order to grant the divorce sought by his wife, who really is committing adultery. He then learns of another man in a similar situation:

> "It only remains to select a partner," said the solicitor; no hint of naughtiness lightened his gloom. "We have on occasion been instrumental in accommodating our clients but there have been frequent complaints, so we find it best to leave the choice to them. Lately we had a particularly delicate case involving a man of very rigid morality and a certain diffidence. In the end his own wife consented to go with him and supply the evidence. She wore a red wig. It was quite successful."[19]

The husband who wishes to get rid of his wife still prefers her company, in this caper, to that of any other woman; she spares him the moral awkwardness and sheer embarrassment of being alone and intimate (these are British people we're talking about here) with a lower-class woman of doubtful character. His "diffidence" makes him want her to pretend to be his mistress, to pretend to be unfaithful to him with him.

The self-impersonating wife is more betrayed than betraying in the film *Out Cold* (Malcolm Mowbray, 1989), in which a woman named Sunny (played by the blond Teri Garr) hires a private detective to spy on her cheating husband. She takes to wearing a black wig; the detective thinks she is the mistress and reports on her to her.

A gender-reversed variant of this theme is the story of a jealous husband who hires a detective to find the man whom he suspects of cuckolding him, only to find that he himself, meeting his wife from time to time, is (wrongly) identified as the other man. This device, which John Galsworthy used in *The Forsyte Saga* (1922),[20] where there really was another man, was given a further twist by Graham Greene in *The End of the Affair* (1951), where there both was and wasn't another man. This is what happened:

> Sarah Miles's husband Henry rightly suspected that his wife had a lover but did not know who it was. The friend he took into his confidence, Maurice, actually was the lover, though Maurice (wrongly) suspected that Sarah was being unfaithful to him, too, with yet another lover. And so Maurice suggested to Henry that he (Maurice) would save Henry embarrassment by pretending to be Sarah's husband and hiring a detective on his behalf, to smoke out the suspected (other) lover. Henry agreed, and the private eye confirmed that there was indeed a lover, until Maurice gradually realized that he himself was the man whom the detective had followed and photographed—the lover pretending to be the husband and mistaken for the lover.

In this case, the real lover for whom the woman has forsaken both husband and lover is God, but the men do not know this and follow the usual shoddy scenario of triple-crossing.

The more common gender pattern, self-impersonation by the woman, occurs in a murder mystery about a woman who impersonates her adulterous husband's mistress (impersonating her) in order not to divorce him but to kill him. In Martha Grimes's *The Five Bells and Bladebone* (1987), the dead body of a man who lives on his wife's money is discovered in the country, and then the corpse of the woman who appears to be his mistress is discovered in London. But the detective discovers that the two women look strikingly similar and surmises that the husband and the mistress plotted to kill the wife and replace her with the look-alike mistress. He suspects, though he cannot prove, that the wife too uncovered the plot and killed the other two, intentionally leaving about clues to mislead the police into mistaking her for the mistress imitating her. At this point, one of the characters in the know remarks, "It's rather unsettling. To think that one could go about impersonating someone else impersonating one's self. It's like dealing off the top and bottom of the deck at the same time. It makes you wonder, doesn't it, if you know who anybody really is."[21] Whoever the remaining woman is, she kills herself, and as she dies, she says, "I'm not her." The chapter ends with the author's remark: "Ambiguous to the end."[22]

The theme of the man who leaves his wife for another woman who turns out to be his wife was boiled down to its bare essence in an incident reported in an obituary for the comedian Milton Berle, in 2002: "Mr. Berle was married in 1941 to Joyce Matthews, a showgirl. They were divorced in 1947, and he married her again two years later. Why, he was asked. 'Because she reminded me of my first wife,' he replied."[23] At the end of Gottfried von Strassburg's thirteenth-century rendition of the tale of Tristan and the two Isoldes (Isolde the Fair and Isolde of the White Hands), Gottfried remarks of Tristan, "And so he stayed with Isolde for some time, because she reminded him of Isolde."[24] It is unlikely that Berle was quoting Gottfried, but in this, if in nothing else, Berle belonged to the same club as Tristan, as well as King Udayana and Count Almaviva.

CHAPTER THREE

The Double Amnesia
of Siegfried and Brünnhilde

And the best and the worst of this is
That neither is most to blame,
If you have forgotten my kisses
And I have forgotten your name.

Algernon Swinburne, "An Interlude" (1866)

IN STORIES OF marital self-imitation, sometimes the mind of the man is obscured, so he forgets and/or fails to recognize his own wife; this happens to King Udayana in Harsha's *Ratnavali*. But sometimes the woman is the one who is fooled, when her husband pretends to be someone else (pretending to be him); this happens to Queen Vasavadatta in *Priyadarshika*. If we combine the two themes, we have a husband who pretends to be someone else (pretending to be him) in order to trick his wife but is also cursed to forget her. And if this encounter takes place in bed, both partners are bedtricked: while she unknowingly (because of the trick) commits adultery with her own husband, he unknowingly (because of the curse) is tricked into committing adultery with his own wife.[1]

Such a case of double amnesia torments Siegfried and Brünnhilde in the most famous of the many versions of their story, Richard Wagner's opera cycle *The Ring of the Nibelung*:[2] Siegfried, drugged, masquerades as Gunther to win Brünnhilde, to whom he has already pledged his love; Brünnhilde does not recognize Siegfried because he is magically transformed into someone else, and Siegfried does not recognize Brünnhilde because he is drugged. In effect, Siegfried is wearing a two-sided mask, with one side that changes his perception of her and the other that changes her perception of him. The double marital amnesia of Siegfried and Brünnhilde was wonderfully captured in a poem by Algernon Swinburne called "An Interlude," of which stanzas 10, 11, and 14 (there are 14 in all) seem most relevant to our story:

> As the glimpse of a burnt-out ember
> Recalls a regret of the sun,
> I remember, forget, and remember
> What Love saw done and undone.
>
> I remember the way we parted,
> The day and the way we met;
> You hoped we were both broken-hearted,
> And knew we should both forget.
>
> . . . .
> And the best and the worst of this is
> That neither is most to blame,
> If you have forgotten my kisses
> And I have forgotten your name.[3]

The story of Siegfried is not necessarily or originally a story of a man who imitates himself. It's about a man who betrays a woman on one or both of the two occasions on which he encounters her. But the need to erase that betrayal, or at least to complicate and justify it, inspired later tellers, most notably Wagner, to invoke the theme of amnesiac self-imitation clouding Siegfried's self-awareness. Let us trace the story from its earlier versions to Wagner, noting as we go along how the theme of self-imitation is woven into it.

THIDREKS SAGA

In the earlier versions, the trick is relatively straightforward and one-sided.[4] In the old Norse *Thidreks Saga* (c. 1250),[5] Siegfried does not, at first, masquerade. He is after Brünnhilde's horse Grani, and after he kills a number of warriors in single combat, he is welcomed by Brünnhilde, tames the horse (which only he can do), mounts (the horse), and rides away. The text says nothing here about any erotic connection between Siegfried and Brünnhilde, but there is an inconsistency on this point: later on—only when she learns that Siegfried has married someone else—Brünnhilde refers to his previous promise to marry no one but her. For after leaving Brünnhilde, Siegfried meets Gutrune and marries her because (as he later tells Brünnhilde) she (Brünnhilde) has no brothers and Gutrune has. Without resorting to the magic of a drug, this text settles for the realistic, if shameful, explanation—that Siegfried dumped Brünnhilde and married Gutrune in order to advance his career. Then:

> Siegfried suggested that Gunther marry Brünnhilde. Siegfried and Gunther went to Brünnhilde, who received Gunther warmly but Siegfried coldly, knowing perfectly well (just as he did) that he had broken his promise, made when they last met, to marry no woman but her. Yet Siegfried persuaded Brünnhilde to accept Gunther, arguing that Gunther was a powerful and brave man. She agreed, and they married. But on the wedding night, Brünnhilde would not allow Gunther to consummate the marriage; she hung him on the wall by their girdles, releasing him only at dawn. After three nights of this, Gunther asked Siegfried to help, and only then did Siegfried tell him that she would remain that obstinate so long as she remained a virgin, but that after she had lost her maidenhead she would not be any stronger than any other woman. The two men decided that Siegfried should deflower Brünnhilde but keep it secret. That night, Siegfried and Gunther exchanged clothes; Gunther left the bedroom and Siegfried entered it; other people thought that Siegfried had left and Gunther had entered. Siegfried swiftly raped Brünnhilde, and when morning came, Gunther and Siegfried exchanged clothes again, and no one else knew what had happened. Only later did Gunther start sleeping with Brünnhilde himself.

Since Brünnhilde is sexually threatening, she must be sexually disarmed and tamed; in folkloric terms, she is a Loathly Lady who must be kissed by a brave knight in order to be released from the spell that makes her dangerous and/or hideous.[6] Though no magic is used for the disguise—the men just exchange clothes—Brünnhilde is entirely taken in by the deception. Since she prefers Siegfried to Gunther and met (and probably loved) Siegfried before Gunther but is forced to marry Gunther, we may regard her marriage, more particularly her wedding night, as an instance of the medieval *ius primae noctis* ("right to the first night") or droit du seigneur ("right of the lord"): the king's right (and duty) to take any woman he wants and more particularly to deflower any man's bride on the wedding night (a major theme of the Figaro-Susanna-Almaviva triangle in *The Marriage of Figaro*). In this sense, Gunther as king is substituting himself for Siegfried the bridegroom by marrying and bedding Brünnhilde, and when Siegfried then substitutes himself for Gunther, he is simply restoring the status quo.

In European mythology the droit du seigneur is usually regarded as an injury to the bride as well as the bridegroom and is often, as here, thwarted with a bedtrick.[7] But the usual substitution is of another woman in place of the bride, and it is usually the women who engineer the substitution.[8] This time, however, the plan is carried out (without the knowledge of the woman) by the men, tricking not the king but the bride herself. Unlike the bridegroom forced, against his will, to allow the *ius primae noctis*, Siegfried willingly assists Gunther, and this aspect of the plot invokes another paradigm, in which Gunther is the bridegroom and is not injured but protected by the man who substitutes for him in bed on the wedding night. For though, erotically and romantically, Siegfried is the true bridegroom and Gunther the unwelcome intruder, legally Gunther is the bridegroom and Siegfried is doing Gunther a favor by replacing him in bed. Many cultures regard defloration as dangerous for the bridegroom, who willingly employs a substitute to draw off the curse of that first blood. Freud rightly connects this custom with the *ius primae noctis* and notes that women, as well as men, may conceive a fear and hatred of the first sexual partner,[9] as Brünnhilde clearly does for Gunther. In this sense, Siegfried is substituting for Gunther with Brünnhilde on the wedding night. It is the king himself, Gunther, who initiates the plan, getting the man who is (though he does not know it) his wife's lover to slip into bed in his place in order to destroy the all-too-present maidenhead. Siegfried, always eager to help, cheerfully plays the bedtrick on Brünnhilde.

A bedtrick is not necessarily a rape, but sometimes it is: if Brünnhilde knew who was in bed with her it would not be rape, but she doesn't, and so she resists—fights hard for a long time—and is raped. Freud suggests that one solution to the paradox of defloration, which makes the woman both bound to the man who does it and also hostile to him, is remarriage, which is why, according to Freud, second marriages are often more successful than first marriages.[10] But an even neater solution is remarriage to the same person, which allows the woman to remain bound to the original man but to discharge her hostility on a past life with him, so that she is no longer hostile to him in his present form.[11] If the remarriage is further hedged by a bedtrick, as it is here, the woman is further protected by her own half knowledge, her ability both to affirm and to deny that both forms of the man are the same man.

At first, Brünnhilde seems to beat off the unwanted seigneur by her own powers; yet in the dark, and without knowing it (or does she, on some level, know it?), she finally yields to the man she really wants, the man who had promised to marry her—Siegfried. Thus her resistance to Gunther forces Gunther and Siegfried to trick not just her but themselves, to trick her into allowing into her bed the man she loves but is not allowed to have. The bitter irony of this is that Siegfried's act is not a seduction but a rape, because Brünnhilde resists him, not knowing that he is the man she wanted; and the rape is all the more horrid because he does know perfectly well that if she knew who he really was, she would welcome him with open arms.

Völsunga Saga

In the Icelandic *Völsunga Saga* (c. 1270), Siegfried has already won the horse Grani for himself before he first meets Brünnhilde. He comes to a mountain surmounted by a castle glowing with fire; he penetrates the ring of flames, enters, and finds an armed figure, asleep; removing the helmet he sees that it is not a man but a woman, whom he awakens. The god Wotan, father of Brünnhilde and the other Valkyries, has cursed Brünnhilde first to sleep and then to awaken only to marry; she, however, will accept only a man who knows no fear. Siegfried being such a man, each promises to marry the other, and he rides away. All of this is straightforward enough: nothing is said about them making love.

A few days later, Siegfried comes to the valley of Hlym, where Brünnhilde is now at home, embroidering images of Siegfried's noble deeds. When Brünnhilde offers Siegfried a cup, he kisses her and proposes that they enjoy one another. She protests that she prefers fighting to living with a man, and she predicts that he will marry Gutrune. Siegfried swears that he will marry Brünnhilde or no one; again they swear oaths to one another, and again he rides away. But when Gutrune comes to Hlym and she and Brünnhilde discuss Siegfried, Brünnhilde says: "Siegfried, the man I have chosen for my husband, will come to you; Grimhild [the mother of Gunther and Gutrune] will give him bewitched mead, and you will marry him and quickly lose him."

When Brünnhilde later, unwillingly, agrees to marry Gunther instead of Siegfried, she recollects the time she and Siegfried pledged their love on the mountain, and then, immediately and without another word, she casually hands over to her foster father to raise a little girl named Aslaug, who is, she says, "the daughter of Siegfried and me." We never hear another word about that child; the medieval European epics, with their obsession with adultery, treat children rather casually, and Aslaug is no exception. Is this a reference to another variant in which Siegfried not only seduces but impregnates Brünnhilde on the mountain? Was the child born from the aftermath of that one kiss in the valley of Hlym? Or is the reference to an episode of this sort that has been erased from this text? We do not know.[12]

In light of the pledge of love between Siegfried and Brünnhilde (to say nothing of the child), the author of the *Völsunga Saga* must take pains to explain why it is that Siegfried nevertheless marries Gunther's sister Gutrune. The rationalization employs a glass of wine: Grimhild, perceiving "how much Siegfried loved Brünnhilde," gave him something to drink, and "because of that drink he could not remember Brünnhilde." Siegfried, drugged by Grimhild, marries Gutrune. They have a son, Sigmund.

Siegfried by now has presumably forgotten not only that he loves Brünnhilde but that he has already ridden through the ring of fire, and so this time Grimhild, not Siegfried, urges Gunther to marry Brünnhilde, and Gunther learns about the fire the hard way:

> Brünnhilde would marry only a man who rode through the blazing fire surrounding her mountain fortress. Gunther failed to ride through the fire on his own horse; he bor-

rowed Siegfried's horse Grani, but Grani would not obey him. Siegfried and Gunther exchanged shapes; Grimhild told them how. And when Siegfried-as-Gunther, riding Grani, got past the flames, he found Brünnhilde, who asked him who he was. He called himself Gunther and asked her to be his wife. She had no choice but to accept him as her husband when he reminded her that he had fulfilled her condition, riding through the fire.

This time it is Brünnhilde who has reason to know who has won her and Siegfried who is ignorant of his attachment to her. Even when Siegfried lends Gunther his horse Grani (whom, in the *Thidreks Saga* but not in this text, Siegfried got from Brünnhilde in the first place), Gunther cannot get to her; only when Siegfried lends him, in effect, his whole body can "Gunther" reach Brünnhilde. The woman, like the horse, will only let the right man mount her—even when he appears to be the wrong man.

Perhaps under growing Christian influence and in order to avoid the promiscuity of the *Thidreks Saga* (in which both men sleep with Brünnhilde), the *Völsunga Saga* goes out of its way to insist that Siegfried most definitely does *not* rape Brünnhilde:

> Siegfried-as-Gunther stayed there for three nights and they slept in one bed. He took his sword and laid it unsheathed between them. She asked why he put it there. He said it was fated that he must celebrate his marriage in this manner or else die. After this he rode away back through the same fire to his companions. Siegfried and Gunther changed back into their own shapes and then rode to Hlym and related what had passed. The same day Brünnhilde journeyed home to her foster father. She told him in private that a king had come to her "and rode through my wavering flames, declaring he had come to win me. He called himself Gunther. Yet when I swore the oath on the mountain, I had said that Siegfried alone could do that, and he is my first husband." When the wedding celebration ended, Siegfried remembered all his vows to Brünnhilde, although he said nothing. Brünnhilde and Gunther sat together at the entertainment and drank good wine.

The three nights in which the *Thidreks Saga*'s Gunther fails to deflower Brünnhilde when he wants to do so have now become three nights in which Siegfried willingly refrains from doing so. The double twist comes because Siegfried, still bewitched by the wine (presumably "good wine"—he did, after all, marry for money), pretends to be someone else in order to lie with his own beloved Brünnhilde—and then does *not* lie with her, since he has forgotten that she is his. Siegfried lays his sword in the bed to ensure his own chastity as well as hers, but he has *already* pledged his love to her (and possibly impregnated her). Under these circumstances, to lay the sword between them is locking the stable door after Grani has escaped. But Siegfried is doubly exculpated in this text, in comparison with the *Thidreks Saga*: he does not know that the woman whom he is tricking into marrying another man is one to whom he has pledged his love, and he does not, apparently, touch her.

After he drank the magic drink, Siegfried lost his mind but not his body, for he did not know that he loved Brünnhilde—no one knew, except Brünnhilde. Now he loses his body but not his mind, for when he takes on Gunther's shape, he still knows that he is Siegfried, though no one else does—again, perhaps excepting Brünnhilde. The lovers in the bedtrick know different things: she knows that she has pledged her love to Siegfried, but she does not know that Siegfried-as-Gunther is Siegfried; he knows that he is Siegfried, but he does not know that he has pledged his love to Brünnhilde. Unlike Siegfried, Brünnhilde remembers perfectly well that Siegfried alone can penetrate Brünnhilde's ring of flames, and so she both knows and does not know that he must be the man who has come to her this second time. She knows that Siegfried *was* her lover and half suspects that he *is* her lover now in the form of Gunther, but she can do nothing about it. Later, she says to Siegfried, "I wondered at the man who entered my hall, and I thought I recognized your eyes, but I could not perceive clearly because of the veil that lay over my fate." Here she seems to be blaming fate for clouding her mind and overriding her own correct perceptions. As for Siegfried, though it was too late for him to stop the marriage of Brünnhilde to Gunther (for at that time he was still unaware that Brünnhilde was the woman he had sworn to love forever), even when he realizes what has happened, he remains silent instead of telling the truth; here for a moment we see through the paper-thin excuse of the drug. For now he is well aware that Brünnhilde is the woman he had sworn to love forever, and it is not too late for him to stop the consummation of the marriage, but he does nothing. Later, dying, Siegfried blames the drug and his amnesia for what he did; yet even he must admit that, once he sobered up, expedience overrode honesty, not to mention love.

Brünnhilde, in this text, does *not* refuse to consummate her marriage with Gunther at the start (as she did in the *Thidreks Saga* and will do in the *Nibelungenlied*), but after she finds out about the deception, she locks him out, refusing to see him or to return to him except on her conditions. Thus in all three medieval sources she kicks Gunther out of bed at one point or another. Yet this time it is she, rather than Siegfried, who has concern for Gunther's honor, and it is she who refuses to contemplate adultery; when Siegfried urges her to "love King Gunther and me," she replies, "I will not have two kings in one hall," speaking both literally and metaphorically. Indeed, in this one text in which Siegfried-as-Gunther definitely does not rape Brünnhilde (though he may have seduced her earlier, in his own right), Brünnhilde has by far the most agency in the final scene, as well as dignity and honor. This may be because Icelandic literature in general depicts strong female characters, in comparison with continental texts, such as the *Nibelungenlied* and even the Norse *Thidreks Saga*. Much of the Eddic poetry on which the *Völsunga Saga* is based is narrated from the viewpoint of the major female characters, Brünnhilde and Gutrune. Such sympathies and conventions paved the way for the *Völsunga Saga*'s depiction of Brünnhilde as a formidable, passionate woman who is determined to avenge her honor against the man who done her wrong.

NIBELUNGENLIED

The Austrian *Nibelungenlied* (c. 1200)[13] never actually describes any meeting between Siegfried and Brünnhilde before Siegfried meets Gutrune; officially, the first erotic encounter Siegfried has in this text is not with Brünnhilde but with Gutrune, whom he wishes to marry. Yet the text drops several heavy hints about such a previous meeting (and presumably a sexual encounter), and there are overtones that suggest that the author of this text knew the Norse variants in which Siegfried and Brünnhilde had met and promised to marry one another.[14] When Siegfried and his party arrive at Brünnhilde's court, one of her maids tells Brünnhilde that "one of them bears a likeness to Siegfried," to which Brünnhilde replies, "If strong Siegfried has come it is at peril of his life, since I do not fear him so much that I should consent to marry him."[15] Why does she assume that he has come to propose marriage to her? Is it just because he (or she) is generally famous or because she knows him personally? Does she remember their previous meeting(s)? In fact Siegfried does not propose marriage to her (his first inadvertent insult to her); he tells her that Gunther wants to marry her, and she says she will marry Gunther if he meets her terms. Thus intertextuality operates even in the heads of the characters in the stories; they, too, like their authors, know of earlier versions of the story. The explicit statement, in this text, that there has never been anything between Siegfried and Brünnhilde forestalls any need for apologies, let alone a drugged drink. But the submerged, suppressed episode surfaces later to make serious trouble.

The *Nibelungenlied* hedges on the maidenhead question. When Gunther says he wants to win Brünnhilde, Siegfried tries to discourage him, for he knows (*how?*) that Brünnhilde will be won only by a man who can beat her at throwing a javelin, hurling a weight, and broad jumping. And anyone who fails to win her in this triathlon will lose his head.[16] Siegfried agrees to help Gunther win Brünnhilde—on condition that, if he succeeds, Gunther will let Siegfried marry Gutrune. Siegfried now masquerades, magically, in not one but two episodes of substitution for Gunther, but the sexual issue is erased from one and blurred in the other, for the *Nibelungenlied* divides Siegfried's proxy wooing on Gunther's behalf into two parts, one martial and one sexual.

The first of the two disguised encounters takes the place of the nonsexual encounter with Brünnhilde that Siegfried had undertaken *for his own sake* in the Norse and Icelandic versions but not in this text. In this first masquerade, a magic cloak of invisibility allows Gunther to pretend to fight while Siegfried, invisible, hurls the weapons:

> Siegfried took the magic cloak of invisibility, which also gave him the strength of twelve men, and any man could do as he pleased in it without being seen. Brünnhilde would have taken the King's life, had not Siegfried come to his aid. But Siegfried went up to him unseen and touched his hand, startling him with his magic power. He said, "Now, you go through the motions, and I shall do the deeds." Gunther was relieved when he recognized Siegfried. Gunther pretended to fight, and Siegfried, invisible, hurled the weapons. No one was to be seen fighting other than King Gunther.

Gunther "recognizes" the invisible Siegfried by his touch and his voice in the darkness of invisibility, as other people recognize lovers in the dark. Siegfried provides a kind of medieval dubbing (i.e., doubling), and Gunther lip-synchs his actions. Having won Brünnhilde in this way, Gunther marries her; Siegfried marries Gutrune, and the two couples retire to bed. But Gunther still needs to call upon Siegfried again to subdue Brünnhilde, this time not martially but sexually. As in the *Thidreks Saga*, Brünnhilde refuses to consummate her marriage, vowing that she will stay a maiden. In this text, however, she must be conquered not physically but mentally; she will not let Gunther touch her until she has "learned the truth about Siegfried." By this she means to know what she has already asked Gunther several times: why Gutrune should be Siegfried's wife. Ostensibly, she is concerned about Siegfried's low status in comparison with that of the king's sister, Siegfried's wife Gutrune; but in fact, when she first saw Gutrune at Siegfried's side, "never had she suffered such torment; she began to weep so that the hot tears fell down her radiant cheeks." Clearly she is consumed with jealousy, but Gunther answers her question only on the first, superficial, political level ("He has cities and broad lands quite as good as mine, for, rely on it, he is a mighty king!"). She continues to hold out because she still wants to know why Siegfried is with another woman. So she hangs Gunther up by her silk girdle and beats him up rather badly; after that, he takes care not to go near her in the bed again. And so, as in the *Thidreks Saga*:

> Siegfried promised Gunther, "I shall see to it that she lies so close to you tonight that she will never deny you her favors again . . . . Lady Brünnhilde will have to submit to you tonight. I will enter your room in my magic cloak so secretly that none shall see through my wiles . . . and then I shall tame your wife for you to enjoy her that night, or lose my life in the attempt." When Gunther insisted, "You must not make love to my dear lady in any way," Siegfried replied: "I promise on my word of honor . . . that I shall not make free with her at all. I prefer your lovely sister to any I have ever set eyes on." And Gunther believed him when he said it.

Siegfried went to Gunther's chamber and extinguished the lights, and Gunther hid himself behind the bed curtains inside the bedroom. Siegfried and Brünnhilde began a game that gladdened yet saddened the King. Although Gunther could not see Siegfried, he could plainly hear that no intimacies passed between them. Siegfried acted as if he were Gunther and embraced her. After a long fight, which Siegfried won, he left the maiden lying there and stepped aside as though to remove his clothes. Then Gunther lay with Brünnhilde and had his delight of her lovely body.

Does she guess that it is Siegfried? A. T. Hatto implies that she might: "She must admit that she has been most shamefully deceived, and deprived of the one eligible mate in the story. . . . Brünhild must divine that only the man who vanquished her at the game of war can vanquish her at the game of love."[17] Just as she might have guessed that he was the only man who could ride to her through the fire, she might have guessed that he was the only man who could wrestle her to a standstill in bed. Yet the text insists that here (as in the *Thidreks Saga*) Brünnhilde seems to be fooled. In her mind, therefore, one man, whom she does not want, has first overpowered her physically and then raped her.

Brünnhilde's passivity and incomprehension demonstrate her total lack of agency in this text, where her rape (by Siegfried-as-Gunther or by Gunther, all the same to her) is designed primarily to clip her wings, to restore the gender equilibrium that has been upset by a woman who dares to be stronger than a man. Siegfried takes from her the girdle that has already appeared as the symbol of Brünnhilde's resistance and superior strength, probably "that same girdle which Gunther could not loosen and by which he was hung on the wall."[18] Both the *Thidreks Saga* and the *Völsunga Saga* depict Brünnhilde as a kind of Amazonian virgin with exaggerated aggressive powers, who resists the consummation of her marriage and must be subdued. But the *Nibelungenlied* regards the Icelandic queen as a weird foreign woman (she is, by the way, the sister of Attila the Hun), a problem to be solved, and has little respect for her honor or power. This undoubtedly reflects the erosion of women's status on the Continent at this time and the dominance of the courtly image of women as things to be fought for, rather than people worthy of fighting. And so Brünnhilde must be sexually disarmed by a man who strips her of her maidenhead, for more than a mere maidenhead is at stake here; as he battles her in the dark, Siegfried thinks, "If I now lose my life to a girl, the whole sex will grow uppish with their husbands forever after, though they would otherwise never behave so." The maidenhead is a symbol of her manliness and must be cut off; only when castrated in this way does she become a woman.[19]

And so, in these texts, Brünnhilde is raped. But by whom? Where the *Thidreks Saga* states blatantly that Siegfried did it, the *Nibelungenlied* puts up a smoke screen.

What actually happened that night? The text tells us that, during the night battle, Siegfried kept his clothes on; when he got out of bed, fully dressed and as if to undress, that was the signal for Gunther to get in, presumably naked. And Gunther "took his pleasure with her as was his due, so that she had to resign her maiden shame and anger. But from his intimacy she grew somewhat pale, for at love's coming her vast strength fled so that now she was no stronger than any other woman." These statements certainly insist that Siegfried did not rape her and that Gunther did. No sword separates Siegfried and Brünnhilde, but they do not spend the night together, and Siegfried apparently leaves her intact. Yet this text assumes that she loses her strength only when she loses her maidenhead and that Siegfried destroys her strength but does *not* take her maidenhead, a logical contradiction. Certainly he overwhelms her so that Gunther can now handle her—which, in the closely parallel *Thidreks Saga*, happens only when she has lost her maidenhead. On the one hand, as Hatto argues, taking a girdle "means in ancient poetic language" taking a maidenhead.[20] The wording of a later conversation between Siegfried and Gunther also strongly suggests that Gunther knows that Siegfried did rape Brünnhilde. And does Gunther really trust Siegfried? He says he does, but he also hides himself behind the bed curtains inside the bedroom, perhaps just to be sure—he cannot see, but he can "plainly hear that no intimacies passed between them." (Siegfried might well have whispered in Brünnhilde's ear the words that the Wizard of Oz said to Dorothy: "Pay no attention to the man behind the curtain.") The king's ambivalence is wonderfully expressed in the statement that it "gladdened yet saddened the King" to watch Siegfried subdue his bride for him.

Hatto regards the *Nibelungenlied* as a conflation of the *Thidreks Saga*, in which Siegfried rapes Brünnhilde, and the *Völsunga Saga*, in which he doesn't. There is the evidence of the girdle and of the Norse tradition, but on the other hand, "It had become unthinkable for many of his listeners that Siegfried should deflower his brother-in-law's wife." And so, "in the conflated account of the *Nibelungenlied*, Brünhild is won twice over, though the motif of defloration is blinded." The poet resorts to "'blinding' the motif before our eyes," invoking a darkness that augments what is already a double blind: the disguise and the drug. Hatto points out this paradox of blindness: "The need for Brünhild to be won by contest [brought] with it the need for the cloak of invisibility, a 'daylight motif' which nevertheless recurs in the darkness of the bedroom scene unnecessarily, apart from the strength it confers."[21] That is, though Siegfried no longer needs the magic cloak he needed in the fight, he says he will use it and then takes pains to put out the lights, producing a natural darkness that renders magical invisibility superfluous. This is a text divided against itself, constantly doubling back to cover its own literary traces.

When Henrik Ibsen retold the story in 1858, he combined the sources, just as Wagner did. (Since Ibsen is, unlike the sources we have just considered, more or less contemporaneous with Wagner, it is best to regard him as a parallel rather than a source.) Only well into the play do we learn that Sigurd and Hjördis (as Siegfried and Brünnhilde are called) already love each other, for neither confesses this love to the other until the very end of the play. Instead of conveniently forgetting that he loves her and she loves him or being drugged so that he forgets this, Sigurd simply does not *yet* know that she loves him, for purely natural, psychological human reasons: mutual shyness.

In Ibsen, as in both the *Völsunga Saga* and the *Nibelungenlied*, the woman is terrifying, and the man who would marry her has to get his more virile friend first to tame her in battle (this time a battle not with her but with her bodyguard and familiar, a white bear) and, by implication, also to tame her in bed:

> Hjördis [Brünnhilde] swore that no man should have her as his wife unless he came to her chamber, killed the white bear that stood by her door, and carried her off in his arms. Gunnar [Gunther] wanted Hjördis but was afraid of the bear. Sigurd [Siegfried] was in love with Hjördis but thought she did not love him. One night, she got drunk with the men, and later, at the request of Gunnar, Sigurd put on Gunnar's armor and went to Hjördis's bedroom. It was dark in the room, black as a raven's wing. Hjördis thought it was Gunnar sitting by her. She was still flushed from the mead. Sigurd stayed the night with Hjördis in her room; after he made love with her, he placed his drawn sword between them and then slept. Before day dawned, Sigurd carried Hjördis off to Gunnar's ship. She did not notice the trick, and Gunnar sailed away with her. That day, Sigurd carried off and married Dagny [Gutrune], as Gunnar married Hjördis.

The feat to win the woman has changed yet again (horse to fire to javelin to bear), but the essence of the problem remains the same. The sword we know from the *Völsunga Saga* still preserves Sigurd's honor (if not Hjördis's). For here, Sigurd really does make love with Hjördis when he is disguised as Gunther. And he is able to do it not because he is drugged but because *she* is drunk. This is what we might expect: it is usually, as here, the victim rather than the perpetrator of a bedtrick who is drugged or made drunk.[22] But Ibsen seems to be the first to assign this theme to the more logical person; all the other variants make the trickster, Siegfried, drunk. The usual moral problems inherent in this seduction are absent, since Sigurd has pledged his love neither to Dagny nor to Hjördis. The bedtrick is used for the most common reason: because a man (here, Gunnar) wants a woman who apparently does not want him. By deconstructing not just the traditional mythology but the political motivations of the masquerade of Sigurd as Gunnar, Ibsen has restored a great deal of Sigurd's honor. Since there is no reason to believe that Hjördis prefers one man to another, why not switch one for the other? The trick becomes bitter only when we realize that she did prefer one man to the other and, of course, resents having been tricked in any case.

Ibsen adds a crucial hint of psychological realism to the story when Hjördis (Brünnhilde) describes to Dagny (Gutrune) the night of what we know to have been the bedtrick, though she does not know it—or, at least, not consciously:

> When a man holds the woman he loves, is it true that her blood turns to fire, that her breast throbs, that she swoons with a strange ecstasy? . . . [I felt this] once. But only once. The night [Gunnar] remained with me in my room. He took me in his arms, he crushed me so hard I thought his armour would burst, and then . . . and then . . . ! That was the only time. Never, never again! I thought I had been bewitched.

Without realizing what she is saying, Hjördis reveals that she could tell the difference between the men in bed: Gunnar was different that night, and for a very good reason: he wasn't Gunnar. She could tell, not because of anything she noticed in him but because of her own unique sexual response to the one man and not to the other. Later, when Hjördis has discovered the substitution, she says to Sigurd, "You have poisoned my whole life! Remember it was you who played that shameful trick. It was you who remained with me in my room, making a mockery of love and laughing slyly to yourself." Is the "mockery of love" a euphemism for making love while pretending to be someone else?

WAGNER'S THE RING OF THE NIBELUNG

If Wagner wanted to avoid the *Nibelungenlied* dilemma (Did Siegfried-as-Gunther rape Brünnhilde or didn't he?), what were his options? On the one hand, he wanted to re-create Siegfried as a noble hero, but on the other, he knew the history of the texts too well to present Siegfried as a man with a clear conscience. He invoked the magic drug that was already there on the props table, using it in the traditional way, to produce a conveniently focused amnesia of an earlier commitment. But he also presented the events in a different order. He manipulated the chronology, weaving together aspects of all three medieval sources, piecing together extant pieces of the tradition and rearranging them—*bricolage*, German style. For political[23] as well as artistic reasons,[24] he downplayed Siegfried's caddishness, all too apparent in the sources, reshuffling the chronology in ways that whitewash the character of his great Aryan hero. But long before Wagner, so much of the blame had already been shifted away from Siegfried that Wagner himself might well have said what Anna Russell used to say in her famous satirical summary of the plot of Wagner's *Ring*: "I'm not making this *up*, you know."[25] Any *bricoleur* worth his salt would say the same, but the truth is that they all do make it up, even Anna Russell. Wagner wrought his changes on a series of earlier sources that were already fiddling with the moral implications of Siegfried's treatment of Brünnhilde; he was rewriting history just as all the storytellers before him had done, swimming both with and against the current of hundreds of years of narration.[26]

In Wagner's opera *Siegfried*, as in the first episode of the *Thidreks Saga* and the *Völsunga Saga*, Siegfried-as-Siegfried, undisguised, wins Brünnhilde for himself, riding through the ring of fire to get to her. They make love, an event that mediates between the *Thidreks Saga*, where Siegfried rapes her, and the *Völsunga Saga*, where they fall in love but do not, explicitly, consummate their love. But Wagner moved up into this first moment, before the bedtrick, before Siegfried meets Gutrune, the sexual conquest of Brünnhilde that, in the medieval sources, occurs only in the bedtrick, after Siegfried has met Gutrune. He also placed here the motifs of terror and desire that characterize the later bedtrick in the *Thidreks Saga* and the *Nibelungenlied*, in which Siegfried-as-Gunther wins Brünnhilde because Gunther is terrified of her. Now it is Siegfried who, at first, finds Brünnhilde formidable and is frightened of her. The *Völsunga Saga* provides Wagner with several crucial details: Brünnhilde will accept only a man who knows no fear, a man she finds in Siegfried, and when Siegfried has stripped Brünnhilde of her armor, he recovers from the ambiguous androgyny of the sleeping figure by exclaiming, in amazement, "That is no man!" ("Das ist kein Mann!" a line that seldom fails to inspire muffled, or not so muffled, laughter in performance).

But where the *Thidreks Saga* and the *Nibelungenlied* argued that Brünnhilde was terrifying until she was seduced, Wagner implies that she can be seduced only *after* she ceases to be terrifying. Only after Siegfried has overcome his fear do they kiss and embrace in full orchestral rapture, as the curtain discreetly falls. This removes the brutal emphasis on the maidenhead and makes way for a far more romantic interpretation of their first encounter. Siegfried conquers her in battle merely for himself (as in the first episode in the earlier texts), not to subdue her for another man (as in the second episode). And then, when he has won her love, he makes love with her, still trembling, but now more in passion than in terror. Presumably, between the end of *Siegfried* (when they fall into one another's arms, singing lustily) and the prelude to *The Twilight of the Gods* (when they engage in a loving, morning-after dawn duet), while the audience at Bayreuth is having their second dinner, he deflowers her. The seduction happens offstage, but the music leaves us in little doubt (after all, Wagner invented movie music). When we meet Brünnhilde in *The Twilight of the Gods*, she has lost her powers even as she loses them, in the other texts, when she has been deflowered. As Anna Russell so delicately puts it, "Love has certainly taken the ginger out of her." Siegfried has every right to deflower Brünnhilde *for himself*, because he has not yet even heard of Gutrune, let alone married her. Since the Wagnerian defloration happens at a different point in the plot (significantly, at the point where the Norse Siegfried rapes Brünnhilde), Siegfried makes love to Brünnhilde with her joyous assent. Keine Problem. Das ist kein Rape.

Perhaps through some foreboding, he promises always to remember her, while she asks him, with the same foreboding that animates the Brünnhilde of the *Völsunga Saga*, merely to "remember yourself" and, she adds, "remember the fire that blazed around my rock." Brünnhilde gives him her horse Grane (an atavism of the *Thidreks Saga* horse), a horse who, she says, slept with her when she slept and was awakened when Siegfried awakened her. Siegfried rides Grane away into the *Götterdämmerung*.

And then he meets Gutrune. At this point, the plot follows that of the *Völsunga Saga*, with only minor modifications: Gunther's half brother Hagen tells Gunther to marry Brünnhilde, warning him of the fire that encircles her rock and advising him to get Siegfried to win her for him, bribing Siegfried with the promise of their sister Gutrune and making him fall in love with Gutrune by drugging him. And so the three siblings (with Hagen but without their mother) plot this, and the magic drink makes Siegfried forget everything: that he ever saw a woman before Gutrune, that any woman ever was near to him. Siegfried drinks, toasting Brünnhilde in words that he speaks softly to himself: "Though I may forget all that you gave me, I shall never let go of one lesson; this first drink to true love I drink to you, Brünnhilde." (Hagen alone knows that Siegfried has already encountered Brünnhilde.) Siegfried then immediately falls for Gutrune. The drug wipes out the stain on his honor that the betrayal of his own true love for a richer, better-connected woman might otherwise bring. (Anna Russell suggests another excuse for Siegfried's sudden passion for Gutrune: She is the only woman Siegfried has ever come across who hasn't been his aunt; Siegfried's mother Sieglinde is, like Brünnhilde and the other Valkyries, a daughter of Wotan.) When Gunther tells Siegfried that he wants to marry Brünnhilde, Siegfried helpfully promises to bring Brünnhilde to him, using the Tarnhelm, the magic hat of transformation, to change into Gunther's form. When Siegfried then sets out for Brünnhilde once more, the Tarnhelm gives him the form of Gunther, covering all but his eyes and disguising, deepening, his voice (which may explain why he is not recognized in an opera). As in the *Völsunga Saga*, he is not only drugged by Gunther but also magically transformed into the shape of Gunther.

Siegfried passes through the flames and accosts Brünnhilde: "A suitor comes; I claim you for my wife. Night is falling; in your cave you must marry me." After a violent struggle, he seizes her, saying, "Now you are mine, Brünnhilde, Gunther's bride." This is a double entendre: if she is "mine," that is, Siegfried's, how can she be Gunther's bride? The first statement is emotionally true—she is his—while the second is politically true: she is supposed to marry Gunther. He is pretending to be her lover, not knowing that he is. But then he seems to remember that he's Siegfried, though not that he loves Brünnhilde. (At this moment, Wagner plays Siegfried's leitmotif, which may indicate what Siegfried is thinking or, perhaps, merely what we, the audience, are thinking.[27]) Even if he does know, on some level, that he is Siegfried, Siegfried has two reasons not to sleep with Brünnhilde: he knows he is not Gunther, her future husband, and he does not know that he, Siegfried, is already her lover and her fiancé. Therefore, he spends the night with the sword chastely between them, going by the book—that is, the *Völsunga Saga*. But Wagner's Siegfried has no need to deflower Brünnhilde for Gunther, for the simple reason that—unlike Siegfried in the *Völsunga Saga*—he has already done it, all by himself, on his own initiative, in the previous opera, with her consent; he now lies with her chastely, though against her will. Then he brings her to Gunther, and the two men change back into their own forms.

The interrogation to which Gutrune later subjects Siegfried on his return plays upon the ambiguity in Siegfried's self-knowledge and his drugged tendency to conflate the two sexual encounters with Brünnhilde, the first half forgotten, the second vividly remembered:

> Siegfried: "I have won you today as my bride. I went through the fire for him, so that I could win you."
> Gutrune: "Did Brünnhilde think you were Gunther?"
> S: "I resembled him down to a hair; the Tarnhelm did that."
> G: "You forced that woman?"
> S: "She felt—Gunther's force."
> G: "But she married you?"
> S: "Brünnhilde obeyed her husband through the full bridal night."
> G: "But you were acting as husband?"
> S: "Siegfried stayed with Gutrune."
> G: "But Brünnhilde was by his side?"

At this point, Siegfried points to the sword and remarks, cryptically: "North between east and west: so near and so far was Brünnhilde to him." Siegfried knows that he did not deflower Brünnhilde (on the occasion of the sword in the bed); but his blocked memory keeps reminding him that he did deflower her (on the occasion when he awakened her with a kiss), and this paradox colors his hedging answers to Gutrune.

Now Wagner makes another significant alteration in the sequence of events. Where Siegfried in the *Völsunga Saga* awakened from the drug *before* Brünnhilde married Gunther, and still did nothing to stop it, here he remains in the dark to the very end and is thus absolved of knowingly betraying her. Brünnhilde, by contrast, in the *Völsunga Saga* did not find out about the bedtrick until *after* she had married Gunther; in Wagner's scenario, however, she finds out right away, before she marries him, and still goes through with it. When Brünnhilde arrives to marry Gunther, she is stunned to see that Siegfried doesn't recognize her and that he is about to marry Gutrune. She faints, into Siegfried's arms, but quickly recovers when she realizes that he does not know who she is. Gradually Brünnhilde realizes what has happened, and she cries out, "Betrayed! Shamefully betrayed!" And to Gunther, "Away, betrayer, betrayer of your self." Brünnhilde sums up the irony and pathos of the inadvertent sexual masquerade when she rightly accuses Siegfried of betraying her and Gunther, and Gunther of betraying himself. She then insists that not Gunther but Siegfried married her and "forced pleasure and love from me."[28]

The argument between Siegfried and Brünnhilde goes on and on like a Shakespearean comedy or an Abbott and Costello routine, because Siegfried and Brünnhilde are talking past one another, switching back and forth between the two different seduction episodes that Wagner has conflated: the first, when Siegfried-as-Siegfried rode through the fire *and made love to her*, and the second, when Siegfried-as-Gunther laid the sword between them and did not make love to her.[29] But on which occasion did he "force" pleasure and love from her? On the first, when she resisted him but then gave herself to him? Or on the second, when he forced her to marry Siegfried-as-Gunther? Siegfried keeps confusing the two.

Later, Siegfried apologizes to Gunther not for betraying him (which he still insists he did not do) but for letting Brünnhilde see through the disguise. Siegfried tries to make sense of the two statements (that he did, or did not, make love to her) by translating them into two degrees of disguise: "I did a bad job of changing myself; the Tarnhelm, I rather think, only disguised me halfway." He thinks that she half recognized him; and she, too, talking of last night, implies that she recognized him by his eyes (as she did in the *Völsunga Saga*), the one part of him that the Tarnhelm did not cover: "One single glance from his glancing eye, which even through the lying form lighted upon me." He only half disguised his voice, too, suddenly speaking to his sword in his natural voice. But Gunther thinks he now understands what has happened, and he moans, "I am the betrayer—and the betrayed." He regards himself as the betrayer of Brünnhilde (for pandering for her with another man) and as the man betrayed by Siegfried (who, Gunther thinks, actually did rape Brünnhilde). Siegfried reassures him: "But women's rage ends quickly; then she will thank me for winning her for you." And he goes off gaily to marry Gutrune with an entirely clear conscience.[30]

Only after she has engineered the death of Siegfried does Brünnhilde learn that Gutrune had bewitched him. (When Gutrune learns of Siegfried's death, she curses Hagen for making her give Siegfried the drug: "Brünnhilde was his true love, whom he forgot because of the drink.") At the time, she did not know that Siegfried loved Brünnhilde. Hagen gets the dying Siegfried to tell him the story of his life, and as Siegfried approaches the episode with Brünnhilde, we begin to think that the sheer force of the narrative will make him remember. (In the *Völsunga Saga*, he had awakened naturally from his amnesia at the end of the wedding celebration.) But before this can happen, Hagen sadistically gives him another drugged drink explicitly intended to awaken his memory clearly, so that nothing of the distant past will escape him. Siegfried drinks it and now begins to remember explicitly the earlier episode that, vaguely recalled, had been swaying his apparently lying answers: "My kiss awakened her." And that memory of the awakening kiss finally awakens *him* fully from his drugged amnesia. But it is too late. He dies, and Brünnhilde calls for her horse Grane, lights the pyre, cries, "Siegfried, your wife greets you!" and rides Grane into the pyre, back into the circle of flames, to join Siegfried in Valhalla. In duplicating, in this last act, Siegfried's first act that brought him to her, riding into the fire, she once again asserts her defiant, masculine nature.

There are questions we may ask of all the versions, beginning with our central question of self-imitation and self-deception. If ignorance is, if not bliss, then at least innocence, the one who wakes up from the amnesia but still goes through with the sexual betrayal is the one who has to take the blame. In general, knowledge is power; the woman who doesn't know is depicted as passive, helpless, disempowered. But when it is a matter of betrayal, then knowledge is a torment and ignorance is power: I did not know, I am not guilty, I did not betray. Thus by altering the sequence of knowledge and action for Siegfried and Brünnhilde, Wagner shifts the guilt of knowing adultery from him to her. Siegfried is the callow, unfaithful lover in the sagas, but Wagner fixes it so that she is the contemptuous, unfaithful lover and he is the one who is duped, who learns the truth only as he dies. To say that he does not know, then, is to say that he is good, a helpless pawn, and she is evil, manipulative. Brünnhilde's subversive intelligence (to say nothing of her colossal physical power) is valued by some of the sources and problematized by others, and we may see both strains in tension in Wagner, who makes Brünnhilde more powerful but also more dishonest and vengeful than Siegfried, simultaneously empowering his heroine and holding her responsible for the tragedy. Brünnhilde is great, and there is much sympathy for her, but she is dangerous and ultimately destroys the world. Siegfried's preternatural stupidity makes him heroic but a kind of holy fool. Significantly, where the *Nibelungenlied* tells us that Hagen tricked Brünnhilde into telling him Siegfried's vulnerable spot, knowing that she would not willingly facilitate his murder, Wagner has her give Hagen this vital clue of her own free will, in the clear knowledge that she is giving Hagen the power to kill Siegfried.[31]

The question of who knew what is tangled up in the question of who did what. Each text expresses a different sort of uneasiness, inconsistency, or ambiguity about the same point: was the encounter between Brünnhilde and Siegfried-as-Gunther sexually consummated or not? In the *Thidreks Saga*, probably the most archaic of the five,[32] the hero, disguised but not drugged, simply rapes his fiancée, quick and dirty, and later sleeps with another woman; he makes no effort to hide or to apologize. Other texts say that he did not touch her, yet these texts fail to erase some piece of evidence that he did rape her or, at the very least, seduce her. And when did each of them realize that they had been lovers in the past? The later versions attempt to resolve the moral problem they begin to see in the received versions, and they do this by obfuscation, generating more and more excuses, like squid (or college students), who, when frightened, emit quantities of ink. Obfuscation is the method of choice for two reasons: first, because a smoke screen of detail is always a good way to deal with an insoluble paradox, and second, because the storytellers are blessed or cursed with a number of details from conflicting versions, some of which they are reluctant to jettison even when those details clearly no longer fit the new agendas. This is yet another use of intertextuality. Thus the *Völsunga Saga* introduces a magic potion to exculpate Siegfried and also denies the rape; the *Nibelungenlied* leaves out the drug but says he had never met her before he perpetrated the bedtrick on her; Ibsen says *she* was drunk that night; and Wagner says Siegfried was drugged and, anyway, besides, he didn't rape her.

THE SWORD IN THE BED

The main excuse Wagner's Siegfried uses is the uncorroborated testimony of his sword; Gutrune finds it rather flimsy, but Brünnhilde accepts it, for at the end she insists, "He was the purest, though he betrayed me. Faithless to his wife, he was true to his friend. He put the sword between himself and his own true love, who was true to him alone." As early as *The Short Lay of Siegfried* in the Elder Edda, or Poetic Edda, from the eleventh or twelfth century,[33] Siegfried lays the sword in the bed.

This sword is a veritable palimpsest of meanings. The sword in the bed that fragments a couple, dividing them into two people, is the inverse of the shattered sword, broken into two (or more) pieces and then put back together. Siegfried's sword, Gram, is such a sword: it had belonged to Siegfried's father, Siegmund, who had taken it out of the ash tree where his own father, Wotan, had placed it.[34] But in Wagner's telling, Wotan's spear had split Siegmund's sword; Brünnhilde and Sieglinde saved the pieces, and Siegfried re-fused, reforged them into his own sword (now called Notung[35]), with which he in turn cut Wotan's spear in two. When Siegfried meets Brünnhilde for the first time, as she is sleeping on her mountain, he tries in vain to unfasten her breastplate; then he takes his sword, cuts the fastenings, and lifts it off. Looking at the shattered breastplate, Brünnhilde says: "A sharp sword cut it into two and dispelled the power from the maiden's body." This dissection has precisely the effect that taking her maidenhead had in the cruder variants in the *Thidreks Saga* and *Nibelungenlied*: it turns her from a man into a woman and (temporarily) from a powerful, active agent into a passive, weak object. The dissecting function continues when, in the *Völsunga Saga*, Siegfried, attacked by Guttorm (another brother of Gunther), uses his sword Gram to cut Guttorm in two at the waist, one side in the room and the other outside. This theme of bifurcation and separation adds weight and meaning to the crucial act of dissection when Siegfried (in the *Völsunga Saga*, Ibsen's play, and Wagner) lays the sword between himself and his woman in the bed.

Wagner's Siegfried draws his sword and says, "Now, Notung, bear witness that I keep my vow. To be true to my brother, separate me from his bride." Later, when accused of having seduced Brünnhilde, he remembers his sword, which he insists was between them, to which Brünnhilde replies, "You are calling on your sword. I know its sharpness very well, and I also know its sheath, in which it slept on the wall, Notung, your true friend, as his master broke his promise." This is a blatant metaphor for his penetration of her, made even more blatant by the secondary meaning of *Scheide*, "sheath," as "vagina." But the sword proves nothing unless Siegfried can prove which night he is talking about; on the first night, he did seduce her, and on the second night, when he laid the sword between them, he did not. So, too, in Ibsen's play, Sigurd places the sword between them in the bed, but only after he has had her. In both cases, the sword has entirely reversed its meaning, locking the bedroom door after the maidenhead has been taken. Ibsen introduces a kind of flat-footed common sense in imagining that the man simply put the sword in the bed as a kind of postcoital joke, making it painfully obvious that the sword is *not* proof of the nonconsummation of a sexual act. Just as Brünnhilde had mirrored, or reversed, Siegfried's act of riding the horse through the flames, so at the very end of the *Völsunga Saga*, she places the sword between them on their double-bed funeral pyre, "as before, when we entered one bed and vowed to become man and wife." Once again there is a conflict between the implications of the sword (chastity) and of the vow (consummation), but this time Brünnhilde can lie down beside her lover in the sure knowledge that there will be no breach of chastity—not just because there is a sword between them but because he is dead.

The deconstruction of the sword as a proof of chastity is evident in the tale of Tristan, told in texts composed only slightly earlier than those narrating the Siegfried story. Tristan's sword, too, is prone to bifurcation: it shatters into two pieces, leaving one part in the head of Isolde's kinsman Morolt (or Morholt) and the other half with Tristan, which later identifies Tristan as Morolt's killer. The pieces that fit together in Tristan's sword when Isolde puts them together are the pieces of the lives of Tristan and Isolde, coming together at that moment; that very sword then separates them and saves them, for a while one day, from the discovery of their adultery (when Isolde has married King Mark, Tristan's uncle). This is how Gottfried von Strassburg narrates the episode (c. 1200 CE):

> They were very much afraid—and events were to prove them right—that somehow someone might discover their secret. To meet this eventuality Tristan thought of a plan, which the two of them adopted. They returned to their couch and lay down again a good way apart from each other, just as two men might lie, not like a man and a woman. Body lay beside body in great estrangement. Moreover, Tristan had placed his naked sword between them: he lay on one side, she on the other. They lay apart, one and one: and thus they fell asleep. . . . As Mark recognized his wife and nephew, a cold shudder ran through his heart and all over his body. He thought to himself, "If anything has passed between these two such as I have long suspected, why do they lie apart so? A woman should cleave to her man and lie close in his arms by his side. Why do these lovers lie thus?" He closed the window through which he had seen them, made the sign of the cross over her, and went away; they found the closed window and his footprints when they awoke. . . . Their greatest trust and hope was that, whoever it was that had discovered them, he had found them lying as they were, so well apart from one another.[36]

Mark makes the sign of the cross over them but leaves them no other sign, merely a closed window.

When this episode is narrated by Béroul (c. 1191), the lovers suspect nothing; they lie apart simply because Tristan has comes back to Isolde too weary from the hunt to do anything but sleep:

> So she lay down, and he, and between them Tristan put his naked sword. To their good fortune they had kept on their clothes. . . . Someone brought the king to them; as he looked at them, he thought: "Does not all the world know that a naked sword separating two bodies is the proof and the guardian of chastity? If they loved each other with mad love, would they lie here so purely?" . . . Then the king took up the sword which separated the lovers, the very one—he recognized it—which had splintered in the skull of Morholt; he put his own in its place, quit the hut, and leaped into the saddle.[37]

Mark's sword thus matches, doubles, Tristan's sword, which is telling a lie, of course: it is a mere momentary accident that he lies beside the queen in chastity at this moment, not evidence of his usual practice. And in effect, Mark's sword lies too, for

Tristan misreads its signal. The king leaves the sword as proof that someone found them asleep together and "took pity on them," but when Tristan awakens and finds the exchanged sword, he says, "He is surely convinced of our guilt. . . . He left us in order to deceive us. He was alone, and he has now gone back for help." And they run away. Clearly, it is quite easy to put a sword in the bed *after* you have finished making love, and this is why Mark continues to be, rightly, suspicious. By contrast, when Tristan lies with Isolde of the Fair Hands and actually does remain chaste, he does *not* put his sword between them.

Despite the clear evidence that the sword can lie, there is a folk tradition that Béroul's Mark calls upon, looking frantically for an excuse to continue in his official ignorance of the affair (useful non-knowing, as usual): "Does not all the world know that a naked sword separating two bodies is the proof and the guardian of chastity?" "All the world" may or may not know it, but the medieval European tradition certainly did. Intertextuality again: the myth of the sword in the bed is well known in Europe by this time, and this, rather than any legal evidence, is the straw that Mark clutches in his desperation.

The story of the sword in the bed survived in German folklore[38] and was recorded by the Brothers Grimm (whose work Wagner knew well) in a long tale they called "The Two Brothers." It appears in the final episode:

A man had identical twin sons. They grew up and became separated; their father had given them a knife, which they stuck into a tree at the place where they parted, knowing that the side of the knife in the direction by which each had gone would remain bright as long as he was alive but would rust if he died. One of the brothers married a princess, but then an evil witch turned him to stone. The other came looking for him; he knew that his brother was in danger when he saw that the other side of the knife was half rusted.

He came to the castle where the princess was anxiously awaiting the return of her husband. The sentries mistook him for his twin and escorted him into the castle with the greatest joy. The princess thought that he was her husband. At night he was taken to the royal bed, but he laid a two-edged sword between him and the princess; she did not know what that could mean, but did not venture to ask.

He found his brother and rescued him; the two men stood together before the King. Then the King said to his daughter: "Say which is your husband. Each of them looks exactly like the other, I cannot tell." She was in great distress and could not tell at first, but then she identified her husband by a token she had given him. Then the King laughed and said: "Yes, he is the right one," and they all sat down together to table and ate and drank and were merry. At night when the princess went to bed with her husband, she said: "Why have you for these last nights always laid a two-edged sword in our bed? I thought you had a wish to kill me." Then he knew how true his brother had been.[39]

The bond between the men is stronger than any sexual bond that either might make with a woman; the knife that joins the lives of the two brothers is doubled by the two-edged sword that also joins them by separating one brother from his brother's wife. This two-edged sword, which has become a more general English expression for a device with ambivalent results, is a brilliant metaphor for the ambivalent relationship between the two brothers who do and do not sleep with the same woman. This variant, too, mentions what surely must have been the reaction of other women who found themselves under the sheets with naked steel: "I thought you had a wish to kill me." And indeed, the blade of chastity does express hostility against a woman.

For the sword in the bed—usually said to be a "naked" sword, as if to force us to confront its sexual symbolism—is a violent image, setting a violent form of chastity against its even more violent, closely related, polar opposite: rape, which appears in these texts primarily in the form of defloration, more particularly defloration through a bedtrick. Just as the masquerade splits the deflowerer into the one who binds and the one who violates, though they are one and the same man, so, too, the sword in the bed separates the man who deflowers from the man who does not deflower, though they are one and the same man. Both rape and the sword in the bed are sexual abuses against women, which objectify them, disregard their feelings, use them as pawns to other ends, and avoid the mutuality and intimacy that is the essence of the ideal relationship between the sexes. Rape and sexual rejection are uneasily intertwined throughout this entire corpus of tales of Siegfried, who sometimes rapes Brünnhilde, sometimes places a sword between them, and occasionally does first one and then the other. The metaphorical sword in the bed, in both the folk and literary traditions, is a problem that the rejected wife must solve. In the medieval courtly tradition, the literal sword in the bed appears to be a solution but is in fact the symbol of a quandary to which there is no solution.

If deflowering a virgin (whether it is regarded as rape or as seduction) represents the dangers of sexual excess, the sword in the bed, by contrast, is a dramatic expression of sexual deficiency, which, in its milder form, rejected wives experience simply as the back of the man in bed or the empty pillow. It expresses a kind of sexual ambivalence that other wives experience in a more subtle and elusive form. The juxtaposition of the rejection and the rape also expresses the ambivalence not only of the hero but also of the heroine: like Isolde, Brünnhilde both loves and hates her lover. Brünnhilde's refusal to accept Gunther as a sexual partner, or to marry at all, in several of our texts, is the female equivalent of the male sword-in-the-bed theme; here, as in her entire demeanor, Brünnhilde usurps male privileges.

The sword, in these stories from the courtly traditions, is not merely a phallic symbol but a symbol of male honor and brotherhood. It represents the purity of the relationship not only between the man and the woman in his bed but between the man and the other man to whom the woman in his bed belongs. In the *Völsunga Saga*, Brünnhilde tells Gunther that Siegfried had laid between them a sword that (in Jesse Byock's translation) was "tempered in venom" but, according to William Morris, "venom had made hard."[40] What a symbol! Tumescent hate, both sterile and deadly. As an erotic symbol, the hard sword of honor becomes bent and twisted, broken, shattered, fragmented, because the lover betrays his brother or the woman he loves or both.

CHAPTER FOUR

Resurrection and the
Comedy of Remarriage

"One Hero died defiled, but I do live,
And surely as I live, I am a maid."
"The former Hero! Hero that is dead!"

Hero and Don Pedro, Shakespeare,
Much Ado about Nothing (1598–1600)

TRUE AND FALSE ACCUSATIONS AND ORDEALS OF ADULTERY

By placing his sword between himself and Brünnhilde in bed, Siegfried absolves himself (for a while, at least) of what may or may not be a valid suspicion that he has cuckolded his king. When Tristan similarly lays his sword between himself and Isolde, the suspicion that he thus temporarily quiets is without question valid; eventually it provokes King Mark to force Isolde to submit to a more formal ordeal (grasping a red-hot iron), which she evades through self-imitation:

> Tristan put on the costume of a pilgrim, stained and blistered his face, and disfigured his body and clothes. He went to the place of the ordeal, and when Mark and Isolde arrived there by ship, the Queen saw him and recognized him at once. She asked the pilgrim to carry her from the ship's gangway to the harbor; he did, but when he came to the shore and stepped on to dry land he dropped to the ground, falling as if by accident, so that his fall brought him to rest lying in the Queen's lap and arms. "Would it be surprising if this pilgrim wanted to frolic with me?" asked Isolde with a smile. "You have all clearly seen that I cannot lawfully maintain that no man other than Mark found his way into my arms or had his couch in my lap." When it was time for her to swear the

oath, she said to Mark, "Hear the oath which I mean to swear: That no man in the world had carnal knowledge of me or lay in my arms or beside me but you, always excepting the poor pilgrim whom, with your own eyes, you saw lying in my arms. I can offer no purgation concerning him." Mark declared himself satisfied with the oath. In the name of God she laid hold of the iron, carried it, and was not burned.[1]

Isolde's play on words ("lying in my arms" in an innocent or sexual sense) becomes a play of bodies when Tristan-as-pilgrim masquerades as a man who has touched Isolde, which of course he is. In Béroul's version, Isolde makes Tristan disguise himself not as a pilgrim but as a hideous leper, who begs from Mark and receives the king's own hood. (One might expect Tristan to use this hood in a later ruse, but he never does.) She asks Tristan-as-leper to carry her across the mud, and she rides him as she would ride a horse,[2] with one leg on each side. Later, then, she swears, "No man has ever been between my thighs, except the leper who made himself a beast of burden and carried me over the ford and my husband King Mark. . . . The leper was between my legs."

Just a few pages earlier, Isolde had sworn another false oath, when she knew that Mark was spying on her and Tristan and could hear her: "I declare before God that I never conceived a liking for any man but him who had my maidenhead, and that all others are barred from my heart, now and for ever."[3] (In Béroul, she asks God to punish her "if anyone except the man who took my virginity ever had my love."[4]) In this case, one lie supports another: since Mark thinks he himself took her maidenhead, which is a lie, he thinks she has been true to him, also a lie. Thus Isolde uses her very infidelity to prove that she is a faithful wife. Gottfried seems to take quite seriously the ordeal that Isolde evades, lying not in the letter but in the spirit; and God seems to be satisfied by it, too. Yet there is surely deep cynicism in Gottfried's remark in reporting this episode: "Thus it was made manifest and confirmed to all the world that Christ in His great virtue is pliant as a wild-blown sleeve."[5]

SITA'S ORDEAL OF RESURRECTION

The lover is even more intimately collapsed into the ordeal in the story of an Indian woman who has a serpent lover (because her husband refuses to sleep with her); when she becomes pregnant, and her husband accuses her of adultery (because he has not slept with her), her ordeal is to survive the touch of a serpent, and she simply arranges to have *her* serpent used in the test: "He hung around her neck like a garland, opened all his five hoods, and swayed gently. She was exonerated."[6] This serpent belongs to the class of helpful animals who, in gratitude for past favors (in this case sexual favors), help out heroes or heroines in tight spots. Such stories seem to mock the classic Hindu chastity test, the ordeal of truth that Rama's wife Sita, most famously, passes honestly.

In the Valmiki *Ramayana*, composed between 200 BCE and 200 CE, a powerful demon named Ravana carries off Sita, the wife of king Rama, and keeps her locked up in his island citadel until Rama kills the demon and brings his wife home. At that point, Rama accuses Sita of violating her marital vows of chastity; he does not really believe that Sita committed adultery, but he fears that if he does not banish her he will lose face among his subjects, who do suspect her, and so he subjects her to an ordeal by fire, which she survives. He then banishes her, not knowing that she is pregnant; in exile, she bears him twin sons who, when they grow up, come to Rama. He recognizes them, brings Sita back, and reinstates her. But when he again expresses public doubts about her, she disappears forever back into the earth from which she was born. He never sees her again, but in her absence he has his artisans make a golden statue of her, which stands in for her at sacrifices.

Over the centuries, troubled South Asians invented various devices to take the edge off Rama's guilt for his false accusation of Sita; some texts introduced a shadow double of Sita who suffered in place of the real Sita, though Rama was still left alone in the end.[7] But the best solution to the problem was devised, some thousand years after the first Sanskrit text, by the playwright Bhavabhuti (probably in the first half of the eighth century CE) in a play called *The End of Rama's Story* (*Uttararamacarita*), which introduced the theme of resurrection from the dead: Sita comes back from her real exile and her now only apparent death so that Rama can apologize to her and be forgiven. By resurrecting Sita, Bhavabhuti gives the tragedy a happy ending at last. This play collapses together the ordeal, banishment, and final dismissal of Sita: Rama abandons the pregnant Sita in the forest on the banks of the Ganges, where he assumes that she will die, the prey of wild beasts. But when he comes back to that place twelve years later, Sita is there, though invisible; he senses her and feels her touch, but he cannot see her. (In any case, he assumes she is dead.) Nor does Rama recognize his sons when he meets them, though he feels a mysterious sense of kinship with them and notes how much they resemble not him, but Sita, and he begins to suspect that they are his sons. At this point, Bhavabhuti introduces a play within the play, in which the real Sita acts the part of Sita in a play about herself and Rama[8] (perhaps inspired by the scene in Harsha's *Priyadarshika* in which King Udayana plays King Udayana). Sita, situating herself within the play, within the past, calls out from backstage, "I am alone, without a protector, about to give birth; I shall throw myself into the Ganges." At this, Rama, overcome with emotion, cries out, "My queen, my queen, have pity," and his brother Lakshmana says, "It's just a play." Rama responds to the Sita in the play as if she were the real Sita (which, in this case, she is, though he does not know this); he recognizes himself, too, in the Rama on stage; when the stage Rama is described in very harsh terms, the Rama in the audience admits, "Yes, that's just like me."[9]

When Sita disappears from the stage, Rama faints. At that moment, Sita herself as herself, not as the Sita inside the play, walks out of the wings to touch the "real" (and unconscious) Rama with her living hand, reviving him (even as she herself has been revived). As David Shulman describes this moment, "The embedded play becomes fully congruent with its external setting which, for want of a better word, we might call 'reality.'"[10] She has forgiven him. The husband's false belief in his wife's death erases his false belief in her infidelity, and this in turn allows her to forgive him. Rama is just as wrong to believe in Sita's death as he is to pretend to believe in her adultery. Thus the moment of Sita's self-impersonation is framed by two parallel episodes: first, before the play, when the invisible Sita touches Rama's hand and he cannot explain his arousal (much as Priyadarshika cannot understand her arousal by the touch of King Udayana, who is invisible to her within the assumed persona of Manorama); and second, after the play, when she awakens Rama with another touch of her hand. But just as Rama mistook the stage Sita for the real Sita, he does not know, at first, if the real Sita is real or not when she comes to him after he has fainted; "What is this?" he says, and "Can this be the queen?"[11] Rama displaces his guilt from his supposedly dead wife onto artistic substitutes for her. The play uses the statue that Valmiki had mentioned and adds a play as well as the passage of time (twelve years) to bring a wrongly accusing husband to his senses.

Wives must forgive their husbands sometimes for the husbands' adulteries and sometimes for the husbands' unjust suspicions of the wives' adulteries (often for both). The first sort of forgiveness is evoked in the tales of the rejected wife whose husband must ultimately admit that he, not she, attempted to commit adultery. The second sort of forgiveness resolves the tales of false accusation, which stand as variants, almost inversions, of the tales of attempted adultery. In these stories, the husband rejects his wife not because he wants to commit adultery, because he thinks that she is undersexed, but on the contrary, because he fears, wrongly, that she has committed adultery, that she is oversexed. The double standard assumed in the stories of attempted adultery is again invoked in the tales of false suspicion: she must not be allowed to do what he has done. Yet in order to prove that she is not what he thinks she is, the maligned wife does precisely what the two-timed wives in the other stories do: she pretends to be someone else pretending to be her. She impersonates herself. But this time she does something else, too: she pretends to die and comes back to life.

In three of Shakespeare's plays—*Much Ado about Nothing*, *Cymbeline*, and *The Winter's Tale* (the last two known as romances)—the husband's suffering when he believes his wife is dead is regarded as fitting punishment for the damage he has done in doubting her and is ended by her resurrection. In *Much Ado about Nothing* (1598–1600), Hero, whose fiancé Claudio has wrongly accused her of sleeping with another man, pretends to die and is mourned. When Claudio learns that she is innocent, he is overcome with grief and shame. Hero's father forgives him for killing his daughter, on one condition:

> And since you could not be my son-in-law,
> Be yet my nephew: my brother hath a daughter,
> Almost the copy of my child that's dead,
> And she alone is heir to both of us:
> Give her the right you should have given her cousin,
> And so dies my revenge. (5.2)

Claudio agrees to marry this woman, but as he takes her hand, she unveils:

> Hero: And when I lived, I was your other wife:
> And when you loved, you were my other husband.
> Claudio: Another Hero!
> Hero: Nothing certainer.
> One Hero died defiled, but I do live,
> And surely as I live, I am a maid.
> Don Pedro: The former Hero! Hero that is dead! (5.4)

Claudio's belief that Hero has died and come back to life wipes out the memory of the false accusation; all of that happened to the "other wife" and the "other husband," the "Hero that is dead." This new couple may or may not live happily ever after.

The plot thickens considerably in *Cymbeline* (1608–1610), which includes pieces of every sort of sexual masquerade known to folklore as well as several of the themes of Shakespeare's masquerading plays, which make it a kind of cross between *All's Well That Ends Well*, *Othello*, and *A Winter's Tale*. (Shakespeare's use and reuse of such themes inspired the authors of *The Compleat Works of Wllm Sakspr [Abridged]* to combine all of the comedies into one hilarious play by rounding up all the usual suspects: identical twins, shipwrecks, cross-dressing, forest banishments, and so forth.) A greatly simplified summary, concentrating only on the issues central to the present discussion, is complicated enough:

Iachimo bet Posthumus that Posthumus's wife Imogen would commit adultery with him, Iachimo; Iachimo won his bet by entering Imogen's bedroom, hidden in a locked chest when she was asleep, then emerging and taking detailed notes on the contents of the room and the marks on her body. When Iachimo presented these "proofs," Posthumus was persuaded. He sent a man to kill Imogen, but the messenger spared her; she disguised herself as a man and escaped; the queen, her stepmother, tried to poison her, and she appeared to die but merely slept long and awoke later. Eventually, Imogen and Posthumus, both in disguise, were brought into the presence of the King; Posthumus, not recognizing her, almost killed her before she was revealed and vindicated.

The deaths begin with Posthumus, so named because his father had died right before and his mother right after his birth. Imogen dies twice, first condemned to be exposed and saved by a merciful executioner (as Oedipus is, and Snow White, and Brangane in Gottfried's *Tristan*), then drugged to resemble death, only to sleep and be revived (like Juliet). These resurrections are needed to wipe out the "stain," as Posthumus calls it, of her presumed adultery.

But when this plot is further developed in *The Winter's Tale* (1609–1611), matters are not so easily settled:

King Leontes of Sicily wrongly accused his pregnant wife, Hermione, of adultery with their friend King Polixenes of Bohemia. Hermione died, their young son Mamillius died, and the newborn daughter to whom Hermione gave birth in prison was taken away to be killed by exposure but was rescued and raised by shepherds in Bohemia. Leontes, learning of Hermione's innocence, grieved deeply. Sixteen years passed, and Hermione's daughter, named Perdita, and Polixenes' son, prince Florizel, fell in love and traveled back to Sicily, where Perdita's true parentage was discovered. Then Hermione's friend Paulina presented Leontes with a statue of Hermione, which, unveiled, turned out to be Hermione, whom Paulina had kept in hiding all those years.

By pretending to be a dead woman pretending to be a live woman, Hermione helps Leontes forgive not her but himself.

Did Hermione die and rise again? Or did she, like Juliet and Imogen, simply take a magic drug that made her seem to be dead when she was only asleep? Unlike *Much Ado*, where we see Hero's friends plotting her faked death, and *Cymbeline*, where we see the mechanisms of Imogen's apparent deaths, *The Winter's Tale* never lets us know, for sure, what happens to Hermione. It does seem to us that she dies; and then we are told that she is alive. Perdita dies Imogen's first death: exposed, but saved through mercy. Hermione dies Imogen's second death: she appears to be dead but, perhaps, sleeps, like a statue or someone in a cryogenic coma. Paulina speaks of this apparent resurrection as resembling the plot of an "old tale" (5.3), perhaps, indeed, the tale of Juliet or Imogen.

But lest we dismiss the faked deaths as just a toothless old tale, they are given teeth by the two real deaths that take place, of Mamillius and of Paulina's husband Antigonus (his demise predicted by the notorious line, "exit, pursued by bear"). And there are other sorts of deaths in this play. Speaking of the restored Hermione, Paulina says to Leontes, "Do not shun her / Until you see her die again; for then / You kill her double" (5.3). Ostensibly, this means that if Leontes rejects Hermione again, he will kill her again, doubly, but it also means that she is now her own double, a woman newly susceptible to further killing by her husband. The word "double" has a similar double meaning in *All's Well That Ends Well*, when Helena says to Bertram, "This is done. Will you be mine, now you are doubly won?" (5.3). "Doubly" here is a pun: Bertram will be won in two ways (by the evidence provided by a child and by a ring) and by a double (Helena doubling as Diana). "Won" also puns on "one." The line in *The Winter's Tale* may also be a reference to the double killing that Shakespeare refers to in *Hamlet* (in the play within the play), though he assigns the lines to the wife rather than the husband: "A second time I kill my husband dead, / When second husband kisses me in bed"(3.2).

Where remarriage to a wrongly cast-off wife is a rebirth after an apparent death, remarriage to another woman is a second death for the first wife. And indeed, remarriage to the first wife after such a long time, long enough for her to have become another woman, is also a kind of death for the woman she used to be. At the end of *Pericles* (a play with a number of parallels to the three under discussion, including a wife wrongly believed to have died), Pericles recovers from his amazement at the apparent resurrection of his wife and says to her, "O come, be buried / A second time within these arms" (5.3). Leontes should have said much the same but does not.

THE SELF-REPLICATING CHILD

Leontes is obsessed with things' resemblance to themselves, both Hermione's resemblance to Hermione and sons' resemblance to their fathers. He keeps talking about how his son Mamillius looks like him and how Polixenes's son looks just like Polixenes. At the same time, Leontes is jealous of Mamillius, whose intimacy with Hermione in many ways resembles Polixenes's, and he is awakened from his jealous fantasy only by Mamillius's death.[12] Leontes's words to Florizel—that he's the spitting image of his father and that Polixenes's wife was, therefore, demonstrably true to her spouse—expose his obsession with family resemblance, more particularly paternal resemblance, as proof of maternal chastity. Leontes even describes the adultery in

terms of a presumed "resemblance" between the two men when he accuses Hermione: "You have mistook, my lady, Polixenes for Leontes" (2.1).

But the resemblance of daughters poses problems as thorny as those of resembling sons. Leontes also notices how Perdita looks like Hermione, and here he wanders dangerously close to the Cinderella theme, behaving like the father who swore to marry only a woman who looked just like his wife, namely, his daughter.[13] When Leontes's courtiers urge him to remarry, he refuses, until Paulina makes him swear that he will never marry again "Unless another, as like Hermione, as is her picture, Affront his eye" (5.1). When Perdita appears, she seems to be such another; Leontes says he might like to have her for himself, whereupon Paulina says "Sir, my life, / Your eye hath too much youth in 't. Not a month / 'Fore your queen died, she was more worth such gazes / Than what you look on now." And he replies, rather lamely, "I thought of her / Even in these looks I made." Here the issue of aging returns in a new key. Perdita is now close to the age of Hermione when Leontes last saw her, while the resurrected Hermione is a different woman: she is older, and time has changed both her and the man who doubted her. The new wife, however, just like a picture (or, as it turns out, a sculpture) of Hermione, is not Perdita but Hermione. Like Rama and other jealous husbands who discover their errors, Leontes displaces his guilt onto a work of art. The statue is the final resemblance, and a near-perfect, indeed, tautological resemblance: nature imitating art imitating nature. But it is not perfect: age is a disfiguring factor. Paulina warns Leontes that his new wife "shall not be so young / As was your former," and when he sees her, Leontes complains, "Hermione was not as much wrinkled, nothing / So aged as this seems" (5.3). Always a man for surfaces, this is the only way he can tell the two Hermiones apart.

Perdita, as wrinkle-free as the former Hermione was, is masquerading but not as her mother. Hers is an unconscious masquerade of class, a princess masquerading as a shepherdess, matched by the conscious masquerade of class performed by Florizel, whom she knows to be a prince pretending to be a pauper. Perdita's masquerade doubles back into a self-impersonation when she dresses up as a princess/goddess on the occasion of a local feast and jokes about the chiasmic masquerades of herself and Florizel: "Your high self, The gracious mark o' the land, you have obscured, / With a swain's wearing, and me, poor lowly maid, / Most goddess-like prank'd up" (4.4). Like Ernest, who doesn't know he's telling the truth when he says he's Ernest, Perdita wrongly thinks she's lying when she says she is a princess. But the truth of her high birth is a secret that cries out to be heard. Polyxenes half senses that Perdita is a noblewoman in disguise: "Nothing she does or seems / But smacks of something greater than herself, / Too noble for this place" (4.4).

Perdita's story is an example of the old tale Freud called the Family Romance, citing the tale of Oedipus as a paradigmatic example: a child is taken from his real, high-born parents and raised by low-born people (or animals) until, years later, he finds his parents, establishes his noble birth, and comes into his inheritance.[14] (Oscar Wilde's *The Importance of Being Earnest* is a Family Romance, too.) Hermione and Leontes are undone by this same Family Romance, precipitated by Hermione's pregnancy at a moment when her husband does not trust her. Hermione's pregnancy is intimately related to her death, both on the level of the plot (she is imprisoned and, presumably, killed because she has become pregnant under suspicious circumstances—her husband's suspicions) and on the level of metaphysics: related in most creation mythologies, death and fertility enter human life at the same time. Because a parent must die, a child must be born to carry on the line.

The more gendered aspect of this belief, that the father lives on in the son only if that son is a true copy of him, is the driving force behind paternal insecurity, well captured by the Latin saying, *pater incertus* ("the father is uncertain," uncertain in both senses—unknowable and nervous) or, in our day, by the South Chicago saying, "Mama's baby, papa's maybe."[15] The son is, in a sense, what Augustine called a "worsened resemblance," a second-rate copy, while the mother is, in this model, either invisible or implicated in this copying process through the stigmatizing of resemblance itself as the "mother of falseness"[16] or, finally, vindicated in her chastity by the "proof" that her son so closely resembles her husband that he could not have been fathered by any other man. The visual criterion is essential in this pre–DNA world, in which paternity is difficult if not impossible to establish; the husband imprints his image on his child even as he imprints his identity on the objects that he stamps with his signet ring. And it is the need to be reassured of that stamp of approval that fuels the father's paranoia.

This visual criterion, basic to the mythology of adultery, occasionally leads to a triple cross. It was widely believed in early modern Europe that a woman who thought of her lover while being impregnated by her husband would give birth to a child that looked like the lover. This "maternal impression," as it was sometimes called, led to the false accusation of some innocent women whose children did not happen to resemble their fathers closely enough for patriarchal comfort, but it must also have kept many adulteresses from being accused and punished. After all, if your child is the spitting image of your best friend, there is a more logical explanation than maternal imprinting. Then, however, it was argued that a woman who knew this would think of her *husband* while in the arms of her lover, in order to conceal her crime, by imprinting the lovechild with her husband's features; and this backlash cast suspicions upon faithful women whose children did resemble their husbands.[17] Thus the belief in maternal imprinting forced chaste women to pretend to be chaste women, imitating themselves. This was the fate of Hermione.

Hero and Hermione replicate themselves as wives when they appear again after being presumed dead. Such apparent resurrections also occur in circumstances other than false accusations of adultery. In Euripides's *Alcestis* (430 BCE), a man who thinks he is marrying a second wife discovers that she is his first wife, returned from the grave:

> Admetus was saved from death when his wife Alcestis insisted on dying in his place. Before she died, she worried that a stepmother might mistreat her children, and Admetus swore he would never remarry. When she died, he said, "While alive, you were my only woman; now that you are dead, no one but you will bear that name . . . . My sons are enough . . . . Your body [*demas*], fashioned by the hands of skilled craftsmen, shall lie in our bed as if asleep, and I will fall on it and clasp it in my hands, calling your name, and so I will think that I have my dear wife in my arms, though I do not have her . . . . And coming to me in dreams, you will make me rejoice, because it is sweet at night to see the person you love, for as long as it can last."
>
> After Death had taken Alcestis away, Admetus was overcome by grief and shame until Heracles brought in a veiled woman and asked Admetus to guard her. Admetus remarked on her remarkable resemblance to Alcestis: "You have the form of Alcestis, and your body is like hers . . . . When I look upon her, she seems to be my wife." Heracles tried to persuade Admetus to remarry; Admetus remained adamant, but when Heracles insisted that Admetus take the woman by the hand and removed her veil, Admetus saw that she was Alcestis, whom Heracles had rescued from death.

Despite the absence of any accusation, false or true, the thematic core of *Alcestis* corresponds to the Zen diagram of the core of the Shakespeare plays.

Admetus's willingness to accept his wife as a substitute for him in death leads him to accept three other substitutes for her: the statue, the figure in his dreams, and the veiled woman. It also produces in him a guilt not unlike that of the jealous husbands who discover their error in accusing their wives of adultery. Alcestis is the very opposite of unfaithful—she gives her life for her husband—and Admetus never doubts this. But his failure to see that the substitute offered for his wife is his wife herself, pretending to be the substitute wife, is also characteristic of the falsely accusing husbands. As Alcestis is dying, someone asks her slave woman if she is dead or alive, to which the woman replies, "You might say that she is living, and also that she is dead." That is, death has come for her but has not yet taken her; which is, of course, true of all of us.

Alcestis's concern for her children is a major factor in her return from the dead. In a related subplot of self-sacrifice, mothers pretend to be the mothers of their own children. This theme can be traced back to the Hebrew Bible, where Moses' mother, having cast him away upon the waters (the Family Romance story), is then employed by his adoptive family (who happen to be the royal family of Egypt) as his wet nurse, that is, as the substitute for his mother. In *The Changelings*, an eleventh-century Japanese novel, a woman adopts and raises the boy whom she herself had given birth to (when she was masquerading as a man).[18] The theme surfaces briefly in Philip Roth's *The Human Stain*, where the mother of a black man (the hero, Coleman Silk) who passes as white and is about to marry a white woman anticipates (correctly) that he will never acknowledge her as his mother; she says, "You tell me the only way I can ever touch my grandchildren is for you to hire me to come over as Mrs. Brown to baby-sit and put them to bed, I'll do it."[19] When this theme makes it to Hollywood in *Imitation of Life* (Douglas Sirk, 1959), just as the black woman passing as white pretends to be black, which she is, her mother on one occasion pretends to be her mother, which she is.

Top stars often played mothers who passed as single women passing as mothers, giving away their (usually illegitimate) babies and then finding ways to bring them up by masquerading as respectable pseudo-mothers of some sort, hovering about in misery making great sacrifices and watching their children treat them like dirt and call other women "Mother." (The theme has male variants, too: Gaylord Ravenal in *Show Boat* [1936, 1951] comes across the daughter he has never seen and asks her to make believe he is her father;[20] so, too, Robin Williams in *Mrs. Doubtfire* [Chris Columbus, 1993] puts on drag to become the nanny of his children, who live with his estranged wife.) Fay Bainter in *White Banners* (Edmund Goulding, 1938), Bette Davis in *The Old Maid* (Edmund Goulding, 1939, based on an Edith Wharton novel), and Olivia de Havilland in *To Each His Own* (Mitchell Leisen, 1946) vied for the honors in this class. *Stella Dallas* (King Vidor, 1937), with Barbara Stanwyck, is a somewhat inverted example of the theme, but the winner, hands down, is *Madame X*, which was filmed a number of times (Leslie Halliwell remarks in despair that "the thing defies criticism"[21]), including two silent film versions in 1929 (directed by Lionel Barrymore) and 1937 (directed by Sam Wood and starring Gladys George), and most famously in 1966 (directed by David Lowell Rich):

Holly Parker (Lana Turner) abandoned her legitimate son because of a brief adulterous affair (and a horrid and conniving mother-in-law), but, when, at the end, she was on trial for murder (a murder she committed in order to keep a blackmailer from telling her son who she was), through a strange coincidence her son (Keir Dullea) was appointed to defend her. Near the end of the trial, she realized who he was, and though he did not yet know who she was, he felt an instinctive love for her. He urged her to tell her son who she was, and she refused. He imagined that, if he were her son, he would accept her and ask her forgiveness. He said, "If I were your son, I'd want to know. Your son should be here." "You're here," she said. "Yes," he said, and kissed her. "Today I've had a son," she said, and died smiling. Later he said to his father (John Forsythe), "I don't know why, but I loved her. From the moment I saw her, I loved her." And his father, who had just figured it all out, said, "I know."

So the mother is not the only one doing the self-imitating; her son pretends to be her son. As Halliwell lamented of this particular version, "The more expensive the production, the more obvious the holes in the plot and the psychology." But the passionate filmgoer, like the committed myth hearer, pretends not to notice the holes, while the true devotee not only expects them but positively revels in them.

RESURRECTED MARRIAGE IN HOLLYWOOD

Combine the tearjerker films of self-replicating, self-sacrificing mothers with *The Winter's Tale*, flip the tragedy over into comedy,[22] and it is just one small step for humankind to the Hollywood genre in which a husband who falsely accuses his wife of adultery exonerates her when, as he believes, she dies and comes back to life. In the films, as in the Shakespearean romances, greatly exaggerated reports of a woman's death and adultery are needed to make the marriage real, but the chronology is different: in the films, the alleged adultery takes place not before but during the presumed death, and so the resurrection (bringing with it the news of the adultery) triggers the jealousy, not the forgiveness. The forgiveness, however, comes, as in the plays, from the passage of time, which in this case simply makes the husband realize how much he has missed his wife and how glad he is to have her back, whether or not she has committed adultery.

Stanley Cavell argues that the Shakespearean structure resurfaced in Hollywood in 1934, "a date at which a phase of human history, namely, a phase of feminism, . . . and the nature of film's transformation of its human subjects met together on the issue of the new creation of a woman."[23] This properly alerts us to the second phase of the comparison, the recognition of the differences between the Shakespearean and the Hollywood examples of the genre. Do the films merely spell out and make explicit possibilities that were there, latent, perhaps, in the earlier genres? Or do the films go beyond what the earlier texts say, imagining possibilities that the earlier texts did not imagine? Do we need women's liberation to make the point the films are making, in particular to challenge the double standard for adultery? Are the films asking entirely new questions? These are not mutually exclusive possibilities, and I believe there is some truth in all of them. So does Cavell, who points out at least one significant difference between the Shakespearean and Hollywood patterns:

Comic resolutions depend upon an acquisition in time of self-knowledge; say this is a matter of learning who you are. In classical romance this may be accomplished by learning the true story of your birth, where you come from, which amounts to learning the identity of your parents. In comedies of remarriage it requires learning, or accepting, your sexual identity, the acknowledgment of desire."[24]

But I would say that Shakespeare, too, was wrestling with the acknowledgment of desire, as were many of the ancient Indian texts (such as the Harsha plays), while some of the films (such as *The Lady Eve*) are very much concerned with learning the identity of your parents.

My Favorite Wife (1940)

A classic film of this genre is *My Favorite Wife* (Garson Kanin, 1940):

> Ellen Arden (Irene Dunne) was presumed drowned in a shipwreck; after seven years, her husband Nick (Cary Grant) had her declared legally dead and married Bianca (Gale Patrick). On the day of the wedding, Ellen reappeared—she had survived on a desert island—and discovered the remarriage. Hastening to the place where Nick and Bianca were about to begin their honeymoon, she confronted Nick. He still loved her and wanted her back, but he was unable to break the bad news to Bianca for some time and devised various ruses to avoid consummating the marriage, while Ellen pretended to be an old friend from the South visiting them. When Nick learned that Ellen had not been alone on that island but had been shipwrecked there with the aggressively handsome and virile Steve (Randolph Scott), he suspected her of committing adultery. Nick told Bianca he was married; the police arrested him for bigamy; in court, the judge declared Ellen alive and offered to annul the second marriage. Nick drove to the mountains with Ellen and their two children, who, Ellen discovered, knew that she was their mother. Ellen locked Nick out of her bedroom until Christmas; he told her he loved her and then appeared in the bedroom dressed as Santa Claus. "Oh, Nick," she laughed. And so to bed.

Like the shipwrecked Viola in Shakespeare's *Twelfth Night*, Ellen returns to civilization in drag, borrowed from the sailors who rescued her; when she walks up to her own children in front of her own house, her daughter asks her, "Are you a lady or a man?" She must reclaim her womanhood from Bianca, and she fights back, first by demonstrating that she was desired by another man and then by demonstrating that she resisted that desire. She must also reclaim the past. When she dresses to meet Nick, who still does not know of her existence, she chooses a dress she used to wear, but when she sees the other women in the hotel, she realizes her skirt is too long and too long ago; it is precisely seven years too long, and she has to cut off that extra piece of hemline to bring herself into the present. But it is not so easy to cut off the fabric of time. She must masquerade to do that.

Nick's two masquerades are transparent. Like Ellen, he appears briefly in drag: when Ellen sends him to the house to get some of her clothes for her, he tries them on and happens to be seen by a psychiatrist whom Bianca has hired to deal with his apparent impotence. And at the end he appears as Santa Claus, a costume that is the very essence and cliché of the obvious lie, a satire on masquerade itself. Ellen also masquerades, but not always so transparently as Nick. After her initial appearance in drag, she appears as a Southern belle (the "old friend"), with a Southern accent as thick and sweet as molasses. This act fools Bianca, but it doesn't fool the children for long; while she is screwing up her courage to tell them she is their mother, they are teasing her with questions about their mother, and when she finally says, "Suppose your mother didn't drown. Suppose she was right here," their giggles wise her up, and she realizes she is the one who has been fooled, by them, into thinking they were fooled. She smiles and says, "You already know, don't you?" And they nod. Even less successful is the masquerade Ellen engineers for someone else, getting a mousy-looking shoe salesman to masquerade as Steve in the vain hope of preventing Nick from finding out how attractive her desert island mate really was; Nick has already seen the real Steve and so is on to her.

Ellen also masquerades, this time transparently, as Bianca. Suddenly faced with two wives, Nick installs them in two different rooms in the same hotel. But when he cannot find the courage to tell Bianca about Ellen's resurrection, Ellen suggests that he practice on her: "I'll be Bianca," and then, "I'm Bianca." Ellen does an absolutely unconvincing and libelous imitation of Bianca, whom she has only glimpsed for a moment; Ellen-as-Bianca speaks in a hoity-toity upper-class voice, to which Nick rightly objects ("She doesn't talk like that," he says) and to which he responds without conviction, unable to pretend that she is not Ellen. Finally, she insists, "Darling, aren't you going to kiss me?" (still in her Bianca voice) and then, when he hesitates, in her own voice, "Do it! Do it!" He kisses her, genuinely, and she says, "Was that for Bianca?" They are interrupted before he can answer, but, of course, it was not for Bianca. Having at last established his desire for her, Ellen is determined not to let Nick sleep with her until he gives up his suspicions (she puts him in the attic, "Perfect for thinking things out"). In the end, he capitulates without actually declaring her innocent: "I don't care what happened and I don't care what people say," he declares; "I was always mad about you and I always will be."

Just as the children "already know" that Ellen is their mother, so Nick, too, already knows not only that Ellen is not Bianca but that she is not Steve's woman, that she has kept her marriage vows. The parallels are clear though asymmetrical: she cannot bring herself to tell the truth to the children, and he cannot bring himself to tell the truth to Bianca. When she relents at the end, she is forgiving him, as Rosina forgives Almaviva, not for his attempted adultery (with Bianca) but for his suspicion of hers (with Steve). To win against the woman who is taking her place, Ellen must first become her and then prove that she is not her.

And the film shows some sympathy for Bianca. When Bianca seeks her annulment, the judge calls the second marriage "kissless" and annuls it. (In the Doris Day remake, Bianca says she was "unkissed, un-anything.") The kissless marriage is Hollywood's coy term for our old friend the sword in the bed (which enters film as the notorious sheet that separates Clark Gable and Claudette Colbert in *It Happened One Night* [1934]), and here its usual ambivalence is somewhat scrambled: now noble restraint is mistaken for impotence. The judge, a Yale man, noting the "kissless" marriage, looks at Nick and mutters, "Harvard man," a clear slur on Nick's virility, and Bianca storms out of the courtroom with a final shot at Nick: "All I have to say to you is, as far as I'm concerned, *you're* legally dead." Yet another twist in the running joke about sex and death. But in his other marriage, it is Nick who suffers from the sword in the bed when Ellen locks him out—just until he learns his lesson.

My Favorite Wife claimed to be inspired by a poem that Alfred Lord Tennyson published in 1864, "Enoch Arden," about a married man who sets off to sea, taking with him a lock of the hair of his third child, newborn; he is shipwrecked on a deserted island, and while he is away the child dies. Twelve years pass, and his wife Annie, presuming that he is dead, marries their best friend Philip; they have a child. Eventually, Enoch is rescued and makes his way home only to discover that his wife has remarried; he watches them from afar for a year and then, as he is dying, sends her the lock of hair as a sign that he had returned and stayed away: "It will moreover be a token to her, / That I am he." Enoch's failure to stand up and be counted disqualifies this poem as a source for anything but the initial situation of *My Favorite Wife* (and even then with a change of gender) and the atavism of the name (Enoch/Nick Arden, which might as easily have been derived from the site of *As You Like It*).[25]

D. W. Griffith made a (silent) film *Enoch Arden* in 1911, and Somerset Maugham wrote a play called *Home and Beauty* (1919) about the return of a husband presumed killed in the war. Other films applied the Tennyson/Maugham genders to the plot of *My Favorite Wife*, as the Hollywood resurrection machine spun almost out of control. Leo McCarey, who produced *My Favorite Wife*,[26] had originally planned the film for Jean Arthur under the working title *Woman Overboard*; but she was committed to another project, for in that same year she made a film with a suspiciously similar plot (though with the reversed, Tennyson/Maugham genders) for someone else: *Too Many Husbands* (Wesley Ruggles, 1940), aka *My Two Husbands* (the husbands played by Melvyn Douglas and Fred MacMurray). Years later, Betty Grable was caught between her presumably dead and then resurrected husband (Jack Lemmon) and her new husband (Gower Champion), both of whom fortunately happened to be songwriters, for the film, which stated that it was based on the Maugham play, was a musical, *Three for the Show* (H. C. Potter, 1955). The variations in the gender of the resurrected person are not particularly significant, since in all variants each of the two partners has found a second mate; it is the different nature of those second relationships (engaged, married, adulterous) that varies and that has different consequences according to the gender of the actor.

Another version of the original Leo McCarey plot (and genders), now called *Something's Got to Give* (the original working title of *My Favorite Wife*), went into production in 1962, directed by George Cukor, with Marilyn Monroe leading a great cast.[27] But the film was never completed, since the vacillations in the marital life of the heroine—married, died, resurrected, remarried—were grotesquely mirrored by those in Marilyn's professional life, scrambled in the wrong order: hired, fired, rehired, and died. *Something's Got to Give* then became the title not of the unfinished movie but of Marilyn Monroe's unfinished life, more precisely the title of a 1990 TV documentary made about her last days, including the aborted film.[28] So art, not life, had the last word there.

A year after the cameras abruptly stopped rolling on *Something's Got to Give*, the near infinite elasticity of the myth[29] was demonstrated by the casting of Doris Day in the role of Ellen that had been intended for Marilyn Monroe, a 180-degree turn from out-of-control sexpot to professional virgin in one swell foop.[30] *Move Over, Darling* (Michael Gordon, 1963), with James Garner (Nick), Polly Bergen (Bianca), and Chuck Connors (Steve), is a dumbed-down version in which all the subtle jokes lightly implied in the first version are spelled out in neon. The relationships, moreover, are misogynized and desexed. As for the misogyny, where Irene Dunne had been a lady explorer shipwrecked on an anthropological expedition without her family, Doris Day would never be so uppity as to go off like that on a career of her own. She was lost when they were all traveling together as a family and their plane went down in the water; the others were rescued, and only she was lost. As for the sex, in *My Favorite Wife*, right after the children acknowledge Irene Dunne as their mother, she says, "Don't you think it's about time somebody started kissing somebody?" and they all hug. The Doris Day film ends with a version of this scene: the kids are in the swimming pool with James Garner (who has just told them that Doris Day is their mother), and Garner says, "Isn't it about time somebody started kissing somebody around here?" At that moment, Doris Day jumps into the swimming pool,[31] they all hug, and the credits roll. In the earlier version, however, there is a different finale: after the family hug, the kids go to bed and Irene Dunne, in a sexy nightgown, teases Cary Grant until he practically breaks down the door to her bedroom. Where Irene Dunne and Cary Grant end up in bed, Doris Day and James Garner end up in the water with the kiddies.

There is a nice a moment of intertextual self-imitation in *Move Over, Darling*. To avoid sleeping with Bianca, Nick pretends to have hurt his back, and Ellen masquerades briefly as a Swedish nurse hired to give him massages. (Where Irene Dunne's Southern accent made her hypersexual in this situation, the squeaky-clean, sports mistress Swedish persona makes Doris Day even more antisexual.) The "masseuse," growing impatient as Nick puts off breaking the bad news to Bianca, gets Bianca alone by offering to give *her* a massage too, and in the course of it drops a heavy hint: "When I was a little girl I went to the movies. Poor Cary Grant thought his wife was dead, but Irene Dunne, she comes back." And Bianca says, "Oh, that just happens in the movies."

THE COMEDY OF REMARRIAGE IN HOLLYWOOD

Cavell maintains that the genre of film he calls the comedy of remarriage (and Pauline Kael called "one of old Hollywood's favorite subjects: the divorced couple who almost bed down with new mates but get back together"[32]) is "an inheritor of the preoccupations and discoveries of Shakespearean romantic comedy."[33] He argues that *The Winter's Tale*, in particular, supplies the precedent for the structure of the films of remarriage,[34] but as we have seen, Shakespeare's comedies and romances (not only *The Winter's Tale* but *Much Ado* and *Cymbeline*) are closer to the films of marital resurrection, or resurrection-and-remarriage. The false accusation of adultery does come from *The Winter's Tale*, but not all the remarriage films include this accusation. The remarriage plot can be more directly traced back to Noel Coward's *Private Lives* (1930), in which Eliot and Amanda, long divorced, meet again when they are about to marry two other people and, instead, run away together; the film (Sidney Franklin, 1931) starred Norma Shearer and Robert Montgomery.

The remarriage comedies are not about death or children, themes that play a major part in the resurrection films. The heroines of the film comedies of remarriage in this regard more closely resemble rejected wives, such as Vasavadatta and the Countess Rosina, who merely replace their husbands' mistresses without getting pregnant. Cavell suggests that for the remarrying couples, "children, if they appear, must appear as intruders," because the couple themselves "wish to be children again, or perhaps to be children together."[35] In one of the classics of the remarriage genre, *The Philadelphia Story* (George Cukor, 1940), the figure of the (resurrected) heroine's child is displaced onto Tracy Lord's sister Dinah (Virginia Weidler), an obnoxiously precocious teenager. In *The Awful Truth* (Leo McCarey, 1937), the children are replaced by a fox terrier, the object of an elaborate custody battle for visitation rights.[36]

What unites the classic examples of both sets of films (resurrection and remarriage) are the false accusations of adultery and the reunion of a man and woman after such an accusation. Freud remarked, "The finding of an object is in fact the refinding of it,"[37] a statement that Cavell thinks "may stand as the motto for the entire genre of remarriage [films]."[38] It certainly accounts for a great deal of the broader mythology of marital self-imitation. Freud also said, "The husband is almost always so to speak only a substitute, never the right man; it is another man—in typical cases the father—who has first claim to a woman's love; the husband at most takes second place."[39] Moreover, as we have noted in Freud's analysis of Siegfried, the experience of the first sexual experience with the first husband often makes the wife hate him, whereas after she has divorced him, the woman "becomes a tender wife, able to make her second husband happy. The archaic reaction has, so to speak, exhausted itself on the first object."[40] Since, therefore, the husband is already a substitute for the ideal husband, perhaps the father (or brother, Freud also suggests), then the substitute for the husband, the husband in disguise, has two advantages: he negates the negation and is the right husband, and he does not bear the onus of breaking in the wife in the first place. This is certainly the case when Siegfried substitutes for Gunther in deflowering Brünnhilde, who ends up with the man she should have had, the man for whom all other men would be substitutes: Siegfried.

But some women may be haunted by the positive feeling (Freud calls it bondage) that, despite her antipathy toward him, the wife feels for her first husband, whose image intervenes to inhibit the love that she tries to direct to another man.[41] The solution is to have the first husband become the second husband, which is precisely what happens in the mythologies of remarriage, the Milton Berle syndrome viewed from the other side of the bed. Freud's insight also applies more broadly to all of the triple-cross masquerades: the self, as viewed not only by the self but by the person for whom the self is the object of love, begins at one remove from the ideal partner, the "right" one, and approaches that sense of rightness only when a substitute is found for the substitute. If this substitute is the first husband after all, who ends up with the woman who turns out to be his first wife after all, the marriage is complete. What Freud called the repetition compulsion, the mind's need to revisit the scene of the crime, is surely also relevant here. Just as the same stories are told over and over, so in real life the same plots are repeated compulsively, as people marry the same partners over and over.

The Awful Truth (1937)

With these considerations in mind, let us turn to the comedy of remarriage in Hollywood and to one of the best-loved examples of this genre, *The Awful Truth*:[42]

Jerry Warriner (Cary Grant) was pretending to be in Florida when he was not; he faked a tan, skin deep. Returning from this escapade to find that his wife Lucy (Irene Dunne) had been out all night with her voice teacher, a charming Frenchman, Armand Duvalle (Alexander D'Arcy), Jerry accused her of adultery. They filed for divorce (she got the dog), and each started dating someone else: she hooked a rich Texan, Dan Leeson (Ralph Bellamy), and he, after a brief fling with a sluttish false-Southern nightclub singer, Dixie Belle Lee (Joyce Compton), became engaged to an heiress, Barbara Vance (Molly Lamont). To break up his engagement, Lucy crashed a dinner at the heiress's home, pretending to be his sister but behaving like Dixie Belle; she even sang the risqué song that Dixie had sung. Jerry and Lucy left together and drove to a country cabin in the mountains, where he half apologized and she relented. And so to bed.

At one point, while Jerry is talking to Dan Leeson's mother, he assures her that Lucy is pure as the driven snow, while crossing his fingers and talking as if he's lying; but in fact she *is* pure as the driven snow, and we never do find out what *he* was doing when he was supposed to be in Florida. We presume that he was committing adultery, but this is a film in which things are seldom what they seem, and Cavell asks, "Why would a married man find it more important to seem unfaithful than to be so?"[43] Surely, however, Jerry is projecting his own guilt onto Lucy. To punish him for doubting her, she prolongs his agony when he wants to get back into bed with her, postponing the moment of reconciliation (though not nearly so long as Hermione postpones it in *The Winter's Tale*). Even when they get together at the end, he still believes she has been unfaithful to him; she locks him out of the bedroom until he suspends, but never really disavows, his accusation, his capitulation implying either that he will trust her not to do it again or that he grants her the same freedom that he has. In the end, as at the beginning, Jerry doesn't know that there is nothing to know, that the awful truth is neither awful nor the truth.

Each of them has two possible new partners, one hypersexualized (in conventional stereotypes: the suave Frenchman for her [the main reason why Jerry suspects him is simply that he's French], the lower-class nightclub singer for him) and the other desexualized (also stereotypes: the heiress for him, the Texan for her [played, as usual, by Ralph Bellamy[44]], both of them rich and therefore presumably physically unattractive, desired only for their money). Her hypersexualized partner is the one that poses the real threat to him, precipitating the divorce, and his desexualized partner is the one that threatens her, precipitating the masquerade; the other two candidates, her rich guy and his floozy, are mere comic relief. This alone tells us a lot about the asymmetrical concerns of husbands and wives. Yet when she makes her move to get him away from the desexualized woman, she masquerades as the hypersexualized woman. Her sexy song and dance act is a "song and dance act" in the metaphorical sense as well, a performed double entendre, repelling Barbara Vance and her posh family with its implication that she is vulgar (which she is not) while at the same time fascinating Jerry with its implication that she is capable of the same kind of healthy sexuality as Dixie Belle (which she is, and which he has apparently not seen in her until now).[45]

Near the end, while she is wearing a sexy negligee and stalling him, and he is keener and keener to get into bed with her, they engage in a conversation about the same and the different:

> Lucy: "Things are just the same as they always were, only you're just the same, too, so I guess things will never be the same again."
> Jerry: "You're wrong about things being different because they're not the same. Things are different, except in a different way. You're still the same, only I've been a fool. Well, I'm not now. So, as long as I'm different, don't you think things could be the same again? Only a little different."

And so forth. On the surface, she is saying that she is faithful, as she always was (the same), but he is suspicious, as he always was (the same), so they cannot return to the time before he suspected her of being unfaithful (things are different). He counters that they can be as loving as they were before (the same) because he has changed and is no longer suspicious (different), which means that when they are as they were before it will be better (different). But on another, deeper level, he is speaking of his appreciation of her as the same woman but with different parts inside her that he never saw before: she is the same (inside), but different (in his perception). Or as Cavell puts it, both partners must say, "I am changed before your eyes, different so to speak from myself, hence not different. To see this you will have correspondingly to suffer metamorphosis."[46]

Cavell acknowledges that the remarriage in *The Awful Truth* is *like* a rebirth or a resurrection and that the woman, as well as the marriage, is re-created.[47] In fact, this film soon spawned a resurrection film, for *The Awful Truth* was in many ways the prototype for *My Favorite Wife*, four years later, which stars the same man and woman, has the same producer, and involves some but not all of the same plot elements: divorce and remarriage, with other partners waiting in the wings for each of the protagonists; his rejection of her because he wrongly believes that she has committed adultery (while he himself has another woman); her determination not to let him sleep with her until he gives up his suspicions; and his capitulation without actually declaring her innocent. Both films end with a scene in which Irene Dunne, in bed, tantalizes Cary Grant until he is willing to do anything to get into bed with her. The rhetorical gags, too, are linked: Ellen-as-Bianca in *My Favorite Wife* speaks in a hoity-toity upper-class voice that is a far closer imitation of Lucy's rival Barbara Vance in *The Awful Truth* than of Bianca in *My Favorite Wife*. And Ellen-as-old-friend-from-the-South mimics the Southern accent Lucy had used in *The Awful Truth* as Jerry's sister, mimicking Dixie Belle who was already faking a Southern accent. This was self-imitation to the seventh degree, for the Southern accent was the natural, and usually concealed, accent of Irene Dunne, who was born in Louisville, Kentucky. Thus we have Irene Dunne(Kentucky)-as-Irene Dunne (Hollywood)-as-Lucy-as-Jerry's sister-as-Dixie Belle-as-Southern Belle-as-Ellen-as-old friend from the South (Kentucky).

The Awful Truth was, in its turn, also indebted to earlier films of this genre, such as *Third Finger, Left Hand* (Robert Z. Leonard, 1936):[48]

> Margot Merrick (Myrna Loy), a successful magazine editor in New York, invented a husband (who was always away on business) in order to keep her male colleagues and bosses from sexually harassing her; she stalled the amorous lawyer Philip Booth (Lee Bowman) in this way. But then she met Jeff Thompson (Melvyn Douglas), a successful painter from a small town in Ohio, who wanted to marry her. She fell for him, too, and was about to accept his marriage proposal when one of her friends casually mentioned to him that Margot had a husband. Furious that she had led him on without telling him this, Jeff made inquiries and discovered that her husband was a mythical beast. Jeff then showed up at her family home, pretending to be her husband. Everyone (except Philip) was delighted to meet him at last.
>
> But Margot's resentment of his trick overrode her attraction to Jeff; she confided in Philip, who persuaded her that the only way to get rid of Jeff was for her actually to marry him so that she could then divorce him (and marry Philip). Jeff took an overnight train for Ohio, and Margot and Philip boarded the train, too, to get him to sign the final papers. Jeff and Margot, together again after a long separation, realized that they did not want to divorce but did not know how to stop the forces they had set in motion. Jeff stalled for a while but failed to find an opportunity to be alone with Margot. Without telling him, Margot sent a telegram to his parents and friends, who were all there at the station in Ohio to greet Jeff's train in the morning, eager to meet his wife. Jeff had no choice but to introduce Margot to them.

And so once again, the divorce, functioning as a remarriage, saves the marriage.

Both Jeff and Margot play to audiences and use social situations to force personal decisions: Jeff presents himself as her husband first to her parents, not to her, and she repays him by using the same trick at the train station in Ohio. Both of them also masquerade as people of lower classes. When they are at Niagara Falls getting married and he meets people from his home town in Ohio, people (including a rather stuffy judge) who know his parents, she talks like a gang moll, with a lower-class accent and vulgar tastes, and the Ohio people withdraw in horror. He supplements his basic masquerade as her husband with a pair of episodes involving Sam, the black porter on the train (Ernest Whitman). First he gets Sam, who has been to law school, to play the part of a fancy lawyer, to act on his behalf when Philip acts for Margot, and Sam outpaces Philip at every step. Later, in his attempt to get into Margot's stateroom late at night, he imitates Sam's voice. Sam, however, is in the room (while Margot is out having a cigarette); Sam opens the door, laughing and praising the imitation: "I could hardly tell which one of us was me." This statement could also have been made by both Jeff and Margot.

Another film in this genre was directed by, of all people, Alfred Hitchcock: *Mr. and Mrs. Smith* (1941), starring Carole Lombard and Robert Montgomery as David and Ann Smith, with Gene Raymond as Jeff, the Other Man. This time, there is no suspicion of adultery to drive the divorce; instead, there is a legal accident: due to a state boundary dispute, it turns out that their marriage has been declared retroactively invalid. Yet as Freud said (surely with Hollywood in mind), there are no accidents, and this one breaks open what is already a fault line in the marriage: right before the discovery of the legal problem, Ann had asked David, out of the blue, if he would marry her again if he could go back in time, to which he had replied, ungraciously, probably not, he'd rather have his freedom. When Ann learns that they are not married, her mother advises her not to sleep with David; she throws him out and refuses to marry him. Both of them start dating other people, and David goes to considerable lengths (including pretending to be drunk, like Lucy in *The Awful Truth*) to keep Ann out of bed with Jeff when all three of them are staying in a ski lodge. Snowed in, Ann and David (re)marry.

The Awful Truth was remade not only with the same cast and significant plot changes (*My Favorite Wife*), or with a different cast and a roughly similar plot (the many remarriage films, such as *Mr. and Mrs. Smith*), but also with a different cast and the very same plot, same characters and all (as *My Favorite Wife* was transformed into *Move Over, Darling*). This was *Let's Do It Again* (Alexander Hall, 1953), a musical starring Jane Wyman and Ray Milland with Aldo Ray as the Texan. The title applies equally well to the main characters (let's try the marriage again) and to the film (let's do *The Awful Truth* again). Other films, too, did it again, and they, too, were the same but different.

The Lady Eve (1941)

The masquerade in *The Awful Truth* is intended not to fool the husband but, on the contrary, to reveal to him who his wife really is. In Preston Sturges's film *The Lady Eve* (1941), by contrast, the masquerade is intended to fool and succeeds, so that a woman who has seduced the hero in one false persona meets him again in a different false persona, and this time he cannot tell if they are the same woman or different:

On the boat from South America, Charles Pike (Henry Fonda), naïve heir to a beer fortune, met a cardsharp, Harry Harrington (Charles Coburn), who was passing himself off as a wealthy and well-bred oilman named Colonel Harrington and passing off his cardsharp daughter (Barbara Stanwyck) as his equally wealthy and well-bred daughter Jean. They decided to cheat Charles. She easily seduced him (she called him "Hopsy" because of the beer), and he fell for her, but then she fell for him, too. She told her father that she wanted to tell Charles who they really were, but he persuaded her to wait until the boat docked in New York, to protect Harry and their accomplice. Charles's bodyguard, Muggsy Murgatroyd (William Demarest), became suspicious and found an incriminating police photo that he showed to Charles, who was thunderstruck. Charles confronted Jean with the photo; she too was shaken but simply remarked, "Rotten likeness, isn't it? I never cared for that picture." She insisted that she had intended to tell him but had waited in order to protect the others. To save face, Charles pretended that he had known all along and had just been "playing her for a sucker." She believed him; deeply humiliated, weeping, she told her father that she hated Charles and would get even.

Some time later, Jean met an old acquaintance named Pearlie (Eric Blore), now passing as Sir Alfred Keith, who happened to know Charles Pike's parents and introduced her to them as his niece, the Lady Eve Sidwich. When she arrived at the Pike home in Connecticut (which she pronounced "Conneckticut"), Murgatroyd recognized her immediately, and when Charles met her, he was stunned, mouth open. He asked if they had met before, perhaps "on the SS *Southern Queen* between here and South America?" She insisted that she had never been in South America or, indeed, North America until then. Then, as he continued to look puzzled, she asked, with maternal pity, "Were you in love with her?" Charles's father remarked, "He was in love with her but he don't remember what she looked like!" (Big laugh). When Charles remarked to Pearlie-as-Sir Alfred that Eve reminded him of a woman he'd met on a boat, Pearlie-as-Sir Alfred became conspiratorial and told him a "gaslight melodrama" about Cecilia the Coachman's Daughter, implying that the Lady Eve and Jean Harrington were half sisters, that a mythical coachman had cuckolded both the Earl (the Lady Eve's father) and, presumably, Colonel Harrington. He swallowed it "like a wolf," Pearlie later reported.

Charles proposed to Jean-as-Eve, they married, and on their honeymoon on the train, she told him lurid tales about many men she had slept with. He got off the train, went home, and started to divorce her, but now she realized that she was still in love with him. She found out that he was leaving on another voyage, and she booked a cabin on the same boat. Back on the boat, he saw her. "Hopsy!" she called to him; "Jean!" he cried out, and kissed her passionately. They rushed down to her cabin, and on the threshold he said, "There's just one thing I have to tell you, to be fair. It would never have happened, except she looked so exactly like you. I'm married." "But so am I, darling, so am I," she murmured, as she closed the door behind them.

The "gaslight melodrama" is yet another variant of Freud's Family Romance, and both of its heroines, the Colonel's daughter and the Earl's daughter, are mythical characters. The real (or, at least, realer) Jean is the con artist who pretends to be both of them and whom we encounter, undisguised, on several occasions, in conversation first with her father and then with Charles (though she never quite gets around to telling Charles the truth about herself) and again at the very end (when he assumes that she is Jean primarily because she calls him "Hopsy," as Jean did and Eve did not). This relatively real Jean is the woman who falls in love with Charles on the first boat and encounters him again on the second boat; what makes her real is the fact that she loves him. She teases him by conflating the two mythical personae: when Charles and Jean-as-Eve first meet, Charles exclaims in confusion, "Have we met?" "But of course we have," she laughs; "your father just introduced us." Thus she knowingly overlays a recent official event (his introduction to her as Eve) with an earlier event (the shipboard romance with her as the Colonel's daughter), just as Isolde knowingly conflates the recent official event of falling into the arms of Tristan-as-the pilgrim and the earlier event of her adultery with Tristan, and Siegfried unknowingly conflates the two different nights he has spent with Brünnhilde.

In addition to Jean-as-Colonel's daughter, Jean-as-Eve, and Jean-who-loves-Hopsy, there is the "other" Lady Eve, who reveals herself on the wedding night to be a woman of easy virtue who had her first lover at sixteen. Hopsy actually refers to this Eve as a different person; he argues that when she was sixteen she was so young that he cannot blame her for something that was "practically done by somebody else." But he cannot deal with the multiplicity of lovers she goes on to reveal. Is she lying about her promiscuity? Surely she exaggerates and jokes, but it is likely that Jean Harrington the con artist has been around the block, sexually speaking, and really has had other lovers. Her impersonation of a promiscuous woman is, therefore, a kind of self-impersonation: the dishonest (and perhaps promiscuous) Jean pretending to be the virtuous Lady Eve pretending to be the promiscuous Eve.

Jean carries out this charade of promiscuity to take revenge on Charles for at least two apparently contradictory offenses: tricking her (as she believes) into a previous act of promiscuity and failing to see through her masquerade as Eve. As for the first, when they fall in love, their passionate kiss and immediate fade-out, as well as their behavior next morning, are coded (in those Hays Office days) by the film convention for sex: we are to believe that they slept together. When Charles later pretends that he had been "playing her for a sucker" (i.e., that he had seen through her impersonation of the Colonel's daughter and tricked her to get her into bed), she believes him; Jean the con artist had gone to bed with him believing that he believed he was in bed with the Colonel's daughter, and she had awakened to believe that he had knowingly seduced the con artist-as-Colonel's daughter only in order to avenge himself on the con artist. Does she ever see through this trick of his? To the extent that she thinks

Charles saw through her original masquerade as several different women, her private joke on him is to tell him that he is just one of several men to her.

But does he ever see through her trick? This brings us to the second reason for her revenge: she is punishing him for, as she believes, failing to put the two parts of her together, for "taking the good without the bad, the lady without the woman, the ideal without the reality, the richer without the poorer."[49] But is she right about that? Do we ourselves ever escape from what Cavell calls "the ambiguity about whether he does or does not believe in her difference from herself"?[50] Even at the end, when Charles embraces Jean as the con artist, he still does not know that she also masqueraded as the Earl's daughter; he is (like other men we have encountered) under the impression that he is committing adultery when he is actually sleeping with his own wife.

Since film makes it possible for two characters to be played by one person, the film convention "allows a person to be treated as though he or she *can* be told, so to speak, apart from himself or herself, even where . . . she looks no different from one role to another."[51] Charles and Murgatroyd discuss this actors' paradox in the case of Jean's performance as the Lady Eve Sidwich in a brilliant comic dialogue that may have been inspired by the similar argument in *The Awful Truth*:

Murgatroyd: "It's the same dame. She looks the same, she walks the same, and she's tossing you just like she done the last time."
Charles: "She doesn't talk the same."
M: "Anybody can put on an act." [He puts a brush under his nose, makes noises in imitation of Hitler (or Charlie Chaplin imitating Hitler)]. "Guess who I am?"
C: "Weren't her eyes closer together?"
M: "They were not. They were right where they are, on either side of her nose."
C: "But why should she do it?"
M: "I don't know. Maybe she wants you to fall for her again."
C: "Do I look that dumb?"
M: "You wouldn't be the first one. I know a guy married the same dame three times, then turned around and married her aunt."
C: "No. They look too much alike."
M: "You said it! There couldn't be two Janes . . ."
C: "No, you don't understand me. They look too much alike to be the same. If she came here with her hair dyed yellow, and eyebrows different or something . . ."
M: "What's hair to a skirt?"
C: "But she didn't pretend she'd never seen me before, which is the first thing anybody'd do. She *says* I look familiar. If she didn't look so exactly like the other girl, I might be suspicious. You don't understand psychology . . . ."

Charles argues that if one woman were to pretend to be another, she would make the other woman look more dramatically different. But he's wrong: a woman pretending to be another woman can accomplish her goal just by doing nothing at all (as Vasa-vadatta did in Harsha's play *The Lady of the Jeweled Necklace*). Murgatroyd is right, and he gets the last word: At the very end of the film, as Charles and Jean close the door to their bedroom, Murgatroyd rushes out, saying, "Positively the same dame."

To return, in closing, to the question of the degree of relevance of feminism to the film versions of the resurrection scenario, the short answer would appear to be, "Some." The sword in the bed remains a weapon that either a man or a woman can wield, but the woman can now use it to new advantage, to clear her good name. She still often suffers her husband's adultery in silence, but now when she defends herself against unjust charges, she can win from him if not an apology at least an admission of regret or even guilt, sometimes even permission to do what he does. Nor does she have to roll over and play dead for nearly so long before he asks her to stay.

CHAPTER FIVE

Amnesia and the Tragedy of Remarriage

A thing like a divorce can break up a marriage.

George-as-Larry (William Powell)
in *I Love You Again* (1940)

THE COMEDY OF AMNESIAC REMARRIAGE

Some of the great romances of remarriage involve amnesia, which plagues forgetful husbands and, occasionally, forgetful wives in literature (such as the tale of Siegfried and Brünnhilde) and in film. Self-forgetfulness of this sort often has the effect of an unconscious masquerade (when the amnesiac constructs a new self) or, occasionally, a self-imitation (when that new self turns out to be the former self, instinctively reconstructed). It occurs in both comic and tragic forms. Let us begin where we left off in the last chapter, with comedy.

The Matrimonial Bed (1930)

The Matrimonial Bed (Michael Curtiz, 1930, based on a play by Yves Mirande and André Mouézy-Eon) tells a twisted tale of resurrection, amnesia, and pretense:

Adolphe Noblet was presumed dead in a train wreck. After five years, his wife Juliette (Florence Eldrige) married Gustave Corton (James Gleason) and had a child. In fact Adolphe was not dead but had merely lost his memory; he had become Leopold Trebel

(Frank Fay), a hairdresser, and had married a woman named Suzanne (Vivien Oakland), who bore him two sets of twins. One day, Juliet met Adolphe-as-Leopold and fainted when she saw his stunning resemblance to Adolphe. Dr. Friedland (Arthur Edmund Carewe) used hypnosis to restore the early memory of Adolphe-as-Leopold but wiped out his memory of his last five years; Adolphe-as-Leopold-as-Adolphe thought he was Adolphe and had no memory of his identity as Leopold. Dr. Friedland told him he had been asleep for five days after the train wreck and tried to keep the truth from him, thinking the shock could kill him. Gustave recognized Adolphe, and the two men took an instant dislike to one another.

Juliette's friend Sylvaine (Lilyan Tashman) told Juliette that she had known Adolphe-as-Leopold for two years, though he didn't remember her. Juliette told Adolphe-as-Leopold-as-Adolphe that Sylvaine was Madame Gustave Corton and the mother of his child. Sylvaine told Adolphe-as-Leopold-as-Adolphe that she loved him and wanted him to take her away; Adolphe-as-Leopold-as-Adolphe told Gustave that his wife (meaning Sylvaine) didn't care for him; Gustave told Adolphe-as-Leopold-as-Adolphe that he had been thought dead for five years and Juliette had married Gustave three years ago. Then Suzanne Trebel, the wife of Adolphe-as-Leopold, arrived; Juliette told her that she (Juliette) was married to Adolphe-as-Leopold-as-Adolphe, who denied that he was the father of anyone's children. Juliette told Adolphe-as-Leopold-as-Adolphe that she loved Gustave and asked him to go away. Suzanne asked Adolphe-as-Leopold-as-Adolphe to marry her again, and he agreed to this on condition that Dr. Friedland would restore his memory as Leopold. When Dr. Friedland objected that he could not do this, Adolphe-as-Leopold-as-Adolphe asked Dr. Friedland to *pretend* to restore him as Leopold. When Juliette thanked him for this, Adolphe-as-Leopold-as-Adolphe told her that he loved her and said good-bye to her and Gustave. Dr. Friedland hypnotized Adolphe-as-Leopold-as-Adolphe, who pretended to be Adolphe-as-Leopold-as-Adolphe-as-Leopold and left with Suzanne and their four sons.

Like Enoch Arden (or the resurrected wives), Adolphe-as-Leopold-as-Adolphe returns from the dead but not, this time, in time to prevent the remarriage of either of his two wives. He has amnesia squared (not, perhaps, doubled, if we reserve that term for an amnesia shared by two people, like Siegfried and Brünnhilde). In the end, he cancels out his squared amnesia not with another amnesia but with the *pretense* of another amnesia, thus pretending to be not who he is (for he now knows that he was, originally, Adolphe, and he still loves his first love, Juliette) but who he supposedly wrongly thinks he is—Leopold. This self-imitating amnesia to the third power allows Juliette and Gustave to remain married, with their child, and Suzanne and Adolphe-as-Leopold-as-Adolphe-as-Leopold to remain married, with their four children. Only Sylvaine remains rejected; perhaps she marries Dr. Friedland?

Remember? (1939)

Double marital amnesia (of the sort that plagued Siegfried and Brünnhilde) occurs in the film *Remember?* (Norman Z. McLeod, 1939), enabling both partners in a marriage to forget that they are married—in order that they may fall in love with one another again:

> Linda Bronson (Greer Garson) was engaged to Sky Ames (Lew Ayres) when she met Jeff Holland (Robert Taylor). Linda and Jeff fell in love, whereupon Sky graciously bowed out. They married but quarreled and soon divorced. Sky, who felt they should be together, slipped into their drinks an experimental memory-loss drug to make them forget their rough times (and the fact that they were married). It worked. They met, fell in love again, and married for the second time. Immediately after this wedding, Linda announced, "I'm going to have a baby."

This is the very last line in the film; then Jeff and Sky react, and Sky dumps some of those memory tablets into his cocktail and guzzles them down. He turns and looks to the camera, and the credits roll.[1] What happens next? Will they ever find out that the child is Jeff's? Will he accuse her of infidelity? We will never know, nor, apparently, will Sky, who conveniently erases his own memory of his surreptitious meddling.[2] The drug worked on the audience, too, for the film, generally acknowledged to be a stinker, quickly slipped away into oblivion. Remember *Remember?*? No.

I Love You Again (1940)

A film made just a year after *Remember?* depicts a both doubled and squared amnesia and a pretended recurrence of that amnesia (to the third degree): *I Love You Again* (W. S. Van Dyke, 1940, based on a novel by Octavus Roy Cohen):

> A charming con man named George Carey (William Powell) had been hit on the head during a brawl on a train in 1931; he became a boring, tightfisted legitimate business-man named Larry Wilson and married Kay (Myrna Loy). In 1940, on a cruise ship without Kay, George-as-Larry fell overboard and got another blow on the head; he woke up and knew himself only as George Carey. His companion in crime, "Doc" Ryan (Frank McHugh), asked him, "Amnesia. That's what you've got?" and George-as-Larry-as-George replied, "No, that's what I *had*." When he found out that Larry Wilson was wealthy, he pretended to be Larry and returned to his hometown to get Larry's money.
>
> But on arrival, George-as-Larry-as-George-as-Larry discovered that he was strongly attracted to Kay and that she was about to divorce George-as-Larry because of his gen-eral coldness, in particular his sexual coldness: for a year, he had insisted on sleeping in a separate bedroom. When George-as-Larry-as-George-as-Larry learned of this, he tried to talk her out of it, saying, "A thing like a divorce can break up a marriage." Then

he discovered that she was engaged to marry Herbert (Donald Douglas). Gradually, he wooed her, constantly attempting, in vain, to get her into bed and buying her expensive presents. She fell for George-as-Larry-as-George-as-Larry and told him that she was through with Herbert, that she had finally found the man she loved. George-as-Larry-as-George-as-Larry cooed like a dove.

Meanwhile, some of his old cronies arrived to help him work an oil scam, and Doc then told Kay about the amnesia. When George-as-Larry-as-George-as-Larry decided to back out on the oil scam, there was a scuffle, and someone knocked him down and out. Lying on his back, he murmured, "Help! Help! I'm drowning! Kay, how did you get aboard ship?" She looked very very sorry that George-as-Larry had apparently come back and replaced George-as-Larry-as-George-as-Larry. The con men departed, and he cooed like a dove. Then she realized that he was faking the amnesia, that he was really George, the man she loved, the con man. Doc smiled at them and said, "You certainly can kick that amnesia around."

George-as-Larry-as-George-as-Larry-as-George-as-Larry is only pretending to have the sort of third-degree amnesia that actually plagued Adolphe-as-Leopold-as-Adolphe in *The Matrimonial Bed* (who then pretended to have yet another round of amnesia). George-as-Larry's insistence on separate bedrooms is the modern version of the sword in the bed, sexual rejection. The ongoing argument about the same and the different takes on a new form here, too; at first George-as-Larry-as-George-as-Larry says, "I've changed a lot," and she says, "You couldn't change." But when she sees how sexy and generous he has become, she keeps telling him, "How you have changed." And when she gets angry with him because he finds her attractive now, after all this time and after she has decided to divorce him, she changes her tune yet again: "I want you to be your old self," she says. "No more of this Jekyll and Hyde business." In fact she had realized his double nature from the start, even before the amnesia-reversal; she tells him she married him because she sensed, behind the rather stuffy man she married, another, exciting man, the kind of man she wanted to marry. "I finally found the man I thought I'd married," she said; "I'm sorry I didn't find him sooner." She meant it metaphorically, but it was literally true.

THE ROMANCE OF AMNESIAC REMARRIAGE

The comedies of amnesia and remarriage are best understood in tandem with the tragedies of remarriage.[3] I would call the genre as a whole neither comedies nor tragedies but romances, the term often applied to Shakespeare's plays about resurrection and remarriage, such as *Cymbeline* and *The Winter's Tale*. They are romances in several senses of the word: they live in the liminal land between tragedy and comedy, they are fantastic, they often involve what Freud called Family Romances, and they are about true love. Serious (if not necessarily tragic) films about amnesia came into particular vogue at the start of the twenty-first century, the Age of Alzheimer's— *Memento* (Christopher Nolan, 2000), *Mulholland Drive* (David Lynch, 2001), *Vanilla Sky* (Cameron Crowe, 2001)—but they were never out of style.

As You Desire Me (1932)

An early classic of this genre is *As You Desire Me* (George Fitzmaurice, 1932), starring Greta Garbo. The film is set in Budapest, in 1928:

> Zara (Garbo) was working as a nightclub singer, drinking heavily, unable to remember the night before, miserable, promiscuous, and living with the sinister novelist Carl Salter (Erich von Stroheim). She had lost her memory of the past years, too terrible to bear recalling. Into this scene the past erupted. A strange man named Tony (Owen Moore) showed up and claimed that Zara was actually Maria, the wife of his close friend, Count Bruno Varelli (Melvyn Douglas). Tony believed Maria had lost her memory during World War I, ten years ago, after suffering the rape of her home and her person by the German army, while Bruno was away at the war. Zara insisted that she could not remember, that she was not Maria, but she went with Tony in order to get away from Salter, despite (or because of) Salter's violent protests.
>
> In the villa on his estate in Italy, Bruno swore that Zara was Maria and tried in vain to coax her memory back. When she saw the life she could have, she wanted it and hoped that she was Maria, but when she learned that Bruno could inherit the estate, which was actually hers, only if he could prove that Maria was alive, she became suspicious of his motives in bringing her from Budapest. Salter appeared with a woman whom he claimed to be the real Maria; she had been in a mental institution and could barely speak. In the end, Zara and Bruno declared that they loved one another, and she remained with him in Italy. Salter and the other woman departed.

The film never really tells us whether Zara is Maria or even whether she thinks she is Maria.

One of the first tests she faces in Italy is that old standby the family dog,[4] but even this proves ambiguous: at first he growls at her, and then, when she calls him to her, he jumps on her and clearly adores her—but after all, she's Garbo. She argues that her striking resemblance to the portrait of Maria that Tony had painted is proof that she is *not* Maria: "How could you expect anyone who'd been through the tortures of the last ten years to remain the same? This Maria would have changed, wouldn't she? The very fact that I am like her now is proof that I am not she." That is, to remain the same (person) we must be different (in our aging appearance); we cannot remain the same on the surface if we remain the same person inside; if the surface is identical, the person inside must be a different person.[5] The portrait of Maria (another classic testing point), painted before the war, is also ambiguous evidence. Bruno prays that the portrait might come to life again, and when Zara comes downstairs dressed precisely like the portrait, wide-brimmed straw country bonnet and all,[6] Tony takes credit for having created the real Maria, now, out of the portrait of the old Maria— the Pygmalion scenario, nature imitating art imitating nature. But as Bruno watches Zara watching the portrait, she recoils against the superficial identification.

War is widely cited as a cause of both amnesia and extreme change: the victim of war may forget who he is or become so different that others do not recognize him[7] (as we will soon discover in *Random Harvest*). Rape, too, is regarded as a trauma sufficient to explain either the forgetting of a part of the self (a fragmentation or displacement into split personalities[8]) or the forgetting of the whole self. It seems that Zara has forgotten both the years before the rape, the years in Italy, and the years of promiscuity after it, up to the recent past in Budapest. The rape is the pivot from which amnesia spreads out in both directions, but once she gets to Italy, it is the recent past that she wants to forget and the more distant past that she hopes to remember—even if it is not her own past. She finally comes to understand that, because she loves Bruno, she must become the person he wants her to be—as he desires her—whether or not she really is Maria. We, therefore, never know if she is masquerading as someone else or as herself.

These issues were more profoundly developed in the play of the same name by Luigi Pirandello, on which the film is quite closely based (adapted by Gene Markey), though with significant departures. In the play, the female lead is called not Zara but simply the Unknown Woman, and she has been living not merely as a nightclub singer but as a whore. The other names are also different (Count Bruno's friend is Boffi, his wife Lucia, called Cia for short), but the most dramatic difference is the ending: suspicious of Bruno's motives, as she is in the film, the Unknown Woman leaves him and goes back to Salter. Clearly this Would Not Play in Hollywood. The Pirandello play also goes into far greater detail about the psychology of self-invention. The Unknown Woman recalls how she tried to persuade Bruno and Boffi that they were wrong to think she was Lucia: "What I said and did finally convinced them both that it was only a likeness, after all—a striking one, certainly, a similarity of circumstance as well as of looks—but nothing more than that." This is common sense speaking: mere physical resemblance proves nothing. But the counterintuitive argument that, in the film, Zara makes just once—"The very fact that I am like her now is proof that I am not she"—the Unknown Woman develops on several occasions in the play. First she tries to persuade Boffi:

Boffi: "He presumes that you have not come back simply because you feared you could never be the same to him after what had happened."
    Unknown Woman: "And does he believe, then, that she could truly still be the same?"

Boffi: "Why not, Signora, if you choose to be?"
Unknown Woman: "After ten years—the same? After all that must have happened to her—the same?"

And then:

> "How can you think it possible that one who has been swept under by the war—after ten years—should remain so much *the same*? If anything, it would be proof that, on the contrary, it is not I? . . . My being so much *the same* is a proof against me."

And finally she compares herself to the woman Salter has brought to them as Cia: "Cia could well be this poor creature for the very reason that she *no longer resembles her at all*."[9] (This argument may have inspired the rather different riffs on the same and the different in *The Awful Truth* and *The Lady Eve*.)

The Unknown Woman goes so far as to insist that she has purposely destroyed physical evidence on her body, evidence that would have proved that she is Cia: "If I have felt your hands searching—here—for some mark you thought you should have found . . . I tell you it is gone! I did not want it any more; and I did all I could to make it go . . . to keep others from finding it, I got rid of it." This would, of course, allow her to go on pretending that she was Cia if she were not, but she presents it as the reverse, as an argument that, being Cia, she did not want to look like Cia. Perversely, she insists: "I want all of you to doubt me so that I may at least have the satisfaction of being the only one left to believe in myself."

She never really believes that she is Cia (or, for that matter, that she is not), but at the same time she gradually decides to reinvent herself as Cia: "I want . . . no longer to remember anything . . . . If he can give a soul again to this body, which is his Cia's, let him take it and fill it with his memories." Later, she offers not only to give up her memories and the memories of the woman whom she is pretending to be or is but to let Bruno fill her up with his memories of her:

> There is nothing left in me of my own. Take me and make me, make me *as you desire me!* . . . no memory of hers any longer; give me yours, your memories, all you have preserved of her as she once was for you! And they shall come alive again in me.

In the film, this is what she does rather than says: she becomes the ultimate erotic object, made of nothing but his desire, and ours as we watch her, Garbo at the height of her unearthly beauty. In the play, however, only because she finally comes to believe that he desires not her but the estate does she leave him. Had he been able to persuade her that his desire for her had no ulterior economic motives, she might have gone on, as in the film, pretending to be not Maria, not Zara, not even the innocent woman in the portrait, but his fantasy of her.

Garbo on several other occasions played a woman who masqueraded as herself. In *Camille* (George Cukor, 1936), Marguerite Gautier (Garbo) begins life as a farm girl, milking cows; then she goes to Paris and pretends to be a courtesan (the point at which we first encounter her). To satisfy the fantasy of her lover Armand (Robert Taylor), she pretends to be a country girl milking cows, reverting to her original persona; and finally, to save Armand's career, she leaves him for the Baron (Henry Daniell) and pretends to be a courtesan again, which she no longer is; by now she is a milkmaid-as-courtesan-as-milkmaid-as-courtesan. Only when she is dying does Armand recognize the woman beneath these flickering layers of self-impersonation. In *Two-Faced Woman* (George Cukor, 1941), Garbo again played one woman pretending to be two women, but this time more explicitly: the no-nonsense Swedish ski instructor pretends to be her own sexy twin sister in order to get her husband (Melvyn Douglas) back from the Other Woman, Griselda (Constance Bennett). But does he fall for it? Clearly he sees through it and still goes along with it; he knows damn well who she is, but he admires her for masquerading, and he is attracted to the other side of her personality that the masquerade reveals, and that is what brings out new aspects of him, too.

Random Harvest (1942)

The Internet Movie Database entry for *As You Desire Me* adds helpfully, at the end, "If you like this title, we also recommend *Random Harvest*." This is smart advice. *Random Harvest* (Mervyn LeRoy, 1942), based on a James Hilton novel by the same name, like *As You Desire Me* pivots around a tear in the fabric of consciousness at the moment of the end of the First World War and an amnesiac who lives again with a lost lover. But this time the amnesiac is the man, and in this regard and others, Hilton may have been inspired not only by Pirandello but by any or all of the comic variants of the genre, such as *The Matrimonial Bed* and *I Love You Again*.

On Armistice Day 1918, a soldier (Ronald Colman) walked out of the Melbridge County Asylum in a thick fog, both mental and atmospheric; he had been found in the trenches in 1917 and brought to the hospital, shell-shocked, with a complete loss of memory and a speech impediment. He met a young dance-hall singer who called herself Paula Ridgeway (Greer Garson); since the people in the asylum had called him Smith, she called him Smithy. He fell ill; she left the theatrical troupe to nurse him, and they lived in a small village in Devon. Eventually, he recovered his speech and fell in love with her; they married and, two years later, had a little boy. Then one day he went to Liverpool, slipped in the rain, and was knocked unconscious by a taxicab; when he regained consciousness, he remembered nothing since 1917 (it was now 1920); he thought he should be in uniform, in the trenches in France, and knew that he was Charles Rainier, captain in the Wessex Regiment, of Random Hall, in Surrey.

He went home to Random Hall and picked up the threads of his old life. But he always kept in his pocket, on a gold chain, the key to the cottage he had lived in with Paula, not knowing what that key was meant to open. Paula searched for him in vain and consulted Dr. Jonathan Benet (Philip Dorn), the psychiatrist who had treated Smith in the Melbridge Asylum. Charles never met Benet in his new life, though once they sat at close tables in a restaurant and Charles half recognized Benet's voice. Benet, who wanted to marry Paula, told her that her husband's memory might have returned, that he might have taken up his old life again: "Those years are a blank. His life with you is forgotten." But she believed that someday she'd find him again. Ten years after he disappeared, Paula saw a photograph of Charles Rainier in a newspaper, realized that he was "Smithy," and took a job as his secretary, Miss Margaret Hanson. She told Charles that she had been married before and had had a little boy who died. When she learned that Charles was about to marry a young woman named Kitty (Susan Peters), Paula got a legal divorce from Smith, as over seven years (the legal requirement) had passed by now with no word from him and he was legally presumed dead. But when the organ music at the wedding rehearsal played the song they had played when he married Paula, Charles looked straight through Kitty, who burst into tears and broke off the wedding.

Two more years passed, and Charles became a Member of Parliament (Liberal). One day he stared at Paula-as-Margaret long and hard, as if he were trying to remember where he had seen her before, and then he asked her if she might ever marry again; she said no. "You and I are in the same boat," he said. "We're both ghost-ridden. We're prisoners of our pasts. What if we were to pool our loneliness, and give each other what we have to give: support, friendship. I'm proposing marriage, Miss Hanson, or should I call it a merger? A member of parliament should have a wife, Margaret, and you have exceptional gifts. You need have no fear that I would make any emotional demands on you. I have only sincere friendship to offer, I won't ask any more from you. It's a selfish proposal, but I can't have you giving me notice, you know; I'd be lost without you. Miss Hanson, Margaret, have I hurt you?" She dried her eyes and accepted him.

His wealth and power grew, with her help, and he became Sir Charles Rainier, and she, as Lady Rainier, gave dinners at Random Hall for the prime minister and wore a diamond tiara as she sat beside Charles in a box at the ballet. People commented on how devoted to her he was and envied her.

She told him she wanted to travel for a while on her own but would first stop at a cottage where she had once been very happy. He went to Melbridge to settle a strike; afterward the workers cheered him. Walking in another pea-soup fog, he began to recognize things. The noise of the cheering workers, the crowds singing, conjured up the chaos of Armistice Day. He found his way back to the asylum: he remembered, "There was a girl!" Then he recalled the cottage, went there, and opened the door with his key. She appeared at the gate. "O Smithy!" she said. "Paula," he said. Kiss. Fade out.

This is amnesia squared: Charles forgets that he forgot. The first episode makes Smithy forget that he is Charles Rainier, and the second makes Charles Rainer forget that he is Smithy forgetting that he is Charles; but it does not simply turn him back into Charles. The triple cross appears to be complete—Charles to Smith to Charles—but it has the Möbius twist of Charles's knowledge that there is a gap in the tape, as it were. He, therefore, does not become himself (the original Charles Rainier) again; he merely masquerades as himself. Charles post-Smithy is really another person, Charles II, perhaps; and the broken Smithy that reemerges at the very end of the film is certainly not the Smithy of the start. Thus Charles at first unknowingly impersonates himself as Paula's/Margaret's husband—and then, at the end, knowingly impersonates Smithy or, rather, becomes Charles-as-Smithy-as-Charles-as-Smithy. Paula, by contrast, knowingly impersonates herself as his secretary and his wife, intentionally transforms herself, and in the end becomes not Paula but Paula-as-Margaret-as-Paula, quite a different woman. There is a symmetry to the squared amnesia: Smithy is married to Paula for three years and Charles to Margaret for three years before he wakes up to his former life in each case.

A number of themes and motifs from the folklore and mythology of self-imitation resurface in this film, often with striking modifications. Unlike Siegfried in the *Thidreks Saga*, Charles does not want to forget his wife, nor is he, like Siegfried in the later variants, the victim of someone else who wants him to forget his wife. Yet he most closely resembles the later Siegfried, for he is a good guy, not a cad, and it is an unlucky accident that makes him forget his wife: like George-as-Larry in *I Love You Again*, he is hit on the head (a *second* time) on the one occasion when his wife is not with him. The effect, however, is much the same as if he had willed it or been cursed to do it (as, indeed, is the effect on Brünnhilde in either case): he leaves his wife and is about to marry someone else (again like Siegfried) when his wife claims him back, not in person but through the sudden resurgence of his memory of her, triggered by music. A modern concept of amnesia—battle fatigue, a blow to the head—thus replaces the magic potion, but the wife is abandoned and suffers all the same.

When Charles says, "You need have no fear that I would make any emotional demands on you," he means, among other things, no sex. Like the medieval knights and Hollywood husbands who put a sword in the bed between themselves and the women they desired but would not touch, Charles will not touch Paula-as-Margaret until she tells him the answer to the riddle, which is, in this case, "Who did I love? Who am I?" When Paula discusses Charles's proposal with Dr. Benet, she says, "It may work out. He may even fall in love with me. Would that be so extraordinary?" The besotted psychiatrist says, "It would be very extraordinary if he didn't," but he also says, "If you marry him, keep to his terms." This is not hard to do, given the sexual passivity of both Smithy and Charles. Paula mocks Smithy as Kitty mocks Charles, each of them complaining that they have to beg him to kiss them when he should have thought of it himself. (When Smithy proposes to Paula and she accepts him and offers her lips to him, he bites into a sandwich instead.) Both Charles and Smithy are emotionally barricaded within the stone walls of their lost pasts; Smithy's face comes fully alive with happiness only once, for the brief moment when he proudly announces the arrival of his newborn son to the registrar of births, and Charles awakens fully only in the very last frame, when he sees Margaret as Paula and has access to both halves of his memory—and, for the first time in the film, kisses a woman who has not asked him to do it. Even then, it is not clear whether Charles will be able to "live with his recovered memory" (as Stanley Cavell puts it) and, therefore, whether the film will have the tragic ending of the Hollywood melodrama of the unknown woman (such as *Madame X*) or the happy ending of the remarriage comedies (such as *The Awful Truth*). *Random Harvest* combines these genres, "negating the negation in the melodramas,"[10] leaving us with the tabula rasa of the beginning of a new plot. Yet even if we are to imagine that Charles and Paula live happily ever after, the long, long lost years—fifteen, more even than in *The Winter's Tale*—make this a bittersweet tale.[11] The resolved, if not happy, ending in *Random Harvest*, as in *The Winter's Tale*, is soured by the years that Charles (like Leontes) loses through his ignorance. Charles/Smithy and Margaret/Paula will go on together, but now they are old.

Cavell acknowledges that *Random Harvest* is paradigmatic of the remarriage genre, of which he lists the central themes:

> This is complete with divorce; with spiritual death and revival; with the question of whether the man or the woman is the active member of the pair; with discussions of life as beginning with the meeting of the pair, the past having nothing in it but their past; with a return to a particular house in the country which holds the key to a saving perception—all matters that turn out to be part of the grain of remarriage comedies.[12]

But he argues that *Random Harvest* is not a comedy, in part because "the man never claims the woman, never declares his right to her desire." Yet Charles does claim Margaret/Paula at the end, making it neither a tragedy nor a comedy but a romance of both resurrection (with a child) and remarriage (the child disappears). That Charles's amnesia is a kind of death is insisted upon: the barman in the first scene says his brandy would bring anyone back from the grave; the butler Sheldon says Charles came back from the dead; Charles's sister says he's come back from the grave; Kitty says he's come back from the dead; and Paula, finally, has Smithy legally certified as dead. The novel analogizes Charles's lost past to a previous life, when Paula asks Smithy about his (first) amnesia, saying, "What does it feel like—to think of the time before—before you can remember?" and he replies: "Like trying to remember before I was born."[13]

The key, which has its own leitmotif of music, comes to symbolize Charles's tantalizingly inaccessible but haunting memories of the past; it is a duplicate key in a new sense, the key to his duplicate self. On the day when Paula and Smithy marry and go to their cottage for the first time, Smithy takes the key out of his pocket, holds it up before them, and says, "Home." But it signifies "home" in a more complex sense than the rose-covered cottage; it is the home that is his lost self. It is also phallic, waiting to be inserted in something. Again and again she sees him playing with the key, caressing it, fingering it like a rosary, and she knows what it is, while he does not. More precisely, his mind does not understand it; his fingers have a kind of somatic memory of the key, which is a bold metaphor, a literal clue (etymologically related to "key") that he carries around, looking for the secret to unlock with it. It is the key to the door that Dr. Benet has in mind when he says, "A door in his mind has opened, but another has closed," or the door that has closed, as Charles himself says, when he gives up the search in Liverpool. The key (which also shifts the musical key) is doing its own bit of self-imitation: the key is the key.

As the magic spell of the amnesia wears thin from time to time, half-memories break through to taunt him. Just as Smithy knows instinctively that he does *not* love anyone else and so feels free to marry Paula, so Charles knows instinctively that he *does* love someone else and so hesitates to marry again.[14] Right before he proposes to Miss Hanson, he admits that he had felt he had known her before, from the first day she came into his office; that was one reason why he hired her. But he does not recognize her, for they are no longer the people they were, Paula and Smithy. Like Zara in *As You Desire Me*, Paula re-creates herself, first in absence from him—she goes to school to learn stenography—and then with him, as Margaret, to become first the indispensable secretary and then the indispensable hostess/wife. He, too, re-creates himself, but during the first period rather than the second: it is Smithy, not Charles, who invents himself on a rare tabula rasa, a second chance to become whoever he wants to be. Smithy becomes a writer, which was (Paula guesses, correctly) what Charles had always dreamed of becoming; Smithy lives out Charles's fantasy of what he might have been. When Paula-as-Margaret and Charles-as-Smithy-as-Charles meet again, therefore, Paula has put on a new mask and Smithy has taken his off; no wonder he cannot recognize her. Ronald Colman's makeup, mostly a bit of talcum powder in the hair about the temples, superfluously signals his aging, for he was actually fifty-one when the film was made. Greer Garson, by contrast, actually thirty-eight at the time, seems much younger as Paula and remains young throughout the film, surely in deference to the vanity of an actress proud of the bloom of her beauty; yet perhaps inadvertently, this changelessness signals her enduring, undimmed, unclouded love for him, in contrast with his love for her that has been sicklied o'er with the pale cast of amnesia.

Why, everyone who sees the film asks, doesn't she tell him? Cavell feels that we never know what precisely she is waiting for, but I think it is clear that she wants to tell him and has good reasons not to.[15] She begs Dr. Benet, "Let me tell him that I was his wife," and he replies, "You can risk it if you wish. But if the sight of you did nothing to restore his memory, what could words do? The impetus must come from within. It cannot be forced upon him from outside." And she agrees: "He'd resent me. He'd accept me. He'd pity me. And he'd resent me."[16] People tell noble (which is to say self-sacrificing, self-destructive) lies of this sort all the time in films of this period, often about death[17] but also about blindness[18] and amnesia: people conceal the truth from amnesiacs "for their own good," for fear that the shock of recognition will kill or permanently alienate the amnesiac. The hypnotizing Dr. Friedland in *The Matrimonial Bed* tries to protect Adolphe-as-Leopold-as-Adolphe from the shock of the truth, and in *As You Desire Me*, Tony says of Bruno's protection of Zara, "He's probably afraid of the shock of bringing back too many memories at once."[19] Paula-as-Margaret is also afraid that Charles, who is after all a different person now, won't love her as Smithy did; she tells Dr. Benet, "I want him as he was; I want his love." Nobly, she gets a legal divorce from Smithy to protect Charles from committing bigamy not with Kitty (as she thinks when she does it) but with herself (as she realizes when he later proposes to her).

What keeps the masquerade going is their British silence, the upper (class) lip not merely stiffened but buttoned up entirely.[20] When he confesses to her, years later, the strong sense of knowing her before that he'd had when he first met her, she remarks, coldly, "You didn't show it." How different things might have been if he had. Smithy's silence during the first amnesia, generated by the shock of war that impairs his speech, is matched by the silence of Paula-as-Margaret in the second amnesia, generated by her shock at his total loss of any memory of her and her fear that he will feel trapped if she tells him the truth of their relationship or tells him who she is and who he really is. And so Paula-as-Margaret keeps from him his knowledge of her, while he, too, constructs barriers against any possible truth telling. When she presses him about his half memories of the past, he says, "I'd rather not talk of it, Margaret; it's not something I can put into words." The film conveniently invokes this convention of noble silence in order to keep the plot going: she mustn't tell him, or there will be no story. Near the very end, when she has decided to leave him ("travel on my own"), she finally throws caution to the winds and teases him with the truth: "Do you feel that there really is someone, and someday you may find her again? Doesn't it frighten you sometimes, that the years are passing, and you may have come so near her, even rushed by her in the street? You might even have met her, Charles. It might be someone you know. It might even be me." "Oh, Margaret!" (he laughs). "I'm talking wildly now," she says, turning away. This is as close as she can come to telling him the truth: pretending that it is just an imaginary possibility ("It might even be me"); and still he doesn't get it. (By contrast, when Ellen in *My Favorite Wife* finally says to her children, "Suppose your mother didn't drown. Suppose she was right here," she realizes from their behavior that they already know.) By suggesting that she might have been his wife, Margaret inadvertently mocks and defuses his own deep suspicion that she might be the one. The truth masquerades as the truth.

The poignancy of the film lies in the contrast between, one the one hand, Paula-as-Margaret, always aware of her passion for the man right next to her and never able to express it, constantly remembering the other life—the key, Liverpool, Melbridge—and, on the other, Charles-as-Smithy-as-Charles, always straining past her in his attempt to touch her ghost. It is an actor's dream, and this may be what made Robert Osborne call *Random Harvest* "a movie movie"[21] and Tom Keogh call it "the ultimate tearjerker" and "one of the great date movies of all time," what we might nowadays call a chick flick. Pauline Kael,[22] the archenemy of all sentimentality, called it "this hunk of twaddle" and "a big clinker" and remarked that Ronald Colman "must be the only person lucky enough to forget that sticky, arch great lady of the screen."[23]

The emotional tension is quite different from that of the novel on which the film is based, a novel that was already what might be called "a movie novel" and was published just one year before the film. For the chronology is significantly different: the novel begins when Charles has already been married for some time to Mrs. Rainer. When Charles's memory is finally triggered (on page 175 of a 300-page book), there is a long flashback (another hundred pages) in which he recalls his life with Paula, from their first meeting on Armistice Day to the Liverpool accident; and finally he finds Paula. Only then, on the very last page, does the reader, along with Charles, realize that Paula is Mrs. Rainier. Mrs. Rainier is never called Margaret by anyone, including Charles; she is cold and distant. It is as if, like Berkeley's tree in the quad (and unlike Alice in the dream of the Red King), Mrs. Rainier cannot become visible to us until Charles wakes up from the dream in which she has become invisible to him. He might have said, as King Udayana says, in Harsha's play, "How is it that I didn't notice that the queen was right here beside me?"

But when Hollywood decided to film the book, there was no question of making Greer Garson only semivisible for half the film; she was at the top of her form and won an Oscar for Best Actress (for *Mrs. Miniver*) in that same year. (She had also made, just two years before, *Remember?* which in retrospect looks like a slapstick preview of *Random Harvest*.) Of course she could not be kept in wraps until the surprise ending, and once we *see* Greer Garson as Miss Hanson in the film (in contrast with the novel, which barely sketches her physical appearance), we must realize immediately who she is. The film, therefore, cuts not to the chase but to the romance, beginning not (like the novel) with the muted Mrs. Rainier of the present but with the passionate Paula of the past, whom we continue to see beneath the veneer of Paula-as-Margaret.[24] The surprise ending is thus reduced, in the film, to a brief interval during which Charles speaks to Miss Hanson on his Dictaphone, and we even hear her voice (distorted by the machine) before we ever see her—and are then shocked, shocked to see, when she walks through the door to him, that she is Paula. What we gain in the film, in place of the surprise ending, is the pleasure of actually watching Paula-as-Margaret waiting for Charles to recognize her, watching him like a hawk.[25]

The value and meaning of several of the motifs in the film are illuminated by comparison with the themes of the novel that the scriptwriters jettisoned.[26] The elements that the filmmakers invented, as we have noted, are the key, Smithy's reaction to the birth of his child, and the vivid sexual presence of Paula-as-Margaret. The elements in the novel that the filmmakers left out, beside those we have just considered, are the play within the play, the political and economic corruption of Charles Rainier, World War II, and the politics of the '30s in England.

In both the film and the novel, playacting is there from the very beginning, for both Smithy and Paula confess to false names, his false because of his amnesia, hers because she is on the stage. Charles's memory is jogged, in the novel, not by the Melbridge strike but by a play within the play, an episode that the film reduces to a brief, frivolous vaudeville number in which Paula impersonates the old Scottish trooper Sir Harry Lauder, thus simultaneously faking her age, gender, and ethnicity. (The other play within the film is the ballet Sir Charles and Lady Rainier watch together, "Swan Lake," the tale of a prince who cannot recognize that what he regards as a single, rather two-faced woman is in fact two different women—the opposite of Charles's quandary.) In the novel, Charles and his assistant Harrison attend a music-hall play, *Salute the Flag*, a lighthearted, patriotic piece about the war. Charles remarks to Harrison, "That stammer . . . they kept it in—and the doorknob coming off as well," and when Harrison says, "Sounds as if you've seen the show before," he says, "Yes, I think I have, but more than that, more than *seeing* it before—I—I—"[27] Suddenly Charles remembers: He and Paula had remained with the theatrical troupe, and one night he had stood in for a player too drunk to go on in a bit part in *Salute the Flag*; terrified, he had stammered and accidentally pulled the doorknob off, but the audience loved it, and that bit of business became incorporated into the scene from then on. Now, years later, the stage business that he himself had inadvertently invented brings it all back to him. The doorknob that unlocks Charles's memory in the novel becomes the key to the locked door in the film.

It is no accident that *Salute the Flag* is about war. Both the film and the novel are set in the period between the two wars, *entre deux guerres*, but where the film is about the aftermath of World War I, the novel is about the coming of World War II; the film ends in 1935, the book on the day when England declares war on Germany, in September 1939. The two themes, the romantic and the political, are intertwined throughout the novel, reaching their climax on the day Mrs. Rainier finds out that Charles has remembered Paula, which also happens to be, as Hilton/Harrison puts it, "that first morning of the second war."[28] For the book is about more than the romance; it is also about England forgetting its better self as Charles forgot his, England that became corrupted even as Charles was corrupted, that fell asleep during that long period of Smithy's amnesia, fell prey to smugness and fascist sympathies (even Charles is furious about the appeasement at Munich) that have laid it wide open to Hitler's threats.

Charles's adventure in (loss of) memory land is also a variant of the tale of *The Prince and the Pauper*: the king goes slumming, often against his will, but always for his edification. (There is self-imitation in that basic model, too, in Mark Twain's telling: the prince's friends, regarding him as a mad pauper, pretend he is the king when he asks them to; they think they are teasing or humoring him, but he really is the king. The French psychoanalyst Jacques Lacan once remarked that a madman who believes himself to be a king is no more mad than a king who believes himself to be a king.[29]) Charles-as-Smithy is a pauper who turns out to be, if not a king, a powerful and wealthy upper-class Englishman, not a blue blood but the son of a very rich man. Paula is symbolic of his social conscience; the novel makes much of the fact that Mrs. Rainier had been his secretary, a commoner (even commoner than people think, for we know, as they do not, that she was on the stage, just one step up from prostitution as far as the people in Charles's world are concerned). Where Smithy in the film becomes a writer, Smithy in the novel becomes a social activist; Smithy and Paula go to London and live in the slums and work to help the poor. All of that is lost and forgotten when he awakens in Liverpool and returns to a life of great wealth and privilege.

It is also lost when he wakes up in Hollywood (at MGM). The film shamelessly changes Charles from a Conservative MP to a Liberal MP, while at the same time giving him a knighthood that he never has in the novel (where there is no Lady Rainier, just Mrs. Rainier). Where Charles (in the novel) expresses guilt about the poor men who ask him for jobs, the film's Charles explains proudly that he stayed with the company not just to keep his own family going but because, "I found that Rainier's kept other families going too, little families in little homes." The novel argues that Charles is no longer himself or a good man when he has all that money, that he and Paula were only happy (and only themselves) when they were poor but honest; it mocks both the class privilege and the wealth of its hero and heroine and seriously questions them. But the film luxuriates in them, as if to say, "Here is this gorgeous couple, elegant and rich, with a nice big house, famous friends, power, diamonds and emeralds; how happy they would be if only he could remember her." The absence of any sensual presence in Mrs. Rainier until the very end is a necessary corollary to the bloodless life Charles is leading; our interest during the first half of the book is sustained entirely by his public life; he has no private life, and so Mrs. Rainier has none, either.

The film ignores the novel's strong social criticism of Charles and makes a hero of him, just as the German tradition incrementally glorified Siegfried. The film reduces all the serious socialist concerns of the novel to the scene in which Sir Charles goes to settle the strike at Melbridge, and the union leader says, "We've got our terms, the strike is settled, and we've won, thanks to one man, Sir Charles Rainier," and they all sing, "For he's a jolly good fellow!" Sir Charles's gesture of solidarity with his workers is what triggers his memory of the time when he, too, was a poor man and a good man, a man married to Paula; in the novel, Charles experiences that solidarity not with his workers but with the acting troupe (a different sort of lower class), and when he remembers them, he begins to remember Paula. There is, therefore, a grim irony in the fact that one reason why Paula does not declare that she is Charles's wife is that she fears Charles will think she is after his money; Dr. Benet, in the film, asks her if what she wants from Charles is his name, his protection. For this is, after all, a major pattern in the folk background: Siegfried married Gutrune for her political connections, and Paula's motives might seem uncomfortably like those of Bruno in *As You Desire Me*: persuade the wealthy amnesiac that s/he is your long lost love so you can get the money.

Another major political issue in the novel that vanishes from the film is espionage. In the novel, but not in the film, Charles tells this spy story about himself:

> During the desperate months of trench warfare in France an English staff officer reasoned that if some spy whom the Germans had learned to trust were to give them false details about a big attack, it might have a better chance of success. The first step was to establish the good faith of such a spy, and this seemed only possible by allowing him, over a considerable period, to supply true information. Accordingly, during several weeks before the planned offensive, small raiding parties crawled across no man's land at night while German machine gunners, having been duly tipped off as to time and place, slaughtered them with much precision.[30]

Charles watched his men being slaughtered and then overheard snatches of conversation both from his own officers and from the Germans, in trenches within hearing distance, that enabled him "to deduce the whole intrigue of plot and counterplot." (This episode explains the epigram that accounts for the title of the novel, an English translation of a German report of an English report—the double twist—that unconsciously puns on the name of Charles's stately home: "According to a British Official Report, bombs fell at Random.") The shock of this betrayal, compounded by the agony of his wounds, his distress for his men, and finally, a head wound that knocked him unconscious, left him with a partial loss of memory. Thus Charles's betrayal by his own officers is the indirect cause of Paula's betrayal by Smithy: in both cases, it is friendly fire that destroys a life. When Charles-as-Smithy-as-Charles recognizes Paula, he recognizes himself and awakens from his spiritual death. England, too, Hilton fervently hopes, will awaken with him to face World War II.

Julia Misbehaves (1948), *Memory of Love* (1948), and *Love Letters* (1945)

Greer Garson made a comedy of remarriage a few years after *Random Harvest*: *Julia Misbehaves* (Jack Conway, 1948), in which, as in *Random Harvest*, she (Julia) was a chorus girl and her husband (William) a wealthy aristocrat (played by Walter Pigeon, her running mate from *Mrs. Miniver*); again she did a vaudeville routine and showed her legs. Without any amnesia, a few years into the marriage, he simply tells her he does not love her; his mind has been poisoned against her by his snobbish mother (Lucile Watson)—the *Madame X* syndrome. Their child does not die, but when he throws her out, she gives the young child up to him to raise because, as she says later, "They had all the money" (*Madame X* again). Years later, when their daughter Susan (Elizabeth Taylor) is grown up and about to be married, Julia returns and rescues Susan from marrying the rich Mr. Wrong, catapulting her into the arms of the (poor) Mr. Right (Peter Lawford), while she herself, chiasmically, escapes from her engagement to the poor Mr. Wrong, the acrobat Fred (Cesar Romero), and she and William get back together. Fred's indignant remark, crystallizing the whole plot, is lifted straight out of *I Love You Again*: where Herbert, in that film, had said to George-as-Larry, "She may be your wife, but she's engaged to me," Fred says to William, "She may be your wife, but she's my fiancée."

There are many ways to juggle the elements of these plots. In *While You Were Sleeping* (Jon Turtletaub, 1995), for example, Lucy (Sandra Bullock) allows the amnesiac Jack (Bill Pullman) to go on thinking she *was* his lover when she was *not*, precisely the reverse of the situation in *Random Harvest*.[31] *Memory of Love* (John Cromwell, 1948), also called *Night Song*, tiptoes around some of the same class issues as *Random Harvest* but with a change in the cause of the man's nonrecognition (not amnesia but blindness) and a change in the woman's economic transformation: now the heroine goes from riches to rags:

Cathy Mallory (Merle Oberon), a wealthy San Francisco woman, met Dan Evans (Dana Andrews), a piano player and composer who had just been blinded in an accident. She fell for him, and when she learned from his friend Chick Morgan (Hoagy Carmichael) that Dan would have nothing to do with a rich, sighted woman, she pretended to be a poor, blind woman named Mary Willey, and they fell in love. She arranged matters so that an anonymous wealthy woman (herself) offered a prize for an original piano concerto in order to get Dan the money to have the operation that would restore his sight. He won the contest and went to New York, where the operation was successful. But he hesitated to return to Cathy-as-Mary and did not write to her. (He never said why, but Chick, who knew that Cathy was Mary, explained to her that now that Dan could see, he didn't want to tie himself down to someone blind.)

Cathy went to New York and appeared to Dan in her true persona as the wealthy (and sighted) Cathy Mallory. He began to fall in love with her. She asked him about the woman back in San Francisco (whom he had never seen), and he said, "I might know her hand or her voice. Her voice was like yours, only a bit lower." She lowered her voice. "Yes, it's like that," he said. He took Cathy's hand as he had taken the hand of Cathy-as-Mary in San Francisco and looked at it thoughtfully, but that's all. She was disturbed by his love for her; she said to Chick, "I want him to go back to her." When Chick reminded Cathy that Mary Willey was "just a gag," she replied, "She was at first. Now she's very real to me." When Dan started to make love to Cathy, she was deeply ambivalent and moved away from him.

Dan was increasingly tormented by memories of Mary. He admitted to Cathy that he was still thinking about the blind woman he had left in San Francisco, and Cathy, hoping that Dan would eventually acknowledge his love for Mary, refused to reveal her impersonation to him. On the night of his premiere (a performance of a movie music concerto, actually played, in full, by Artur Rubinstein and Eugene Ormandy in Carnegie Hall), Dan suddenly took the train back to San Francisco. When Cathy learned from Chick what Dan was doing, she flew back and was there ahead of him. He went to her house, saw her, and broke into a smile.

Blindness makes possible a masquerade that poverty makes necessary. This logic may well be an echo of the silent film *City Lights* (Charlie Chaplin, 1931), in which the blind woman (Virginia Cherill) mistakes a tramp (Chaplin) for a millionaire and recognizes him, years later, by the touch of his hand. Here, Dan looks long and hard at Cathy's hand but does not figure it out; Cathy-as-Mary appears in his flashbacks as a blur that we and the camera, but not he, can recognize as Mary. At one point, Cathy says to Dan, "So that's how it is. I remind you of someone," and still later he says to her, "I keep thinking I've known you. It's like when you think something has happened exactly the same way before." This is a paradigm that has happened more or less exactly the same way before and will happen again.

Cathy Mallory indulges in a great deal of lying and manipulation, wielding the evil power inherent in money; she has the upper hand, in knowledge as well as power, vividly expressed by the metaphor of her flying, asleep, above him and ahead of him as he crosses the country, awake and trailing behind, on a train. When they are on her penthouse balcony, she says, "I don't like looking down at people from a high place. They look too insignificant." And he replied, "Let's go down there and be significant." But it is she, not he, who is anxious to "go down there and be significant." The odd thing is that everyone in the film (including Ethel Barrymore, in a supporting role) comes to regard the fantasy persona, the "gag," the poor, blind woman, as more real than the original persona, and the film ends with Cathy-as-Mary still inside that frame, still pretending to be poor (though, presumably, she will soon start writing checks). Who is Dan smiling at in the final frame—Mary or Cathy-as-Mary? Or Cathy-as-Mary-as-Cathy? Is he so glad that Mary has turned out to be Cathy, even though it means that Mary knows he almost fell for Cathy? Or is he just glad to see Mary? The ending is far more ambiguous than that of *Random Harvest*.

There may be echoes here, and in *Random Harvest*, of other films in which the class conflict neatly circles back in on itself. In *My Man Godfrey* (Gregory La Cava, 1936), a wealthy socialite (Carole Lombard) hires a homeless tramp (William Powell) to be her butler and is surprised how quickly he learns to imitate upper-class ways and how quickly she falls in love with him; he turns out to be a blue blood ("one of the Park Parks of Boston," a Harvard man) pretending to be a butler pretending to be a Harvard man. Similarly, in *Sullivan's Travels* (Preston Sturges 1941), the privileged film director John L. Sullivan (Joel McCrea), who wants to make a film about a chain gang,[32] masquerades as a tramp to find out how poor people suffer. But then (during a brief bout of amnesia after a blow on the head—another sort of movie would have picked up this theme and run with it) he is mistaken for a real tramp and becomes a real convict on a chain gang. By the time he remembers who he is, no one will believe him until he pretends to be his own murderer (that is, he confesses to the murder of the film director, who has been reported dead) in order to get his picture in the papers so his friends can come, invoke his privilege, and get him out of the chain gang.

A simplified version of the romantic strand of *Random Harvest* is *Love Letters* (William Dieterle, 1945), in which, as in *As You Desire Me*, the amnesiac is a woman. The plot, which also draws heavily on *Cyrano de Bergerac*, goes like this:

During World War II, a soldier named Allen Quinton (Joseph Cotton) and a young woman named Victoria Remington (Jennifer Jones), who had never met, fell in love through love letters that he wrote to her on behalf of his friend Roger Morland. When Roger returned and married her and she discovered what a bounder he was, there was a fight; he was killed and she lost her memory. Allen was told that both Victoria and Roger had died in a tragic accident, which no one would talk about. He met a woman who called herself Singleton, and he did not realize at first that she was his old pen pal Victoria Remington, though eventually a mutual friend (who had a crush on Allen herself) told him the truth and warned him never to speak to Singleton about her past: "If her memory ever came back, it should come back gradually, from within, of her own accord. If anyone told her of her past now, the shock would be so terrible that she'd probably lose her mind." Singleton was haunted by the memory of another man whom she had loved, who had written wonderful letters to her, and she feared that Allen, too, was still in love with someone else, someone she didn't know, named Victoria Remington ("I'll help you find her," she said, cheerfully).

They fell in love, but Singleton's guardian (Gladys Cooper) warned Allen that he was proposing to marry two women, Victoria and Singleton, and that only one, Singleton, could give her consent; how could Singleton give Victoria's consent? And what if Singleton turned back into Victoria? Allen feared, too, that if he told her he had written those letters that made her love their author, she would hate him for his deception, and so he remained silent. Still, they married. One day Singleton wrote out a verbatim passage from one of the letters she had written to Allen-as-Roger long ago. Then Allen quoted from one of his letters to her, and she realized he was the author she was seeking. Now she remembered everything, but she did not hate him for his deception. They embraced joyously.

As in *Random Harvest*, one of the lovers is an amnesiac and the other is a masquerader, and again, the masquerader does not tell the amnesiac the truth for several overdetermined reasons (spelled out, in both cases, by someone else in love with the amnesiac's lover), primarily the fear of alienating the amnesiac. Allen lets Singleton go on believing she is substituting for Victoria, while he himself fears he is impersonating Allen-as-Roger, and both of them are right. There are two triangles here in Singleton's mind, composed of just three people, though she thinks there are four: in the first triangle, Singleton is torn between men she thinks of as Allen and Roger (actually between Allen and Allen-as-Roger), and in the second, she imagines that Allen is torn between Victoria and Singleton (actually between Victoria and Victoria-as-Singleton). After a while, she figures it out all by herself, though, as usual, long, long after we do.

The appeal of the theme never seems to die. In *Groundhog Day* (Harold Ramis, 1993), Phil Connors (Bill Murray), a jaded weatherman, finds himself trapped in a constantly self-replicating February 2. At first this appears to be the happy dream of stopping the clock, extending life, but then it becomes the nightmare of the eternal return: he is doomed to spend the rest of eternity in the same place, seeing the same people do the same thing every day. This arrangement has, however, romantic advantages. Since no one else remembers the previous February 2, in effect, everyone but him has amnesia, including Rita (Andie Macdowell), whom he is determined to seduce. He learns, day by day, all her tastes, which he uses to re-create himself as her dream man; she does not remember that she herself told him what she likes, and she falls for him—until she smells a rat.

This scenario was inverted (and fleshed out with bits of *Memento* [Christopher Nolan, 2000]) in *Fifty First Dates* (Peter Segal, 2004), in which Henry Roth (Adam Sandler) and Lucy Whitmore (Drew Barrymore) fall in love. As the result of a recent accident, she has no short-term memory, a factor that, as in other films, makes for endlessly renewed erotic freshness; when he first kisses her, each day, she says, "There's nothing like a first kiss." But now her amnesia poses a problem for her non-amnesiac partner. One day, Lucy wakes up in bed with a man (Henry) she regards as a total stranger; naturally, she screams. He realizes that he must start all over again to persuade her, every day, that she has already fallen in love with him; in effect, he must make her fall in love with him every day. Yet in the end she remembers him in her dreams, a place that, like the body, seems to preserve memory even when it has been erased from the mind. Luckily for Hollywood, the viewing public also has this convenient recurrent amnesia: it keeps forgetting that it has seen these films of amnesiac lovers many times before.

CHAPTER SIX

Reincarnation

[A] secret, partial, tangible and true aspect of our resistance to
death, is the long, desperate, daily resistance to the fragmentary and
continuous death that insinuates itself throughout the whole course
of our life, detaching from us at each moment a shred of ourself,
dead matter on which new cells will multiply and grow.

Marcel Proust, *In a Budding Grove* (1923)

Déjà Vu All Over Again

Where the mythology of lost love and recovered love, lost memory and recovered
memory, is generally limited to a single life, the mythology of reincarnation employs
the same imagery but jumps the barrier of rebirth, imagining the survival of consciousness on the other side. In this mythology, the new self is literally a part of the
past not merely of the present life but of another, previous life. Such stories suggest
that each of us, in our present lives, may at any moment be awakened to the memory
of another, lost life, that we all constantly reinvent ourselves out of the scraps of the
past, so that, in a sense, we are always imitating our past selves. The signals we send to
ourselves from our former lives are wake-up calls, like the message the Chippendale
Mupp, one of the creatures in *Dr. Seuss's Sleep Book*, sends to himself: at bedtime, he
bites the end tuft on his *very* long tail, so that the ouch will work its way up the whole
tail and, finally, wake him up in the morning.[1]

These myths ask: Where is memory, in the mind or in the body? How can our
bodies remember things that our minds have forgotten? Indian philosophy locates

memory in the *manas*, a combination of mind and heart: like the heart, it is a physical organ in the body, and like the mind, it is where you learn calculus, and like both mind and heart, it is where you fall in love—thus doubly blurring the Cartesian distinction between mind and body. Hinduism assumes that when the body dies, the soul transmigrates, taking with it the dead person's karma, the moral record of good and bad actions committed in all former lives. Although the transmigrating soul usually loses its memory as it crosses the boundary of rebirth and sheds its body, some particularly gifted people can remember their previous births. Some branches of Indian philosophy, therefore, locate memory along with karma in (or more precisely on) the soul, without, however, totally divorcing it from the body.

Belief in reincarnation has long appealed to non-Hindu consciousness. Karmic thinking continues to surface among us in New Age circles, in Hollywood (both in films and in the personal beliefs of stars like Shirley MacLaine), and in what might be called American folk belief. Most scholars of Hinduism and Buddhism tread lightly upon the karma theory for reasons of inter-cultural tact (or raging relativism, depending on your point of view). Some (including myself) go farther and grant the theory some degree of useful wisdom, at the very least as a powerful metaphor and at the most as an expression, mutatis mutandis, of ideas that we, too, hold about the compelling force of the past.

All of us are subject to what the Hindus call *vasanas*, "perfumes," scents that are "the impressions of anything remaining unconsciously in the mind, the present consciousness of past perceptions."[2] This force accounts for our sense of déjà vu, among other things, the sense that one sometimes has, on seeing someone or someplace for the first time, that one has seen it before. These are the "impressions of lingering emotions" that a king in a Sanskrit play (a man who has forgotten his wife), has in mind when he says:

> Even a happy man may be overcome by passionate longing
> when he sees beautiful things or hears sweet sounds.
> Perhaps he is remembering something he was not conscious of before that
> moment,
> the loves of a former life, firmly rooted in the impressions of lingering emotions.[3]

The bits of experience that Hindus call the karmic memory traces cling to our transmigrating souls even in new bodies, loose threads trailing not merely from a former life within this lifespan but from a previous life, a previous incarnation. (One commentator remarks that it is impossible to shake off these impressions even after thousands of lives.[4])

The unconscious memories of past lives, the *vasanas*, predispose the transmigrating soul to act in one way or another in its new life. Similarly, the transmigrating soul in the myth of Er in Book Ten of Plato's *Republic* (c. 375 BCE) retains some sort of magnetic attachment to its old body and, with it, to its old personality, like Eeyore to his detached tail. For before our minds are washed clean as we drink the waters of Lethe, we are given the choice of who to become in our next life; but we choose to become the same sort of person we were before or, as the case may be, the very opposite of the sort of person we were before. One way or another, the force of our previous personality constrains and skews our rational choice:

> The choice was both laughable and amazing, since most people chose according to the habits of their former life. The soul that had been Orpheus chose to be a swan, because he so hated the race of women—at whose hands he had met his death—that he did not want to be conceived and born of them. And Er saw a swan changing into the life he chose as a man. When all the souls had chosen their lots, they went to the Plain of Oblivion and drank from the River of Forgetfulness, and then they all fell asleep.[5]

Plato describes many other, similar cases, each choice based on the experience of a previous life: Atalanta, seeing the great fame of an athlete, is unable to resist the temptation; the jester Thersites chooses the form of a monkey; and so forth. Agamemnon becomes an eagle; does he remember that he was symbolized by an eagle in Aeschylus's eponymous play about him? So, too, Augustine (in the *Confessions*) speaks of habit as a kind of internalized necessitating power of the past, a chain that drags you into the past; and the *contrapposto* in Dante's *Inferno* doom many sinners to an eternity whose torment consists primarily in being forced to do forever in Hell what they chose to do on earth—or its diametric opposite. Even if we cannot remember who we were, we are reborn in the shadow of our previous personality. The soul gets typecast.

Orpheus's choice of a swan may have been influenced by Plato's knowledge of the importance of that animal in Indian theories of transmigration,[6] in which the swan (*hamsa*), more like a wild goose, really, symbolizes the transmigrating spirit that returns year after year. A Hindu text from about 700 CE imagines the reincarnating soul meditating on its next life not on the far shore of Lethe but in the womb of the soul's future mother, where it (not yet he or she) not only remains fully conscious but remembers its previous lives in agonizing detail:

> Then it begins to remember its many previous existences in the wheel of rebirth, and that depresses it, and it tosses from side to side, thinking, "I won't ever do *that* again, as soon as I get out of this womb. I will do everything I can, so that I won't become an embryo again." It thinks in this way as it remembers the hundreds of miseries of birth that it experienced before, in the power of fate. Then, as time goes by, the embryo turns around, head down, and in the ninth or tenth month it is born. As it comes out, it is hurt by the wind of procreation; it comes out crying, because it is pained by the misery

in its heart. When it has come out of the womb, it falls into an unbearable swoon, but it regains consciousness when the air touches it. Then Vishnu's deluding power of illusion assails him, and when his soul has been deluded by it, he loses his knowledge. As soon as the living creature has lost his knowledge, he becomes a baby. After that he becomes a young boy, then an adolescent, and then an old man. And then he dies and is born again as a human. Thus he wanders on the wheel of rebirth like the bucket on the wheel of a well.[7]

Chagrin at the memory of previous mistakes and despair at the realization that one will make them all again in this life, too, is what makes the baby cry as he enters the world. The *Laws of Manu* (c. 375 CE), the classical Sanskrit text of Hindu law, promises many upwardly mobile transmigrations, but not for everyone: "Through the repetition of their evil actions, men of little intelligence experience miseries in womb after womb in this world."[8]

Reincarnation is generally regarded as a fresh start, but the tabula is not always quite so rasa as more simplistic treatments of the doctrine assume. The goal of liberation theology, Hindu style, is to untangle the knots of karma, to achieve *moksha*, freedom from the same old same old in life after life. For a Hindu, this means to break out altogether from samsara (the cycle of transmigration), but it could also mean to be free to go forward without the compulsion for self-imitation. For in our culture, too, people find it difficult to kick the Lethe habit. Peggy Sue (in Francis Ford Coppola's *Peggy Sue Got Married* [1986]) says, "If only I knew then what I know now," but when she does get a chance to live her life over again, by going back in time so that she knows what the future holds for her, she falls for the same two-timing husband. Mae West once said that if she had her life to live over again she would make all the same mistakes, but she would make them sooner.

In many ways the *vasanas* that return to the reborn soul correspond not just to the unconscious as we have come to understand it but more particularly to the repressed unconscious that *returns*, in Freud's formulation. Freud himself likened this process to reincarnation, citing (as an example of the "remoteness of time" over which the repression operates) a line from Goethe about the survival of love: "For you were, in times lived through before, my sister or my wife."[9] Freud also referred (in "The Unconscious") to a "memory trace" (*Erinnerungsspur*) that was not yet a part of conscious memory. Other scientists approached this problem in different ways. The brain surgeon Wilder Penfield (1891–1976) in 1955 electrically stimulated a particular part of the temporal lobes and found that about 8 percent of his subjects experienced "memories." But were these actual memories, hallucinations, or merely the affectual component of "memory" that could be superimposed upon new experiences to produce the sensation of déjà vu?

The Hindu "perfumes" correspond in many ways to the social chemo-signals that Martha McClintock has studied, olfactory clues to social behavior that are handed down genetically (which is, in a sense, through rebirths), generally unconscious clues that influence our emotions. Appropriately, McClintock named one group of these chemo-signals, closely related to what she has called pheromones, after the *vasanas* of Hindu philosophy:

> The term is used to explain why a person has a tendency to react to a situation in a particular way. We find it useful to adopt this philosophical term in our classification of human social chemo-signals because both its etymology and its functional definition are so close to the findings from our empirical psychological data.... *Vasanas* are those unconscious chemo-signals whose functional effects are related to or predicted by their odor qualities when they are experienced consciously.... The power of subconscious odors to evoke emotional memory-derived experience in humans is widely recognized.
> ... Because they are not necessarily conscious, the term *vasana* may be more appropriate than "unconscious odors," which is an oxymoron.[10]

Perfume is notoriously evocative and identifying; the last line in Murgatroyd's argument for the identity of Jean and Eve in *The Lady Eve* is, "She even wears the same perfume." These parallels bring to mind the taste (so closely related to smell) of Marcel Proust's madeleines from Combray, which evoke and recover for him the rich memories of his childhood. Proust also speaks of reincarnation, remarking that, upon waking each morning, his thoughts about himself "would begin to seem unintelligible, as the thoughts of a former existence must be to a reincarnate spirit."[11]

The "social chemo-signals," or *vasanas*, which are evidence of "the effect of a previous life on one's current life," are handed down in the DNA.[12] We might equate this genetic inheritance with the karma we get from the two people with whom we share our physical substance, our parents. This prenatal parental karma (an ocean full of the reefs and sharks that Greek tragedy warned us about) is further compounded, especially in early childhood, by our postnatal parental karma (an ocean full of the obsessional reefs and incestuous sharks that Freud warned us about). We are (as the karma theory demands), more often than not, ignorant of the precise nature of our parental karma of both types, either because it was made before we were born or because we have forgotten (or—Freud would say—repressed) it. There is a long continuum: closest are the things we remember that our parents did for/to us relatively recently, and then the things that they did when we were so little that we cannot remember them clearly or at all, then the things (like smoking or contracting AIDS) that our mothers did to us while we were in the womb (here we move back into prenatal parental karma), then the things that our parents did before we were conceived, and finally both the genetic stock and the cultural memories transmitted from earlier generations—the things that happened during the pogroms in Russia, the traumas suffered during the Great Depression. Prenatal parental karma gives us our susceptibility to certain diseases and, perhaps, to certain sorts of people; postnatal parental karma, too, may be negative,[13] but it also accounts for the transmission of talents, positive memories such as those stirred by music and art, and irrational love, or the ability (or curse) to fall in love at first sight, generally with a highly inappropriate person.[14] It is this final piece of the karmic inheritance—irrational love—that is celebrated in the myths (and films) that depict lovers who recognize one another across the barrier of death.

THE MAN WHO FORGOT HE WAS GOD: THE MONK'S DREAM

A complex pattern of self-impersonation through reincarnation, and a circular model of the survival of consciousness, is formulated in the *Yogavasishtha*, a Sanskrit text composed in Kashmir between the tenth and the twelfth centuries CE, a time when Hindus and Buddhists were in close contact.[15] This is the tale of a man who dreams he is the god Rudra, a form of the god Shiva, who is, in this text, the supreme god:

> One day a monk decided to imagine what happens to ordinary people. And so he imagined that he was a man named Jivata, who lived for a long time until one day he drank too much and fell into a heavy sleep in which he saw a Brahmin who read all day long. One day that Brahmin fell asleep after a hard day's reading and dreamed that he was a prince; the prince fell asleep one day after a heavy meal and saw himself as a powerful king. The king, having gorged himself on his every desire, fell asleep and saw himself as a courtesan who fell into a deep sleep in the languor that followed making love; she saw herself as a doe who fell asleep and dreamed she was a clinging vine (for animals dream too, and they always remember what they have seen and heard). The vine saw herself as a bee who was trampled by an elephant and, dying, saw himself as an elephant in rut; that elephant in rut was cut to pieces in battle, and, dying, saw a swarm of bees and became a bee again. The bee became a goose who was shot by a hunter and died and was reborn as the swan on which the god Brahma, the Creator, rides.
>
> One day the swan saw the god Rudra and realized, "I am Rudra." And he became Rudra, living in Rudra's palace, and as Rudra he could see every one of his former experiences. Then he went to the place where the monk was sleeping and woke him up; and the monk realized that he had been mistaken to think he was Jivata. Then Rudra and the monk found Jivata asleep and woke him up, and the three of them went to wake up the Brahmin, and so forth, until they reached the swan of Brahma. Then Rudra said, "Now go back to your own places and enjoy yourselves there with your families for a while, and then come back to me. And at doomsday, all of us, the bands of creatures who are part of me, will go to the final resting place." And they all went back, but after a while they will wear out their bodies and unite again in the world of Rudra.[16]

The swan, a natural and cross-cultural symbol of periodic return, is the emblem of both the individual soul and the mind of god, in this case Rudra. The very substance of this god is (according to a doctrine that begins in the Upanishads, c. 600 BCE) the stuff that our own consciousnesses are made of—*brahman*, a kind of world-soul (sometimes translated "godhead") which is distributed within each of our individual souls or selves (*atman*). In this metaphysical world, we remember both our dreams and our rebirths—much the same thing—when we awaken from our primary amnesia, which makes us forget that we are god.

The story does not reveal to us the entire rebirth of each of the characters; none of them is born, and most of them do not die within the story. Significantly, the first person the monk dreams of is named Jivata, a word derived from the word for a life or a soul, *jiva*. Some of the subjects are women (and female animals), with whom the male actors have no lasting attachments, merely brief physical encounters. These people dream and become what they have habitually dreamed about and are thinking about as they die. We awaken from ignorance, or from sleep, or from life; the same verb (*budh*) covers all three. One door opens, and another shuts, as the doctor says in *Random Harvest*; we awaken from one dream not to full wakefulness but only to fall into another, as Charles Rainier fell from one amnesia into another. The chain-gang guard in *Sullivan's Travels* (1941) is thinking along this track when he tells Sullivan, "Maybe you ain't a picture director. Maybe that's just an idea that came to you when you got hit on the head. We had a guy here, used to think he was Lindbergh."

The creatures in the monk's dream form a pattern that is a masterful combination of order and chance. Though anything *can* happen, certain things are more *likely* to happen; this is how karma skews and orders the chaos of the universe. The text tells us: "Again and again these lives revolve in creation like the waves in water, and some [rebirths] are strikingly similar [to what they were before], and others are about half the same; some are a little bit the same, some are not very much alike at all, and sometimes they are once again just the same." This flexibility, together with the elements of pure chance and the gravity of karmic tendencies, makes certain coincidences not only possible but probable. For the text tells us that after the bee had become an elephant and was then reborn again as a bee, he went back to the same lotus pond where he had previously met with his unfortunate accident, "because people who are not aware of their karmic traces find it hard to give up their bad habits." So, too, the beautiful woman becomes a doe because she envies the beauty of the doe's eyes, and the text remarks, "Alas, the delusion that results from the karmic traces causes such misery among creatures."[17] Each of the people in the dream chain is reborn in a particular form *because they all want something*. There is a hunger, unsated in their present lives, that propels them across the barrier of death into a new birth where this still unfulfilled longing leads them to do what they do. By extension and implication, all of us, too, helplessly spin out of our desires the lives we have inherited from our former selves. And so in each new life, we pretend, once again, to be who we are, repeating lines from an earlier script even when we think that we are improvising or that we are not performing at all. We cannot escape from our own previous character, our desire, which sticks like tar to the transmigrating soul. Our memory of those ancient desires is also partly accidental, partly not so accidental; Hinduism offers several different praxes designed to help us remember our former lives, just as psychoanalysis claims to help us remember our dreams. For most of us, however, such memories remain largely unconscious and inaccessible.

The God Who Forgot He Was God: Chandrashekhara and Taravati

All of us tend to forget that we are god, according to the doctrine of Hindu idealism in the *Yogavasishtha*. But divinity is a continuum; some creatures are more divine than others, and some gods are more divine in certain texts than in others. The philosophical and mythological assertion that all humans are (conscious or unconscious) incarnations of a deity is enacted in the many rituals in which the worshipper masquerades as the god (through the use of masks, for instance). Sacrificial rituals complicate the pattern by introducing a third party—the animal victim—and imagining that the victim takes the place of the sacrificer (the ram standing in for Isaac, who is in a sense already standing in for Abraham) and/or that the god becomes present in the victim (the lamb or the wafer and the wine). But the ritual in turn often gives rise to a mythology that questions, reverses, or even laughs at these assumptions. Indra, the king of the Hindu gods, is one of several gods designated as the recipients of the horse sacrifice (in which the queen pantomimes copulation with the dead stallion) but unique in that he is himself famed for having performed more horse sacrifices than anyone else and is jealous of this preeminence.[18] He thus normally combines the roles of sacrificer and recipient, where the usual human worshipper is sacrificer and victim. But in one text,[19] Indra adds to his two usual roles that of the victim:

> During the coronation of king Janamejaya, his queen approached the designated stallion and lay down beside him, according to the rules of the ritual. But Indra saw how beautiful the woman's body was, and he desired her. He himself entered the designated stallion and mingled with the queen. And when this transformation had taken place, Indra said to the priest in charge of the sacrifice, "This is not the horse you designated. Scram."[20]

The official substitution is the stallion's impersonation of the sacrificer, the king, who is himself the emblem of the god Indra on earth. Indra jumps over these links to become the stallion himself, mocking the representational conventions of the horse sacrifice—to the distress of the king, who immediately forbids anyone to perform another horse sacrifice. Indra is thus imitating (the king who is imitating) Indra. We may see this as one of those moments when common sense butts in or as an intertextual moment in which a tradition makes fun of one of its own assumptions about ritual self-impersonation.

In the *Bacchae* of Euripides, an actor plays the god Dionysos, who impersonates one of his own worshippers (dressed in imitation of the god Dionysos) and wreaks havoc among them. Shiva, who resembles Dionysos in many ways,[21] does similarly self-referential damage in a myth that short-circuits the chain of sacrificial identifications, much as the myth of Indra did: Daksha, the father of Shiva's wife Sati, gives a sacrifice in which the sacrificial victim is a goat, standing in as a surrogate for the sacrificer (in this case, Daksha); but Shiva, who has not been invited to the sacrifice, crashes it in fury and beheads not the goat but Daksha himself, literalizing the symbolism by making the sacrificer the actual victim.[22] The *Yogavasishtha* depicts humans who forget that the god Shiva, as Rudra, is the very substance of consciousness, but in other texts, Shiva himself forgets who he is and engages in unconscious self-imitation when his wife Parvati tricks him by masquerading as another woman.[23] Parvati, however, already *is* another woman, for in her former life she was Shiva's wife Sati, who committed suicide by fire (at Daksha's disastrous sacrifice) and was granted her wish to marry Shiva again in her next life, as Parvati.[24]

The chain continues when Shiva and Parvati become incarnate not merely in all human beings but in particular human beings (called partial incarnations) who slip in and out of consciousness of their incarnational status. A Sanskrit text composed in Assam in the tenth or eleventh century CE explores the human complications that can arise out of such a partial (re)incarnation:

> Once when Shiva and Parvati had quarreled and she had gone away, Shiva, tormented by unsatisfied desire, mistook the beautiful goddess Savitri for Parvati (who closely resembled Savitri) and begged her to make love with him. When he tried to take her by force, she cursed him to make love with a human woman, since he had behaved like a human man. Shiva became partially incarnate as a prince named Chandrashekhara ("wearing the crescent moon as his crown," an epithet of Shiva). When the prince grew up, he married Taravati, a partial incarnation of Parvati. One day when Taravati had bathed in a river, the sage Kapota saw her and was overcome by lust for her. He said, "You must be a goddess or a demon woman who has become mortal in order to enjoy the pleasures of the flesh. You must be Parvati." She replied, "I am not a goddess but merely a mortal queen, Taravati, wife of King Chandrashekhara." Fearing the sage's curse if she failed to submit to his sexual demands, Taravati sent her sister in her place, but when the sage realized the deception he cursed Taravati: "Since you deceived me

with a trick when I desired you, and you did not desire me enough to commit adultery with me, therefore Shiva will rape you, coming to you in the form of a hideous Skull-bearer, and you will immediately bear him a pair of monkey-faced sons." But she said, "I swear by the vows that my father made to Parvati when he obtained me for his daughter. I swear that I will never make love to any man but Chandrashekhara, even in a dream."

Then Taravati told Chandrashekhara what had happened, and he made a high terrace to protect her, an impenetrable place where he always went to make love to her. One day, as Taravati worshipped Shiva and Parvati, she did not distinguish between Shiva and Chandrashekhara. Then Shiva came there with Parvati, to whom he said, "Taravati is your human incarnation. As I wish to make love to no woman but you, enter into her form now so that I can beget the two sons in you." Parvati did so, and Shiva then approached Taravati in the form of a hideous Skull-bearer. Taravati, into whom Parvati had entered, received him with great joy and immediately gave birth to twin monkey-faced children, whereupon she fell into a deep swoon. Then Parvati left the body of Taravati and deluded her so that she did not recognize herself (as an incarnation of Parvati). When Taravati saw the two sons and Shiva in his loathsome form, she realized that the sage's curse had come true. Shiva said, "You have kept your vow never to desire any man but Chandrashekhara, for I am Shiva and I am Chandrashekhara." But when Shiva vanished, Taravati was again overcome by delusion, and she wept in grief and anger.

Then Chandrashekhara said, "What has happened to you, Taravati? Who has raped you, like a jackal attacking a lioness?" When she told him what had happened, he thought, "Shiva has no beloved but Parvati. But because of the sage's curse some demonic magician has taken on the deceptive outer form of Shiva and defiled my dear wife. How else could she have given birth to these demon sons with monkey faces? How can I keep her as before?" A voice in the sky, however, assured him that Shiva himself had begotten the sons, and a sage explained that Shiva had been born as Chandrashekhara and Parvati as Taravati because of Savitri's curse. The king and his wife closed their eyes and saw Taravati as Parvati and Chandrashekhara as Shiva wearing a tiger skin and riding on a bull. But when they opened their eyes again, they thought, "We are mortals."

As time went by, Chandrashekhara favored his other three sons over the two boys engendered by Shiva. The twins went away and begat sons of their own, and then Shiva came to them and made them immortals, leaders of his hosts.[25]

In the first impersonation, Taravati's sister explicitly takes her place, while the sage Kapota's attempted rape and subsequent curse of Taravati foreshadow and predict Shiva's successful rape and impregnation of Taravati. Shiva and Parvati impersonate Chandrashekhara and Taravati on four, increasingly specific levels: First is the general philosophical doctrine that all creatures are made of *brahman*, and hence the king and queen are part of the godhead embodied in Shiva and Parvati. Second is the implicit metaphysical incarnation based on the belief that all men and women are forms of Shiva and Parvati,[26] rather than of other deities, for human beings are all marked with the signs of the god Shiva and his consort, the male and female sexual organs, lingam and yoni.[27] Third is the myth in which Shiva himself becomes a Skull-bearer when he beheads the god Brahma, a myth that certain of his devotees, also called Skull-bearers, reenact by carrying a skull when they beg.[28] And last, the proximate cause, is the explicit impersonation of Chandrashekhara by Shiva, necessitated by Kapota's curse.[29]

When Kapota suggests that Taravati may be Parvati incarnate, he is speaking in clichés to flatter her rather than speculating on her actual incarnational nature; but he is speaking more truth than he knows. She, too, misses the individual truth in the general cliché; she refuses to accept his identification and must learn it the hard way. She makes a vow to protect her from the rape predicted in Kapota's curse, but her ignorance of the identity of her husband Chandrashekhara and the god Chandrashekhara causes her to word her vow in such a way that it fails to protect her from the curse, even though she reveals in that vow the very clue that should teach her her own identity: the fact that she was born when her father propitiated Parvati. Like Isolde, Taravati creates a loophole for adultery, referring explicitly to her husband but implicitly to her lover of the same name (for Hindus are often named after their god). But unlike Isolde, she has *not* committed adultery and does not realize the double meaning of her words. Her curse is to be raped, and as long as she remains ignorant of the identity of her seducer—as both her husband and her god—she regards the seduction as a rape, though the goddess, by entering the mortal woman, transforms the sexual act into a willing and joyous union. This transformation is made possible by the theology of the repulsive that characterizes the mythology of Shiva, particularly the erotic frisson that Parvati (here in the form of her incarnation, Taravati) gets from the dangerous, antinomian god.[30] The application of this theology to the tale of Taravati has troubling implications for a feminist, clothing the rape in mythological veils. And it even troubles Taravati within the text: when she is in Shiva's embrace, she learns who she is, but she forgets it again when she returns to the mortal world and is left holding the baby—two babies, as usual in this mythology—to explain to her husband. (A similar ambivalence is experienced by Brünnhilde, who experiences as rape her seduction by Siegfried, whom she does not recognize because he is disguised as Gunther.) Stories such as this give rise to the widespread, though unjustified, opinion held by many Europeans, including Freud, that the fear of deflowering a virgin that plagued certain men—such as Gunther in the *Nibelungenlied*—was dealt with in some parts of India by obliging the newly married woman "to sacrifice her hymen to the wooden lingam,"[31] the form of Shiva in the temple.

Like so many husbands in this mythology of self-impersonation, Chandrashekhara wrongly doubts his wife's fidelity. At first, he suspects a literally demonic lover in the form of Shiva (a fifth level of impersonation) and only realizes the truth when a sage tells him the tale of yet another case of mistaken identities (level six) to illuminate his own: Shiva mistaking another woman (in this case, Savitri) for Parvati, as he often does. The king and queen obtain a brief joint vision of their true natures, but they cannot sustain it; they cannot bear to look upon naked divinity, even their own naked divinity. Conventional life obscures it; the human ties of the king's natural sons supersede the dim mystical vision, and the king rejects the sons of his god. Chandrashekhara knows that Shiva fathered his sons, but he doesn't realize that he *is* Shiva and that his cuckolder is not only his god but himself; eventually, therefore, he rejects the children as any common-or-garden-variety cuckolded husband might do. Chandrashekhara has raped his own wife but does not know it—here due to theological rather than magical (or alcoholic) amnesia. When there is no longer any specific need for Taravati and Chandrashekhara to know who they really are, the uncomfortable truth is veiled from them. Yet they retain a part of the vision: after they have opened their eyes and consider themselves mortal, they still know that they are portions of Shiva and Parvati.[32] This much of the truth is tolerable and accessible to all mortals, without the need for the actual encounter with Shiva himself that is enacted in the myth.

The mythology of Shiva's human incarnations (or impersonations) was so well known in India that contemporary folk traditions satirized it. In a story collected by A. K. Ramanujan in Karnataka in the 1950s, a rich merchant had the town crier announce through the village that he should be worshipped in all the temples instead of Shiva. One day, Shiva took on the merchant's appearance—an exact look-alike, with the merchant's face, manner, and voice—and went to the merchant's house and talked with his wife (probably a euphemism for sex, as it often is in South Asia and elsewhere). When the merchant returned, the villagers thought he was a false double and beat him. Finally, the merchant called on Shiva, who appeared to him and healed his bruises.[33] The tale takes the heavy theological hypothesis of the identity of the worshipper and the god and leavens it with the old chestnut of the bedtrick and the almost as old chestnut of the man who inadvertently imitates himself and is beaten for it (as the Japanese priest Kongo-in was beaten because he was mistaken for a fox pretending to be Kongo-in).

The incarnations (or avatars) of the god Vishnu, particularly Rama and Krishna,[34] have a more particular awareness of their own divinity, yet even they often forget their divine natures. In the *Mahabharata*, Krishna often forgets he is god until someone else remembers, a mortal or, occasionally, another god, or Krishna himself.[35] In later texts, such as the tenth century *Bhagavata Purana*, however, Krishna never forgets. Indeed, when Krishna is still a little child, he sometimes remembers not only that he is god but that he was previously incarnate as Rama, recalling, when he is drifting between sleeping and waking, his earlier birth as Rama.[36] He is also firmly in control of his knowledge of his own divinity when he deals with other people (including his mother), whom he allows to forget who he is because they cannot sustain the intensity of their brief visions of his true nature,[37] just as Shiva allowed Taravati and Chandrashekhara to forget their vision of themselves as gods. Krishna also indulges in a neat bit of self-imitation: pretending to be a human cowherd, he teases the naked cowherd women by making them pretend that he is god—which he knows he is—and forcing them to worship him by raising their cupped hands in a gesture that simultaneously reveres the god and lets the naughty boy see their nakedness.[38]

Rama, too, often forgets his divinity. When Rama publicly doubts that his wife Sita remained faithful to him while the demon Ravana held her captive, the gods ask how he can do this, adding, "Can you not know that you are the best of all the gods?" Rama, uncomprehending, says, "I think of myself as a man, as Rama the son of king Dasharatha. Tell me who I really am, and who my father is, and where I come from."[39] Sheldon Pollock has argued convincingly that in order to achieve his purpose of killing the demon Ravana, Rama must become truly human, for Ravana has secured a boon that no one but a human being can kill him. And to be truly human is to forget that you are god, which Rama must do—at least until after Ravana's death. Moreover, taking on a human body is the consequence of wrong knowledge,[40] for true knowledge would have brought enlightenment and freedom from the wheel of rebirth. The very act of incarnation would destroy the incarnation's true knowledge of his divinity, but in addition (as we have seen), in the process of being born, the newborn child must lose his knowledge. Therefore, an embodied avatar cannot possibly remember who he has been; the very fact of human birth robs him of the capacity to remember his past existences. Other commentators argued that Rama had intentionally become ignorant[41] or that he merely pretended to forget who he was.[42] In other retellings of the narrative, too, Rama insists that he merely pretended to subject Sita to an ordeal and, presumably, pretended to forget that he was god.[43]

THE ROMANCE OF REINCARNATION IN INDIA: THE TWO LILAS

Rama's accusation of Sita is the direct cause of her death. But if suspicions of infidelity can kill, affirmations of fidelity can give new life. In Hindu mythology, a woman may swear by her unbroken fidelity to her husband and, by the power of that truth, may be reunited with her present husband in heaven, after their deaths, or with his reincarnation when they become reincarnate; to this day, Hindu women pray for this boon. We have seen Sati reincarnate as Parvati; similarly, Valmiki's Sita is said to be the reincarnation of a woman who wanted to marry Vishnu but, when Ravana raped her, committed suicide by fire (as Sati had done), vowing to be reborn to destroy Ravana.[44] In a variant of that story, Ravana's victim is reborn not as the real Sita but as her shadow, who endures the fire ordeal in Sita's place; Sita then asks Rama to marry the shadow Sita, too, but he insists that he will have only one wife in this life; he promises, however, to marry the shadow Sita in his next incarnation.[45] The human women in these myths do not usually recognize, or remember, their born-again husbands, nor do their husbands usually remember/recognize them, but sometimes they do, and gods and goddesses often do.

Hindu mythology depicts a number of men who marry their wives again in their next births. In an extreme case of the self-replicating wife, a woman named Lila creates another woman named Lila to marry her husband in his next rebirth:

> Queen Lila was the wife of King Padma. When he died, Lila prayed to the goddess of wisdom and learning, Sarasvati, who explained to her that in a former birth she and the king had been a famous sage and his wife. Now Padma was reborn as another king, and, since Lila had not died, the king had taken a new wife, whose name happened to be Lila (II) and who happened to look just like the first Lila (I). The goddess used her magic powers to transport Lila (I) to the palace where the reborn king lived, and there they spoke with Lila (II). When that reborn king died, Lila (II) also died, since she was merely a product of his dream. Then both of the Lilas returned to the tomb of King Padma, whom the goddess revived. "Who are you? And who is this? And where did she come from?" he asked. Lila (I) said, "I am Lila, your queen from a former life. This second Lila is your queen by my art, just a reflection that I produced for you." Then Lila (I) and Lila (II) and the king took as much pleasure in the stories of his former lives as in the pleasures of making love, for eight thousand years.[46]

Like Nick in *My Favorite Wife*, Padma is suddenly faced with two wives, but in this case they are identical in both form and name. This story, surely a travesty of the self-imitation rebirth pattern, is told in the *Yogavasishtha*, where the concept of the reification of mental images allows the king to experience a happy ménage à trois with his two wives, both of whom are named Lila, "play" or "art," a term used for the illusory sport of an artist (such as a sculptor or a playwright), a magician, or a god. In Indian folktales, too, and from time to time in real life in India, a woman would choose her husband's second wife for him (either when she was dying or when he wanted two wives instead of just one) to make sure that the new wife would be someone she approved of, as Sita asked Rama to take the shadow Sita as a second wife.

Here the goddess Sarasvati makes it all possible. The women understand it all far better than the king, whose flabbergasted response on the occasion of his revival seems to inject a moment of banal common sense into the otherwise no-holds-barred fantasy. Lila II only exists because, like Milton Berle's showgirl, she reminds Padma (and Lila [I]) of his first wife.

THE ROMANCE OF REINCARNATION IN HOLLYWOOD AND BOLLYWOOD

Karma and rebirth are, as we have seen, roughly translatable into other sorts of beliefs about the influence of the past that are compatible with what passes for common sense in America and Europe, particularly in Hollywood, which has a much lower standard for such things as reason. We have already explored the genre of resurrection films, in which a woman dies and come back to life within a single lifetime. Other films (such as *On a Clear Day You Can See Forever* [Vincente Minelli, 1970]) deal with complete reincarnations, long-term avatars—a death and then a rebirth as an infant who grows up. *Dead Again* (Kenneth Branagh, 1991) gives long-term reincarnation a gender twist: she becomes reincarnate as the man, he as the woman, and still they fall in love again. And yet other films are about partial reincarnations, short-term avatars, moments when, for a while, one person's mind gets into another person's body, someone of another gender (*Goodbye Charlie* [Vincente Minelli, 1964], remade as *Switch* [Blake Edwards, 1991]), or age (*Big* [Penny Marshall, 1988], *Vice Versa* [Brian Gilbert, 1988], *18 Again* [Paul Flaherty, 1988][47]), or gender and age (*Prelude to a Kiss* [Norman René, 1992]), or race (*Watermelon Man* [Melvin van Peebles, 1970]), or career (*Sliding Doors* [Peter Howitt, 1998], *Me Myself I* [Pip Karmel, 1999], *The Family Man* [Brett Ratner, 2002]), or an entirely different life (*Lost Highway* [David Lynch, 1997]). In time-travel films, the partial rebirth takes place in the protagonist's past.

One subgenre, which occurs in both long-term and short-term avatars, focuses upon the belief that although the reincarnated soul loses its memory, traces of memory may linger in the form of déjà vu. In films on this theme, people who love one another hope to be reborn with their partners, and because random bits of past karma stick to the soul, they recognize (or half recognize) their partners after they have been reborn. One variant of the short-term species has reappeared in several incarnations, a recycling that gives a double meaning to the useful phrase déjà vu: "Didn't we already see this film?" "No, honey, that was . . . ." First comes Harry Segall's play called *Halfway to Heaven* (1938), then Segall's script for *Here Comes Mr. Jordan* (Alexander Hall, 1941, with Robert Montgomery), then the films called *Heaven Can Wait*, first by Ernst Lubitsch (1943, with Don Ameche), then by Warren Beatty (1978, with Warren Beatty). The most recent variant, *Down to Earth* (Chris Weitz and Paul

Weitz, 2001, with Chris Rock), which was written by Elaine May and Warren Beatty (both of whom had worked on the 1978 version of *Heaven Can Wait*), has been called "A story of premature reincarnation,"[48] which well summarizes all the others, too. The basic plot of *Here Comes Mr. Jordan* sets the paradigm:

Here Comes Mr. Jordan (1941)

A Boxer named Joe Pendleton (Robert Montgomery), flying in his private plane to his next fight, crashed and went to heaven by mistake; he had been intended to survive the crash and live another forty years, but a Heavenly Messenger (Edward Everett Horton), new on the job, had jumped the gun and botched the job. Unfortunately, when Joe went back for his body, it had been cremated, and so the HM had to find him another one, recently deceased. Joe entered the body of a millionaire named Bruce Farnsworth who had just been murdered by his wife and secretary, and in that body he met his old trainer from the prizefighting days, Max (James Gleason); he also met a woman, Betty (Evelyn Keyes). When he had brought the murderers to justice, he left that body and entered the body of another boxer named Lefty who was otherwise slated to have been killed in the ring; and in that body he met Betty again.

The convention in this film privileges the soul over the body: no matter whose body Joe enters, to the camera he looks just like Robert Montgomery. Beginning as a boxer (named Joe, Robert Montgomery), he briefly and knowingly pretends to be a millionaire (Robert Montgomery), and then, for the rest of his life, unknowingly pretends to be a boxer (named Lefty, Robert Montgomery), which he is. When he is a millionaire, he knows he is acting, as he is in a kind of privileged limbo from which he can see his past life, his liminal heavenly status, and his temporary new life, all at once; but when he goes into the second, lasting incarnation, as Lefty, he knows nothing but that life, losing all memory of both of his previous lives. Joe had played the saxophone for a hobby, badly, and just one tune; when Max cannot, at first, believe Joe's soul is in the body of the millionaire, Joe convinces him by playing his favorite tune on the saxophone, as badly as ever, and by reminding him of events that only the two of them could know about. But in Joe's final incarnation as Lefty, when he himself does not remember who he has been or recognize Max, Max recognizes him, in part because Joe had tipped him off that this transition would take place and in part because Max recognizes the lousy saxophone playing. The hero in each of the three main variants of this film[49] begins as something different—a boxer (Robert Montgomery), a quarterback (Warren Beatty), or a comedian (Chris Rock)—but each of them becomes temporarily incarnate as the same character: an evil rich man. This is a pattern we may recognize from *Random Harvest*, the rags-to-riches reincarnation, and here, too, it has a moral tone: the boxer/quarterback/comedian is a good person who must clean up the moral mess made by the not-so-good rich man, whose body he temporarily inhabits, before he can move on—which is to say back—to become the person he was meant to be.[50]

The woman spans the last two incarnations; before he leaves the body of Farnsworth to enter the body of Lefty, Joe asks her to promise to recognize him if she ever sees him behind the eyes of someone else, and she remembers that later and does recognize the true soul behind the masking face. In *Heaven Can Wait* (1978), the quarterback's voice is (as usual in these myths) a clue to his identity. When Betty (Julie Christie) meets the reincarnated soul of the man she has come to love as Farnsworth, now in the body of a quarterback she has never met before, she says his voice sounds familiar, and he (again without any memory of the past) replies, "I thought I knew you, too. People are always thinking they knew someone before." But she knows she recognizes him: "You're the quarterback," she realizes. "Yes. How'd you know that?" he asks.

The Reincarnation of Peter Proud (1975) and Chances Are (1989)

The recognition of the reincarnated self—both by the reincarnated person and by those who love him (or her, though most of the films under consideration are about men)—remains the focus of two closely related treatments of the long-term variant of the theme, complete reincarnation, both instances involving incest. The first is *The Reincarnation of Peter Proud* (J. Lee Thompson, 1975):

> A man named Peter Proud (Michael Sarrazin), about thirty years old, began to have detailed visions of a town in New England where he had never been, and also to remember being murdered by a woman in a boat in a lake. He cried out, in a voice not his own, "Marcia, don't; I didn't mean what I said." He had a terrible pain in his hip, for no apparent medical cause. He found the town and found the woman, Marcia (Margot Kidder), now sixty years old, whose husband (named Jeff) had died in an "accident" in a lake some thirty years ago; she had a daughter, Ann (Jennifer O'Neill), who had been three months old at the time of Jeff's death and was now about thirty. Peter recognized Marcia, and she half recognized him. He found out that Jeff had married her for her money and played around with other women and was generally no good.
>
> One day Peter fell asleep beside a pool and cried out, in the same voice, the same words as before: "Marcia, don't; I didn't mean what I said." Marcia realized then that he was her husband reincarnated. He fell in love with Ann, who was drawn to him as if to her father. He hesitated at first but then made love to her. Ann took him to visit her grandmother (his mother, though she didn't know it), a senile, half-blind old woman in a home, who no longer recognized anyone. But the minute he walked into the room, she said, "Jeff! Why haven't you come to see me for so long!" Trying to explain this incident, a witness praised him for carrying it off so well: "He made it seem real, just as if he was her son."

Peter decided to exorcise the ghost by swimming in the lake where Jeff had been killed. Marcia accused him of incest ("You seduced our daughter," she said) and killed him (again).

Reincarnation makes Peter, in effect, half his own age, while his wife ages normally. Jeff-as-Peter is strongly drawn to the women of all three generations: mother, wife, and daughter. The mother is the only one who immediately recognizes the reincarnated son, with the true, nonsexual love that knows its object, a love that the literature of recognition generally limits to mothers, children, and dogs. For his part, when he pretends to be pretending to be her son, he is imitating himself. The other two women, wife and daughter, are drawn to him sexually, drawn to his body, which blurs their vision of his soul. His wife is now An Older Woman to whom he is, of course, no longer sexually drawn, and she recognizes him from words he speaks in his sleep, when his unconscious mind, the mind of the previous body, speaks out to a woman no longer present (the Marcia of thirty years ago) words that are recognized by the woman beside him (the Marcia of the present).[51] As in *Heaven Can Wait*, the reincarnated voice is recognized as if it were a part of the soul; but the body accessible to the eye is unrelated to the previous body, which was lost in transition. (Though not entirely lost: Jeff had been wounded in the war, with shrapnel in his hip, which explained Peter's pain: he had Jeff's scar.) But unlike the camera in *Heaven Can Wait*, this camera recognizes the body, not the soul: a different actor (Tony Stephano) plays the part of Jeff in his previous life.

Perhaps the switch of actors is necessary to avoid a direct visual depiction of incest, since one actor is Ann's father and the other her lover. But is Peter's relationship with his daughter incest? Peter both is and is not Jeff, and therefore, he both is and is not sleeping with his daughter. Surely no one named Peter Proud could stay out of sexual trouble for long, in any case. The film seems to agree with his wife, who believes that it is incest and kills him again, this time presumably for good. Incest is always a danger when, as here, people are reincarnated and, therefore, become the age of their children; or when someone travels back in time, as in *Back to the Future* (Robert Zemeckis, 1985), where Marty (Michael J. Fox) meets his mother before she married his father and is horrified to see that she is more attracted to him than to his father; or when someone is frozen and thawed out in the future, as we will soon see. But it can also happen simply when a man marries someone of another generation, someone old enough to be his mother, as Oedipus did, to take a case at random.

Tom Milne regarded *Peter Proud* as "the silliest approach to the subject in any medium ... all flashbacks trampling the action with the finesse of a rogue elephant."[52] The film *Chances Are* (Emile Ardolino, 1989) is a somewhat improved version, which Halliwell merely damns as an "excessively contrived romantic comedy; we have all been here before and there is nothing noteworthy about this particular variation on a familiar theme." "We have all been here before" is not a bad thing to say about a movie about reincarnation or, indeed, any film on a mythic theme. But there is always that Möbius twist; it's not *exactly* the same.

Louie Jeffries (Christopher McDonald) married Corinne (Cybill Shepherd); the best man, Philip (Ryan O'Neal), was also in love with her but held his peace. A year later, when Corinne was pregnant, Louie was hit by a car and killed. He demanded to be reincarnated immediately, and in the rush the angel forgot to inject him with the Lethe potion. He was reborn as Alex Finch (Robert Downey Jr.).

When Alex was twenty-three years old, he met a woman named Miranda (Mary Stuart Masterson), whom he kissed passionately; then he met Philip, who invited him to join him for dinner at the home of a friend. When they entered the house, Alex found that Miranda was the daughter of Corinne, who was still living in the house she had lived in with Louie, still in love with the ghost of Louis, still unaware that Philip was in love with her. Alex started to have vivid memories of Corinne, which disturbed him; Corinne noticed that he sprinkled salt on his corn just as Louie did, and she was surprised when he knew what drawer the little silver corn holders were in, but she didn't puzzle it out. (He privately tested his own identity by predicting, correctly, what he would find in another drawer: maps, keys, sunglasses, and light bulbs.) When Miranda tried to kiss him now, he pushed her away; when she climbed into bed with him, he kicked her out. He tried to convince Corinne that he was Louie: he played on the piano the tune that Louie used to play. Still she couldn't believe it. Then he said, "Remember this?" and kissed her, and she responded and believed he was Louie.

Corinne told her psychiatrist, "I don't know if it's just his body I'm attracted to, or his soul, or if it's just me." She went out with Alex, and a hot dog seller speaking to Corinne referred to Alex as "your son," which upset her, though as she repelled his advances, she said, "I'm old enough to be your mother." (Correspondingly, Miranda complained, "He treats me like I'm his daughter.") Alex persuaded Philip that he, Alex, really was Louie. Corinne realized that she loved Philip; she told Alex, "It's not that I don't love you; I do. But people change. Not as much as you, generally, but we've both changed. You're just not my husband any more." Then Alex fell downstairs, hit his head, and was taken to the hospital; while he was there the angel came, dressed as a doctor, and injected him with the Lethe potion. He woke up without any of Louie's memories but certain that he loved Miranda. Corinne said, smiling, "You're the first boyfriend of Miranda I ever liked." Philip married Corinne, and Alex was best man.

When Alex offers Philip proof that he is Louie, repeating a conversation they had had years ago, Philip responds, "What are you, CIA?" Common sense here substitutes espionage for other explanations, trumping the usual proofs, such as the remembered tune (a motif recycled from *Here Comes Mr. Jordan*) and the trivia test

("Where are the corn holders?"). But ultimately, it doesn't matter whether Alex is Louie; time has passed, and he is thirty years Corinne's junior. The barrier of death is not the only significant one that has been breached; as Corinne points out, death is simply an extreme form of the changes time produces anyway, in all of us. And it is that change that cuts the tie between them, as it does for married couples in less metaphysically charged situations.

But Alex is the same age as Miranda, and so they are perfectly matched—except, of course, that she is his daughter. In contrast with Peter Proud, who sleeps with Ann though he knows she is his daughter, Alex resists the incestuous connection with Miranda, and so he survives. (Again, two different actors play the two incarnations, so Louie, Miranda's father, does not resemble Alex, her lover.) But as soon as Alex's memory has been erased, he no longer regards his relationship with Miranda as incestuous, and so he can marry her—with the beaming approval of Corinne, even though she has *not* forgotten that Miranda is Louie/Alex's daughter. Clearly this film believes that incest is only in the mind, not in the reincarnated soul or the new body. Innocence is, as it was for Siegfried, bliss.

Late for Dinner (1991) and *Forever Young* (1992)

The angels who postpone death in some reincarnation films are replaced in other genres by mad scientists with cryogenic coffins. Their technique is a modern variant of the magic inflicted upon Sleeping Beauty and Brünnhilde, cursed to remain frozen in sleep until, some day, their princes will come. Reincarnation is replaced by apparent cryogenic resurrection of the dead in *Late for Dinner* (W. D. Richter, 1991) and *Forever Young* (Steve Miner, 1992),[53] which begin in the same way but end quite differently. Here is *Late for Dinner*:

> In the early 1960s, Willie Husband (Brian Wimmer) was mortally wounded, and a doctor experimenting with cryogenics froze him. Willie awakened in 1991 and began to search for his wife Joy (Marcia Gay Harden) and his now grown daughter Jessica (Colleen Flynn). He found Jessica first and danced with her to old records; when he found Joy, he asked her to divorce her husband and marry him, and after some initial resistance, she consented. Kiss. Fade out.

Willie dances quite sensuously with Jessica (incest alert!), but nothing more. The generation gap produced by the Rip van Winkle effect becomes far more significant in the other direction, with Joy, who resists him because he looks so young and she looks so old. (She says the Iocasta line: "I'm old enough to be your mother.") He, however, insists that he loves not the surface but what is inside her, what she does and says. Earlier, someone had remarked, "The only reason for time is so that everything doesn't happen all at once." And that's a good reason, which Willie and Joy seem to forget at the end of the film. Why is it suddenly OK for Willie to get back together with the woman now old enough to be his mother, when it wasn't OK for Louie in *Chances Are*, just two years earlier? Is feminism finally making a case for older women and young guys in Hollywood? But then, one might ask, why are there no films in which *she* gets frozen young while *he* ages?[54] That's an easy one: because that is the dog-bites-man variant, the status quo in our world. Old guys marry young chicks all the damn time, without reaching for anything more magic than a Viagra pill, let alone a cryogenics lab.

The golden feminist moment didn't last. A year later, *Forever Young* (Steve Miner, 1992) lost its nerve and backed out of the June-December reunion:

> In 1939 a test pilot named Daniel McCormick (Mel Gibson) agreed to become cryo-genically frozen because he believed his fiancée Helen (Isabel Glasser) was dying. "I don't have a single memory without her," he said; "If she gets better, wake me up." He woke up, by chance, fifty-two years later in 1992, still looking young. But then he began to age rapidly, and when he found the notes of the scientist who had frozen him (and who had died without telling anyone about him), he read: "AGING IRREVERSIBLE." He learned that Helen had lived, married, buried her husband, and moved back to the old house he knew, where she was still living now. Still aging at an alarming rate, he stole a plane, flew to Helen, and proposed to her just as he reached his true age. She accepted him. Hug. Fade out.

Presumably they will live out their golden years together; they are eighty-five now. The film might better have been titled *Forever Old*.

"AGING IRREVERSIBLE" is hardly a shocking new discovery; we need no cryo-genics subject come from the grave to tell us about it. The hero of *Forever Young* stays frozen twice as long as the hero of *Late for Dinner* and still gets his woman back; but since Daniel and Helen end up the same ripe age or, to put it differently, since he ends up as old as he would have been had he never gone near the cryogenics machine, there is no point to the freezing at all and no problem of age disparity in the couple. (While he is still cryogenically young, there is, as usual, another woman [Jamie Lee Curtis] young enough to have been the daughter of the man he used to be, but since she is not his daughter, and since he resists her obvious attraction to him, and since he very quickly gets very old, the problem goes away.) Daniel goes into the "vampire suddenly showing its age and crumbling to dust" routine, but he's no 800-year-old Transylvanian slipping out of his magic world; he's just an octogenarian who looks like an octogenarian, a man who is his age, in love with a woman the same age. Only in Hollywood would this be newsworthy.

Madhumati (1958) and Karz (1980)

Reincarnation also thrives in Bollywood, which had tackled the theme in films long before Hollywood discovered it and had, after all, inherited it through an unbroken line of transmission dating back to the Upanishads. When Bimal Roy made *Madhumati* in 1958, reviewers noted that the theme was already a conventional plot, a typical Hindi Film Potboiler, in which the hero experiences a sense of déjà vu leading to his flashback of a former life; the film also exploits other classical Indian ideas about reincarnation. But, as always, something new (or, as the case may be, something old) is added:

Devendra (Dilip Kumar), an engineer driving to meet his wife Radha and their child, took shelter from heavy monsoon rains in a deserted mansion. He began to think that he had been there before and talked to the caretaker about an old portrait that had once hung where there was now just an empty space on the wall. He then found the portrait and realized he had painted it himself—in a previous life. It was a portrait of Ugranarayan, who had owned the mansion. Devendra then remembered everything and told his story to the caretaker:

Anand (Dilip Kumar), an artist, had fallen in love with Madhumati, nicknamed Madhu (Vijayantimala), a tribal girl. Ugranarayan, a ruthless and arrogant landowner, lured Madhu to his mansion by telling her that Anand had been injured and was lying in a bed there. She went to the bedroom, pulled back the covers and found—Ugranarayan. He chased her until she fled to a high terrace and fell to her death. Anand believed she was still alive. One day in the forest he sketched a portrait of Madhu from memory; as he put it down, there appeared, right behind it, a girl who looked exactly like Madhu but insisted that she was Madhavi (Vijayantimala). When she saw the sketch, she realized that she did resemble Anand's lost love. (Her friends assured her that people not even related to each other could look alike.) She went to Anand's house to return the portrait. There, a servant told her the story of Madhu's disappearance. The ghost of Madhu appeared to Anand and told him how she had died. Just as the ghost vanished, Madhavi appeared. Anand persuaded her to appear to Ugranarayan as the ghost of Madhu (he gave her the clothes that Madhu had worn that night) to shock him into confessing. Ugranarayan agreed to let Anand paint his portrait. During the sitting, Anand pretended to hear ghosts stirring in the house, the sound of anklets, and then a woman he assumed to be Madhavi-as-Madhu appeared and accused Ugranarayan, goading him until he relived the murder scene in his mind, the chase up the stairs, her jump from the upper terrace to her death. "You buried me beside the lake," she said, "so no one would know." Shaken, he confessed the truth and was arrested by the police. Then Anand turned to Madhavi-as-Madhu and asked her, "How did you know all those details about what happened to Madhu after she came here? How do you know what I don't know?" While he stood staring at Madhu-as-Madhavi, Madhavi, dressed as Madhu, rushed into the room, saying, "I'm sorry I'm late; the car broke down." Anand stared at the two women until Madhu ran out of the room, and then he said to Madhavi, "So she was here. Madhu." Now Madhu became transparent, and Anand heard her voice calling him and singing. He followed Madhu up the stairs to the terrace, to the very spot from which she had fallen to her death before. She vanished, and Anand fell to his death from the same spot.

Devendra finished his story and said: "That's how I died. I didn't get Madhu. As I breathed my last, all I wanted was Madhu, in the next lifetime. And now she is mine, my wife. Our love has transcended death. We have been reunited." Daylight came, and he hurried to meet her. There she was, with the same face (Vijayantimala). "Radha! I feel as if I'd found you all over again," he said. "We've been together in birth after birth." Then the baby cried. Devendra laughed and said, "Oh! I had forgotten."

Dilip Kumar plays only two roles, Devendra and Anand (whom the villain briefly impersonates in a bedtrick), while Vijayantimala is a truly polymorphous presence. On the outer frame, mentioned at the start but seen only at the end, she is Radha (Devendra's wife). In the inner frame, however, she is first Madhu (Anand's love), then Madhavi (a look-alike), then the ghost of Madhu. The woman Anand assumes is Madhu-as-Madhavi (first in the forest and then when she dances in tribal costume) is simply Madhavi. (Since she lives in the same time frame as Madhu, she cannot be her reincarnation, though she keeps popping up just as Madhavi's ghost or portrait disappears.) But the woman he then assumes to be Madhavi-as-Madhu in Ugranarayan's palace, where he has asked Madhavi to masquerade, is actually Madhu's ghost-as-Madhavi-as-Madhu. Madhu is thus masquerading as herself, via the detour of Madhavi. Anand stages a single play within a play to catch the conscience of the king, but Madhu's death scene is a set-piece that has four performances: Devendra tells it to the caretaker, Anand's servant tells it to Madhavi, Madhu's ghost-as-Madhavi-as-Madhu tells it to Ugranarayan, and finally we actually see Madhu's ghost leap from the terrace (again).

The debt here is not merely to other Hindi films (whenever Madhu appears, first in life and then as a ghost, we hear her voice, singing, before we see her, and her songs are dubbed by the great Lata Mangeshkar) but to the older Sanskrit tradition of self-imitation, the tales of Vasavadatta and Sita, even down to such details as the use of multiple portraits to mirror other self-replicating forms—here in the form of a powerful metaphor for amnesia, the empty space on the wall where a portrait should have been.

Many of these themes were repeated, with reversed genders (now the woman murders the man), decades later, in *Karz* (Subhash Ghai, 1980):

Ravi Varma (Raj Kiran), the young owner of a rich tea plantation in Ooty, married a young woman named Kamini (Simi Garewal), who murdered him (by running over him with a car at a shrine of the goddess Kali) and inherited the plantation. His widowed mother, weeping over the mangled corpse, begged him to return to pay the debt (*karz*) of revenge for this untimely death. Ravi Varma was reborn and grew up to become a popular rock star named Monty (Rishi Kapoor). One day, while performing a song entitled "Om, Shanti Om," he experienced flash visions of his previous life, particularly the murder scene. When he sought medical help, some doctors regarded him as psychotic, though others suspected that he might in fact be remembering his former life. In any case, they prescribed rest, which he sought—in Ooty. There he met Kamini, now some twenty years his senior but maintaining an artifice of youthful attraction through her great wealth. He also met a very young woman named Tina (Tina Munim), whom he felt he had met before and with whom he instantly fell in love. As the visions recurred with mounting intensity, he began to recognize the places he had seen in his trances. He convinced Tina and her Muslim stepuncle of the truth of his reincarnation and of the need for revenge. With their help, he seduced Kamini, drove her mad, and finally lured her to her death—in a car, next to the same shrine of Kali.

The theme song, the punishment that fits the crime, the basic reincarnation plot, above all a lot of singing and dancing, are traditional elements of a Hindi film. It is also traditional for a Hindi film to quote a certain amount from classical Hindu sources, such as the devotional song based upon an Upanishadic phrase ("Om, Shanti Om," sung, however, in a jazz syncopation and not in a temple but on a most untraditional stage resembling a giant gramophone record). Other mythological tropes stir deeper, perhaps even unconscious, resonances with older Indian sources. For instance, Kamini's seductive nightgown is black on one side and white on the other, the visual icon of the splitting goddess who strips away her black half to become Kali, the Black One, while her other half remains the Golden Girl, Gauri. This image evokes, for Indian viewers, the mythology of the ambivalent goddess as well as the vertically split figure of the morally and sexually androgynous deity, good and male on the right, evil and female on the left.[55]

Madhumati (1958) anticipates, and hence may have been a source of, much of the plot of *The Reincarnation of Peter Proud* (1975). *Karz* (1980) in turn shows the influence of both *Madhumati* and American films about reincarnation, particularly *Peter Proud*, and may in its turn have contributed to *Chances Are* (1989). Thus the so-called pizza effect,[56] the cross-cultural form of intertextuality, produces Indian versions of Orientalized Hollywood variations on already somewhat Orientalized Indian films. Since the Indian theme of reincarnation has meanings for Americans, too, in however transfigured or even degraded forms (the globalization effect, America's assembly-line cultural imperialism replacing indigenous diversities), Hollywood develops a strand that is then woven back, like an imported ribbon, into the constantly re-twisted Bollywood braid. After the first twist, it's self-imitation all the way down.

CHAPTER SEVEN

Face-Lifts

There will be time, there will be time
To prepare a face to meet the faces that you meet.

T. S. Eliot, *The Love Song of J. Alfred Prufrock* (1917)

THE AGING WIFE

"How could you expect anyone who'd been through the tortures of the last ten years to remain the same? The very fact that I am like her now is proof that I am not she." This argument that Zara (Garbo) makes in *As You Desire Me* (1932) is implicit in many of the tales of self-impersonation. The woman the rejected wife actually impersonates in many variants is the wife herself before the torments of normal aging, exacerbated by her husband's rejection of her, made her change and age. Marcel Proust felt that these changes might be so profound as to trigger misrecognition:

> The transformations effected in the women particularly, by white hair and by other new features, would not have held my attention so forcibly had they been merely changes of color, which can be charming to behold; too often they were changes of personality, registered not by the eye but, disturbingly, by the mind. For to "recognize" someone, and, *a fortiori*, to learn someone's identity after having failed to recognize him, is to predicate two contradictory things of a single subject, it is to admit that what was here, the person whom one remembers, no longer exists, and also that what is now here is a person whom one did not know to exist; and to do this we have to apprehend a mystery

almost as disturbing as that of death, of which it is, indeed, as it were, the preface and the harbinger.[1]

The protagonist in a contemporary novel by Javier Marias, who is not sure whether the prostitute he has just gone to was his wife, muses on the way we change in time:

> It was only four or five months since I last saw her although people can change a lot in that time if that time is in some way anomalous, a time of illness or suffering or denial of what came before. I was sorry suddenly that she didn't have some scar or mark or easily visible mole, had that been the case I would have taken her home and undressed her, even at the risk of finding out her identity for certain. Or perhaps I just didn't remember those identifying marks on her body, we forget and never really notice anything very much, why remember if nothing is as it is . . . . [I]f I was I and she was she, she might have her doubts about me too, we barely notice the changes that take place in ourselves, I'm not aware of it in myself, even though those changes might be profound and serious ones.[2]

Those changes, "profound and serious" but barely noticed, are at the heart of this mythology, far deeper than the superficial difference between a wife and a prostitute, let alone a wife and a mistress. They mark the difference between ourselves and ourselves.

In John Corigliano's opera *The Ghosts of Versailles*, the three women (Marie Antoinette and Rosina and Susanna from *The Marriage of Figaro*) sing a trio together:

> As autumn brings its windy chill
> And water freezes on the hill,
> Women love and hate their men,
> Wishing they were young again.
>   O time, O time, O thieving time,
>   Give me back my stolen years.
> As winter brings a longer night,
> And women read by candlelight,
> They come to know, like sun, like rain,
> That nothing lasts, not love nor pain.
>   O time, O time, O thieving time,
>   Give me back my stolen years.

They cannot have the past; they cannot change the past; they cannot even have, or change, the present; they must love and age and die. "Thieving time" is the greatest of all tricksters, time that ages us and changes us, that magically transforms us into other people, our older doubles.

The self-impersonation of a woman as she ages and loses her beauty is expressed in another opera that is, like *The Ghosts of Versailles*, closely related to Mozart's *The Marriage of Figaro*: Richard Strauss's *Der Rosenkavalier* (with a libretto by Hugo von Hofmannsthal). There are a number of explicit citations of Mozart in the Strauss opera—intertextuality again: Mozart's Cherubino in gender triple cross (a woman on the outside frame playing a man who, in the inside frame, plays a woman) becomes reincarnate in *Rosenkavalier* in Oktavian, who is the noblewoman's lover, as Cherubino is suspected of being, and is played with the same gender triple cross. But here let us focus on the theme of the aging and rejected noblewoman. In *Rosenkavalier*, the Marschallin's suspicion that she is about to lose Oktavian to a younger woman inspires her to meditate upon the nature of time. Right after that, the Baron Ochs comes to ask the Marschallin, his cousin, to help arrange his marriage with a young woman named Sophie. When the Baron leaves, the Marschallin muses on the different ways in which men and women age and wonders how it can be that the horrid old Baron Ochs will marry the young and beautiful Sophie (the woman to whom, though she does not yet know it, she herself is about to lose Oktavian):

> There he goes, the bloated worthless rogue, and gets the pretty young thing and a tidy fortune, too, as if it had to be. And flatters himself that it is he who makes the sacrifice. But why do I upset myself? It is just the way of the world. I well remember a young woman who came fresh from the convent to be forced into holy matrimony. [She looks in the mirror.] Where is she now? Yes, seek the snows of yesteryear! It is easily said, but how can it really be, that I was once the little Resi and that I will one day become the old woman, the old woman, the old Marschallin. "Look, there she goes, the old princess Resi!" How can it happen? How does the dear Lord do it? While I always remain the same. And if He has to do it like this, why does He let me watch it happen with such clear senses? Why doesn't He hide it from me? It is all a mystery, so deep a mystery, and one is here to endure it. And in the "how" there lies the whole difference.

And when Oktavian returns to her, she warns him, "Today or tomorrow you will go and give me up for another woman who is younger and more beautiful than I."

"The way of the world" is what we have come to call gender asymmetry, an aspect of the double standard—a phrase to which these myths of doubling give new meaning: the Baron Ochs can get a woman decades younger than him, but the Marschallin (who is barely thirty!) is already over the hill and must give up a young man just a few years her junior.[3] The problem of being the same (*die gleiche*, i.e., the same inside) and appearing to be different is the same for everyone, but each of us experiences it differently (*der ganze Unterschied*); in particular, men and women experience it differently. The Marschallin even wishes that she did not see the trick, wishes to be fooled, like the self-deluded victims of many bedtricks;[4] she wants God to conceal her concealment from her. Though she herself does not actively masquerade, she is going to engineer the transvestite sexual masquerade of her young lover; more to the point, she realizes that she is about to experience the helpless and inevitable masquerade of a young woman as an old woman.

Zara/Garbo (in *As You Desire Me*) saw the other half of the Marschallin's point of view: where Zara argued that if we do not change on the surface, we cannot be the same person, the Marschallin puts the emphasis only slightly differently, arguing that we do not change inside when we seem to change on the surface. The Marschallin's viewpoint is taken in yet another direction in Muriel Spark's novel *Aiding and Abetting*, when people argue about the possibility of finding Lord Lucan, who has disappeared after committing a murder: "You must remember that if Lucan's alive, he may have changed more radically in appearance than the mere passage of years can explain. He would have undergone perhaps extensive plastic surgery." "Then how would his friends recognize him?" "That's the point. They would expect to not quite recognize him immediately; they would expect him to have undergone facial surgery. Which leaves the way wide open for a crook, posing as Lucan. . . . A fake Lucan might be entirely convincing."[5] And so, when they do see the real (undisguised) Lucan, and even see him playing Santa Claus, the ultimate fake disguise, they think they are imagining it, projecting his image on other people merely because they're looking for him. Like Hopsy in *The Lady Eve*, they assume that, since he looks the same, he cannot be the same man.

Angela Carter tells the tale of aging twin sisters, Flora and Dora (Dora narrates the story), who meet their even older stepfather, Perry, after a long time. He greets them with the usual cliché:

> "Floradora! You haven't changed one bit!" I was about to say him nay, draw his attention to the crow's feet, the grey hairs and turkey wobblers but I saw by the look in his eye that he meant what he said, that he really, truly loved us and so he saw no difference; he saw the girls we always would be under the scrawny, wizened carapace that time had forced on us for, although promiscuous, he was also faithful, and, where he loved, he never altered, nor saw any alteration. And then I wondered, was I built the same way, too? Did I see the soul of the one I loved when I saw Perry, not his body?[6]

That's a very good question. Cartesian though the terms of its expression here may be, the same dichotomy between body and soul cuts deep into the folk literature of cultures, like that of ancient India, that puzzled over this quandary long before Descartes. These texts express the subjective reactions of wives to their own aging as they see it mirrored in the eyes of husbands who do not love them enough to recognize the parts of them that time cannot alter. Yet when these men reject their wives for other women, those women turn out to be their wives.

The Marschallin in *Rosenkavalier* confesses that she sometimes gets up in the middle of the night and stops all the clocks. How do we stop the face of the clock—or, rather, the clock of our faces? William Butler Yeats, in "Before the World Was Made" (1933), tells us how, and why:

> If I make the lashes dark
> And the eyes more bright
> And the lips more scarlet
> Or ask if all be right
> From mirror to mirror,
> No vanity's displayed:
> I'm looking for the face I had
> Before the world was made.
>
> What if I look upon a man
> As though on my beloved
> And my blood be cold the while
> And my heart unmoved?
> Why should he think me cruel
> Or that he is betrayed?
> I'd have him love the thing that was
> Before the world was made.

The impulse to darken the lashes is also the impulse to pretend that the blood is warm when it is cold, and as the mythology of the face-lift also catches up the threads of other masquerades, it frequently intersects with self-impersonation, including the unconscious self-impersonation occasioned by amnesia. For in the mythology of face-lift, the masked, "lifted" face of one partner functions to produce the same effect that other texts achieve through the amnesia of the other partner. The second stanza of the Yeats poem connects this mildest degree of masking with the theme of sexual betrayal that so often dogs the heels of self-impersonation. And the poem as a whole suggests a link between the re-creation of the world and cosmetic face-lifts; we might say that, from the god's-eye view, or sub specie aeternitatis, not only each human death but even each doomsday is nothing more than a cosmic face-lift, a superficial alteration that leaves the essential untouched.

Face-lifts (by which I mean any cosmetic surgery to make the face look younger, a midcourse correction, a partial renewal[7]) are nothing new. Medical techniques that have made them a reality are relatively recent, but mythological texts spanning many centuries and many cultures (from ancient India to Hollywood) have imagined what the consequences might be if those who wished for a new face got their wish; cultures far from the worlds of actual cosmetic surgery have conceived myths about face-lifts.[8] An Inuit myth gives new meaning to the "lift" in "face-lift," for in this tale a mother "lifts" her daughter's face in the sense of stealing it, as in "shoplifting." Moreover, she also attempts to "lift" (in this second sense) her daughter's husband, her son-in-law:

> Kiviok came to a land where there were only two people, an old lady and her daughter. He married the daughter, but one day while he was out hunting, the old lady killed the daughter and skinned her head down to the neck. She pulled her daughter's head skin over her head to fool her son-in-law, so she would look like her daughter and could marry Kiviok. When Kiviok approached, the old lady put on the head and walked to meet him, but because her looks didn't really change, she could still be recognized as an old lady. He told her to remove her kamiks, and when she did, her legs were skinny and brown like straw. After she told Kiviok what she had done, Kiviok married the old lady, but not for long. He left her to go back to his parents.[9]

Kiviok is fooled by the face-lift, but he can tell the difference between the legs of an old woman and a young one. Another variant of the myth contrasts with the face not just the legs but the body as a whole:

> Kiviok came to be very fond of his young wife, and was therefore very much surprised when he came home one day and found only one of the women. Her face was exactly like that of his wife, but her body was shrunken and bony. Thus he discovered that it was the old woman who had killed her daughter and pulled her skin on over her own. Kiviok then left that place and went home to his own village. He rowed and rowed and at last recognized his own village, and when he recognized it, he fell to singing.[10]

Again the mother's masquerade is literally only skin-deep and quickly penetrated.

In some variants of this myth, the sloughing of the skin—a major ingredient in the face-lift that is meant to restore youth—brings not youth but death. Sir James George Frazer cites a variant from the Central Celebes [Sulawesi]:

> In old times men, like serpents and shrimps, had the power of casting their skin whereby they became young again. There was an old woman who had a grandchild. Now the old woman went to the water to bathe and she hung her old skin upon a tree. When she returned to the house her grandchild kept saying: "You are not my grandmother, my grandmother was old and you are young." Then the old woman went back to the water and drew on her old skin again.[11]

The women fight about the surface, the skin, but what is at stake runs far deeper—death. Frazer cites other myths very like this one (including one fetchingly entitled

"The Composite Story of the Perverted Message and the Cast Skin"). Another story in this series was recorded in 1909:

> To Kabinana and To Karvuvu are brothers. Their mother had cast her skin and now she was a young woman once more. But To Karvuvu cried he would not have his mother like this and he brought her old skin back again. To Kabinana said: "Why have you put the old skin back again on our mother? Now the serpents will cast their skin and our descendants will die!"[12]

Several other versions also depict a son who rejects his mother when she sheds her skin ("I don't know you. . . . You are not my mother").[13] In retrospect, we can see that the version from Sulawesi simultaneously distances and exaggerates the problem by making the older woman not a mother but a grandmother and erases the overtones of incest by making the younger person not a son but a daughter.[14] The psychoanalytical anthropologist Geza Roheim glosses these stories for us: "A child or grandchild refuses to recognize the rejuvenated grandmother or mother in the young woman. In the last version quoted above and belonging to this group the difficulty lies in the Oedipus complex. If mothers were to cast their skins and hence mankind were to live forever, sons would want their mothers for their wives—hence we must die."[15] Many of these tales assume, almost as a truism, that the face-lift confuses the generations in such a way as to foster incest.

Malinowski recorded a related myth from the Trobriand Islands (now part of Papua New Guinea) that spells out, at least in Malinowski's retelling, the implications for the origins of death:

> After a span of spiritual existence in Tuma, the nether world, an individual grows old, gray, and wrinkled; and then he has to rejuvenate by sloughing his skin. Even so did human beings in the old primeval times, when they lived underground. When they first came to the surface, they had not yet lost this ability; men and women could live eternally young.
>
> They lost the faculty, however by an apparently trivial, yet important and fateful event. Once upon a time there lived in the village of Bwadela an old woman who dwelt with her daughter and grand-daughter; three generations of genuine matrilineal descent. The grandmother and granddaughter went out one day to bathe in the tidal creek. The young woman remained on the shore, while the old woman went away some distance out of sight. She took off her skin, which carried by the tidal current, floated along the creek until it stuck on a bush. Transformed into a young woman, she came back to her granddaughter. The latter did not recognize her; she was afraid of her, and bade her be gone. The old woman, mortified and angry, went back to her bathing place, searched for her old skin, put it on again, and returned to her granddaughter. This time she was recognized and thus greeted: "A young girl came here; I was afraid; I chased her away." Said the grandmother: "No, you didn't want to recognize me. Well, you will

become old—I shall die." They went home to where the daughter was preparing the meal. The old woman spoke to her daughter: "I went to bathe; the tide carried my skin away; your daughter did not recognize me; she chased me away. I shall not slough my skin. We shall all become old. We shall all die."

After that men lost the power of changing their skin and of remaining youthful. The only animals who have retained the power of changing the skin are the "animals of the below"—snakes, crabs, iguanas, and lizards: this is because men also once lived under the ground. These animals come out of the ground and they still can change their skin. Had men lived above, the "animals of the above"—birds, flying foxes, and insects—would also be able to change their skins and renew their youth.[16]

This variant blames women, as usual, for death and goes on to divide the blame between the foolish young woman and the vindictive old woman (the mother does nothing and remains silent, leaving the generations on both sides to fight it out). In an attempt to solve the problem of old age, the women inadvertently invent death. The disguised grandmother in this story might lead us to view the story of Red Riding Hood in a new light, not as a conflict between the kindly granny and the wicked old wolf but as a conflict within granny herself, who has her own big teeth with which to devour her little granddaughter.[17]

Oscar Wilde's *The Picture of Dorian Gray* (1890) is one of the great face-lift myths in English literature: the gorgeous young Dorian, literally the golden boy (d'Or-ian), never does get Gray. He stays young forever, while the physical signs of both his natural aging and his unnatural depravity are transferred to a portrait he hides from all other eyes. In the end, he stabs the portrait, and he himself dies; at that instant the portrait becomes beautiful, the man hideous. The portrait documents not just what would have happened to Dorian in any case but the extraordinary degeneration brought about precisely by his desire never to degenerate. It was his effort to stay the same, to stop time, that accelerated his inevitable decay; it seemed to work for a while, but then time caught up with him and passed him. His evil, as well as his age, destroyed his face, and the main component of that evil was his narcissism, his wish never to age.

Angela Carter's Dora is pursued by the husband of a woman who, like many wives of straying husbands, undergoes a face-lift. This face-lift, however, makes her resemble not her younger self but (functioning like the bedtricks often turned by such wives) the woman her husband fancies (Dora):

A hand-made, custom-built replica, a wonder of the plastic surgeon's art. The trouble she'd gone to! She'd had her nose bobbed, her tits pruned, her bum elevated, she'd starved and grieved away her middle-age spread. She'd had her back molars out, giving the illusion of cheekbones. Her face was lifted up so far her ears had ended up on top

of her head but, happily, the wig hid them. And after all that she looked very lifelike,
I must say, if not, when I looked more closely, not *all* that much like me, more like
a blurred photocopy or an artist's impression, and, poor cow, you could still see the
bruises under the Max Factor Pan Stik, however thickly she applied it, and the scars
round where the ears should be. Oooh, it must have hurt! . . . [She] loved her man so
much she was prepared to turn herself into a rough copy of his beloved for his sake. . . .
[He] and the imitation Dora lived happily ever after, once he'd got over the shock, and
if you believe that, you'll believe anything.[18]

It never really works, neither in fictional tales nor in real life. Olivia Goldsmith
wrote a novel, *The First Wives Club* (1992, successfully filmed, by Hugh Wilson, in
1996), about women who take revenge on their husbands for dumping them for
younger second wives. In 2004, at the age of fifty-four, she died from complications related to anesthesia in the course of elective surgery "to remove loose skin
under her chin."[19]

Kobo Abe's novel *The Face of Another* (1966 in Japanese, 1992 in English) inves-
tigates the psychological pathology of a face-lift made necessary by an industrial
accident. At first, the victim of the accident wears an obvious mask to hide his hideously disfigured face; but then he has a plastic surgeon make him a more realistic
face mask that he can put on and take off at will, and in this face he seduces his own
wife. Furious at his own success, he is even more deeply wounded when she leaves
him—and tells him, in a letter, that she had recognized him behind the other face
all along. The husband explains, in a letter to his wife, his own self-justification:
"The mask was no longer a means by which to get you back, but only a hidden
camera through which to watch your betrayal of me. I had made the mask for the
purpose of recovering myself. But it had willfully escaped from me."[20] And finally:
"I knew very well that exposing the true character of the mask would probably hurt
and humiliate you."[21] In a film made from the Japanese novel (*The Face of Another*
[*Tanin no Kao*], Hiroshi Teshigahara, 1966), the plastic surgeon says to his nurse
(with whom he is having an affair), "I hope he will use the mask to find himself, not
to escape from himself." The latter option is, however, what the face-lift is designed
to achieve in this film, as in so many myths: it represents a man's vain attempt to
transcend himself. In a subplot of the film, a woman with a hideously scarred face
seduces her brother and, later, commits suicide. So this, too, is an intolerable situation; to have a face-lift, or not to have it, is fatal (and leads, as usual, to incest). The
more brutal form of the face-lift myth, the Inuit version, is imagined in the film
when the surgeon finds a man whose skin tone he wants to copy and says to him,
"Just give us the shape of your face; we don't want the details; we wouldn't skin you
for 10,000 yen." But this is precisely what the surgeon has done to the man who

commissioned the new face: skinned him—removed his own skin and given him another—and charged him 10,000 yen—overcharging him in a way that we refer to by the slang term of "skinning."

Face-Lifts: The Films

Mythology heavily colors face-lift films. In *A Woman's Face* (George Cukor, 1941), *The Face of Another* (Hiroshi Teshigahara, 1966), *Ash Wednesday* (Larry Peerce, 1973), *The Promise/Face of a Stranger* (Gilbert Cates, 1979), *Shattered* (Wolfgang Petersen, 1991), *A Face to Die For* (Jack Bender, 1996), and other films of this genre, the plastic surgeon at first functions as a kind of deus ex machina, restoring youth, giving life (and sometimes love: often he marries his transformed patient, the Pygmalion paradigm); but in the end, he dispenses loss and death, also divine gifts. In *A Woman's Face*, the plastic surgeon (Melvyn Douglas) calls the woman he transforms (and marries—Joan Crawford) his Galatea (as well as his Frankenstein, here making the common error of mistaking the maker—the Baron Frankenstein—for his monster. Still, he has the right instinct when he reaches for a myth.). Stanley Cavell, too, cites both Frankenstein and Pygmalion as prototypes for "the abutment of films of remarriage with films of the creation of the woman (or the human) by other means," of which he regards Hitchcock's *Vertigo* as the greatest example,[22] and I would include the face-lift films as immediate runners-up.

Face-lifts in Hollywood films are often designed to carry off a deception and almost inevitably end in disaster. In *The Scar/Hollow Triumph* (Steve Sekely, 1948), a man gives himself a scar in order to match the scar on the face of the man he murders and then impersonates; too late, he discovers that he has been impersonating a murderer like himself, in that sense unknowingly impersonating himself; and so he, too, is murdered, for the other man's crime.[23] In *Dark Passage* (Delmer Daves, 1947), we never see the face of the accused murderer Vincent Parry until he has had the plastic surgery that transforms him into—Humphrey Bogart; until then, we see the world through his eyes. (Later we see a newspaper "Wanted" photo of the presurgical Parry, who looks rather like Robert Duval.) But the only true self of Parry that we know, inside the frame and also outside (since Bogart's was by then one of the most famous faces in America), is a mask he never takes off.

Return from the Ashes (1965)

The twists are more twisted and more noir in *Return from the Ashes*, a British film made in 1965 (directed by J. Lee-Thompson, from the novel by Hubert Monteilhet), where the mood, appropriately, is halfway between the romance of the '40s films and the murder of the '80s films:

Dr. Michele Wolf (Ingrid Thulin), a Jewish woman doctor in Paris in the 1930s, married Stanislaus (Maximilian Schell), a younger man who was after her money. She was deported to Dachau during the Nazi regime, and thinking her dead, he had an affair with Fabienne (Samantha Eggar), her daughter by a previous marriage. But Michele survived and returned secretly, though so hideously changed by her experience in the camps that she hid from her husband until her old friend Charles, a plastic surgeon (Herbert Lom)—who recognized her even in her deformed condition—transformed her face back into what it had been. Before she could reveal herself, however, Stanislaus caught sight of her and took her to be a woman who looked just like his wife, whom he still believed to be dead. He asked her to impersonate the dead woman in order to help him claim her fortune and went so far as to teach her to forge the other woman's signature. When he suggested that she should have a concentration camp number tattooed on her arm to complete the disguise, she casually remarked that she had already seen to that, and showed him the scar. This made him uneasy, and eventually, when she dyed her hair blonde again, he realized she really was his wife. Indeed, as he always used to say to her, "If a woman has beautiful eyes, there is always something the same about her, no matter what else happens." When Michele claimed him back from her daughter, Fabienne, saying sadly, "He's the first man in your life; he's the last man in mine," Fabienne plotted Michele's murder in order to keep him to herself. Stanislaus killed Fabienne and attempted to kill Michele, who was saved by the plastic surgeon.

Michele's surgery removes one set of scars, but her identity is revealed by another scar, the concentration camp tattoo. Here again, the shadow of incest falls across the face-lift: Michele comes into murderous conflict with her own daughter—her younger self, who looks like the woman she was before she aged. Leonard Maltin[24] calls the plot "far-fetched," but it is one of the more psychologically realistic treatments of the mythic theme.

Ash Wednesday (1973)

Ash Wednesday (Larry Peerce, 1973) is even more realistic and deals with more common aspects of plastic surgery:

Barbara Sawyer (Elizabeth Taylor), a woman of a certain age, learned that her husband Mark (Henry Fonda) wanted to divorce her and marry a younger woman. She underwent massive and painful plastic surgery in the hope that it would restore her youth and the idealized form of her own face, so that Mark would love her again. She had a brief affair with a younger man while waiting for Mark to join her at a ski resort. When Mark arrived, he expressed pleasant surprise at her transformation and said he hoped she would be happy. He then left to marry the younger woman.

Elizabeth Taylor was born in 1932, so she was forty-one when she made this film in 1973; Henry Fonda, born in 1905, was sixty-eight, some twenty-seven years older than

Taylor. Barbara Sawyer's age is vague; she has a daughter of twenty-five, so she is perhaps forty-five, only a little older than the real Liz Taylor at this time. A montage during the credits shows a series of sepia photos beginning with the very young Liz Taylor marrying a very young Henry Fonda and then more photos in which they appear gradually older and older, until they are both rather soft and gray. When the film begins, we see an aged hand and then the face of Taylor, covered with makeup to make her look much older. After the surgery, her face, of course, turns out to be the face of Elizabeth Taylor, the woman every other woman in America wanted to look like (though Elizabeth Taylor herself once confessed that the woman she herself wished she looked like was Audrey Hepburn). Her face seems much younger than the face of a forty-one-year-old woman; has life here imitated art as usual?

But even in this gorgeous form, Barbara does not keep her man. She hopes that if she gets back the same face she had when he loved her before, he will love her again or that, as she puts it, he will be able to open his eyes again when he takes her to bed. When she confronts him after the surgery and he still wants to leave her, she says, "Look at this face. Isn't it almost the face you married?" His reply chills her to the bone: "You look exactly like the woman I married. But then, you always did, you always will. No amount of surgery is going to change the way I see you." This seems at first to be the same positive approach to the enduring beauty of the self that is often expressed in movies of this genre: "I see, and love, your soul, no matter how you look on the surface." In fact, however, Mark's statement has the negative implication that since, to him, her face is always the same, it has become invisible, and so he wants someone with a different face entirely. Barbara's disappointment has been foreshadowed by two statements she overheard from other, more cynical patients in the clinic: "We all simply refuse to accept reality" and "No matter what she does, a younger woman will always walk into the room."

Face of a Stranger (1979)

Another rather stereotypical face-lift story is *The Promise* (Gilbert Cates, 1979), which was more descriptively retitled *Face of a Stranger*:

Nancy (Kathleen Quinlan) and Michael (Stephen Collins) were madly in love. They were in a terrible automobile accident, in which her face was totally shattered and he suffered a blow to the head that rendered him unconscious for several weeks. While he was unconscious, Michael's rich, evil mother, Marion (Beatrice Straight), persuaded Nancy (a penniless orphan) that Michael would never want to see her again without a face, and she made Nancy promise never to speak to Michael again, in return for which Marion hired a famous plastic surgeon to give Nancy a new, different face. The plastic surgeon fell in love with Nancy. When Michael regained consciousness, Marion told him Nancy was dead. Eventually, Michael met Nancy, who now called herself Marie; he did not recognize her but kept half recognizing her behind her face; he fell in love with her again and pursued her. One day, he saw, in the surgeon's home, a painting that Nancy had started and Marie had completed; he realized who she was. They met at the place where Michael and Nancy used to meet, and they embraced. Fade out.

This is a remake (skin-deep) of *Random Harvest*.[25] Her changed face takes the place of his amnesia, but the result is the same: she knows, while he doesn't, that he has fallen in love again with the same woman, and she is not allowed to tell him. The surgeon who loves her is a transformation of the besotted psychiatrist in *Random Harvest*, who poses obstacles to her true love's ultimate realization of her identity. Here he is merely an ally of the true villain, the evil mother-in-law who engineers the heroine's disappearance, a character borrowed from *Madame X* (David Lowell Rich, 1966).

Shattered (1991)

Aspects of the plot of *The Promise* are developed in more interesting ways in *Shattered* (Wolfgang Peterson, 1991):

A man who had been in a terrible automobile accident woke up horribly disfigured, without a memory or a face. His wife Judith (Greta Scacchi) showed him (and the plastic surgeons) photos of his face and told him who he was: her husband Dan Merrick (Tom Berenger), a wealthy San Francisco businessman. The surgeons reconstructed his face according to the photos, and he began to have memories of making love to Judith on a beach in Mexico. But when he found photos of her making love to another man, he became jealous and disturbed. One day he smashed his mirror image to bits. He learned that she had been having an affair with a man named Jack Stanton, and she told him that he had shot Stanton. Now he dreamed of watching someone shoot a man who looked like himself, Dan, and when he woke up he searched for Stanton's body until he found a body that had been preserved in formaldehyde; it had the face that he had now, Dan's face. He realized that, behind his reconstructed face, he was Jack Stanton.

Shocked, he fell and hit his head, and now again he remembered making love on the beach, but this time when he saw the face of the other man, he knew it was not only Jack Stanton's face but his own face, and he heard her say, "Jack, I love you." As Jack, he remembered clearly that she, not he, had shot Dan and tried to persuade him to run off with her. He had protested, "I'm out of your life," and in her furious resistance there had been a struggle in the car and an accident in which she rolled free and he was disfigured and concussed. Now he realized that he had smashed the face in the mirror because it was not his face but the face of the man he had cuckolded. Again there was a struggle in the car, but this time, he was the one who rolled free; the car exploded, killing her.

Dan is not actually imitating himself, except in the sense that some of the rejected wives self-imitate, the wife taking the place of the mistress (taking the place of the wife). But he is wearing a two-sided mask, like Siegfried (who was both masked and given an amnesiac drug): Dan's amnesia prevents him from recognizing himself, and his reconstructed face prevents others from recognizing him.

"I don't get it," Dan keeps saying. "Why did she do all this?" Why, indeed? If you don't have your face or your memories, who are you? What is there, beside the mind and the face, that she loves? Is it just the body? Or is it the idea that he is her lover, not her husband? Some of the implicit questions left unanswered in this film were explicitly posed, and partly answered, in the novel on which the film was based, *The Plastic Nightmare* (by Richard Neely, 1969—designated on the cover as "a masterpiece of fifties high pulp"). Judith, in the novel, explains to Jack (after he has figured out that he is Jack) how she did it: after the crash, she saw some old photos of Dan: "They'd been taken seven or eight years ago, when Dan was a lot thinner. I thought how remarkably he resembled you. He was your height, was then about the same weight, had the same color eyes and hair and similar features. You could have been brothers. I don't wonder I found him attractive in those days."[26] It would, therefore, be easy to change his face, but how did she know he would have lost his memory? (As Dan says, "I had emerged from coma conveniently amnesiac.") And even if we know how she did it, *why* did she do it? In the novel, she admits the stupidity and the failure of her plan: passion wears off fast, and they start sleeping in separate bedrooms. Finally, she tells him, "It would never have worked anyway. . . . You began to remind me too much of *him*. I found I was *glad* when you moved into this room. Everything was breaking down all over again, just as it had with Dan."[27]

The brief second honeymoon ends because the body and the mind corrupt the face; the face cannot go on being the face of the beloved when the mind is programmed to be someone else. *Shattered* is the embodiment of a cynical cliché: that sexual love never lasts, because lovers turn into spouses. Judith has an unusual chance to turn the spouse back into the lover, and she takes it. Stanley Cavell saw the amnesiac love potion in the film *Remember?* (Norman Z. McLeod, 1939) as "whatever the thing is that makes love possible, or recognizable—as providing the gift of pastlessness, allowing one to begin again, free of obligation and of the memory of compromise."[28] This same pastlessness for both marital partners was created, in *Mr. and Mrs. Smith*, by the legal cancellation of a previous marriage. Jack-as-Dan unwittingly expresses to Judith the fantasy that she, as well as he, hopes to live out: "You know what I like about amnesia? After seven years of marriage, I get to fall in love with you all over again."[29] Scientists tell us that our bodies are entirely regenerated, cell by cell, every seven years (the period that some Americans regard as the limit for male sexual fidelity, what George Axelrod called the *Seven Year Itch* [Billy Wilder, 1955]). When the bedtrickster in the film *Dream Lover* (Nicholas Kazan, 1994) confesses to having entirely manufactured her past and her personality, she excuses herself by saying, "They say you change every molecule every seven years.... [Masquerading as someone else is] just like putting on new clothes, a new perfume." The helpless amnesia that Jack-as-Dan jokes about, a younger and more cheerful cousin of Alzheimer's, is one solution to the Seven Year Itch, and the face-lift is another attempt to turn back or at least to suspend this ticking meter.

A Face to Die For (1996)

A Face to Die For (Jack Bender, 1996, TV) borrows from *Shattered* the theme of the person who gives the lover the face of the spouse and from *Return from the Ashes* the woman who pretends to have the scars she really has:

> When Emily (Yasmine Bleeth) was six years old, she was in an automobile accident that scarred her hideously and killed her father. In her teens, she fell for a man named Alec (James Wilder), who proposed to her ("Any man would want to marry you if he could see you the way I do," he insisted, when she protested), used her to get some money, let her go to prison for him, and ran off with her pretty sister Sheila (Chandra West). A surgeon (Richard Beymer) said he could reconstruct her face but warned her that she might not recognize herself; "Make me somebody else," she replied. He did. Her first words on seeing her reconstructed face in the mirror were to him: "I think I love you," and soon he told her that he had fallen in love with her. One night he proposed to her; she accepted, but when she discovered that he had given her the face of his dead wife, she was horrified; "You don't love me, you love my face," she exclaimed. She ran away from the surgeon and took a new name, Adrian.
>
> Now a beauty, she met again a man named Paul (Paul Mallory) who had loved her when she was scarred but never dared to tell her; now he told Emily-as-Adrian that he loved her and that she reminded him of a woman he used to know and love; Adrian's mannerism of hiding her face with her hair evoked the image of Emily, and her drawings reminded him of Emily's. Then Emily-as-Adrian met Alec again; he did not recognize her but found out (from Sheila) that she was Emily. Emily-as-Adrian made a date to meet Alec in a hotel room. She put on makeup to make her face look like Emily's scarred face, and in this form, Emily-as-Adrian-as-Emily, she entered the hotel. When Alec arrived, she suggested that he make love to her in that form, as he used to do; he repulsed her brutally, there was a struggle, and he was shot. Emily-as-Adrian-as-Emily wiped off her makeup and left the hotel as Emily-as-Adrian. No one had seen Adrian come in, just Emily, a woman who was so horribly scarred that the clerk later said, staring right at Adrian, "I'll never forget that face." Emily-as-Adrian went off with Paul; when she tried to confess what she had done, he interrupted her to say that he already knew.

When the plastic surgeon gives his patient the face of his dead wife, he forces her to engage in an inadvertent masquerade that she discovers only later. This time Emily is the one who is fooled. But then she masquerades on purpose (as herself) in order to murder her unfaithful lover, putting a scar over the face over the scar. Paul, who loved her, recognizes her, and Alec, who didn't, doesn't. Even when Alec finds out that Adrian is Emily, he mocks her, saying, "You're still the same scarred, ugly girl you always were." To Paul, however, who had always known who she was and knew that she was now Emily-as-Adrian-as-Emily, she is still the same beautiful woman she always was.

Face/Off (1997)

A more mythological example of this genre is Face/Off (John Woo, 1997), in which the faces of a terrorist and an FBI man are surgically transposed:

> Castor Troy (Nicholas Cage), a terrorist, was in a coma; Sean Archer (John Travolta), whose son Castor had killed, underwent plastic surgery to switch not only faces with him but voice and body: "I've implanted a microchip in your larynx," said the doctor, and so Sean could speak with Castor's (that is, Cage's) voice. Then the faceless body of Castor (who came out of his coma) forced the doctor to give him Sean's spare face. Each man slipped into the life of his deadly enemy.

The procedure is in effect an exchange of masks, leaving souls and/or brains intact; the brain of each is in the body of the other. The men seem to grow into their masks as the film progresses, taking up one another's lives with a kind of natural, almost instinctive recognition; this happens because they were, from the start, so deeply immersed in one another's lives that they had in many ways already become one another even before they changed faces. Their intense hatred, like intense love, makes them enter into one another's souls. A similar premise drives Heat (Michael Mann, 1975), in which the cop and the crook (Robert De Niro and Al Pacino) are dedicated to killing one another because they have the same personality and largely the same values. Hindu mythology calls this "hate-devotion" (dvesha-bhakti); the evil Kamsa goes to heaven when he dies because, having devoted his life to the attempt to kill the incarnate god Krishna, he thought constantly of nothing but Krishna, the perfect mental attitude of a devotee.[30] And the mythology of Face/Off is patent: Castor has a brother named Pollux (the mortal and immortal twins, the Gemini, now evil twins actually named Troy, after the sister of the Gemini, Helen of Troy) and a son named Adam, while Sean has a wife named Eve.

As Janet Maslin sums it up, in a review neatly entitled "Good and Evil Trade Places, Body and Soul," "Castor is free to wreak havoc with Sean's suburban family and at F.B.I. headquarters. Bingo. . . . Sean once looked like Mr. Travolta, but now he looks like Mr. Cage. That means that he sees the horrible sight of his own son's killer every time he looks in a mirror."[31] When Sean (with Castor's face) sees himself as Castor, he shatters the mirror; at one point, the two men stand on two sides of a double mirror and shoot at one another through it—each shooting at the image he hates, apparently his own reflection but really the reflection of his enemy, whom he resembles not only outside but inside, through years of obsessive hatred. (This is precisely what happened to the victim in *Shattered*, who also smashed the mirror that revealed to him—though he did not yet know it—not his own face but that of his hated rival.) The teenage daughter of the FBI agent keeps changing her face, too—but she does it with green paint and weird earrings, the usual teenage self-mutilation, and her father asks her, "Who are you supposed to be now?" She is caught up in another familiar subtheme of the face-lift, incest: she shoots Sean, mistaking him for Castor, naturally enough, but when Castor (whom she mistakes for Sean, her father) makes sexual advances to her, she stabs him. Maslin remarks that, in films, the exchange of faces is "a gimmick that hasn't been seen before,"[32] but as myth and film, it certainly *has* been seen before. In *Mask of Death* (David Mitchell, 1996), a cop (Lorenzo Lamas), given the face of the criminal who had killed his wife, slept with the criminal's girl, killed a number of cops, and complained, "I'm becoming him."

Satyam Shivam Sundaram (1978)

A Hindi film, *Satyam Shivam Sundaram* (Raj Kapoor, 1978), whose title Keats might have translated as "Truth Is Beauty, Beauty Truth," is about a scar hidden not by a face-lift but by a combination of a veil (this is India, after all) and self delusion:

> Rupa (Zeenat Aman) was a gloriously beautiful woman who had a hideous scar on the right side of her face from a bad burn received in childhood. Rajeev (Shashi Kapoor), an engineer sent to repair the dam near Rupa's village, heard her singing in the temple of Krishna and Radha and thought, "With a voice like that, she must be lovely." Then he saw her moving about half-naked, though she quickly veiled her face before he could see her scar. They began meeting in the forest by a waterfall and fell in love. He asked her to marry him and begged her to unveil; she said she would not remove her veil until her wedding night. They married, and when he removed her veil and saw the scarred side of her face, he recoiled from her, insisting that she was not his Rupa, that there were two Rupas and her people had married him to the wrong one. "Who are you?" he asked. "I am the same woman," she insisted. Unveiled, she sang for him, and he closed his eyes and murmured, "Rupa!" but when he opened his eyes and saw her, he shuddered in horror and ran out into the forest.
>
> The unveiled, married Rupa changed to the clothes and veil of the other Rupa (the veiled, unmarried Rupa, the forest Rupa) and went to meet him. He embraced her passionately and told her, as he had told the unveiled, married Rupa, that they had married him to the other Rupa. She begged him to return to his wife, but he refused. And so,

reluctantly, she promised to meet him every night by the waterfall, as before. She ran home and changed back into her wedding clothes, put back the wedding decorations on her face; when he returned, he slammed the bedroom door in her face and refused to speak with her or look at her. That was the wedding night.

One day, when the veiled, unmarried Rupa asked him what she had that his wife did not have, he said, "Does she have your qualities, your mind, your lovely eyes, your beauty [*rupa*]?" He put out the candle and they made love. Again and again he begged her to show him her face, but she said: "Accept your wife. The day you start loving her, this veil will fall on its own." But this, he said, he could never do. He sent the unveiled, married Rupa back to her father's house, where she soon discovered that she was pregnant. When Rajeev learned of this (from his delighted mother), he stormed into the unveiled Rupa's house and accused her: "Whose bastard do you want to make me responsible for?" He dragged her to the temple, and in front of her father (who was the priest of the temple) and all her relatives, he publicly accused her of having a secret lover: "How can she be carrying my child? Have I ever touched her?" When she protested that the child was his, he made her swear to this in front of the images of Krishna and Radha. Finally, she confessed that there was only one Rupa, that she was the one who had met him in the forest, but he did not believe this either. At last, in fury, she cursed him: "When my heart breaks, the earth quakes, the heavens open, the world is destroyed. I'm going. You won't ever find your wife again, nor your love."

Immediately a terrible storm broke out, torrential rains entirely out of season, of a force never seen before. People said it was the wrath of the gods or the curse of a good woman. The river rose dangerously high, and Rajeev announced that he would have to open the floodgates of the dam to prevent even greater damage; everyone must leave the village and take refuge on higher ground. Panic-stricken crowds carried Rupa along with them on the bridge toward higher ground. Rajeev heard her voice as she sang and recognized it and, at last, her. He begged her to forgive him. The floodgates opened, the waters rose above the bridge, and they were swept away. Together they swam to safety, landing on the roof of the temple. The sun came out, the clouds dispersed, and the images of Krishna and Radha emerged from the subsiding waters.

In a number of earlier Hindi films, a man resists an arranged marriage and refuses to meet the prospective bride, who pretends to be someone else and wins him over before he realizes that she is his intended wife. *Satyam Shiva Sundaram* adds to this formula a number of complications that resonate richly both with the mythology of self-impersonation and with Hollywood films that had already drawn from that well of storytelling. (Philip Lutgendorf likens this film to "an Indian folktale costumed by Fredericks of Hollywood.") Like Sita, Taravati, and Hermione, Rupa is rejected by her husband, who unknowingly impregnates her and accuses her of adultery; and like the rejected wife (Vasavadatta, Rosina) who is mistaken for her husband's new love or purposely masquerades as her husband's new love, she masquerades as another woman in order to sleep with her husband.[33] Rupa speaks for all of these wives when she complains, "The love that is my lawful right as his wife I have to beg for as his mistress." In this case, however, Rupa does not replace an existent rival mistress but simply masquerades as a nonexistent mistress or another aspect of herself, like Jean in *The Lady Eve*, Paula in *Random Harvest*, and the mutilated women in *Return from the Ashes* and *A Face to Die For.*

Rupa is a woman of stunning physical beauty who appears half-naked most of the time, a fact that is commented on (pejoratively) by a woman in the film; even in a dry sari Rupa is a knockout, and she is usually wet (from that convenient waterfall).[34] At first, Rajeev hardly looks at her veiled face, since he has her whole gorgeous body to look at. Naturally, he doesn't recognize her when he marries her, as it's the first time he's seen her with her clothes on, leaving his attention free to wander to her face. Like Udayana, like Charles Rainier, Rajeev cannot see that his wife is his mistress even when she is right in front of him, and so he decides there are two Rupas, his wife in the house and his mistress in the forest. The veiled, unmarried Rupa has been interpreted as representative of profane, earthy, imperfect love, "a sex object embodying the 'modernity' contemporary India has to come to terms with (resulting in censorship problems)." The unveiled, married Rupa, by contrast, represents sacred, ideal love as well as the lost cultural traditions of India that have become corrupted, evident in the "glitzy temple architecture" in which "ejaculatory symbols are inflated to gigantic dimensions."[35]

When Rajeev is finally ready to accept his wife, the fear that she is dead, that she has been or will be lost in the flood, seems to shock him, as it shocked Leontes, into acknowledging her innocence. It also shocks him into admitting what he already knows on some deep level, that the two women are one. Her singing triggers his memory, as music does for Charles Rainier. (We know that Rajeev has finally recognized her because he reruns most of the film in his head at top speed.) Then Rajeev says, "I have sinned terribly; I looked for physical beauty and failed to perceive the beauty of your mind." But he has not in fact experienced the physical beauty of the veiled Rupa he loves; he has merely imagined it, as she herself insists: "You imagine that I am beautiful, but I am ugly." At the very start, he follows a woman who looks a lot like Rupa from the back and talks to her for quite a while, boasting, "I can recognize you by your footsteps," until she turns around and he sees her face; then he lamely mutters, "I made a mistake," and beats a hasty retreat. He makes a much bigger mistake with Rupa, for he projects his own imagination of her not only onto other women but onto her.

The veiled Rupa instinctively covers her scar when she first sees him, veiling herself at first out of mere modesty or vanity (as well as a deeper self-effacement that comes from guilt: her mother died giving birth to her). But she soon finds herself plunged into a tragic self-imitation. "If I just hide the scar on my face, I become the woman of his dreams," she says sadly. She hopes, in vain, that he will be able to continue to love her when he sees the scar, which she reveals to him as soon as they have married. Still, like Paula, she does not tell him that she is his wife because, "Whatever little hope I have of winning him back would be lost." At first she says that she will unveil on her wedding night and then, since there is no real wedding night, at the time when he starts loving his wife—that is, in both cases, she will unveil when he can desire her by looking past the scar, through the scar, to her. And in the end, he does; looking right at the scarred face, he says, "My Rupa is very beautiful, seen through my eyes. The lamp of her soul lights up her face."

There are a number of conscious citations from Hindu mythology in this film. Rupa's face is bisected down the middle like the split forms of deities such as the androgynous Shiva or Hari-Hara (Vishnu-Shiva) or the mythologized murderess in the Hindi film *Karz*. The lovers begin and end up in the temple of Krishna and Radha, the deities to whom she also makes her oath—Sita's ordeal of adultery here in a mild form. The songs she sings to Rajeev in the forest are also about these gods. In one, Krishna's mother explains to him that Radha's dark eyes, gazing at Krishna, made him dark, another example of projection from the eyes as well as a projection onto Krishna of Rupa's own problem (and, therefore, a hint that Rajeev misses): a transformation of her skin. Her name, too, has mythological overtones, for *rupa* in Sanskrit means both beauty and form. Beauty is, of course, central to the film (*Sundaram* in the title means "beauty"), but so is form: to say that there are two Rupas is also to say that there are two forms—of the same woman. The power of the curse of a wronged woman, a good woman, is an ancient mythological theme, and Rajeev knows it: when the storm breaks, he remembers her curse. (As the *Encyclopaedia of Indian Cinema* puts it, "The curse materializes in the form of a dam bursting, causing floods.") The floodgates that open then are a patent metaphor for the return of repressed understanding, repressed love. But the flood is not merely an internal doomsday; it is there in the world. When people see the storm raging, they say, "It looks like doomsday." The gods, too, emerge from the doomsday flood to create the world anew. Rupa and the world are reborn at this moment.

A final note on the frame-jumping power of self-imitation. Lata Mangeshkar, the most famous singer of Hindi films (whom we have already encountered as the singer in *Madhumati*), was not very pretty but had a gorgeous voice; she was called "the Nightingale," a plain bird with a lovely song. She did the singing for this film, dubbing for the gorgeous but not particularly musical Zeenat Aman.[36] Many people suspect that the film is about Lata Mangeshkar.

The classic face-lift myth, the story of Dorian Gray, reinforced by the Inuit and New Guinea stories, expresses and challenges the belief that in order to remain yourself you must stay the same and in order to stay the same you must change your face into the face that belonged to the person you were. The films, too, demonstrate that this is a foolish, impossible, or even fatal desire. Yet the argument is still hotly debated by people contemplating actual plastic surgery, including people on reality television shows like *Extreme Makeover, Nip/Tuck,* and *The Swan.* As the reviewer of a book about medical enhancement remarked of such people, "To many of them, and to their doctors as well, aging was a disease, unnecessary and henceforth treatable."[37]

Some face-lift myths are about people who want to change into other people (Bogart in *Dark Passage,* Yasmine Bleeth in *A Face to Die For*) but end up masquerading as themselves after all. And both the heroines in stories and the real women patients who undergo plastic surgery frequently express from the start the desire to have their own faces as they once were in the past. Modern surgical techniques, like mythological magic powers, generally construct a new face, but many myths imagine the exchange of one face for another that already exists, and surgery can create a face in imitation of another model, too. Some people want to have a face-lift to look like Marilyn Monroe or Elizabeth Taylor or even, in one documented case, Barbie (a throwback to the woman-as-statue-as-woman scenario). Sometimes they want to look just like a *part* of someone else: when Myrna Loy was the queen of Hollywood, herds of women stampeded to plastic surgeons, demanding the Myrna Loy nose.

Recent surgical techniques have made it possible actually to give someone an entirely new face, a face transplant with all the risks and drawbacks of a heart transplant, a transfer of, at the least, the skin and underlying fat or, at the most, the muscle as well, from a live donor.[38] This dangerous procedure might be justified for people with severe facial disfigurements necessitating multiple skin grafts that become masks, rigid and expressionless—so the surgery would in this case remove a mask, not create one—though if it miscarried it would create an even more inhuman mask. The "yuck factor" and moral intuitions triggered by this process have already inspired apprehensive comparisons with Frankenstein, Michael Jackson, and John Woo's film *Face/Off.* Arlene Judith Klotzko underscores the mythological underpinnings of these reactions:

> It's about our increasingly precarious sense of identity, the same anxiety tapped by reproductive cloning—you would go on even after your death but it would be another

you. Psychological concerns about double and mistaken identity are not new—they have been the staple of comedy for thousands of years. What is new is medicine's ability to give substance to these fears. What makes you you? In the age of gene-speak, most of us think it is our genes but if that were true, identical twins would be exactly the same and, of course, they are not. Personal identity extends far beyond genetics—to our personalities, behaviour, our memories and, of course, our faces. What would it be like to look in the mirror and see a new and very different face? It would be unsettling, but the disfigured recipient of a face transplant has already endured this experience.

The final question that Klotzko raises is the question raised by the myths: How would your family and all the other people who love you recognize you?

Sometimes candidates for plastic surgery want to look like someone of the opposite sex. The male-to-female transsexual in Pedro Almodovar's *All about My Mother* (1999), who has had dozens of cosmetic surgeries, declares: "You are more authentic the more you resemble what you have dreamed you are." The sex-change operation is the ultimate (downward-displaced) face-lift. Marjorie Garber questions the special acceptability of face-lifts in contrast with operations that change not one's age but one's sex: "Why does a 'nose job' or 'breast job' or 'eye job' pass as mere self-improvement, . . . while a sex change (could we imagine it called a 'penis job'?) represents the dislocation of everything we conventionally 'know' or believe about gender identities and gender roles, 'male' and 'female' subjectivities?"[39] Short of a penis job (a term nowadays more usually applied to penis-enhancing surgery than to a sex-change operation), genders (rather than sexes) are often bent through the milder, more superficial, method of transvestite masquerades. Complete gender masquerades, however, in contrast with superficial or temporary cross-dressing, generally require some fairly heavy lifting in the makeup department, ranging from false eyelashes to breast implants and sexual surgery.

And more extreme, if more narrowly focused, mutilations continue to be made in a variety of contexts: ritual clitoridectomies, erotic penis piercing, and most grotesquely, the revival of the much-reviled Chinese custom of foot binding (itself reflected in the story of the mutilation of Cinderella's sisters' feet to make them fit into the glass slipper), which has now resurfaced in the practice of cosmetic surgery to make the feet fit better into designer shoes. Some people even resort to plastic surgery to look like someone of another species. Jocelyne Wildenstein married a billionaire (Alex Wildenstein) who eventually began to stray. Pushing fifty, she had a number of plastic surgeries, and at first this seemed to work, but then she learned that he was still sleeping with other women. Since she knew he loved the big cats on his Kenyan estate more than anything, she asked her surgeon to transform her into a big cat. He enlarged her lips and pulled back her face at the eyes to resemble a cat's eyes.

Most people, however, just want to look like their younger selves. Barbara Sawyer in *Ash Wednesday* is the paradigm of plastic surgery patients who try not to change, who fear change and view with alarm the fact that they do change, for the worse, experiencing the inevitable deterioration of helpless aging, which they hope the face-lift will reverse. They have not heeded the warning made by the scientists in *Forever Young*: "AGING IRREVERSIBLE." Such people want to become the people they once were and feel that they still are, beneath the skin: "This wrinkled person that you see is not the real me; the real me is the person in my high-school graduation photograph." The body lies. Surgery lies too, but the lie of surgery cancels out the lie of the body to produce the truth, the body from the past. Most people who opt for cosmetic surgery feel that the face they display on the surface is just a mask hiding the real person hidden within them, a younger, more beautiful person, just as men or women who opt for transsexual surgery feel that their male or female body is false, concealing the true female or male body within. They do not realize that the face-lift actually changes them, like the people in the films, into someone else, away from the people they really are now—people with souls and faces that are formed and scarred by experience.

The protagonist of a story by Max Beerbohm puts on a mask to win the love of the woman he loves. His misgivings, at the sight of his masked reflection in a stream, express the paradox of self-imitation implicit in the face-lift:

> A great shame filled him that he should so cheat the girl he loved. Behind that fair mask there would still be the evil face that had repelled her. Could he be so base as to decoy her into love of that most ingenious deception? He was filled with a great pity for her, with a hatred of himself. And yet, he argued, was the mask indeed a mean trick? Surely it was a secret symbol of his true repentance and of his true love. His face was evil, because his life had been evil. He had seen a gracious girl and of a sudden his very soul had changed. His face alone was the same as it had been. It was not just that his face should be evil still.[40]

This is the face-lift rationale: my face is not my real face. The mask in the Beerbohm story has some of the unfortunate side effects of the injectable drug known as Botox, which paralyzes facial muscles and thus erases wrinkles: "The mask could not smile, of course. It was made for a mirror of true love, and it was grave and immobile."[41] But it is the face of the person he hopes to become.

Charles Siebert describes watching a face-lift operation: "With each snip, I imagined the ghosts of the myriad worries that furled this woman's forehead flying free: there, the times she troubled over school exams; there, the long waits for loved ones who were late; and there, the years of confusion and doubt."[42] And he records the misgivings of a woman who was thinking about having the surgery: "'But then,' she said, a nicely furrowed frown indicating a still-intact corrugator muscle, 'I looked at my nose in the mirror and thought, That's my father there, and that's my mother right there in the upper eyes.'"[43] Family resemblance here serves to anchor personal identity in the surface of the face that changes with age, not with surgery. The lines of age are like the scars that identify imposters through the mythology of recognition, beginning with the scar on Odysseus's thigh. When the brainwashed husband and wife in the film *Duplicates* (Sandor Stern, 1992) are trying to figure out who they are, he notices that he doesn't have any of the scars his memories tell him he should have (a mark on his chin from a bad cut, an appendectomy scar, etc.). He asks her, "Do you have any memories of scars? I don't have the scars I'm supposed to have." She asks him, "What happened? Did they heal our scars? Did they heal us?" Then they realize, "That's why our bodies are different from what our minds remember."

The literature of face-lift surgery keeps reverting to both classical mythology and film mythology. An article about Botox cited Dr. Nancy Etcoff, a professor of psychology at Harvard Medical School and author of *Survival of the Prettiest: The Science of Beauty*, who remarked, "There is also the potential for what some doctors call the Dorian Gray effect. Because Botox wears off, more injections are required to maintain its effects or the patient's face will return to its wrinkly state." The writer of the article commented, "In a variation on 'The Stepford Wives,' it is now rare in certain social enclaves to see a woman over the age of 35 with the ability to look angry."[44] (The reference is to the film [Bryan Forbes, 1975] in which real women were replaced by robots of standardized beauty, sexual enthusiasm, and mindlessness.)

A Clairol advertisement for a dye to make gray hair black or blond or red again proclaims: "Gray Hair Lies." That is, time lies, age lies, death lies; Gray can, with Clairol, remain D'Orian forever. The outer surface of the old woman lies by concealing the young soul beneath, and the dye restores the truth of youth. The face-lift offers a quick fix to stave off the inevitable flood, the deeper change that Saul Bellow's Armenian cynic spoke of: "On any certain day, when you're happy, you know it can't last, but the weather will change, the health will be sickness, the year will end, and also life will end. In another place another day there'll be a different lover. The face you're kissing will change to some other face, and so will your face be replaced. . . . You make your peace with change."[45] "Your face will be replaced" has so many meanings here: your own present face will be replaced (a) by your aging face, (b) by the face of another person with whom your lover will replace you, or as a result of the first and in order to prevent the second, (c) by a face-lift. Most of us cannot claim, with Bellow's protagonist, that we have made our peace with change.

The mythology of the face-lift imagines people who attempt to swim upstream against the current of time by changing their faces back in the other direction. What is the relationship between our identities and our faces? The face-lift is an attempt to dodge the responsibility mentioned by W. H. Auden (a man whose skin was dramatically etched by his life): "After fifty, you're responsible for your face." (Coco Chanel is also quoted as saying that at twenty you have the face that nature gave you and at fifty you have the face you deserve.) In the film *Dave* (Ivan Reitman, 1993), the wife of a man who has been replaced by an imposter realizes that the imposter lacks the emotional "scars" of all their years together; he has had "something that amounts to moral cosmetic surgery." The man in *Late for Dinner* (W. D. Richter, 1991) who finds his wife visibly aged after thirty years says he is jealous of the man who made her smile all those years to give her the lovely laugh lines around her eyes now. The scars that a face-lift removes are the body's memory, in a form visible to others, of what the mind may have forgotten, including, for instance, the scars that wedding rings often make on the hand after a long time. Our scars may be the strongest signs of who we really are: perhaps, at the final reckoning, the whole body will disappear, and only our scar tissue will be there to testify for us.

The character of Sosia in Kleist's play *Amphitryon* expresses to his look-alike (Mercury) the impossibility of doing what Kiviok's mother-in-law did: "I can't annihilate / Myself, transform myself, slough off my skin / And hang my skin around your shoulders."[46] And this being so, he eventually realizes, he must be who he thinks he is, and Mercury cannot be Sosia, as he claims. But the people who opt for face-lifts do not reason as Sosia does, because, unlike him, they do not know who they are when they are confronted with their doubles; the mirror that throws in their faces the faces of aging people seems to be a fun-house mirror. The mythology of the face-lift exploits the tension between two aspects of our ambivalent attitude to the soul, two ideas of the self, two sets of beliefs, often held in common: (1) your soul is deep inside, invisible, and that's you; and (2) your soul is your face, the public self, the way others perceive you, the barrier—and bridge—between you and the rest of the world. The myths tell us that there is no way of being sure which of these options is true at any moment but that each is, in its way, true. The process of aging and changing presents us with new versions of ourselves, both the same and different. Some people totally reject the selves of the past, the former lives, the ex-wives or -husbands, and become each new person, each new face. Others totally reject the present self and strive to squeeze themselves back into the selves of their youth, through the magic of the Nautilus machine, the younger and younger lovers, the haunting of high school reunions—and above all, the face-lift. Even when we succeed, however, the myths tell us, our short-lived triumph is Pyrrhic, soured by the loss of a precious part of our genuine selves—our faces. This fact is encapsulated in the original title of the film *The Scar* (1948): *Hollow Triumph*. But some people acknowledge the truth and value of all the faces at the same time and strive to recognize themselves in all of them.

Incest dogs the face-lift because of the confusion of generations, mothers looking just like their daughters, as they so proudly boast on returning from their surgeries and spas. Even when this doubling back does not result in actual incest, it arrests our ability to move forward in time into a position where we can become our parents and eventually accept our deaths. In *Harry Potter and the Prisoner of Azkaban*, Harry sees, across a lake, someone who saves him from present danger. Harry vaguely recognizes him and is convinced it is his dead father. When he later goes back in time to that moment, through an episode of time travel that traces a kind of Möbius twist in the chronological sequence, he runs to that place to see who it was, and there's no one else there; *he* is the one who saves himself. He had mistaken himself for his father.[47] This is, after all, the only real kind of time travel there is: each of us becomes, in adulthood, someone who lived some thirty years before us, someone who must save our own life. The face-lift attempts to send us back to that moment in time and keep us there, so that we can no longer save our life in the present moment.

CHAPTER EIGHT

Mind Lifts

We're more than memory banks. From the first moment that we
saw each other, we were drawn together.

Bob Boxletter to Marion Boxletter in Duplicates (1992)

UNDERNEATH THE HEAVY romantic veneer, many amnesia films are driven as much
by legal, political and material concerns as by erotic ones: the estate in *As You Desire
Me*, the political and economic transformation of Charles in *Random Harvest*, the
money for the operation in *Memory of Love*. In *Love Letters*, Singleton does time
for the murder of Roger, though in the end we learn that she was innocent. And to
return the compliment, love and/or sex keep getting into the films about money
and politics. Murder, evil science, and espionage, like all criminal activities (more
recently, terrorism and drug trafficking), generally inspire lies of one sort or another
and occasionally require masquerades that involve self-impersonation, particularly
erotic self-impersonation.

MURDER: *VERTIGO* (1958)

Alfred Hitchcock is the master of the noir side of the film genre of the tragedy of
remarriage, and his masterpiece is *Vertigo* (1958):

> Scottie Ferguson (James Stewart), an ex–San Francisco policeman who had quit the
> force and was recovering from an incident of vertigo, was hired by an old schoolmate of
> his, Gavin Elster, to tail Gavin's rich young, blonde wife Madeleine. Gavin said she had

developed a mysterious obsession with an ancestor of hers who had committed suicide, Carlotta Valdes. Scottie began to follow Madeleine (Kim Novak) and watched her stare for hours on end at a portrait of Carlotta wearing a fabulous necklace. Gavin told him that Madeleine used to put on the necklace and look at herself in the mirror. Scottie and Madeleine met and fell in love. She ran away from him to an old mission church, and he chased her up a staircase to a high tower, but at the last moment his vertigo made him hesitate, and he did not actually see her fall to her death. The verdict at the inquest was accidental death while of unsound mind.

One day, Scottie met a woman who looked just like Madeleine, though her hair was brown and her makeup cruder. "You remind me of someone," he said to her. She insisted that she was Judy Barton from Salina, Kansas, and she showed him a photo of herself as a brunette, with her mother. He was persuaded, but as soon as they parted after their first meeting, Judy recalled, in a flashback, what had really happened: known to suffer from vertigo, Scottie had been set up to witness, at the top of a tower to which he was afraid to climb, the murder of Gavin's real wife, the real Madeleine Elster, whom he had never met and whom Judy had impersonated all along. Gavin, waiting at the top, had switched the women at the moment of truth, just out of sight of Scottie, who thus had been unknowingly present at the murder and could testify in court that Madeleine had committed suicide. Judy began to write him a letter confessing all of this, but she never sent it.

Scottie persuaded her to let him change her superficially to resemble Madeleine—first the clothes, then the hair and makeup. When the makeover was complete, he kissed her and made love to her. That evening, she asked him to fasten on her the necklace that Carlotta (in the painting) had worn, and he stood behind her and looked over her shoulder as she saw herself in the mirror. He recognized the necklace. Saying nothing, he drove her to the mission tower where Judy-as-Madeleine had pretended to jump and the real Madeleine had been pushed to her death. There he told her what he had figured out about the impersonation and the murder, and she confessed it all to him. As she kissed him, and he began to kiss her back, she was startled by the figure of a woman who appeared in the shadows at the top of the tower, and she plunged to her death.

The twists of the plot of *Vertigo* are foreshadowed by the abstract patterns that dance across the screen during the credits, a series of vortices that come out of the pupil of a woman's eye and culminate in a revolving Möbius strip. That shape is then prominently repeated in the swirl in the French twist hairdo worn by the three women who replace one another in the film: Carlotta, Madeleine, and Judy.

Like so many remarrying husbands (including Milton Berle), Scottie finds a woman who reminds him of herself. But Judy can never be the woman he loves. When he meets her, after the murder, we see her as masquerading as herself—that is, with her hair dyed brown (presumably its true color, as in the photograph with her mother), in order to become not-Madeleine; it is brown over blonde over brown. For Judy Barton from Kansas is surely not the same after she has played Madeleine and fallen in love with Scottie; she is forever after part Madeleine, no longer just Judy but Judy-as-Madeleine-as-Judy. Scottie then forces her to add yet another layer: blonde over brown over blonde over brown, or Judy (in Kansas)-as-Madeleine (when Gavin had made her over)-as-Judy (when Scottie met her again after the murder)-as-Madeleine (after Scottie had made her over). This woman is still not just like Madeleine; she lacks Madeleine's faraway look and elegance; she has a different walk; she still has too much of Judy Barton in her to suit Scottie.

Moreover, she has not enough of Carlotta, whose ghost further complicates the already layered roles of Judy and Madeleine. Hitchcock once said, of *Vertigo*, that he wanted to make a film about a man consumed by a dream. (In a film made in the very same year as *Vertigo*, Richard Quine's *Bell Book and Candle* [1958], Jimmy Stewart plays a publisher who is literally bewitched by a witch played by Kim Novak.) But the woman, too, is consumed by a dream: Judy dreams that she has become Madeleine, who is in turn said to be consumed by her dream of Carlotta. (In *The Legend of Lylah Clare* [Robert Aldrich, 1968], Kim Novak dusted off her *Vertigo* persona to play an unknown actress hired to play, in a film, the part of Lylah Clare, a famous actress who died mysteriously; the spirit of Lylah possesses her, and she knows things that Lylah has never told anyone else; then she kills herself just as Lylah had done, having gotten into the same scrape with the same man.) Rupa, in *Satyam Shivam Sundaram*, tells Rajeev that he is in love with a woman who never existed; and that is what happens to Scottie in *Vertigo*.

Gavin teases Scottie from the start when he says that at times his wife "becomes someone else." This is Gavin's Freudian slip: he is lying when he implies that Madeleine (when she goes into her trances) becomes Carlotta, but he is telling the truth in the double entendre of the line, a confession that Judy (when she performs the masquerade) becomes Madeleine. Since Carlotta (like Judy) is a brunette, but Judy-as-Madeleine does not change her hair color when she goes into her trance as Carlotta, the woman whom Scottie follows at the start is Judy-as-Madeleine[-as-Carlotta] (brunette-as-blonde[-as-brunette]). Where Gavin hints that Madeleine is the reincarnation of a dead woman, Scottie first sees Judy, after the murder, as the resurrected form of what he (rightly) perceives as another dead woman, Madeleine. And one reason why Judy-as-Madeleine-as-Judy-as-Madeleine does not look quite right is because what Scottie really wants to see is Judy-as-Madeleine-as-Judy-as-Madeleine[-as-Carlotta]. All of these false images coalesce to deal a final blow when Judy falls to her death because in the shadow of the tower she mistakes a woman (who turns out to be a nun, a mysterious veiled woman) for—for whom? Madeleine? Carlotta? Judy Barton from Kansas? All of the above.[1]

Judy-as-Madeleine-as-Judy-as-Madeleine experiences the classic double bind of the masquerading double (here squared): she knows she is not loved for herself. She asks him if he loves her "because I remind you of her? It's not very complimentary. Couldn't you like me, just me, the way I am?" And even when he insists, "No, Judy, it's you, too. There's something in you," she knows she has lost, and she capitulates: "If I let you change me, will you love me?" But he cannot. He laments, "You were the copy, you were the counterfeit," but by that time she is no longer merely the copy (Judy-as-Madeleine), as she had been when he first fell in love with her; by then she is genuinely in love with him as herself. Who, then, is that self? There was a real woman there before Gavin created Judy-as-Madeleine; as Scottie remarks to Judy, "He made you over just like I made you over, only better." Judy-as-Madeleine-as-Judy feels that she is the same as Judy before the first makeover, Judy-as-Judy, and begs him to love her in that form, but he cannot; not only does that woman no longer exist, but Scottie is obsessed with the nonexistent Judy-as-Madeleine[-as-Carlotta].

And then there is the awkward matter of the murder as well as Scottie's fury at having been tricked and his jealousy of Gavin, who had betrayed him not only by using him to commit a murder but by, in a sense, cuckolding him. ("You were his girl," Scottie says to Judy; "What happened to you? Did he ditch you?" and she does not answer.) For when Scottie thought he was sleeping with Gavin's wife Madeleine, Gavin was (Scottie now thinks, perhaps rightly) actually cheating on the real Madeleine and sleeping with Scottie's woman, Judy-as-Madeleine. Scottie tolerated the idea that Madeleine was still sleeping with Gavin as her husband, but now he can't stand the idea that Judy-as-Madeleine might have been sleeping with Gavin as her lover.

Scottie only figures it out when he encounters the necklace for the first time in the flesh, as it were, after he has seen it only in representation, worn by Carlotta in the portrait.[2] He closes the circle of the masquerade as well as the necklace when he fastens the clasp on Judy's neck. Why does Judy put it on? Has he been such a fool that she doesn't expect him to recognize the necklace? After all, he has seen it only in the painting. Or does she want the necklace to do the remembering for him and put it on for that very reason? Does she want, subconsciously, to break up the illusion, to tell him who she really is so he will love her for herself? Does she tell the truth with the necklace in order to end the masquerade by making it blatant, so that she can stop merely pretending to be who she really is, the woman he has loved all along, and be accepted as that woman? Is wearing the necklace her Freudian slip? (Like Gavin, she is prone to them; she tells a hidden truth when Scottie wants to kiss her after she has dressed for dinner and she refuses because, she says, "I've got my face on." Indeed, as both of them now know, she has someone else's face on.) Scottie is close to the truth when he says, of her wearing the necklace, "That's where you made a mistake. You shouldn't keep souvenirs of a killing. You shouldn't have been"—he hesitates for a moment—"that sentimental." That "sentimentality" (he cannot say "love") is what made her wear it, both to remind herself of the time when he loved her and, unconsciously, to remind him.

But why does Scottie not recognize Judy-as-Madeleine-as-Judy-as-Madeleine before he sees her in the necklace? The answer for him, as for her, is overdetermined.

1. He does, but he is repressing his knowledge. When Judy appears to him with her hair up in the Möbius twist, the final touch on her transformation into Madeleine, she is out of focus, misty, his vision of her as Madeleine; when she comes into focus, we see (but does he?) that she is not exactly like Madeleine. Only then does he kiss her, and we see a brief image of the mission church, an indication that he senses, subconsciously, that she is Judy-as-Madeleine. As he kisses her, the camera revolves through a full 360 degrees, recapitulating the circling swirls of the Möbius twist, the ultimate vertigo of sexual obsession that makes him forget what he knows, that sucks him back into the vortex of self-deception.[3]

2. He sees only surfaces, and the necklace is the surface clue. Between his loss of Madeleine and his encounter with Judy, Scottie keeps mistaking other women for Madeleine; to him in his obsession, they all look alike. Even when he is with the still unreconstructed Judy, he looks longingly at a woman whose hair and clothes are like Madeleine's; he misses the inner woman right beside him and goes haring after a bit of peroxide and a tailored suit. (In this he resembles King Udayana, who, as his wife bitterly pointed out, projects the image of his new love over all other women, including the queen, and Rajeev in *Satyam Shiva Sundaram*, who projects his own imagination of Rupa not only onto other women but also onto Rupa herself.) Scottie acknowledges his superficiality when he says that Gavin made Madeleine over better than he himself had done: "not only the clothes and the hair, but the looks and the manner and the words." He settles for the clothes and the hair, ignoring the looks and the manner even now, and notices only the necklace.

3. He can only accept the painful truth by distancing it through several receding frames. He doesn't recognize the necklace when he looks right at it; it all comes together only when he sees Judy looking in the mirror at the woman that both of them see as Madeleine wearing the necklace, and he remembers seeing Madeleine looking at Carlotta in the portrait wearing the necklace.

That first portrait scene in *Vertigo* echoes the scene in *As You Desire Me* (1932) in which Bruno watches Zara watching the portrait. But the second scene in *Vertigo*, in which Scottie sees Judy and the necklace in the mirror, echoes a parallel scene in *Random Harvest* (1942) in which Charles puts an emerald necklace on Margaret, standing behind her as she faces the mirror, and we see them reflected in it together, and she, too, sees them, though he does not look up. In both films, the image in the mirror reveals the other, forgotten woman, the true image, just as the images in magic mirrors in folktales reveal the true self, or the soul, or (in the case of Dracula) the absence of a soul. Neither Charles nor Scottie can recognize the woman in the mirror, the other woman, the soul of the woman. But unlike Charles, Scottie at least recognizes the necklace, and then he does recognize the woman.

Until that moment, Judy has watched him not recognize her with the same agonized look that Margaret directed at Charles, and for the same reason: Scottie refuses to sleep with her. "No, no," he says, when she implies that he means to keep her as his mistress; like Charles, he assures her that he wants her friendship, nothing else. "Nothing else?" she says. "No." "Not very complimentary," she says (as she had said of being loved merely for her resemblance to another woman, the direct cause of her present objection). Like Margaret, Judy is wounded by this rejection, but, unlike the Englishwoman, the American girl says so. Later, too, she complains, "You don't even want to touch me." Like Charles, Scottie keeps her as his sexless companion, laying the sword in the bed—until he recognizes in her the other woman, the one he loves.

BLACK SCIENCE: *DUPLICATES* (1992) AND *DARK CITY* (1998)

Gavin and Judy-as-Madeleine manipulate Scottie's memory through simple psychology and the power of suggestion, tricking him into thinking that he has seen what he has not seen and that he was with one person when was with another. Science fiction stories and films about manipulated memory imagine assaults on memory both more violent and more complex. The moral ambivalence evoked by the possible results of cloning inspires many of these films about double selves, but such queasiness long pre-dates cloning. We can see it in nineteenth-century Gothic novels about disastrous doubling (all of which were made into popular films): Mary Shelley's *Frankenstein* (1919), Robert Louis Stevenson's *The Strange Case of Dr. Jekyll and Mr. Hyde* (1887), and Bram Stoker's *Dracula* (1897). And this old distrust of evil science is newly exacerbated by contemporary fantasies of the manipulation of memory. In J. G. Ballard's futuristic short story "Thirteen for Centaurus" (1962), scientists encapsulate people in a spaceship heading for a distant star that they will not reach during their lifetimes. To combat despair and depression, some of the people on the ship are led to believe they are actually still on earth, in a mock spaceship from which they may escape; but in fact they *are* on earth, victims of an experiment in the psychology of people shut up in a spaceship.[4]

Films made in the late 1970s, the 1980s, and the early 1990s (the longue 1980s, as it were) moved the action off the planet Earth but still raised the same old Cartesian questions addressed by the mythology of reincarnation. Amnesia erases the mind, and plastic surgery erases the face, but brainwashing and more diabolical tricks of modern science not only cloud the mind but create memory traces from scratch or transfer them from one body to another, implanting false memories. An antiscientific paranoia generated triple crosses in written science fiction even before it came onto the screen, but Hollywood took up the theme and ran with it. An extreme expression of this solipsistic nightmare was *The Matrix* (Andy and Larry Wachowski, 1999), in which the lead character gradually discovers that everything he perceives (and the viewer perceives) is computer generated. Eventually the rebels liberate him from his attachment to the computer, and you see for the first time that he is one of millions who are suspended naked in individual pods, curled up in a fetal position and hooked up as energy sources. But *The Matrix* did not explore the personal and emotional implications of this violence to the sense of self; other, less glossy films, both before and after, delved into this problem and romanticized it.

In *Star Trek: The Motion Picture* (Robert Wise, 1979), Ilea, the navigator of the starship *Enterprise*, is kidnapped by aliens and replaced by a double. When the double sees a member of the crew that the original Ilea once loved, her eyes soften with love. Noting this, Spock suggests:

> Its body duplicates our navigator in precise detail. Suppose that beneath its programming the real Ilea memory patterns are duplicated with equal precision. They may have formatted too precisely. Ilea's memory, loyalty, obedience, friendship, might all be there. ... If we can control it, persuade it, use it.... Reviving Ilea's memory patterns within the alien probe remains our only means of contact with our captor.

And it works, more or less; the probe and the object of Ilea's desire, Will Decker ("Will Deck Her," the antecedent of the stud Will Riker), evolve together into a higher life form, still presumably madly in love. Other films expressed a greater hostility to the "alien probe"—often a thinly veiled metaphor for secret government science projects, or for cold war brainwashing—that manipulated our own memory patterns. In Ridley Scott's *Blade Runner* (1982, based on Philip K. Dick's 1968 novel, *Do Androids Dream of Electric Sheep?*), the android woman is given someone else's memory through surgery performed on the brain; this early classic of the film genre (combined with the founding classic of the literary genre, Mary Shelley's *Frankenstein* [1818]) was immediately satirized in Carl Reiner's *The Man with Two Brains* (1983), whose hero plants the disembodied brain of the woman he loves in the gorgeous body of his horrid wife.

The magician Sky Ames in *Remember?* (Norman Z. McLeod, 1939) used white magic, a liquid drug, to perpetrate the double amnesia of a married couple, as did Gutrune and her mother for Siegfried and Brünnhilde. Sky acted out of goodwill toward the couple and Gutrune toward what she thought was in Siegfried's best interests (if not Brünnhilde's). But the double amnesia of a married couple is achieved through malevolent science, black science, if you will, in *Duplicates* (Sandor Stern, 1992):

Bob and Marion Boxletter (Gregory Harrison and Kim Greist) had a little boy named Joey who disappeared, together with Marion's brother Brian, leaving no trace. Through a series of accidents, Marion found the man she thought was Brian, but since that man didn't remember her, Bob didn't believe it was Brian. Then the Boxletters saw Joey, and finally Bob was convinced. "One look-alike—that can happen," he said. "But two?" As they delved deeper, they were kidnapped by Dr. Congemi (Kevin McCarthy), a mad scientist (funded by the U.S. government) who had kidnapped Brian and Joey. Dr. Congemi removed the Boxletters' memory banks and installed, in their places, the memory banks of two people who had recently died, named Charles Corbin and Elaine Stratton. The Boxletters-as-Corbin-and-Stratton forgot they were married or had a son (he "remembered" that his wife and son had been killed in an accident), but as soon as they met one another, they fell in love. Gradually, they realized that their hearts, but not their minds, remembered their former selves, their former loves (the Boxletters), while only their minds remembered their former official partners (Corbin and Stratton): "I see her face, hear her voice, smell her perfume," he said, "but I don't feel it." "Yes," she replied, "I remember the fear in his eyes, the pain, but it's like a movie: I'm an observer, and I'm touched, but I'm completely uninvolved."

Trying to figure out who they were, they noticed that they didn't have any of the scars their memories told them they should have. They found Joey again and, resisting all of the scientist's counterarguments, insisted on having their original memories reinstalled. They killed all the villains. As they embarked on the (successful) retransfer, Boxletter kissed his wife and said, "Remember that I love you."

If robot memory can be manipulated, if false memory can be implanted as easily as false consciousness, then the memory lodged in the mind is less reliable than the other sort of memory that lodges in a kiss or a touch. Brainwashing both plays upon and advances the assumption that the mind is the brain, and the brain is vulnerable, mutable; better to trust the body. The feeling of a kiss and the scars that don't match memory—these somatic clues combine to break through the massive forces of black science to reveal the truth of love. These films, therefore, go beyond science to argue for a romantic location of the memory in the sexual body. In contrast with the stories of Siegfried, in which a romantic and/or sexual liaison inspires a loss of memory (of a previous romantic and/or sexual liaison), here it is what keeps memory alive.

This film seems to begin where *Remember?* leaves off (and *Twilight of the Gods* begins), exploring the mental world of a couple who have forgotten one another and meet again. The procedure in *Face/Off*, which is in effect an exchange of masks, leaving souls and/or brains intact, is the opposite of the procedure used in *Duplicates*, which leaves the faces intact but reprograms the brains. The result, however, is the same: the brain of each is in the body of the other. What is the relative reality of "them"—the owners of the bodies into which the souls/memories of the dead people have been transferred—and "us"—the souls/memories that have been put into the bodies—or is it the reverse? There is a tension between physical, corporeal criteria (fingerprints, scars) that are at first accepted but then rejected and emotional criteria that are at first rejected but then accepted. At the very start, Bob Boxletter disregards Marion's statement that she has found their child, because he assumes that she is projecting over reality the false image of what she wants to see, as we so often do when we lose someone we love. But it is the "reality" that becomes the projection, and for a while the ineradicable image of the beloved child is all that is real.

The key argument is between Dr. Congemi and the Boxletters-as-Corbin-and-Stratton:

> Congeni: "Do you want death? Your body's dead. You're Charles Corbin. Your memories are alive. Your mind is alive, and that's the real person. Boxletter is just flesh and blood."
> Marion Boxletter: "He's right, Charlie. I'm Elaine Stratton, with all my memories—life. If they do this thing, then we'll be dead."
> Bob Boxletter: "We already died our natural deaths. We have no right to be here. The Boxletters do. Their bodies are here with us, their memories are in these computers. They deserve to live."
> Marion Boxletter: "But we're alive. Here, now, we're alive."
> Bob Boxletter: "What about our souls? Where are they? These people are not right. We're more than memory banks. From the first moment that we saw each other, we were drawn together. That wasn't Charlie Corbin and Elaine Stratton, it wasn't any memory bank. It was them. Whatever he is, whatever she is, they love each other, as strongly as we ever could."

And this proves to be the ultimate, convincing argument.

The experience of the Boxletters is more like triplication than duplication; it sets forth a trichotomy of mind, body, and soul. While the soul is off wherever souls go, the mind is alive and well, controlling someone else's body (and soul? We do not know.). The Boxletter memories would be uncanny under any circumstances because of the strange familiarity of someone else's memories; they are even uncannier, however, because they are on a disk. And both sets of memories are real. Right before the final retransfer, Boxletter insists: "I want to retain all my memories from the moment I woke up in your hospital. I don't want to forget any of this." That is, he wants the matched set of memories, his and his. In the end, the good woman scientist, Dr. Randolph (Cicely Tyson), tells the evil male scientist, Dr. Congemi, what she regards as the central question their work raises: "Does the emotion of love depend upon the existence of memory?" Dr. Congemi says, "Our memory banks are the sum total of our sensory input. To suggest that love works on a level outside that input is romantic tripe." But Dr. Randolph continues to argue that love transcends memory, that we can remember with the body things that we cannot remember with the mind, as a hand can remember how to dial a number that the brain cannot retrieve. The cliché is that the body never forgets how to ride a bicycle—or make love. And sure enough, as soon as the Boxletters' memories have been erased and they kiss, he says, "It's more like—it's as if I've known you all my life," and she says, "Yes, I know. It's as if I'd known you before, sometime." Romantic tripe, indeed—but it has staying power.

It resurfaces in a literally and figuratively darker film about mind-swapping, *Dark City* (Alex Proyas, 1998):

> John Murdoch (Rufus Sewell) woke up one day with amnesia. Gradually, he learned that he had a wife, Emma (Jennifer Connelly), whom he had left when she had an affair with another man; he found her, and she apologized to him for the affair. But then he discovered that none of this had happened, not the marriage nor the affair. Mysterious aliens called the Strangers were studying humans, doing thought experiments on them, playing games with them. The Strangers had programmed Emma's memory, but John had awakened before his memory was fully programmed; hence his sense of amnesia. Still, John loved Emma, and when he learned that they had erased her memory again, so she no longer recognized him, he said, "She doesn't know who she is." Again the Strangers erased his memories, and this time he did forget her, but he remembered his name. They met and liked one another and walked away together.

The Strangers, actualizing the Marschallin's fantasy in *Rosenkavalier* and the weatherman's experience in *Groundhog Day*, can stop clocks and change the world while others sleep. One crazed, but perhaps not crazy man says, "It's like I've been dreaming this life, and when I wake up, I'll be somebody else, somebody entirely different." This is the experience of the dreaming monk in the *Yogavasistha*.

The ending is rather ambiguous. After winning an apocalyptic battle of the minds with the chief Stranger, John seems to know what has happened and why Emma is there, but she does not. As in *Duplicates*, the couple's shared love survives their shared amnesia, but now a double amnesia erases the factor that had driven them apart—in this case, her apparent sexual betrayal of him, the crucial factor in so many of these stories. The unspoken, unrecognized, indestructible link between John and Emma is proof of the survival of what John tells the Strangers is the part of humans they do not know about, the part that makes them human, not the brain, "not here" (he taps his forehead). What makes this survival more complicated is the absence of an original self in which this emotion is lodged. John's amnesia is squared, like that of Charles in *Random Harvest*: since the wife he forgets is a nonexistent person, presumably replacing some other, no more "real" memories, his forgetting of her is a kind of amnesia of his amnesia. But unlike Charles, John himself has no other, more real "I" with which to recall the false memory of Emma. All there has ever been for either of them is a series of memory implants. Who or what is it, then, that continues to love Emma?

The old plot of *Remember?* resurfaced and met *Dark City* (even down to the detail of the beach where the couples meet at the end of each film) in Michel Gondry's *Eternal Sunshine of the Spotless Mind* (2004):

> Joel (Jim Carrey) discovered that his hot-tempered girlfriend Clementine (Kate Winslet) had hired a psychiatrist, Dr. Howard Miezwaik (Tom Wilkinson), to erase her memories of their relationship, on a whim, because he had begun to bore her. Appalled by her failure to remember him, Joel asked Howard to remove her from his memory. But as each memory of her slipped away, Joel relived it: he met Clem in earlier and earlier phases of their love and enlisted her help in attempting to preserve his memory and hers. They failed, but as the last memory vanished she told him to go to Montauk Point, where they had first met. Now they met there again, thinking it was for the first time—until the psychiatrist's assistant Mary (Kirsten Dunst) gave them tapes that had preserved what had been erased from their minds. Now, even though they knew what had happened, knew that she had been bored with him and he infuriated by her, they laughed and went on together.

Joel manages to hang on to his memories of Clem, or a trace of them, for a long time, despite the frantic efforts of the psychiatric crew—Howard and Mary and their two assistants, Patrick and Stan. He succeeds in part because the mind-hackers are criminally sleazy, messy, and irresponsible, a parody of the glistening, antiseptic evil scientists we know from other mind-theft films. Instead of monitoring Joel during the all-night erasure, Stan and Mary drink his liquor, smoke dope, and stage an orgy, while Patrick is in bed with Clem, whom he has seduced in the course of her mind-erasure. Then Mary learns that she has previously had an affair with Howard, who had erased her memory of it; it is this discovery that inspires Mary, angry and suddenly sobered up, to hand the tapes over to all their clients, including Joel and Clem. Thus, the desire of the scientists, too, indirectly preserves the memories of their subjects. And even when those subjects know that it will end badly, they choose, like Peggy Sue, to do it all over again. Once again the irrational power of love fights both evil science and the inevitable flow of time, clinging to the past, to memory.

Double penetration agents often double back, as in the incident in the novel *Random Harvest* in which the British spy pretends to be a German spy pretending to be a British spy. A classic of this genre is E. Phillips Oppenheim's *The Great Impersonation* (1920), in which German espionage agents groom one of their own to take the place of an English gentleman, but the real Englishman, figuring it out, pretends to be the German pretending to be him. The potentially infinite regress in this scenario was a running joke in the old "Spy vs. Spy" features of *Mad* magazine and in the novels of writers like John le Carré (particularly *The Little Drummer Girl*), whose spies double and triple back until one loses track of what side they are "really" on. But le Carré had been a "real" spy, and triple backs of this sort happened in real-life espionage as well. The joke became quite sinister when the principle of doubling back was applied during the Vietnam War. The U.S. forces laid mines that would be triggered by motion from only one direction, when the enemy came toward them. The enemy, knowing this, would turn the mines around so they exploded when the U.S. forces advanced. The U.S. forces, knowing this, began to lay the mines facing toward themselves, so when the enemy turned them around, they would face toward the enemy.[5]

Doubling back in this way allowed spies to hide the truth in plain sight, masquerading as the truth. When people asked Guy Burgess, who was spying for the Soviets, how he seemed to have so much money all of a sudden, he laughed and said, "I'm a Russian agent," so, of course, no one thought he was. As Slavoj Zizek remarked of Burgess's self-presentation, "'What better cover for someone like me than total indiscretion?' This is, of course, the very Lacanian definition of deception in its specifically human dimension, where we deceive the Other by means of the truth itself."[6] Guy Burgess might have been consciously or unconsciously quoting the scene in Carol Reed's *Odd Man Out* (1947) in which Johnny McQueen (James Mason), the much-hunted leader of the Irish underground, is riding in a taxicab that the police stop at a roadblock; when they ask the cabby (who has not noticed the identity of his fare), "Who's in the back?" "Johnny," jokes the cabby, and the police laugh and wave him on. In *The Sum of All Fears* (Phil Alden Robinson, 2002), a man who is secretly a CIA agent has to break a date with his girlfriend and wonders what to tell her. His senior CIA colleague advises him to tell her the truth, and he does: "I'm actually a CIA agent and I am on my way to Russia on an assignment," he tells her, and she replies, "Oh, that is so lame."

For films about espionage, self-imitation is a gift on a silver platter. Hitchcock used the trick of self-imitation in a scene in *Notorious* (1946) in which Alicia (Ingrid Bergman), bitterly estranged from her former lover Devlin, an American agent (Cary Grant), marries Alex Sebastian, a Nazi spy (Claude Rains), only in order to spy on him for the Americans. Devlin and Alicia are about to steal some incriminating evidence when Alex interrupts them. "I'm going to kiss you," Devlin says. "No," she says, "he'll only think—" "That's what I want him to think," Devlin says, and fakes a passionate kiss. But then she kisses him for real, and he responds. They are meeting as spies, pretending that they are meeting as lovers, which, though they do not know it, they still are. Espionage masquerades as sex masquerading as espionage. As Anthony Lane glosses this scene, "Rains sees them, and his face falls with the sadness of betrayal; thanks to their pretense of passion, he does not yet suspect them of spying. But they *are* passionate; the deceit is true."[7]

A triple cross results when the film invokes both the inner frame of the spy and the outer frame of the actor playing the spy. This happened during the making of *Doctor Zhivago* (David Lean, 1965), most of which was filmed in 1964 in Spain (they mopped the brows of the actors during the snow scenes, shot in 100-degree weather). For the scene in which the students march down Gorky Street singing the Communist anthem, the "Internationale," and are trampled to death by the charging Cossacks, they rounded up hundreds of Spanish extras and began to teach them the "Internationale." Soon they realized that the extras already *knew* the "Internationale." They were old Spanish civil war fighters who had long pretended to be loyal to Franco and were now "pretending" to be communists, singing the song they had sung a quarter of a century ago, now imitating again the very people (the 1918 Russian communists) they had imitated in 1938.[8] That triple cross was the only way those old communists could express their true political sentiments in Spain in 1963.

In Charlie Chaplin's film *The Great Dictator* (1940), a barber who looks like Hitler is mistaken for Hitler. (Chaplin said that Hitler was one of the greatest actors he had ever seen.) Years later, a woman who had known Chaplin recalled that when she had seen, after the war, actual documented film footage showing middle-class Jews forced to go down on their knees to scrub a sidewalk with toothbrushes, "It was almost like something out of *The Great Dictator*. One almost laughed, it was so terrible." And the historian Bernard Vorhaus, commenting on silent footage of Hitler giving a speech, said, "Hitler looked ridiculous, just as Chaplin would look if he were playing Hitler in a film."[9] In *To Be or Not to Be* (Ernst Lubitsch, 1942), a Polish Jewish actor named Joseph Tura (Jack Benny) plays a Nazi, first onstage and then off. When, in the offstage masquerade, he is caught and rightly accused of being an imposter, while he is awaiting sentence he finds the dead body of the Nazi whose place he had taken. He shaves off the real Nazi's real mustache and puts a fake mustache on him, so the Nazis, quickly pulling off the mustache, conclude that the other man is the imposter and set Tura free. Thus Tura has forced a real (dead) Nazi to pose as an imitation of himself. That episode was repeated in the Mel Brooks remake in 1983, which added another episode of self-imitation: when the actors escape at the end, they take with them a group of Jews they have been hiding. They dress the Jews as clowns, put them in the act, and parade them down the aisle through the audience of SS men. One woman panics and starts to babble in Yiddish; Gestapo eyebrows begin to rise until another clown, thinking fast, claps a big yellow star on her and on another Jew and points to them and shouts, "Juden! Juden!" and laughs, and all the SS men laugh, and the Jews—pretending to be clowns pretending to be Jews—escape. The joke about yellow stars then became real just a few years later for Hans Rosenthal, who survived World War II by hiding in a hut in southwest Berlin. Susan Neiman tells his story:

> The day after the liberation he found himself surrounded by Russian troops with machine guns. Trying to smile, he pointed to the yellow star he'd re-sewn to his jacket, but they pushed him to the wall. Hans Rosenthal was lucky; at that moment a Jewish officer of the Red Army passed by. "Can you say the Sh'ma?" he asked. Hans Rosenthal could. The officer released him and warned him to take off the star. The division had liberated Maidanek, where the SS officers tried to save themselves by putting on prisoners' clothing. After that it was ordered that everyone wearing yellow stars was to be shot on sight.[10]

In real life, as well as literature, inadvertent self-imitation can be fatal.

The concept of comedians playing their characters in a dangerous real-life situation was ratcheted up one notch in *Three Amigos!* (John Landis, 1986), a film about three unemployed silent film stars whom a Mexican woman mistakes for genuine bandit-killers and brings to her village to fight a villain who is not an actor (as they had assumed) but the real McCoy. Switching gears, they re-use stunts from their films to foil the fiend. The theme was modernized in *Galaxy Quest* (Dean Parisot, 1999), in which actors from what is clearly the *Star Trek* series find themselves actually transplanted to a distant galaxy whose inhabitants, devoted Trekkies who have mistaken the TV series for "historical documents," have modeled themselves and their equipment on the series. The actors are able to help their galactic fans overcome their powerful and evil enemy by repeating their old TV lines, treating the real equipment just as they had treated the cardboard stage props, and calling out to one another, in moments of grave and violent danger, to employ stratagems from "Episode 11" or "Episode 17." The film, therefore, employs real film actors (Alan Rickman and Sigourney Weaver, among others) playing TV actors playing their own TV characters against real extraterrestrials (played, of course, by actors). At one point, the villain forces the actors to tell the truth to the extraterrestrials, to admit that they're just actors and that the spaceship on the television image is just a tiny model. But later, when the actors have conquered the villain, the extraterrestrials smile and say, "What a very clever deception that was, to say that your spaceship was just a tiny model!"

Take the complexities of memory implants in the film mythology of black science and combine them with body snatchers, time warps, dream warps, and finally, espionage, and you get *Total Recall* (Paul Verhoeven, 1990), based on Philip K. Dick's short story, "We Can Remember It for You Wholesale" (1966). The short story is relatively straightforward: it begins when the protagonist returns from what he thought was a dream of a trip to Mars but turns out to have been real; he tells his wife, "'I have both memory-tracks grafted inside my head; one is real and one isn't but I can't tell which is which. . . . Just tell me and make it absolute; I did go or I didn't—tell me which one.' *But they may have altered your memory-track also*, he realized." And so on; the regress of triple crosses is potentially infinite. In order to divert the impulse from his memory of the trip to Mars, his handlers offer to let him live out his "most expansive daydream," and his first wish is predictable: "Women. Thousands of them, like Don Juan himself. An interplanetary playboy—a mistress in every city on Earth, Luna and Mars." He gives that up, out of exhaustion, but when they hypnotize him they find out that the Don Juan scenario is not his fantasy but his real history . . . and there the story ends.

The plan to let him live out, again, what he thinks is a fantasy and his evil handlers know is a reality is expanded in the film, which begins with a vacation ad: "You can buy the memory of your ideal vacation, cheaper and safer than the real thing, without the lost luggage, lousy weather, and crooked taxi drivers. With Rekall, everything is *perfect*." Perfection in this case includes choosing a new identity to enjoy the ultimate Ego Trip, "because what is always the same on all vacations is you—you're the same." But this time, the alternative identity the hero chooses takes him on an Alter-Ego Trip:

A man named Douglas Quaid (Arnold Schwarzenegger) kept dreaming that he had been on Mars with a beautiful brunette, though he knew he had never been on Mars and he was married to a beautiful blonde named Lori (Sharon Stone). He told the dream to Lori, who kept asking him about the brunette. He went to an agency called Rekall that promised to implant in his brain the false memory of a glorious two-week vacation as a secret agent on Mars. When they asked him what sort of exotic woman he wanted to have his adventure with, he chose a heterosexual brunette, athletic, sleazy and demure. "41 A," they decided. But as they strapped him into an implant chair and the process began, they realized that he really *had* been a secret agent on Mars, with the brunette, and that the Agency had erased his memory of all that. Now, in a panic, they themselves erased his memory that he had ever been to Rekall. They released him, dazed, and on the way home, he killed a group of men who attacked him.

When he told Lori what had happened, she tried to persuade him that the people at Rekall had disturbed his mind and inspired paranoid delusions. But when he showed her the blood on his hands and asked, "You call this a delusion?" she tried to kill him.

When he put her gun to her head she told him she was not his wife, that their marriage was just a "memory implant" six weeks old. When he protested, "Our wedding, falling in love, my job—just an implant by the Agency?" she insisted, "Your whole life is just a dream. The job is real." "Then who the hell am I?" he demanded. "Beats me," she replied. "I just work here." Men came to get him, but he knocked her out and fled. The Agency man who arrived on the scene kissed Lori, who was actually *his* wife, and the head of the Agency told him to take Quaid alive, for a reimplant.

Quaid was given a videotape that his Martian double (the man Quaid had been on Mars) had prerecorded for him. It began: "Howdy, Stranger. This is Hauser. If things have gone wrong, I'm talking to myself . . . . Whatever your name is, get ready for the big surprise: You are not you. You are me." Hauser told Quaid that he had worked for Mars intelligence, the Agency, until he met a woman who showed him that he had been on the wrong side, and he defected. Now Hauser told Quaid to get to Mars.

Quaid followed the trail on Mars to a brunette woman named Melina (Rachel Ticotin), a member of the resistance movement, and when he saw her he stared as if he half recognized her; she, of course, recognized him, called him Hauser, and was furious with him for having disappeared from her life. Quaid protested that he had lost his memory, that he had forgotten that he loved her. He asked her to help him remember, but when he mentioned his wife, her fury returned, and she threw him out.

Lori appeared and tried to persuade him that the Martian episode was all a dream, but Melina showed up and killed Lori. As Quaid and Melina ran away together, she said the leader of the movement was going to enable Quaid to remember things from the period when he was Hauser, "like that you love me." "I don't need him for that," he replied and kissed her. When he told the leader he wanted to remember in order to be himself again, he was told, "You are what you do. A man is defined by his actions, not his memories." In the final battle, Quaid and Melina were captured and put into memory-erasing chairs for a moment until Quaid got them out. "Are you still you?" he asked her, as they fled. "I don't know," she replied. He kissed her and smiled.

When Quaid manufactures the secret agent scenario, he is unconsciously drawing upon his memory, masquerading as himself. (Hauser's eyebrows are a little gentler than Quaid's, and his face more relaxed and intelligent, but he has the same faint Austrian lisp.) The message Hauser sends to himself in the future is like the wake-up calls we send to ourselves from our former lives or the message the Chippendale Mupp sends to himself by biting his long tail. (In another film based on a Philip K. Dick story, John Woo's *Paycheck* [2003], a spy named Jennings [Ben Affleck], whose memory has been erased, discovers clues that he had left for himself before the erasure so that he would be able to reconstruct the crime he is now wrongly accused of having committed.) From the standpoint of Melina, Quaid behaves very much like Siegfried or Tristan (or other medieval cads) who "forget" their life with a woman in one place (Melina, the brunette on Mars) when they meet a woman in another place (Lori, the blonde on Earth). (From the standpoint of the filmgoing public, the blonde and brunette are the usual semiotic signifiers of two different mental worlds—the blonde, especially when she is Sharon Stone, representing the evil world.)

When Quaid gives the familiar anti-commonsense argument of mere coincidence to explain how he dreamed of being a secret agent and then turned out to be a secret agent, the man from Rekall says, "Brunette, athletic, sleazy *and* demure. Just as you specified. Is that coincidence?" In this he attempts to dehumanize Melina even as the Rekall people had reduced her to a grotesque bra (or shoe?) size (41 A). Yet Quaid retorts that the brunette was real because he had dreamed of her even before he went to Rekall, because he had had an image of her in his mind before the people at Rekall asked him to choose the woman he wanted to be with on Mars. His two women are jealous of one another, even though each regards the other as part of a dream. "I can't believe you're jealous of a dream," he protests to Lori, but dreams are always real, particularly sexual dreams, and particularly in a world of memory implants. Even when he decides the blonde is unreal, the brunette must still prove she is real, through her kisses, which validate some level of memory and truth.

The tension of these science fiction films derives in part from a conventional situation: for most of the film, the hero is all alone, doubting his own perception against the testimony of all the rest of the world—until he gets an ally, usually a woman who is in love with him. He may be in danger of losing his mind, but he feels he can trust his body, and his body trusts the woman. *Total Recall* deconstructs this scenario at first, providing the hero with two different women validating two different scenarios, but when one woman wins out and kills the other, we end up in the familiar scenario after all. Other approaches to the sexual mythology of self-imitation imply that reality inheres both in the body and in the fantasy, both in the brunette and in the blonde, or that the multiple partners in adultery or promiscuity may be the physical parallel to a split personality or multiple minds. But *Total Recall* is a naively realistic film: where you might think there was room for multiple identities, it all turns out to be a simpleminded case of amnesia. A Hollywood action film demands one straightforward answer—ambiguity doesn't play well in a drive-in—and the final vote argues subtly and persuasively for the body (Arnold Schwarzenegger's body, after all: how real can you get?) rather than the mind as the true record of human memory and identity. The naïveté lies in reducing the moral issues to a binary choice—which was real?—and giving one answer: it was the body, it was the brunette.

Yet the ultimate assertion—I am X—springs from the hero's moral choice: Quaid wonders who are the good guys and who the bad guys, and in particular, he wonders if his old double, Hauser, whom he cannot remember, was on the right side. The head of the Agency tells Quaid that Hauser had not defected but had only pretended to do so in order to infiltrate the resistance movement for the Agency (another triple cross). The choice of who Quaid is is, therefore, in part a choice of who he wants to be, and that choice is dictated by the moral quality of each man (Hauser/Quaid)—though the key to that quality reverts back to the quality of the woman. The choice of the gorgeous brunette inspires him to make the right choice of moral sides; in the end, she is the most persuasive reality of all. The real you, and the better you, is the one that has not only the better-looking woman but the woman playing on the right team.

True Lies is a phrase that well expresses the theme of self-imitation, and the film by that name (James Cameron, 1994) is Schwarzenegger's self-satire on the genre of Schwarzenegger spy-cum-action-films:

> A spy named Harry Tasker (Schwarzenegger) neglected his wife Helen (Jamie Lee Curtis), who thought he was merely a businessman. Bored and depressed, she tottered on the brink of an affair with a used-car salesman (Tom Arnold) who pretended to be a spy and claimed credit for certain acts, reported in the press, that were actually committed by Harry Tasker. To keep Helen happy, Harry trumped up a spy scenario for her to play in and summoned her to the hotel room of a mysterious stranger. When she came to the hotel room, he sat in the dark and played a tape recording of the voice of a French colleague (knowing she would recognize his own voice). As he watched her strip, he saw her with fresh lust in his eyes, and then he made her close her eyes while he kissed her. At this moment, the real spies who were his enemies broke in on them and interrupted the seduction.
>
> Later, Harry became suspicious of his wife's fidelity and had her interrogated as if she were under suspicion for spying. In the course of the interrogation, he kept asking her if she had had an affair with another man and if she loved her husband. In return, when the enemy injected him with truth serum, she took that opportunity to ask him if he had had an affair with another woman. Together, they killed all the bad guys and were last seen doing the dance of self-parody, the tango.

Tasker is a political masquerader from the very start, and when he takes on the additional sexual masquerade, he begins to impersonate himself, producing a fantasy figure who may be his secret self but is also his wife's fantasy lover (as well as a surrogate for the Other Man who threatens to cuckold him, a stock character in remarriage films, here a used-car-salesman-as-spy). None of it is very real. When she finally discovers his true profession she asks him, "Have you ever killed anyone?" to which he replies, with deadpan self-satire, "Yes. But they were all bad."[11] The lies of spying are used to force sexual truths when husband and wife politically "interrogate" one another about sex. But he has been lying to her for years (about spying), while she has told the truth (about sex). This asymmetry is all too familiar.

What do we learn about memory and self-imitation from these American films about evil science and espionage? Somatic memory is a theme these films share with some of the medieval myths of amnesia, but there is an important difference in the nature of knowledge in the two genres. In *Total Recall*, the evil Sharon Stone knows the truth, while in *Dark City*, the virtuous Jennifer Connelly does not; this pattern seems to perpetuate for women the medieval model for men, which equates ignorance and innocence. But the male protagonists of these films have a different justification, for they are fighting against apparently invincible, invulnerable evil forces, so powerful that only some chance slip up by the enemy—a shred of memory that slips past the shredder or the barrier that should be impregnable—makes possible the hero's resistance. In this context, knowledge—both personal memory and a broader knowledge of the lay of the land—is essential to survival. Knowledge and memory, therefore, become signs of goodness in the hero as he fights against the evil power, in contrast with the medieval myths in which only ignorance and/or amnesia could justify the protagonist's actions against his woman.

Although science fiction films show us more "scientific" functions of self-imitation than the earlier texts provided, the basic philosophical choices remain limited. Given the fact that Hollywood was spawned by a culture that confidently places the memory in the mind, that assumes that the mind owns the body, that we are our minds no matter what body we happen to be occupying at the moment, it is at first surprising to see the films arguing so romantically for the somatic home of memory and demonstrating that the body owns the mind. It is even more surprising to find science fiction movies, which in general depict the memory as a part not merely of the mind but of the mind viewed as an entirely automatic machine, asserting the romantic belief in the power of the memory of love to transcend the mind.

But our surprise begins to fade when we realize that the memory-in-the-mind school was shouted down by other voices in Hollywood in the years in which these films were made. One of these voices, which reigned at a particular historical moment, was anticommunism. Clones who have the bodies of Americans but the minds of aliens provide a powerful metaphor for brainwashing, which appeared explicitly in films like *The Manchurian Candidate* (John Frankenheimer, 1962) and *The Ipcress File* (Sidney J. Furie, 1965). This metaphor is implicit in the earlier classic of this genre, *Invasion of the Body Snatchers* (Don Siegel, 1956), in which ordinary Norman Rockwell townspeople are replaced by identical doubles grown in pods from Mars. The clones' lack of emotion is a clue to the film's function as a thinly veiled anticommunist tract: the possessed who hand over their minds to Mars are political naïfs who become mesmerized by a message from Moscow. The anti-communist party line traditionally depicted communists as emotionless (recall the deadpan Garbo in *Ninotchka* [Ernst Lubitsch, 1939]); the body snatchers, the Blob, the Thing became, in the 1950s, a common metaphor for the (Russian) controllers of communist zombies. The aliens/Jews are foreigners, marginal figures who invade the planet Earth just as they invade our minds. The pod people pretending to be ordinary townspeople are like communists pretending to be loyal Americans: you thought you were looking at a neighbor you knew well, but it might be someone else imitating that neighbor. A really good person who seemed to believe in democracy might really be a commie who was imitating a really good person who believed in democracy. But of course, in real life there were no Martians; it was just Aunt Mary, pretending that she was just Aunt Mary when you knew that she was really a communist. That *Invasion of the Body Snatchers* was also read, by liberals, as a tract against the spread of McCarthyism, with the clones as red-baiting McCarthyites (opposed, as chance would have it, by a man played by an actor named McCarthy), is a testimony to the chameleon powers of myth.[12] *They Live* (John Carpenter, 1988) inverts the political agenda: the aliens are Reaganite entrepreneurs and yuppies who quote, verbatim, lines from Reagan's 1980 "Morning in America" election speech, and the resisters say, "They're saying we're a bunch of commmies." A brainwashing, mind-bending television station sends out rays that keep people from seeing the truth (seeing who is and is not an alien) unless they wear magic sunglasses and contact lenses. In the paranoid/conspiracy scenario, memory is erased by a malevolent, manipulative, panoptical higher power.

What "paranoid gothic"[13] was for those in the sexual closet, paranoid bourgeois was for anticommunist witch-hunters.[14] The somatic memory faction, as well as anticommunism, was also supported by an older anti-intellectualism that was deeply imbedded in the Hollywood dream factory and by the equally apple-pie American trust in the practical, embodied world, in materialism. The pervasive eroticism of Hollywood is, moreover, committed to a worldview that always points us toward sex as the fixed thing that keeps the world in order or, failing that, makes it go 'round. Memory, one of the props of that world, must, therefore, be held in the thrall of the body.

CHAPTER NINE

Passing
Race and Gender

I feel as if I am falling, trembling, melting. I am so ashamed as I see myself becoming a woman. Alas, my chest is sprouting breasts, and jewelry is growing right out of my body.

Chudala-as-Kumbha-as-Madanika, *Yogavasistha* (C. 1200 CE)

WHERE INDIVIDUAL PEOPLE may willingly masquerade, society as a whole often forces people of one group to pass as people of another group. Self-imitation often arises in the course of passing, a term usually applied primarily to racial passing, black people pretending to be white, but more recently also applied to gender passing, gay people pretending to be straight or people of one gender pretending to be people of the other gender.[1] Sometimes, as in Mark Twain's *Pudd'nhead Wilson*, racial passing and gender passing overlap,[2] and drag may also parody race. In a variant of the usual gender asymmetry, many black drag queens parody white women, while relatively few white drag queens parody black women. In both race and gender, social pressures force individuals to masquerade, usually (though not always) as someone of a higher and/or more powerful class. And in both race and gender, the simplistic paradigm (black passing as white or woman passing as man/man as woman) is destabilized by the intrinsic insubstantiality of the original categories and dichotomies that are the basis of their construction. Black passing for black is the racial equivalent of women pretending to be women, a not uncommon gender trope. These stories demonstrate that everyone who passes is, in a very real sense, self-imitating; since there is neither an ur-purity of race nor an unambiguous gender identity, anyone "black" passing as white is in effect white-as-black-as-white, and a female passing as male is, to some degree, a male-as-female-as-male. We will begin here with racial passing, both in recorded history and in fictional narratives, and then consider gender passing.

BLACK AS WHITE AS BLACK

In William Faulkner's *Light in August* (1932), the foundling Joe Christmas may or may not have some Negro ancestry. He thinks he does and passes for white. When he tells the white woman who is his secret lover that he fears he is of mixed race, she says, "How do you know that?" and he realizes, "I don't know it," and then he says, "If I'm not, damned if I haven't wasted a lot of time."[3] More than time is wasted by this self-masquerade of a (perhaps) white man who thinks he is a black man pretending to be a white man: soon Joe is castrated and killed by racists who think he is black and know he has slept with a white woman.

Mary Ann Doane notes that relatively few films have been made about the quandary of passing because of the visual dilemma that it poses: What does the actress look like when she is supposed to look like a black person who looks like a white person? The simple answer is, a white person. The irony of racism inheres in the fact that people who do not *look* black at all are defined as black by nonvisual criteria, invisible genealogical criteria, though the convention still assumes that they may be identified by skin color. Thus casting a white woman as a passing black woman results in white as black as white: "There is one body too much."[4] A third extra body produces a double back in the two films based on Fannie Hurst's novel *Imitation of Life* (John Stahl, 1934, and then the imitation by Douglas Sirk in 1959). On one occasion, white friends ask the black woman passing as white to serve at table; she carries the tray of food on her head and announces, "I learned it from my mammy and she learned it from her massuh befo' she belonged to you." As Doane comments on this scene (in the 1959 version), "The representational convolutions involved in this scene are mind-boggling. The spectator is faced with a white (Susan Kohner the actress) pretending to be a black pretending to be a white pretending to be a black (as incarnated in all the exaggerated attributes of Southern blackness). Ontology is out of reach."[5] These reversals of reversals produce a kind of vertigo, so the "true" race is obscured or, more precisely, revealed to be the unknowable and meaningless illusion that it is.

As long as the illusion prevails, however, it tends to produce self-imitations. Philip Roth's *The Human Stain* (2002) is about a black man named Coleman Silk who passes as a white man, a Jew; he often tells people that, "down in Virginia at the close of World War II, because his name didn't give him away as a Jew—because it could as easily have been a Negro's name—he'd once been identified, in a brothel, as a nigger trying to pass and been thrown out." After years of dropping these heavy hints, which no one ever seems to have picked up, he actually tells his secret to a woman he falls in love with. She befriends a crow that has been raised in captivity and doesn't know how to caw properly but "imitates the schoolkids that come here and imitate him. When the kids on the school trips imitate a crow."[6] The overtones of "Jim Crow" are surely relevant to this parallel double back imitation, as is the irony of the plot: Silk is fired from his academic post when he uses the word "spook" (intended in the sense of "ghost" and perceived as a racial slur). He is undone by that inadvertent pun, though his whole adult life has been, in a sense, the embodiment of an intended pun on the word *black*.

We may double back from fiction to real life in noting that Coleman Silk bears a striking resemblance to Anatole Broyard, who died in 1990 at the age of sixty-nine. A famous and influential literary critic, Broyard regarded himself as black: all his ancestors on both sides for over 200 years were defined as black, and his family was identified as Negro and identified itself as Negro. But his father, a light-skinned man married to a "high yellow" woman, during one period passed as white in order to join a union to get work in Brooklyn, and Anatole passed as white for all of his adult life. Some of his acquaintances (including his second wife, who was white) knew the truth, but he kept it from his children. He often expressed antiblack sentiments, even to the point of racism, which his wife justified with the logic of irony: "He had paid the price to be at liberty to say things that, if you didn't know he was black, you would misunderstand. I think it made him ironical." But, as Brent Staples pointed out, this is a dangerous game: "When you change something basic about yourself into a joke, it spreads, it metastasizes, and so his whole presentation of self became completely ironic. *Everything* about him was ironic." And Ellie Schwamm noted the price he paid for this irony: "a paradox: the man wanted to be appreciated not for being black but for being a writer, even though his pretending not to be black was stopping him from writing. It was one of the very few ironies that Broyard, the master ironist, was ill equipped to appreciate."[7] For Broyard's writing was blocked because his creative gift was paralyzed, squeezed, as in a vise, within the claws of those ironic commas. He could never write the great novel everyone expected of him because he could not write in his own voice. He was living the novel, and so he could not write it. To tell his story would mean telling more than he wanted to tell.

Broyard wrote, as a white man, about black people, and it was often said that he had the talent of writing as if he were black. More than that, he wrote about Negroes who passed. In a 1950 *Commentary* article entitled "Portrait of the Inauthentic Negro," he said of one such man: "[H]is companions are a mirror in which he sees himself as ugly." Surely Broyard's literary creations were also such a mirror for him. And like Coleman Silk, he could not resist dropping hints about the truth, bitter in-jokes. In one article, he said he avoided his mother and father because they were "too colorful."[8] As Henry Louis Gates Jr. put it, "He perfected the feat of being self-revelatory without revealing anything." But what alternatives did he have? Gates spells it out: "Here is a man who passed for white because he wanted to be a writer, and he did not want to be a Negro writer." It makes no more sense to say that a person with just a drop of white blood or one white ancestor (which Broyard probably had) and passes as white is running from his blackness than to say that a person with just a drop of black blood or one black ancestor (which Broyard said he probably had) and passes as black is running from his whiteness. It is all socially constructed.

Gates sums it up well: "If he was passing for white, perhaps he understood that the alternative was passing for black."[9] This option, black passing for black, was available to him but rejected. And so if, as I suspect and has been widely speculated,[10] the Roth novel is a roman à clef inspired by Broyard, it is about a white man (Broyard) pretending to be a black man (Broyard) pretending to be a white man (in life) pretending to be a black man (on the page), masquerading (in the book) as a black man (Coleman Silk) pretending to be a white man pretending to be a black man (in his brothel anecdote). Perhaps Roth wrote the story of Anatole Broyard's life for him (as Gertrude Stein wrote Alice Toklas's autobiography for her), telling Broyard's truth at last in Coleman Silk's fiction.

WOMEN MASQUERADING AS MEN AS WOMEN: CHUDALA

Through triple cross-dressing, people can pretend to be their own genders via other genders. That is, a man can pretend to be a woman pretending to be a man and a woman can pretend to be a man pretending to be a woman. This is a double drag, or, as the *New York Times* headline reviewing the 1995 musical *Victor/Victoria* called it, a masquerade "in Drag, in Drag." Marjorie Garber argues that the transvestite is *always*, in one sense, in double drag, caught in an infinite regress of representation.[11]

A brilliant example of double drag is the story of Queen Chudala, which is narrated at great length and with many labyrinthine triple crosses in the *Yogavasishtha*:

> Queen Chudala and her husband King Shikhidhvaja were passionately in love, like two souls in one body. In time, the queen became enlightened and acquired magic powers, including the ability to fly, but she concealed these powers from her husband, and when she attempted to instruct him he spurned her as a foolish and presumptuous woman. Yet he remarked that she seemed to have regained the bloom of her youth, and he assured her that he would continue to make love to her. Eventually, the king decided to seek his own enlightenment and withdrew to the forest to meditate; he renounced his throne and refused to let her accompany him, but left her to govern the kingdom.

After eighteen years she decided to visit him; she took the form of a young Brahmin boy named Kumbha ("Pot") and was welcomed by the king, who did not recognize her but remarked that Chudala-as-Kumbha looked very much like his queen, Chudala. After a while, the king became very fond of Chudala-as-Kumbha, who instructed him and enlightened him, and she began to be aroused by her handsome husband. And so Chudala-as-Kumbha went away for a while. When she returned, she told the king that a sage had cursed her to become a woman, with breasts and long hair, every night. That night, before the king's eyes, Chudala-as-Kumbha changed into a woman named Madanika, who cried out in a stammering voice, "I feel as if I am falling, trembling, melting. I am so ashamed as I see myself becoming a woman. Alas, my chest is sprouting breasts, and jewelry is growing right out of my body."

Chudala-as-Kumbha-as-Madanika slept beside the king every night in the same bed like a virgin, while Chudala-as-Kumbha lived with him during the day as a friend. After a few days Chudala-as-Kumbha said to him, "Your majesty, I sleep beside you every night as a woman. I want to marry you and to enjoy the happiness of a woman." He consented to this, and so one day Chudala-as-Kumbha bathed ceremonially with the king, and that night Chudala-as- Kumbha-as-Madanika married him. And so the couple, whose previous state of marriage was concealed, were joined together. They lay down on the marriage bed of flowers and made love all night.

Thus they lived as dear friends during the day and as husband and wife at night. After they had lived happily in this way for a while, Chudala decided to test the king's detachment. She used her magic powers to create the illusion of a garden with a beautiful bed, and on that bed lay Chudala-as-Kumbha-as-Madanika making love passionately with a young man handsomer than the king. The king saw them and turned away, but was unmoved. "Please continue; do not let me interrupt your pleasure," he said to the flushed and apologetic Chudala-as-Kumbha-as-Madanika; "Kumbha and I are great friends, free from all passion; but you, Madanika, are nothing but a woman created by a sage's curse." Chudala-as-Kumbha-as-Madanika said, "Women are fickle by nature; they have eight times as much lust as men. Please don't be angry with me." "I have no anger, my dear girl," said the king; "but—only because good people would disapprove—I do not want you to be my wife. Let us be good friends, as we were before, without any passion."

Chudala was delighted with the king's immunity to lust and anger, and she changed immediately from Chudala-as-Kumbha-as-Madanika to Chudala. The king said, "Who are you and how did you get here? In your body, your movements, your smile, your manner, your grace—you look so much like my wife." "Yes, I am truly Chudala," she said, and then she told him all that she had done. He embraced her passionately, and said, "You are the most wonderful wife who ever lived. The wife is everything to her husband: friend, brother, sympathizer, servant, guru, companion, wealth, happiness, the Vedic canon, abode, and slave. Come, embrace me again." Then he made love to her all night and returned with her to resume his duties as king. He ruled for ten thousand years and finally attained release.[12]

This text takes no notice of the fact that Chudala and the king are childless. They are said to be passionately in love, and she is his lover, a relationship that the text at the start seems to regard as complete. There is, therefore, no conflict here between the personae of the mother and the whore or the wife and a mistress, as there are in many myths of this genre. And so, instead of wishing to be both her husband's concubine and the mother of his children, Chudala wishes to be her husband's mistress both in the sense of lover and in the sense of teacher, schoolmistress. She has already played the first role but is now denied it, and he refuses to grant her the second role; when he goes off to meditate, god is the other woman. In the Hindu view, Chudala is like a man to begin with: aggressive, resourceful, and wise. She is a magician; in other times and places, she might have been called a witch.

But the queen wants to get her husband into bed as well as to enlighten him; the story is, after all, not merely a parable of enlightenment but a very human, very funny story. And the text is not so antinomian as to image a consummated male homosexual relationship. Eventually, Chudala manages to enjoy her husband as a male friend by day and as a lover and wife by night, and she does this by getting him to marry her again, since their already existent marital relationship is, as the text says, "concealed" (like the marriage of Paula and Smithy in *Random Harvest*). The double woman whom she creates— Chudala-as-Kumbha-as-Madanika—is her real self— the negation of the negation of her femininity; the jewelry that actually grows out of her body is what she would have worn as Queen Chudala at the start of the story. This double deception works well enough and may express her full fantasy: to be her husband's intellectual superior under the sun and his erotic partner by moonlight. But since the two roles belong to two different personae, she wants to merge them and to play them both as her original self. That is, she wants to reintegrate herself and abandon her double.

To do this and to test the king, she creates two more magical doubles: a double of the already double woman Chudala-as-Kumbha-as-Madanika and a double of the king, her lover. The king passes the test not because he is so far above jealousy as to allow his wife to sleep with another man but because he realizes that the woman who has betrayed him is not only not really his wife but not even really a woman. As a result of his vision of the adultery of the false Madanika, the king comes to realize the purely illusory nature of the "true" Madanika and rejects her—for being illusory or for being promiscuous? We do not know. Chudala isn't jealous; she watches him make love with another woman—herself—but doesn't mind, while he watches her make love with another man—an illusion—and seems to mind. She is free of jealousy for a number of reasons: she is more enlightened than the king, she knows from the start that none of it is real, she knows that the illusory woman is herself, and finally, the text may still assume the double standard: a woman should not mind, like a man, if her spouse is unfaithful.

The king is still willing to maintain his friendship with Chudala-as-Kumbha, for he thinks that Kumbha is one step closer to reality than Chudala-as-Kumbha-as-Madanika is (Madanika being what he takes to be a double of the "real" Kumbha). And he is half right: Chudala-as-Kumbha-as-Madanika is closer to the original Chudala in gender, but Chudala-as-Kumbha is closer in intellect. Though the king claims he is not jealous, he rejects Madanika as Rama rejects Sita, ostensibly for public reasons. Chudala is repairing the split between them by revealing the illusory nature of sexual love. The playful juggling of the genders demonstrates both the unreality of appearances and the falsity of the belief that one gender is better than the other; the male and female forms of Chudala are, in a sense, all alike in the dark. Moreover, the woman is wiser than the man, enlightens the man, and so forth. This extraordinary openness to gender bending in ancient India may be an indirect benefit of the rigid social order: since social categories are taken for granted, there is more room for role-playing.[13] But not, when we look closer, all that much room. Chudala has to become a man herself—like a bodhisattva—to teach her husband, and she has to become a woman again to sleep with him. Moreover, the relationship between Chudala and the king is never the relationship of a real husband and wife. She functions like a goddess, giving him her grace and leading him up the garden path of enlightenment, setting up a divine illusion and then revealing herself to him as the gods reveal themselves. She can fly. She even can stay young.

THE STAGE AS WORLD: CALL ME ROSALIND

Gender has a penchant for the theater and the theater for gender, and both gender and the theater have a weakness for triple-crossing. Theatrical triple-crossing, on stage or screen, takes place when an actor pretends to be a character pretending to be an actor. If the character and the actor are of two different genders, it's triple cross-dressing, which happens a lot. In the plays of Shakespeare, as in some early operas, men played the parts of women, so when such a character masqueraded as a man, a man was playing a woman playing a man. Shakespeare explicitly acknowledged the reinforcement of the two parallel frames on several occasions,[14] and Shakespearean audiences were clearly aware that men—preferably young boys whose voices had not yet changed—were playing the parts of women—sometimes the parts of women playing men. Yet they suspended that awareness or, rather, half suspended it. Tom Stoppard's film *Shakespeare in Love* (John Madden, 1998) adds yet another twist to the spiral: a woman (Gwyneth Paltrow) plays a woman (Viola de Lesseps) playing a man (Thomas Kent) playing a man (Romeo) and then playing a woman (Juliet), the final twist inspiring Shakespeare (in the film) with the idea for *Twelfth Night*, in which a male actor played a woman (Viola) playing a man. It might better have inspired the counterpart to that play, *As You Like It* (1598–1602), where that final man doubles back yet again to play a woman. Here are the bare bones of that plot:

> Orlando and Rosalind fell in love, but Rosalind disguised herself as a boy, Ganymede, ostensibly in order to avoid being raped or otherwise attacked if it were known that she was a mere woman and also to escape from a malevolent ruler. In the Forest of Arden, Rosalind-as-Ganymede encountered Orlando, for whom she *openly* pretended to be Rosalind in order, she said, to dissuade Orlando from the love of women in general and the love of Rosalind in particular—all the while, of course, using her wit and charm to make him fall deeper and deeper in love with her in her male persona. As Ganymede, she also inadvertently attracted the love of a shepherd woman, Phoebe, whom she tried in vain to dissuade and to encourage to marry the shepherd boy who loved her, Silvius. In the end, Rosalind revealed herself and married Orlando, and Phoebe married Silvius.

When Orlando tells Rosalind-as-Ganymede of his love for Rosalind, she promises to cure him of his love, "if you would but call me Rosalind and come every day to my cote and woo me." And when he says, "With all my heart, good youth," she reminds him, "Nay, you must call me Rosalind" (3.2).[15] But Rosalind-as-Ganymede-as-Rosalind is not the same person as Rosalind-as-Rosalind. Rosalind-as-Ganymede-as-Rosalind is more daring, more playful, more flirtatious, more confident, emboldened both by the double mask and by the level of masculinity embedded in the mediating second personality, able to say things to Orlando that she was not able to say to him when she met him as Rosalind.

Ganymede's name signals his mythological sexual ambiguity, the name of the boy lover of Zeus, a broad hint that the putatively false homoerotic passions in *As You Like It* are for real. (Later writers certainly took the hint: Oscar Wilde's Dorian Gray, otherwise thoroughly embroiled in homoeroticism, falls in love with a woman when he sees her playing Rosalind, and Virginia Woolf's bisexual Orlando begins life as a man but becomes a woman who, on occasion, cross-dresses and passes as a man among women.) On the outside level, the public level, it would seem that a male Ganymede is loved by a female Phoebe; on the inside, a female Rosalind is in love with a male Orlando. Rosalind-as-Ganymede thus experiences simultaneously two different sorts of gender/sex asymmetry, one public, one private (rather like the quandary of cross-dressed characters who must choose between the men's room and the women's room[16]). Unlike Chudala, Rosalind remains within her male persona for much of her seduction of Orlando.

Despite the playfulness of the plot, which might encourage a reader to ignore the illogical or irrational success of the masquerade, Shakespeare tackles head-on the real problems posed by the fact that no one notices that Ganymede is Rosalind. Rosalind's disguise has two layers: she pretends to be, in general, someone of the other gender, a boy, and she pretends to be a particular individual of the other gender, Ganymede. The more general passing is made possible, as she tells us from the very start, because she is unusually tall. People do, however, remark upon Ganymede's femininity. Orlando's brother, Oliver, comments, "The boy is fair, Of female favour, and bestows himself Like a ripe sister," and when Rosalind-as-Ganymede faints (or, as she puts it, counterfeits—feints—a faint) in front of him, and he says, "Counterfeit to be a man," she lamely remarks, "I should have been a woman by right" (4.3). Here, Oliver is asking a man (or so he thinks) to pretend to be a man. Adding this to the tab we've been running, you have a male actor as a woman as a boy as a boy. (Or as another cross-dressing actress was once described, you have a boyish woman who passes herself off as a girlish boy.[17])

The second, more particular masquerade is noted when Rosalind's father thickly remarks of Ganymede, "I do remember in this shepherd boy Some lively touches of my daughter's favour," and Orlando replies, "My lord, the first time that I ever saw him, Methought he was a brother to your daughter" (5.4). Family resemblance to the rescue, as usual in recognition comedies. But Rosalind and Orlando have met and fallen in love before she starts wearing trousers, which makes more problematic the fact that Orlando does not see through the gender masquerade. Orlando's uneasiness is expressive of the latent androgyny of both Rosalind and himself, but it is also a powerful testimony to a love that transcends gender but not sexuality, a love made all the more titillating by the woman's safe hiding place behind man's clothing.

Rosalind at the start is fond of word games, but she plays them only with her friend Celia. Face-to-face with Orlando, Rosalind-as-Rosalind is almost as tongue-tied as he is (she speaks only short sentences, which lack wit though they are still eloquent), and their romance goes nowhere at all. Orlando, too, can express his love for Rosalind-as-Rosalind only in her absence and in poems so bad that even Rosalind mocks them, though not to Orlando's face (3.2). In her presence, Orlando is mired down in his own paralyzing and verbally graceless love-sickness; "What passion hangs these weights upon my tongue? I cannot speak to her, yet she urged conference," he moans to himself. Rosalind-as-Ganymede-as-Rosalind, however, can use her witty wordplay to draw him out. Her masquerade changes Orlando, but it changes Rosalind herself even more and transforms her entire world.

Near the end of the play (5.2), the supple verbal devices of Rosalind-as-Ganymede-as-Rosalind trick Orlando into admitting his love for both Rosalind-as-Ganymede-as-Rosalind and Rosalind-as-Rosalind, expressing in words his subconscious realization that Ganymede is Rosalind. First, she half hypnotizes Orlando through a repetitious series of formulas in which each of the three lovers, Silvius, Phoebe, and Orlando, declares three times that each one is made of sighs and tears, and passion and fantasy, for his or her beloved ("And I for Phoebe," "And I for Ganymede," "And I for Rosalind"), each time naming the object of this passion, while Rosalind, making up the quartet, resolutely declares, "And I for no woman." Finally, when Orlando is caught up in the rhythm somewhat in the manner of a game of Simon Says, after the other two have said to their physically present lovers (Silvius to Phoebe and Phoebe to Rosalind-as-Ganymede), "If this be so, why blame you me to love you?" substituting for the specific name the second person pronoun, Orlando blurts out, "If this be so, why blame you me to love you?" and Rosalind pounces: "Who do you speak to?" she asks, forgetting her grammar, and he replies, lamely and with a very poor pun, "To her that is not here, nor doth not hear." But of course, she is here, and she hears.

Though the pronoun *you*, unlike most proper names (including those in question), can refer to either gender, it must refer to someone present, within earshot (in this case, Rosalind-as-Ganymede). Yet Orlando rather lamely claims that he meant it to refer to Rosalind (allegedly absent, actually present). This Freudian slip, therefore, may or may not mean that Orlando knows that Ganymede is Rosalind (just as Brünnhilde half-recognizes Siegfried-as-Gunther, and Charles Rainier half-recognizes Paula-as-Margaret). For the ambiguity of *you* is matched by the ambiguity of the gender of the actor, whom the audience may or may not perceive, at any given moment in the play, in terms of physical sex or conventional gender. Each flickers back and forth between levels of reality. When, therefore, Orlando says "you" to Rosalind-as-Ganymede-as-Rosalind, he is speaking to a character that is two parts male (the gender of the actor and of Rosalind-as-Ganymede) and two parts female (the gender of Rosalind and of Rosalind-as-Ganymede-as-Rosalind).[18] Shakespeare exploits this ambiguity at the very end, when he has Rosalind begin by saying that it is not the "fashion to see the lady the epilogue" and then remark, "If I were a woman, . . ." acknowledging the gender of the male actor.

We in the audience empathize with Orlando's growing confusion: is this a man or a woman? And *does it matter?* The fun is in the joke, but who is in on the joke, and who is its butt? The audience and Rosalind are in on the joke against Phoebe and Orlando, but the audience alone is in on yet another joke,[19] and this time Rosalind is the butt: for the audience alone knows that she is being played by a male actor. Of course, Phoebe (played by a boy), in love with Ganymede, is also present at the charade, adding yet another point of view to the contrasting views of the audience (who know all four layers of Rosalind's masquerade: actor, Rosalind,

Ganymede, Rosalind) and Orlando (who knows some and suspects others). Phoebe sees only the surface.

The Forest of Arden, the place of magic, resembles, in many ways, the far darker heath in *King Lear* (1603–1605). In both plays, the protagonists flee from the court to the world al fresco, from culture to nature, more precisely to human nature (in geographical nature). But that nature is Rousseauvian in *As You Like It*, where the court is brutal while the sheltering forest brings out a kindness and camaraderie, and Hobbesian in *Lear*, where human nature seems at first polite enough at court but is revealed in all its savagery stripped naked on the naked heath. The parallels grow closer if we accept the view of some scholars that Cordelia is double-cast as the fool (they never appear on stage together), giving her, like Rosalind, a male alter ego in the forest. If the truer self is discovered through the masquerades in the forest, then all of the characters in both plays are really forest people who usually pretend to be courtiers and now pretend to be (courtiers pretending to be) forest people, as Marie Antoinette played at being a shepherdess. The first half of *As You Like It*, at court, is Lear-like in its human darkness and bleakness, while the second half, in the forest, is pure carnival, mocking its own too-easy resolutions, its unbelievable instant conversions of all the villains. In this protean world, in which evil can instantly be transformed to good, female can easily be transformed to male and back again. Stanley Cavell likens this "green world" in Shakespeare to Connecticut in Hollywood's early romantic comedies (and the mythical "Conneckticut" in *The Lady Eve*), the magic forest where a dead marriage is brought back to life.[20]

Angela Carter's *The Passion of New Eve* invokes Rosalind in the magic forest when Eve (a transsexual transvestite, formerly a man, now a woman wearing a man's costume) looks in the mirror and sees

> the transformation that an endless series of reflections showed me was a double drag. . . . It seemed at first glance, I had become my old self again in the inverted world of the mirrors. But this masquerade was more than skin deep. Under the mask of maleness I wore another mask of femaleness but a mask that now I would never be able to remove, no matter how hard I tried, although I was a boy disguised as a girl and now disguised as a boy again, like Rosalind in Elizabeth Arden.[21]

Makeup (the face-lift) becomes a mask that becomes a face, and Eve in Eden becomes Rosalind in (the Forest of/Elizabeth) Arden.

Perhaps the inevitable twist to this tangled skein was provided in 2003 by the playwright actor David Greenspan in his play *She Stoops to Comedy*, in which a lesbian actress who has decided to audition for the role of Orlando in a production of *As You Like It* spends most of the first scene offstage, preparing her disguise in the bathroom. When she finally emerges in slacks, a short-sleeved shirt, furry arms, and a butch haircut, she is most convincingly male, for the simple reason that David Greenspan plays this part, "without a stitch of drag."[22] Rosalind-as-Ganymede-as-Rosalind meet Greenspan-as-lesbian-as-Orlando.

Yet even these twists were topped by a stage comedy, *El Vergonzoso en palacio* or "The Bashful Man at the Palace," by Tirso de Molina (1584-1648), the man who made Don Juan famous:

> Serafina, daughter of the Duke of Avero, boasted coldly that she had never been in love. She disguised herself as a man to act a male part in a palace farce in which she ardently embraced her governess Juana, who was playing a woman's part. Unbeknownst to her, Antonio, one of her rejected suitors, had commissioned an artist to paint her portrait— and when he saw her so passionate in her male costume, he told the artist to paint her like that. When he courted her the next day, however, she rejected him icily; furious, he threw down the portrait and left. But Serafina picked up the portrait and instantly fell in love with the handsome young man who so closely resembled herself. Juana, who had helped Antonio procure the portrait, lied, suggesting that this was a portrait of Dionis, an exiled relative, and told Antonio to come back that night, pretending to be Dionis. Antonio-as-[Serafina-as]-Dionis persuaded Serafina to marry him. Only then did she learn that the real Dionis had secretly married her older sister.[23]

What are we to make of this labyrinth of genders and disguises? Serafina cannot connect with her lover except through gender-bending art forms (play and/or portrait) that release her own androgynous sexuality. This makes her a kissing cousin of Balzac's Sarrasine, Shakespeare's Rosalind, and King Udayana in the Harsha play. But her patent narcissism and homoeroticism, which she shares with Wilde's Dorian Gray, push her one step further than those cousins and make her fall in love with her lover only when she sees him as a transvestite transformation of herself. This is a woman who not only pretends to be who she is but falls in love with the man she is.

THE WORLD AS STAGE: BEAUMARCHAIS AND THE CHEVALIER D'EON

Let us turn now to offstage life in all the world, which is, as we learn from *As You Like It*, a stage. In a case from recorded eighteenth-century French history, the Chevalier d'Eon turned out to be a man who pretended to be a transvestite. This is the story:

> Once upon a time, more precisely on October 5, 1728, a child named Charles Geneviève Louis Auguste Andréa Thimothée d'Eon, also known as Charles de Beaumont, was born to a low-ranking nobleman in the town of Tonnerre in Burgundy. The child grew up to have a distinguished career as a diplomat and spy and a captain in the dragoons and was honored with the title of Chevalier for his bravery in the Seven Years' War. In

1770, rumors that he was a woman began to circulate in France and England, and in 1776 Louis XVI officially announced that d'Eon was and had always been a woman. The Chevalière, as she now became known, left France and lived the rest of her life as a woman in London. When she died, on May 21, 1810, it was discovered that she was anatomically male. [24]

After d'Eon announced that he was a woman, he insisted that he did not want to wear women's clothing but had the right to wear his dragoon's uniform. Still wearing men's clothing in France, apparently concealing but actually revealing his sex (male but allegedly female), he encouraged people to conjure up the two negatives that cancelled one another out. Then he dressed in women's clothes only, he insisted, at the king's insistence, but since he continued to dress as a woman when he was in exile in England, with no French king to make him do it, one is inclined to believe that he did protest too much, rather like Br'er Rabbit begging Br'er Fox not to throw him into his beloved briar patch. It was and still is widely believed that d'Eon first disguised himself as a woman in Russia in order to gain access to the empress Elizabeth,[25] making him a man pretending to be a woman pretending to be a man pretending to be a woman. Kates points out that if d'Eon went to a cross-dressing ball (and there were many at that time), "he would not have to pose as someone else, but rather, his original self would now be regarded by others as female." But what was this "original self"? At many salons, "women began to masquerade as d'Eon, telling risqué stories and flirting with male guests."[26] But what were they masquerading as?

The sexual triple cross explains how d'Eon got away with it. Apparently, as long as no one with any status in Paris had any knowledge of d'Eon's male anatomy (and the strange thing is that no one, apparently, did: he was either celibate or very, very careful), he was safe from accusations or rumors from people who had known him in the provinces. (Half of his names are women's names, but the French *do* that.) Well, his mother lied for him, as mothers do, but the truth was that he set it up in such a way that he could not lose. He was able to project his fantasies upon the people he fooled without actually changing anything, just making other people imagine him differently. People later remarked that he had looked more feminine in his uniform than he did later in a dress. Like the fools in the tale of the emperor's new clothes, who persuaded themselves and one another that they didn't see the emperor's nude body, the French courtiers imagined that d'Eon's invisible nude body was what he told them it was (female) and discounted what they actually saw (male). Jacques Lacan remarked on the Chevalier d'Eon in the context of self-referentiality[27] and cited Alphonse Allais: "Somebody points at a woman and utters a horrified cry, 'Look at her, what a shame, under her clothes, she is totally naked!'"[28] Lacan argued not that "the emperor has no clothes" but, rather, that "the emperor is naked only beneath his clothes,"[29] and he applied this scenario to the Chevalier d'Eon, who was, indeed, naked under his clothes.

The Chevalier created a brazened-out social fiction that no one dared to challenge. Even when he later cross-dressed and behaved in an unabashedly masculine fashion, so that people remarked that d'Eon still seemed more like a man than a woman, even when they noticed that the Chevalière shaved, had a beard, a voice, and a chest like a man, and urinated standing up, still they went along with it. Kates sums up the situation well:

> What is amazing about the reactions of [James] Boswell and [Horace] Walpole is that they did not follow their instincts and declare that d'Eon was actually a man dressed as a woman. Rather, despite what they perceived, they identified d'Eon as an Amazon, a thoroughly masculinized woman. They assumed female in what they could *not* see; they perceived male in what they could see. To them, d'Eon was anatomically female, but socially a man.[30]

Whereas in fact he was anatomically male but socially female. Politics, too, supported the masquerade. D'Eon was a spy for many years, living what Kates calls a double life and I would call a double double life, as spy and diplomat and as man and woman. As a spy, he knew how to be what later came to be called, appropriately, a "double penetration agent." In London, too, he played into the scenario of political double entendre: an article published in England referred to him as "this amphibious being, male in London, female in Paris," while a piece of doggerel in Paris argued that it was believed (presumably in France) that he was male, but England declared him to be female.[31] Each nation feminized the other and blamed the transvestism, like syphilis, on the other.

This story out of history is about fantasy, sexual fantasy, and d'Eon's autobiography is a masterpiece of that genre. At times his life reads like a French comedy, and there is much irony in the fact that one of the players in this drama was Pierre-Augustin Beaumarchais, the author of the play *The Marriage of Figaro*, in which the page Cherubino (always played by a woman in the opera version of the story) is dressed in women's clothing and is intended to substitute for Susanna in the tryst (until, fearing that Cherubino is about to be sent away, the countess Rosina decides to substitute for Cherubino substituting for Susanna). Beaumarchais not only thought that d'Eon was a woman but spread the rumor that he and d'Eon were in love and contemplating marriage and, later, that d'Eon was trying to marry him. Most significantly, Beaumarchais negotiated the document in which Louis XVI announced that d'Eon was a woman. But the true genre of the work of art that d'Eon made of his life was not slapstick or opera buffo but myth; he created a myth of his birth and an imaginary childhood. The story he told was the widespread tale of a daughter whose impoverished parents made her dress as a son,[32] which is a myth in the classical sense of the word—a story that has been told and retold for many centuries in many cultures:

> [A]ccording to d'Eon, his father squandered whatever he found in his wife's dowry, and by the mid-1720's was in debt up to his ears. The way out of debt, it turned out, was to have a son. Françoise's family will stipulated that a large inheritance of some 400 louis would go to the d'Eon family only if Françoise had a son. . . . Although born female, the new infant was to be raised from the start as a boy . . . . Thus according to d'Eon, he was born female, but he never knew what it was like to exist as a girl because from the first breath his family raised him as a son.[33]

But of course, none of this was "true." Even the least suspicious of hermeneuts can see that d'Eon was projecting onto other people (his mother and two other women) his own fantasy of self-re-creation.

The central image of d'Eon's androgyny was recognized as mythical even in his time; in September 1777, a London magazine had a picture of d'Eon "with a kind of gender line running vertically down the middle of his body,"[34] just like the depiction of sacred androgynes in India. Myth or history, the Chevalier d'Eon's triple-cross-dressing led to the eponym *eonism*, coined by Havelock Ellis in 1928 as a synonym for transvestism[35] and enshrined in the *Oxford English Dictionary*: "Transvestism, esp. by a man. So Eonist, one who wears the clothes of the opposite sex." But they have missed the whole point: he was masquerading in the clothing of the *same* sex. He just had to tell people to imagine the switch on and the switch back; he never even had to change out of his trousers.

WOMEN MASQUERADING AS WOMEN, MEN AS MEN

In 1970 the *Times* of London called *eonism* nothing but a "minor deviation."[36] After all, he was French. Oddly enough, the victim of another Eonist was also French: Bernard Boursicot lived for two decades with a Chinese man named Shi Peipu, who persuaded him that he was a woman pretending to be a man.[37] It was, of course, only a matter of time before the true story of Boursicot and Shi Peipu became first a play and then a film, both named *M. Butterfly*. At the end of the play, after dressing as Song (the Shi Peipu figure) playing the part of Madama Butterfly in the Puccini opera, Gallimard (the Bernard Boursicot figure) eviscerates himself, just as Madama Butterfly is usually depicted as doing (when her lover sails away), imitating her father's ritual suicide in the manner of a traditional Japanese warrior. Thus Gallimard is imitating a Chinese man (Song) who imitated a Chinese woman (Song) imitating a Japanese woman (Madama Butterfly) who imitated a Japanese man (her father). This act moves the identity and power from male to female and back again in a manner that finally erases the gender (and Orientalist) categories altogether. In another sort of limbo between life and art, the documentary film *Paris Is Burning* (Jenny Livingstone, 1990) depicts a man who usually dresses as a queen but who comes to the ball as a man in a three-piece suit, briefcase and all.

Other films also depict gender triple cross-dressings. In Blake Edwards's 1982 film *Victor/Victoria*, set in the 1930s (and based upon a film that was actually made in the 1930s, Reinhold Schunzel's *Viktor und Viktoria* [1933]), Victoria Grant (Julie Andrews) says that "a woman pretending to be a man pretending to be a woman" would be "preposterous," but the wise old queen, Toddy (Robert Preston), replies, "It's so preposterous that everyone will believe it." The masquerade, as usual, transforms the woman into a woman: Victoria-as-Victoria is a rather mousy, prissy conservatory singer. But she learns from her gay male friend how to translate her own masculinity into a flamboyant sexuality, and Victoria-as-Victor-as-Victoria sings a hot jazz number that frees her to fall in love with a Chicago gangster. When the word gets out that Count Victor Grezhinski (Victoria's male persona) is not a man, the police want to prosecute her for fraud because she's supposed to be a fake but is real. (The logic in this persists in contemporary arguments about "bio queens," women who perform in female drag in both drag king contests and drag queen contests and whose authenticity is often challenged, presumably because they are self-imitating.) And people keep trying to see, offstage, the tell tale genitals: the man who falls in love with her spies on her in the bathroom, his mistress sees her in the nude, and the police certify her male genitalia in her dressing room (where her male cross-dressing friend, Toddy, stands in for her). But transvestism here really does not seem to be about genitalia at all; it's about theater and about showmanship (which are also about sex and gender), and this is why the final scene, the best scene, is a show. When Victoria decides to give up the stage, Toddy again takes her place: a man pretending to be a woman pretending to be a man pretending to be a woman. (If we want to stretch it as far as it can go, we could say that an actor [Robert Preston] is masquerading as a drag queen [Toddy] masquerading as an actress [Julie Andrews] masquerading as a drag queen [Victoria] masquerading as a Spanish woman.) Since Toddy is an *old* queen (as he points out from the start), he is funny, whereas Victoria, a *young* queen, poses a real sexual threat to the macho hero who falls in love with her. Moreover, this final masquerade is acceptable because there is no illusion: it is hilariously obvious that it is a guy pretending to be a woman. It is pure theater.

The fourth wall was often breached in this regard, too. We all know now (and many people knew then) that a triple cross was at work when the gay Rock Hudson pretended to be a straight man (Rock Hudson) acting the part of a straight man

(Brad Allen) who pretended to be a gay man (Rex Stetson) in *Pillow Talk* (Michael Gordon, 1959).[38] (When Brad says, "I don't know how much longer I can keep up this act, he is speaking on several levels.) Men in drag imitated the great sex queens like Marlene Dietrich and Mae West, but to very different effect. Dietrich, notoriously bisexual, joked about it; at a "come-as-the-person-you-most-admire" costume party in Hollywood in 1935, she went dressed as Leda *and* the Swan. But Mae West (who never wore male drag) became, particularly as she aged, a self-parody, regarded as an imitation of a man imitating her, "the greatest female impersonator of all time."[39] She was not, however, just another female impersonator. Parker Tyler more subtly characterized her as the reconciliation in a single body of the gay son and his gaily painted, warmly all-forgiving mother.[40] She was thus a very special sort of androgyne. Was she doing it on purpose? Who was laughing at whom? Frank S. Nugent wondered aloud in the *New York Times*, "It's one thing to burlesque sex and quite another to be burlesqued by it." As Claudia Roth Pierpont put it, "It is important to note that she was no longer fully in on the joke, or in on the biggest joke: her physical transformation and her blindness to it." Mae West herself felt that Catherine the Great was really a prototype of Mae West, but when, in her sixties, she portrayed a seductive woman of twenty, people thought she looked more like a drag queen than ever. This was in part because old women were played on stage by mature men; thus drag queens played not just women but *old* women, satirizing age as well as gender, and the aging Mae West was caught in this trap without realizing it. She was also caught in another unexpected trap, for cross-dressing often mocks class, too; many drag queens satirize "rich old women," for whom Margaret Dumont in the Marx Brothers movies provided a kind of conscious self-parody. Mae West struck back, insisting that gay men had stolen the camp style from her, when she had borrowed that style from them in the 1920s.[41]

This logic, that "gay men" (not at all the same thing as drag queens, let alone transvestites) were imitating Mae West imitating men (or gay men) imitating women, argues (and not for the first time) that it is men who set the standards for women, *plus royalistes que la reine*. The masquerader in *M. Butterfly* remarks: "Why, in the Peking Opera, are women's roles played by men? . . . Because only a man knows how a woman is supposed to act" (2.7). In Oscar Wilde's *A Woman of No Importance* (1893, two years before its male counterpart, *The Importance of Being Earnest*), Lord Illingworth remarks, "All women become like their mothers. That is their tragedy. No man does. That is his." Angela Carter takes Wilde's insight and runs with it in a conversation between twin sisters, now old and making themselves young with makeup; Dora tells the story: "'It's every woman's tragedy,' said Nora, as we contemplated our painted masterpieces, 'that, after a certain age, she looks like a female impersonator.' Mind you, we've known some lovely female impersonators, in our time. 'What's every man's tragedy, then?' I wanted to know. 'That *he* doesn't, Oscar,' she said."[42]

Outside the frame of the stage and the page, people often triple cross-dress as their true genders. Garber recalls that when Gloria Steinem was given a 1973 award from Harvard's Hasty Pudding (a prize often given to cross-dressed actors and actresses, as Hasty Pudding specializes in drag shows), she remarked, "I don't mind drag—women have been female impersonators for some time." And Garber comments that transvestism shows us that "*all* women cross-dress as women when they produce themselves as artifacts,"[43] or, as Elaine Showalter puts it, "'[W]omanliness' is the putting on of veils, only 'masquerading in feminine guise.'"[44] It could be argued and has been argued that every woman since Pandora has masqueraded as herself, concealing within the deceptive superficial image of a woman the true nature of—a woman. Here is a gendered double standard: although some men may masquerade as women, the feminist claim is that drag is overwhelmingly female drag. This truth came home to me during carnival week in Provincetown, August 2003, when both men and women dressed in drag, and most of the women were wearing not men's suits à la Dietrich but exaggerated eyelashes, wigs, sequins, and high heels, just like the men in drag—or like the bio queens.

In 1929, Joan Rivière published her article "Womanliness as Masquerade," in which she argued that womanliness "could be assumed and worn as a mask, both to hide the possession of masculinity and to avert the reprisals expected if she was found to possess it—much as a thief will turn out his pockets and ask to be searched to prove he has not the stolen goods." And therefore, she concluded, there was no difference at all between "genuine womanliness" and the "masquerade."[45] Lacan reacted to and expanded upon Rivière: "The fact that femininity takes refuge in this mask . . . has the strange consequence that, in the human being, virile display itself appears as feminine."[46] The Lacanian reading also argues that a woman is a man from whom something is missing (a man who is "castrated") and who masquerades in order to conceal this lack,[47] using her own body as a disguise. This prompted Judith Butler to suggest that masquerade might construct this exaggerated femininity in order to disguise bisexual possibilities that threaten the assumed heterosexual basis of the masquerade.[48] And Mary Ann Doane points out that Rivière ignored the joyful and playful aspects of this masquerade, limiting it to its anxious and painful aspects.[49] Our texts give equal time to the playful and the painful aspects of the gender masquerade, though different cultures weight them differently, Shakespeare emphasizing the playful, Hollywood in the 90s the painful—*The Crying Game* (1992), *Boys Don't Cry* (1999). The gender masquerade may also be used to deconstruct the idea of gender entirely or merely to invalidate one particular gender (guess which one?). A woman who dressed as a man remarked, "I suppose I could wear dresses, but then

I think I would just look like a man dressed in drag. . . . If I dress up and put on high heels, or makeup, or things like that, they will call me madame. But I'm not going to be a transvestite to myself." And Holly Devor, who interviewed her and other women who dressed as men, comments, "One is left wondering whether these women believed that average women, in the course of their normal everyday lives, look like transvestites and prostitutes. . . . Sadly, their view of 'typical females' was tainted by misogyny."[50] Or I would say, by a certain sort of mythology.

And this mythology is very old indeed. The *Kamasutra*, composed in Sanskrit in North India in the third century CE, presents the usual stereotyped gender roles (the passive, delicate woman, the active, rough man, and so forth), but it also acknowledges that people do, sometimes, reverse gender roles, particularly in the sexual position with the woman on top: "She does to him in return now whatever acts he demonstrated before. And, at the same time, she indicates that she is embarrassed and exhausted and wishes to stop."[51] The commentary, written in the thirteenth century CE, spells out the gender complications:

> All of this activity is said to be done with a woman's natural talent. The acts he demonstrated before are acts that he executed with roughness and ferocity, the man's natural talent; she now does these acts against the current of her own natural talent. She hits him hard, with the back of her hand and so forth, demonstrating her ferocity. And so, in order to express the woman's natural talent, even though she is not embarrassed, nor exhausted, and does not wish to stop, she indicates that she is embarrassed and exhausted and wishes to stop.

Since the text goes on to inform us that the woman "unveils her own feelings completely when her passion drives her to get on top,"[52] the commentator is saying that, when she acts like a man, she pretends to be a man and then she pretends to be a woman pretending to be a man.

By cross-dressing, the heroines in so many of these texts discover resources that they didn't know they possessed, a nature that needs to be liberated. They go through a male persona to release their full female sexuality. Because the idea of the fake always implies the idea of authenticity, to call a woman unwomanly you have to know what womanliness is. This is the lesson the drag queen teaches us. When a woman is being a woman among men, she is masquerading as the man's image of her or as her idea of the authentic woman. This is not, however, merely a feminist problem. The same thing can happen, though in different ways, far less often and with far less serious consequences, to men. It is surely difficult for many men to imitate men as an idealized social form, to live up to the macho football scenario. And although at present women in most parts of the world construct themselves more artificially than men, men have their masquerades, too, and in earlier periods men's costumes were often more elaborate than women's. Jean Cocteau's Beast (in *La Belle et la Bête*, 1946) dresses up in the elaborate costume of the eighteenth-century French court when he constructs himself as a human male in contrast not with a human female but with a bestial male. Indeed, if anatomy is destiny, then we need only look to the animal kingdom to see that the male may not be deadlier than the female but is usually a snappier dresser—think of the peacocks and the stags. But then, to the extent that anatomy is *not* destiny, that men and women are not (merely) peacocks and peahens, stags, and does, we do construct ourselves. Which is to say that we all masquerade not merely as our own multiple personalities but in a broader sense as our own genders and in some cases as other genders as well.

Conclusion
The Zen Diagram of the Self

Incognito ergo sum.

Sidney Morgenbesser (1922–2004)

The Truth beneath the Mask

Beyond what these stories tell us separately and in thematic clusters, what do they tell us all together? We assume that masquerades lie, and they often do, at least on the surface. But often masquerades tell a deeper truth, that masquerading as ourselves reaffirms an enduring self (or network of selves) inside us, which does not change even if our masquerades, intentional or helpless, make us look different to others. Yeats may have had this in mind when he wrote, "I think that all happiness depends on the energy to assume the mask of some other self; that all joyous or creative life is a re-birth as something not oneself, something which has no memory and is created in a moment and perpetually renewed."[1] After all, the very word *persona* originally designated the mask worn by actors in Greek tragedies, but the word means "that through which [*per*] the sound [of the actor's voice, *sona*] is heard." That is, the actor's presence was an integral part of the mask; he animated it, and it animated him.

Erving Goffman speaks of "the field of public life" wherein our public self must play its part, versus a place "backstage" where the individual can relax before having to put on the theatrical persona; only when we are alone can we take off the mask.[2] Goffman assumes that the private self is unmasked, that we are most genuinely ourselves when alone, an assumption I do not share. Rather, I think, we are never ourselves merely to ourselves but always in relation to others, even if only imagined others. Like Bishop Berkeley's tree in the quad, we exist only when someone sees us. We become the person we see mirrored in the eyes of others, ideally someone we love or someone who loves us. In the mythology of face-lifts and mind-lifts, love is what endures and survives when either consciousness or appearance is destroyed. In the mythology of reincarnation, people recognize one another across the barrier of death not with their minds or memories but with their hearts, their love, embedded in the body. Such stories seem to endorse the psychoanalytic construction of the construction of the self through the reflection that we see in those whom we love and who love us. They tell us that what endures of the self is love.

Jacques Lacan wrote about this relationship in what he calls the mirror stage, in which the dyadic relation of an infant to his mirror image (in a mirror or in his mother's face) makes him believe that he has a stable social identity, equated with his image. In this stage, the mother generates the illusion that she makes us real, the illusion that there is something on the other side of what we perceive that will complete us.[3] But as the child loses this mirror in growing away from the parent, discovering that he (with Lacan it is always he) is not in fact joined to his mother at the hip, or anywhere else, it is also the site of the loss of a stable sense of self. For the mirror stage is superseded by the symbolic stage, the world of language and hierarchy, which is reached by mastering the codes of culture represented by the father and by the phallus. This is the "other" who is, according to Lacan, "in the position of mediating between me and the double of myself, as if it were with my counterpart."[4] The Lacanian paradox is that one becomes trapped between the terror of losing one's mirror image and the desire for language, which requires the loss of that image. But this gain is also a loss, as Toril Moi argues: at this stage, "The speaking subject that says 'I am' is in fact saying 'I am he (she) who has lost something'—and the loss suffered is the loss of the imaginary identity with the mother and with the world. The sentence 'I am' could therefore best be translated as 'I am that which I am not', according to Lacan."[5] To be what one is not, as in this syllogism, is to be someone who masquerades as himself or herself.

We need an audience to play out the self and a mask to give us that refreshed, vivid sense of self that is inspired by actively playing a role, the frisson of the masquerade. Moreover, we project our best self outside of us to present it to the world. Upward hypocrisy[6] can be a very good thing. We wear a mask because we feel vulnerable and, paradoxically, want to attract the one person who will love us as we are without our mask; this is the double bind. For some people, like Goffman and like the women dancing behind the Ginger Rogers masks in *Shall We Dance?* the mask is a lie; but for some, like Ginger Rogers behind the mask, it is the truth.

If the normal face, the social face we put on "to meet the faces that [we] meet," as T. S. Eliot puts it, is already a covert mask, then the blatant mask may free another, more complex and passionate self, lure it out of its repression, create a safe house for it to live in. The mask reveals the truth hiding beneath the mask that is the face. The particularly hidden or repressed or subversive parts of the self may emerge most easily in a masquerade, which makes accessible parts of experience that are not always available. The fantasy is of the right to speak freely, to spill our secrets, to reveal our secret selves. There is a South Indian saying that you can say anything when you wear a mask over your face. In Venice, people wear masks to make possible encounters they have always wanted but not dared to initiate. Religious possession often functions as a mask in this way (and sometimes actually employs masks), especially for women, who are often strictly censored by their cultures except at those moments when the gods (or, more often, goddesses) speak through them, saying things that they would not be allowed to say in their own voices.

The attendant who demonstrates oxygen masks on airplanes before takeoff used to promise, "An attendant will tell you when it is safe to take off your mask"—but no one ever does. For most of us, it is never really safe—or true, or possible—to take off the mask. We prefer, rather, merely to glimpse the reality in the mask. We need our masks. If we always tried to be one single self, without our masks, the world would grind to a halt. With them, the world proceeds from self to self.

APPOINTMENT IN SAMSARA

The mythology of resurrection, remarriage, and reincarnation tells us that people often want to change but cannot, that reincarnation inevitably becomes self-imitation. Some of the face-lift films seem to be saying the same thing, that people want to change into other people but cannot, that they end up masquerading as themselves after all. The classic face-lift myth, by contrast, the story of Dorian Gray, is about people who do not seek change but fear it, who try in vain to avoid it, but they, too, fail to get what they want, experiencing the inevitable deterioration of helpless aging. Such myths tell us that we can neither change into someone else nor stay who we are but that only by trying in vain to change into someone else can we become who we are.

People who seem to change, in these stories, turn out to be people who are actually replaced by other people or by amnesiac forms of their earlier selves. They are different people, merely perceived by others as people who change. Let us first consider the myths that argue against the possibility of change and then the texts that argue for a way of changing without changing. For there is some truth in all of these fantasies, and they have different implications for our own possible uses of masks.

Many myths tell of our futile attempts to escape something that is an integral part of ourselves. The circular workings of fate force us back to the place where we are meant to be, however fast we may run in the other direction. There is a famous Orientalist parable on this theme, based on an ancient Arabic tale (though one not included in the *Arabian Nights*)[7] that Somerset Maugham told in his play *Sheppey* (1933) and that John O'Hara cited, a year later, as the epigraph for a novel to which he gave the title *Appointment in Samarra*:

> [Death speaks:] There was a merchant in Baghdad who sent his servant to market to buy provisions and in a little while the servant came back, white and trembling, and said, Master, just now when I was in the marketplace I was jostled by a woman in the crowd and when I turned I saw it was Death that jostled me. She looked at me and made a threatening gesture. Now, lend me your horse, and I will ride away from this city and avoid my fate. I will go to Samarra and there Death will not find me. The merchant lent him his horse, and the servant mounted it, and he dug his spurs in its flanks and as fast as the horse could gallop he went. Then the merchant went down to the marketplace and he saw me standing in the crowd and he came to me and said, Why did you make a threatening gesture to my servant when you saw him this morning? That was not a threatening gesture, I said, it was only a start of surprise. I was astonished to see him in Baghdad, for I had an appointment with him tonight in Samarra.

The phrase "appointment in Samarra" has come to signify the inevitability of death, but there are also other appointments from which we flee in vain, as Oedipus, fleeing the prediction about his mother and father, ran right to his mother and father. The past exerts its force whether we run toward it or away from it. Slavoj Zizek applies the story from Maugham to Oedipus: "The prophecy becomes true by means of its being communicated to the persons it affects and by means of his or her attempt to elude it: one knows in advance one's destiny, one tries to evade it, and it is by means of this very attempt that the predicted destiny realizes itself."[8]

The myths of self-impersonation apply this particular brand of fatalism to the selves from which we try, futilely, to escape, as Alice tried to get out of Looking-glass House, only to find that every path that seemed to lead out into the garden soon brought her back into the door of the house. In *Sullivan's Travels* (Preston Sturges 1941), Sullivan keeps trying to get away from Hollywood, but every time he hitch-hikes or jumps a freight train it takes him back to Hollywood. Finally he says: "No matter where I start from, I always end up back here in Hollywood." These stories tell us not merely that we can't run away from some impersonal fate, some malevolent gods, some old ladies snipping threads up in Olympus, or a veiled woman who makes a sign to us across a crowded marketplace but that we cannot run away from the people we are now to become someone else. The stories stress the inescapable gravitational pull and centripetal force of the circular drive toward self-impersonation. They argue that our hope of getting away from ourselves is always doomed to failure, that Thomas Wolfe was wrong, that in this sense at least, we cannot help but go home again. They affirm the Greek hell of Sisyphus, rolling the same rock almost to the top of the same mountain over and over again. When we have a chance to pretend, to become someone else, we still end up as the selves we were, reinventing the same wheel—the wheel that is the metaphor that Hindus and Buddhists use for the process of reincarnation, the cycle of samsara. This relentless wheel rolls, juggernaut-like, over the hopes held out to us by the current trend of reinvention, plastic surgery, therapy, self-help programs, twelve-step programs, change your nose, transform your life, get a life.

These texts do not necessarily imply that no one can ever change; people try, and some succeed, all the time in these tales (and, of course, in real life). But they teach us that there are headstrong headwinds working against us, that the force of the past is a deep, strong undercurrent pulling against change, as F. Scott Fitzgerald tells us at the end of *The Great Gatsby*: "So we beat on, boats against the current, born back ceaselessly into the past." Since samsara is not only a wheel but, more basically, a flowing river (the Sanskrit word literally means a "flowing together"), I would translate the concept from Islam to Hinduism and rename it the Appointment in Samsara.

LOOPHOLES

But several positive variants of the myth of self-imitation offer us escape hatches out of the circular trap of the Appointment in Samsara. These might also be called loopholes in Mikhail Bakhtin's sense, possible alternative meanings of our own words and hence of our story, our life. The loophole "accompanies the word like a shadow."[9] And since the loophole meaning may have a loophole, too, an alternative to that alternative, and so forth, the sum total of loopholes may form what Bakhtin calls a "vicious circle of self-consciousness," an infinite and self-reflexive regress, one alternative leading to another.

The Rabbi from Cracow

A Jewish story stands the samsara parable on its head by giving the protagonist the narrative position (though not the persona!) that Death has in the Arabic tale. In this first loophole, the person (or treasure) that we seek in vain when we run away to Baghdad (or, in this case, Prague, though it might have been Arden or Conneckticut) is awaiting us when we return home empty-handed in Samarra. This reading promises us that though we must, indeed, come home again, we can find there what we had hoped to find when we tried, in vain, to get away. The round-trip to the marital bed via the attempted—or imagined—extramarital affair is the voyage home via a fantastic odyssey, the discovery of the self that can be found only via the detour of the other. The story is Martin Buber's tale of the Rabbi from Cracow:

> Rabbi Eisik, son of Rabbi Jekel, lived in the ghetto of Cracow, the capital of Poland. One night, as Eisik slept, he had a dream, which told him to go far away to the Bohemian capital, Prague, where he would discover a hidden treasure, buried beneath the principal bridge leading to the castle of the Bohemian kings. After the dream had recurred twice, the pious Rabbi went to Prague and discovered sentries guarding the bridge there, day and night. He did not dare to dig, but he watched the bridge all day, until the captain of the guards asked him why he was there. When Rabbi Eisik told him about his dream, the officer laughed and said, "What sensible person would trust a dream? Why look, if I had been one to go trusting dreams, I should this very minute be doing just the opposite. I should have made such a pilgrimage as this silly one of yours, only in the opposite direction, but no doubt with the same result. Let me tell you my dream."
>
> Then the Bohemian, Christian officer of the guard told the Rabbi that he had dreamt of a voice: "It spoke to me of Cracow, commanding me to go there and to search there for a great treasure in the house of a Jewish rabbi whose name would be Eisik son of Jekel. The treasure was to have been discovered buried in the dirty corner behind the stove. Eisik son of Jekel!" the captain laughed again. "Fancy going to Cracow and pulling down the walls of every house in the ghetto, where half of the men are called Eisik and the other half Jekel! Eisik son of Jekel, indeed!" And he laughed again. The Rabbi listened eagerly, bowed deeply, thanked his stranger-friend, and hurried straightway back to his distant home, where he dug in the neglected corner of his house and discovered the treasure which put an end to all his misery.[10]

Buber's parable suggests that our own knowledge of our submerged identities always exists on some subconscious level, but some of us must learn these identities from someone else. So, too, the story, the narrative, always preexists but often must be heard from someone else.

People who have lived in many different countries, carrying all their houses about in their minds like snails their shells, sometimes wonder where home is; perhaps where we were little, with our mommy and daddy? But this, too, is a fantasy. Home, now, in this age of globalization, must always be somewhere else, like Prague when you are in Cracow, or Cracow when you are in Prague. There is no one home (in both senses of "one"—nobody home and no single home); the planet is our home. Many myths support this natural human tendency, the wish to find home, to get home, the *nostos* of the Family Romance, sailing home to our parents to be acknowledged as their child. For some it may be true, but for most of us it is a fantasy, inspired by the deeply repressed suspicion that we are not, in any real sense, our parents' children, that we live in a world entirely different from theirs, and that, as the man said, we cannot go home again.

A variant of the story of the Rabbi from Cracow occurs in the novel of *Random Harvest*, when Harrison shows Charles a story he's written in a style that is a cross between Tolstoi and Gogol:

> A Russian soldier returning from the front after the Revolution . . . roamed about the country trying to find where he lived. . . . All he could give was the name of the village and a description of it that might equally have applied to ten thousand other Russian villages. . . . He was run over by a train and carried to a neighbouring village, where he died without knowing that it actually was the one he'd been looking for.[11]

This is the story of Charles's life. The home that Charles is dying in without recognizing it is his wife. T. S. Eliot, in "Little Gidding" (in *Four Quartets*), wrote of this circling back to a town that was to him what Cracow was to the Rabbi:

> We shall not cease from exploring
> And the end of all our exploring
> Will be to arrive where we started
> And know the place for the first time.

Second Naïveté

What the myths depict as discovery or recognition we may also read as change, transformation. To uncover a self that has been concealed until now is also to become a new self that is in some, but not all, ways identical to the self making that discovery and that change. Characters in myths do not change, like the protagonist of a bildungsroman, but they do learn. The self is a work in progress, a process, not just a thing, even a slippery thing like a mask.

The Rabbi's return is an example of what the philosopher and theologian Paul Ricoeur called a "second naïveté": an innocence that has traveled through loss of innocence to an apparently unchanged but actually quite different sort of innocence.[12] This is the second loophole: the self to which we return is not the same self from which we began. It is the Heracleitus effect: we cannot step twice into the same river, especially when that river is samsara. The stories teach us that even when we seem to meet the same self again and again, dovetailed in among the alternating layers of masks, like the filling in a mille-feuille or a seven-layer cake, it is not the same self; the mask has taught it to speak truth to power. The difference between the two selves was subtly captured by Woody Allen in his description of the mythical beast called the Great Roe, which has the body of a lion and the head of a lion but not the same lion.[13]

Rosalind-as-Ganymede-as-Rosalind is bolder, more playful, more confident than Rosalind tout court (or Rosalind-as-Rosalind), emboldened both by the double mask and by the level of masculinity embedded in the mediating personality. King Udayana-as-Manorama-as-Udayana is able to make love to his new woman under the eyes of his queen and get away with it, as he fails to do in his own persona. Madhumati-as-Madhavi-as-Madhumati is able to take revenge for her death as Madhumati herself could not do. Charles in *Random Harvest* is not the same as Smithy but is a different person, a third person after Charles and Smithy. Charles might simply have gone on being what everyone he knew regarded as his first self, and we might regard as his third self, had he not instinctively felt that the second self, between them, was somehow truer, better, in some way closer to his ideal self. The Charles Rainier whom Paula embraces after living with him for years as Mrs. Rainier is not the Charles Rainier who was wounded in the trenches at Arras. It matters at which stage of Charles's amnesia we meet him, and it matters whether the Filmistan villagers are villagers pretending to be film extras or film extras pretending to be villagers. And sometimes, as in films like *Memory of Love* or *Total Recall* or C. S. Lewis's Narnia books or the later volumes of Frank Baum's Oz books, the protagonist remains at the end in what began as the secondary level of reality.

The man who had a sex-change operation in order to become a lesbian, or the man who married a lesbian and underwent a sex-change operation to become a woman, may seem tautological to some people ("All that trouble just to end up in bed with a woman anyway"),[14] but not if we acknowledge the existential authenticity of the process of change itself. As Lacan wisely remarked, after a transformative experience you cannot always go back to being who you were, and a great part of your truth is recognized in the alternative state. He draws this conclusion out of the Chinese paradox of the philosopher who dreams he is a butterfly and awakens to wonder if he is Choang Tsu who had dreamed he was a butterfly or a butterfly dreaming he is Choang Tsu.[15] This is Lacan's gloss on that story:

> When Choang-tsu wakes up, he may ask himself whether it is not the butterfly who dreams that he is Choang-tsu. Indeed, he is right, and doubly so, first because it proves he is not mad, he does not regard himself as absolutely identical with Choang-tsu and, secondly, because he does not fully understand how right he is. In fact, it is when he was the butterfly that he apprehended one of the roots of his identity—that he was, and is, in his essence, that butterfly who paints himself with his own colours—and it is because of this that, in the last resort, he is Choang-tsu. This is proved by the fact that, when he is the butterfly, the idea does not occur to him to wonder whether, when he is Choang-tsu awake, he is not the butterfly that he is dreaming of being.[16]

The loss of innocence, the change that takes place during the double masquerade, puts the twist into Bakhtin's "vicious circle of self-consciousness" that makes it into a Möbius strip, that makes the path of the surface change sides infinitely, so that one side leads to the other and back again, and we come back to the same line on a point farther on.

The Happy Hypocrite

The third loophole is the hope that wearing a mask can change us not into the mask but into someone who has been transformed by the experience of masquerading. The man in Kobo Abe's novel *The Face of Another*, who wears a handsome mask over his hideously deformed face, says: "I prayed for the fairy-tale miracle of awakening one morning to find the mask stuck firmly on my face, to discover it had become my real face. . . . But the miracle, of course, did not happen."[17] The mask does change the personality of the man who wears it, so that in a sense he becomes his mask (this is emphasized in the film version of the novel), but his face remains the same. The more literal transformation of the face itself does happen, however, in a whimsical story by Max Beerbohm, "The Happy Hypocrite," which argues that the face undergoes a transformation to make the mask coincide with the face. Here is the plot:

> Lord George Hell was wicked. He fell in love with a good woman named Jenny Mere, but she said, "I can never be your wife. I can never be the wife of any man whose face is not saintly. Your face, my Lord, mirrors, it may be, true love for me, but it is even as a mirror long tarnished by the reflexion of this world's vanity. . . . That man, whose face is wonderful as are the faces of the saints, to him I will give my true love." Lord Hell went to Mr. Aeneas, the mask-maker, who gave him the mask of a saint—"spiritual, yet handsome." He had it altered a bit so that it was also "a mirror of true love . . . the mask of a saint who loves dearly." He determined to wear it for the rest of his life. But his old girlfriend La Gambogi still recognized him immediately and called him by name, saying, "I cannot let go so handsome a lover. . . . Why, you never looked so lovingly at me in all your life!" He pretended not to know her.
>
> Jenny Mere instantly loved him. He told her his name was George Heaven. They married and lived together in a cottage in the woods. After a month, La Gambogi found them. She said to him, "Your wife's mask is even better than yours." La Gambogi begged him, in front of the astonished and uncomprehending Jenny, to unmask just once for her, to show her the dear face she had so often caressed, the lips that were dear to her. When he refused, she clawed at his face. The mask came off, revealing his face: it was, line for line, feature for feature, the same as his mask had been, a saint's face. At first he thought he must still have his former face, and he told Jenny to forget him, but she said, "I am bewildered by your strange words. Why did you woo me under a mask? And why do you imagine I could love you less dearly, seeing your own face?" He looked into her

eyes and saw in them the reflection of his own face. He was filled with joy and wonder. She said, "Kiss me with your own lips."

As in the story of Dorian Gray, the face reveals the soul, the moral substance of the person. That being so, to change the face is to change the person. Many actors imitate the facial expressions of the characters they portray in order to experience their emotions and then to re-project them on the stage.[18] In one reading, Aristotle's *Nicomachean Ethics* implies that a person who tries to lead an ethical life is imitating a virtuous person, wearing the mask of a virtuous person; and that as the years go by he will actually become the virtuous person, the mask to which he so aspires.[19] A similar logic underlies the Hindu argument that if the demon Ravana were to take on Rama's form, he would take on Rama's mind as well, and presumably, paradoxically, he would stop wanting to change into Rama.[20] A variant of the same logic surfaced in a conversation between a woman Ph.D. student of my acquaintance and her advisor, an older and wiser woman. The student's boyfriend had treated her very badly indeed, and her advisor called him a schmuck. No, responded the student, he just acts like a schmuck. On the contrary, replied the advisor, the definition of a schmuck is someone who acts like a schmuck.[21]

A Balinese dancer who works with masks once said that the face inside the mask must become the same as the mask; the dancer has to generate the emotion within himself and project it through the mask. There are also particular times offstage when the performance of a conscious self-imitation, or anti–Method acting, comes in very handy. A person who has undergone a trauma, such as a rape, may experience it like a death, so that she feels as if she had become a different person and tries to keep going by pretending to be who she was, trying to behave as she knows she used to behave, until she can remember how it actually feels to be who she is. There is a danger here, of course; we must distinguish between putting on a mask of what we already are, or want to become, and becoming a mask we do not intend to become.[22] (Kurt Vonnegut, in *Mother Night*, shows us that we are what we pretend to be and, therefore, should be very careful about what we pretend to be.) Pierre Marivaux pointed out this danger in wearing a mask: "Deception often leads to being deceived; the trickster is duped because his own reflection blurs: 'I had a mask that hid my face and I no longer knew who I was when I looked at myself in the mirror.'"[23]

This happens in *The Mask* (Chuck Russell, 1994). Stanley Ipkiss (Jim Carrey), a mild man whom everyone pushes around, finds a magic mask that changes him into a cartoon character who cannot be killed, a violent and hypersexual superhero who wreaks mayhem among criminal types who oppose him. At first he welcomes the transformation, as Dr. Jekyll at first enjoyed his ability to summon his alter ego Hyde at will and then to dismiss him. Even in his real life, without the mask, he begins to behave with the kind of aggression he learned from the mask, which in retrospect seems merely to free a repressed aspect of his own personality, replete with the powers that he has always fantasized having. ("It brings your innermost desires to life," Ipkiss explains.) But then the mask takes over and rages out of control, just as Hyde began to appear unbidden, and Ipkiss's world turns topsy-turvy. The nice woman who likes him (Amy Yasbeck) turns out to be dishonest, merely using him, while the criminal woman who was using him (Cameron Diaz) is true to him. They, too, were wearing masks. A psychiatrist on television says, "We all wear masks, metaphorically speaking. We suppress our darker sides." When Ipkiss goes to see him in person, the psychiatrist insists, "It's a metaphor, not to be taken literally," but the myth, as usual, brings the metaphor to life.[24]

The Deep Surface

The fourth loophole is the realization that the mask may prove to be more alive than the face, the surface deeper than the depth. By masquerading as ourselves, therefore, we gain access to a more deeply submerged self. Oscar Wilde put these words into the mouth of Lord Henry in the *Picture of Dorian Gray*: "It is only shallow people who do not judge by appearances. The true mystery of the world is the visible, not the invisible." A character in Edgar Allan Poe's "The Purloined Letter" (1845) had already said it: "There is such a thing as being too profound. Truth is not always in a well. In fact, as regards the more important knowledge, I do believe that she is invariably superficial."[25] In other words, things *are* the way they seem, only more so (or, as the case may be, less so). This insight was turned on its head by a woman in a novel by Peter De Vries. When the narrator remarks to her that a particular man "has a lot more depth," she replies, "Only on the surface. Deep down, he's shallow." This means both that shallowness, the surface, is deep, and that apparent depth is shallow. When another character in the de Vries book remarks, "Hubert thinks everything is affectation; he takes nothing at face value," yet another replies, "But nothing can be taken at face value. Least of all pure naturalness. That's the ultimate affectation. It's the attempt to cover our masks with a bare face."[26] Here again, the debt is to Wilde's Lord Henry, who said, "Being natural is simply a pose, and the most irritating pose I know."[27]

A woman in a Richard Stern novel, invoking Colette's concept of "passionate dupery," quips: "Men don't realize sincerity isn't spontaneous; it's only after women master passionate dupery that we skip to sincerity."[28] Stern, de Vries, and Wilde may have been inspired by Nietzsche, who remarked that all that is deep loves the mask, needs a mask,[29] and who praised the Greeks for knowing how to "stop courageously at the surface, the fold, the skin, to adore appearance, to believe in forms, tones, words, in the whole Olympus of appearance. Those Greeks were superficial—*out of profundity.*"[30] Lord Henry's bon mot suggests that the surface—in this case, the mask—is the real image, the face beneath it the false image. This is what Henry Abramovitch has called "the transformation of identity through disguise—how we must appear as we are not, in order to become more truly who we are . . . [to] allow surface to touch depth."[31]

Paul Ricoeur suggests a rather different way of allowing the surface to stay in touch with the depth of a text. He proposes a dialectic between the hermeneutic of suspicion, the idea (developed by Jürgen Habermas, Sigmund Freud, and Karl Marx) that the meaning is hidden beneath the surface, and the hermeneutic of retrieval, the idea (developed by Friedrich Schleiermacher and Hans-Georg Gadamer) that the meaning is on the surface. Ricoeur advised tacking back and forth between the two[32] or (as Jacques Derrida puts it) finding meaning in the space between the two. This is another form of second naïveté: once you've worked your way through the suspicion, you can go back to a retrieval that finds meanings *below* the level of suspicion.

The Authentic Postmodern Copy

Postmodernism has called our attention to the copy that is, in some sense, more real than the original, just as the surface is deeper than the depth. And this is our fifth loophole: to be a copy is to be more, not less, authentic than the original. At the very least, only when you see the fake do you understand what is authentic: for A not to be B, you have to know what B is. Roland Barthes raised the issue in his analysis of the statue and portrait that copied the castrato in Balzac's *Sarrasine.* Terry Eagleton has summarized the postmodern attitude to the copy in concise, clear language, for which one is always grateful but particularly grateful in writings about postmodernism. He says:

> Since there can be no talk of authenticity without the concept of a fake, the phony is the true ground of great art. . . . Postmodernism awards high marks for non-originality. . . . Postmodernism is entranced by imitation but sets itself sternly against mimesis, or the notion of realist representation, so that what copies reproduce is not the world but other copies, in a ceaseless chain of simulacra.[33]

The authenticity that the true copy has lost is not entirely lost, however. Now it is the proud possession of the fake, as Eagleton points out: "Being only human, even the most savvy and sophisticated of forgers find themselves back-sliding into truth and stumbling into reality in moments of forgivable weakness." Hillel Schwartz has plumbed the depths (or, as the case may be, the surface) of the culture of the copy, and Judith Butler and other postmodern feminists have argued that "gay" is to "straight" not as "original" to "copy" but as "copy" to "copy."

That this insight has been rediscovered rather than discovered by recent authors and critics should surely be evident from all the texts I have cited so far; it is a staple not only of myths and films but of English literature. In 1893, Henry James, in "The Real Thing," described a truly aristocratic couple, fallen upon hard times, who agreed to sit for the aristocrats in an artist's illustrations for a novel. The couple pointed out that they were "the real thing," but they were not convincing, not lifelike, and so he hired, instead, a lower-class woman, who played aristocrats very well. The actual aristocratic lady "was always a lady certainly, and into the bargain was always the same lady. She was the real thing, but always the same thing."[34] Finally, the artist used the male aristocrat as the model of a servant, and eventually the two aristocrats, no longer called to model, performed menial tasks for him and actually became his servants until he sent them away. Similarly, in all the many variants, literary and cinematic, of *The Prisoner of Zenda* (beginning with the novel by Sir Anthony Hope [1894] and continuing on screen, first and best when Ronald Colman buckled on his swash in the 1937 film directed by John Cromwell[35]), the copy (the man who stands in for the king) is a far better man than the real king, who, when he is finally reinstated, vows to copy the copy in order to rule his subjects as he should.

The Multiplicity of Masks

The sixth loophole is the realization that each of us is already a lot of people, that we have all these people inside us. And so when, failing to be the other person we hoped to change into, we fall back to our default position, we find a different form of ourselves awaiting us, a different one of our many selves. We are imprisoned in our self, but it is very big prison. When we put on a mask we have a choice, like Lon Chaney, of a thousand faces, and in a sense, they are all our own. The multiple forms or layers of the self are like the multiple variants of a story or the multiple interpretations of a myth, all somehow alike and all somehow different. Thus Charles in *Random Harvest* must learn that, as Stanley Cavell puts it, "the woman who has been resourceful nurse to him, then faithful secretary, then brilliant hostess for him, is one and the same woman, the one with whom he had once bestirred himself to have a child,"[36] just as Chudala's husband came to understand that his wife was friend, brother, sympathizer, servant, guru, companion, wealth, happiness, the Vedic canon, abode, and slave. There are limits: we cannot, perhaps, choose to be Einstein or Marilyn Monroe. There are people who believe we can only choose to be either Jekyll or Hyde, but I think there is a little more wiggle room in there.

Some stories begin and end with the relatively simple assumption that the mask is false and that the face underneath it is real. Never venturing beyond this first level, these stories give us a happy ending: we find the true self, take off the mask, and all ends well—or not so well, as in the case of Oedipus. Others turn this assumption on its head and argue that the mask is what is true, the face underneath it false. In either case, the stories that assume a mere duality of selves—self versus mask—imagine pairs that are mutual referents of one another, such as two genders or nature/art, nature/culture, yin and yang. The polarized variants are fairly easy to play with: Jekyll to Hyde, communist to anti-communist, virgin to whore.

But even the dualistic toggle, if it happens more than once, destabilizes the dualistic paradigm, so that Rosalind plucks out one of her selves as Rosalind, then another as Rosalind-as-Ganymede, and then another as Rosalind-as-Ganymede-as-Rosalind. The copy of the copy produces an infinite regress once we break out of the simple dualism of surface and depth and acknowledge the equal authenticity of each version of the text. And some stories reject the ultimate reality of the mask or of the face beneath it and move on to more complex insights. We see in them an implicit belief in a single self that is revealed and concealed in intricate ways, but we also see glimpses of dual and, occasionally, multiple "authentic" selves. These selves are manipulated by, but also manipulate, self-imitation, self-cuckolding, and self-reference, all connected, all different, each inspiring a different piece of the total narrative puzzle. Such stories break open the theme of single identity to reveal an infinite possibility of variations, an infinite regress (or *mise en abîme*, or endless displacement) implicit in any narrative in which x imitates y while y imitates x, and so forth. The spies in our stories are usually of the dual kind (an Englishman pretending to be a German pretending to be an Englishman), while the stories about transmigration are of the potentially infinite kind.

It may be, as many have argued, that it is natural for human beings to think in twos,[37] but not all important things actually come in twos. Barbara Johnson asks the right questions about this:

> What is the relation between a divided unity and a duality? Are the two 2's synonymous? Is a "Bi-Part Soul," for example, actually composed of two wholes? Or is it possible to conceive of a division which would not lead to two separate parts, but only to a problematization of the idea of unity? . . . If the doubles are forever redividing or multiplying, does the number 2 really apply? If 1 = 2, how can 2 = 1 + 1? If what is uncanny about the doubles is that they never stop doubling up, would the number 2 still be uncanny if it did stop at a truly dual symmetry?[38]

In this way Johnson deconstructs the toggle-switch model of the self, or the cybernetic on-or-off that makes life seem like a game of Ping-Pong.

Many films mock multiple identities, often through the use of a hall of mirrors. Groucho Marx encounters multiple Grouchos in the famous mirror scene in *Duck Soup* (Leo McCarey, 1933), and there are multiple Ginger Rogerses in *Shall We Dance?* (Mark Sandrich 1937), multiple Rita Hayworths in the mirrors in *The Lady from Shanghai* (Orson Welles 1947), and multiple (but different) Leslie Carons in *An American in Paris* (Vincente Minnelli 195), a film in which Oscar Levant (whose 1990 autobiography was titled *Memoirs of an Amnesiac*) fantasizes that he is the pianist, the conductor, all the members of the orchestra, and all the members of the audience, all of whom are the same. In John McTiernan's 1999 remake of *The Thomas Crown Affair* (already a double of the 1968 version with Steve McQueen), Pierce Brosnan outfoxes the police by hiding in plain sight as a man in a bowler hat straight out of a Magritte painting—surrounded by hundreds of other men wearing Magritte bowler hats. In *Being John Malkovich* (Spike Jonze, 1999), Malkovich (playing Malkovich) goes through the portal that puts him inside his own mind and finds himself in a dining room in which everyone is wearing his face and all they are saying is "Malkovich Malkovich Malkovich." There are also multiple doubles of Jack Nicholson in a theatrical number staged in *Something's Gotta Give* (Nancy Meyers, 2003).

Marcel Proust wrote (in 1923) of the multiple selves:

> [A]t every moment, there was one more of those innumerable and humble "selves" that compose our personality which was still unaware of Albertine's departure and must be informed of it; I was obliged ... to announce ... to all these "selves" ... the calamity that had ... occurred ... [S]ome of these "selves" ... I had not encountered for a long time ... For instance, ... the "self" that I was when I was having my hair cut. I had forgotten this "self," and his arrival made me burst into tears, as, at a funeral, does the appearance of an old retired servant.[39]

These selves are the Greek chorus in Proust's erotic tragedy; they are his readers even before we are.

Virginia Woolf, in *Orlando* (1928), wrote of the role of the name in discerning one particular self among many selves:

> [I]f there are (at a venture) seventy-six different times all ticking in the mind at once, how many different people are there not—Heaven help us—all having lodgment at one time or another in the human spirit? Some say two thousand and fifty-two. . . . Hence the astonishing changes we see in our friends. But . . . the selves of which we are built up, one on top of another, as plates are piled on a waiter's hand, have attachments elsewhere, sympathies, little constitutions and rights of their own, call them what you will (and for many of these things there is no name) so that one will only come if it is raining, another in a room with green curtains, another when Mrs. Jones is not there, another if you can promise it a glass of wine—and so on; for everybody can multiply from his own experience the difficult terms which his different selves have made with him—and some are too wildly ridiculous to be mentioned in print at all. . . . [Sometimes], for some unaccountable reason, the conscious self, which is the uppermost, and has the power to desire, wishes to be nothing but one self. This is what some people call the true self, and it is, they say, compact of all the selves we have it in us to be;

commanded and locked up by the Captain self, the Key self, which amalgamates and controls them all.[40]

Since we do have all these masks, personae, selves, within us, how foolish we are to let the "Captain self" lock them up, how foolish we are to tell lies in order to preserve the one mask that we think is who we really are and/or who we should be perceived as. The eponymous hero/ine of Virginia Woolf's novel experiences the layers of gender reversals faced by his namesake in *As You Like It*, in which Orlando characterizes his Rosalind as "of many parts," having distilled within her "many faces, eyes, and hearts," including "Helen's cheek, but not her heart; Cleopatra's majesty; Atalanta's better part."

Robert Jay Lifton, in *The Protean Self*, posits a multiplicity of selves within us that lead us to identify with other selves outside us, so we are doubly not one, inside (a multitude) and outside (connected to a multitude). Moreover, the protean self "can draw images from far places and render them its own 'memories.'"[41] So we can steal memories from other places and make them our own, as the villains do in the science fiction films and as metaphysically gifted people do in the myths of transmigration. The eponymous hero of Woody Allen's *Zelig* (1983) becomes black when he is with black people, fat when he is with fat people, and so on, because each individual calls up a response from that same aspect inside him. Zelig does, in a mythically exaggerated form, what we all do all the time.

But many people cling to the old dualistic model of the self and the mask. The face-lift mentality denies the present, the reformed alcoholic (or the fanatical religious convert) the past, but neither can accept the multiplicity of selves. The fanatical belief that I am (only) the new I, the now I, makes it impossible to keep, let alone to cherish, so much as a hair of the head of the then I, the old I. As Oliver says of himself in *As You Like It* (4.3), "'Twas I; but 'tis not I. I do not shame to tell you what I was, since my conversion so sweetly tastes, being the thing I am." This is also the mentality of the old communists who became rabid anticommunists when they were disillusioned by Stalin, and of the people who clean up some particularly messy aspect of their lives with such monomania that they hate their former partners, the people who knew them when. Such people seem to fear that they will turn into pillars of salt if they so much as glance back at their former selves. This self-loathing is shared by certain scholars who renounce the work, often extremely good work, they did under the influence of the sort of scholars who later turned out to have the wrong sort of politics—the deconstructionist Paul de Man, the Indo-Europeanist Georges Dumézil, the psychologist C. G. Jung.

A very different problem is posed by people who suffer from multiple personality (or borderline personality) disorders, like those of the woman whose story was told in *The Three Faces of Eve* (1957) or the people described in the aptly named book *Lost in the Mirror*:[42] people who have so many selves that they have no abiding sense of self, who feel hollow inside, all mask and no stable self. It is, of course, notoriously difficult to draw an objective line between healthy (rather than merely culturally accepted) and pathological fantasies. But I would venture to suggest that in the stories of pathological multiple selves, the multiplicity is experienced passively, helplessly, and with that special terror that Freud called "the uncanny" (*Unheimlich*). The pathological amnesiacs feel lost in the maze of selves, like Queen Vasavadatta suddenly confronted with the nightmare of a double she did not dream up. We can see the transition to this state from the happier multiplicity when John L. Sullivan in *Sullivan's Travels* first pretends to be a poor, disenfranchised person, which he experiences as a frivolous, happy lark, and then suddenly and helplessly becomes a poor, disenfranchised person and finds himself in a very real hell. Involuntary masks are also imposed by race and gender, not to mention the masks our parents bequeath to us, often simultaneously making us incapable of wearing them.

By contrast, the people who actively and knowingly accumulate all their former selves, who don't kill off their past selves, believe that all their selves are them, even though all selves are not created equal. The Marschallin accepts as her selves the little girl and the old woman and the woman of the present moment, about to lose her young lover. The transmigrating self consists of all forms of us. We can't remember them, but we were them, and we will be them. The past is in us, and the future. So the trick is to convert the dualistic paradigm into the open-ended, multiple model, by decentering the conventions of the self, and this is what masquerading does.

Tautological Self-Coincidence

Sometimes the triple-cross masquerade is the only way a person can bring the various selves together, like the moment when, as a camera is focused or the examining ophthalmologist splits the eye chart into two identical charts, the two separate images finally join and lock into place together. This is the seventh loophole: often the only way people can coincide with their own stories, or with their own selves, is through self-imitation. Zizek tells us, "The Lacanian definition of a fool is somebody who believes in his immediate identity with himself; somebody who is not capable of a dialectically mediated distance towards himself, like a king who thinks he is a king."[43] And so we must find ways to mediate that distance. Bakhtin points out some of the ways in which the author may "coincide" with a character he creates, which is as difficult for the author to achieve as lifting himself up by his own hair.[44] But the characters in our stories are, themselves, authors of their masquerading selves, and I want to argue, so are we all. Bakhtin wrote of this, too, of the difficulty people "in life," as opposed to fiction, have in coinciding with other people or, finally, with themselves: "I can remember myself, . . . but . . . I shall never coincide with myself."[45] David Shulman, too, speaks of a kind of momentary tautology[46] or "tautological self-coincidence":[47] "In order to overcome self-alienation, we must learn to pretend to be ourselves. The self is a kind of coincidence, and most of us find it very difficult to coincide with ourselves except by masquerading."[48]

Zizek finds it not only difficult but impossible: "In a universe in which all are looking for the true face beneath the mask, the best way to lead them astray is to wear the mask of truth itself. But it is impossible to maintain the coincidence of mask and truth."[49] Our stories, however, seem to be siding with Bakhtin and against Zizek. What we might call, with Shulman, "tautological masquerading" brings our chaotic selves into alignment at a tautological moment, when our many identities flow together. But it is not really a tautology, because the circling back of the self brings the masquerader back to a different self.

Hiding in Plain Sight

Hiding in plain sight may reveal or conceal the truth, and each has its uses. This is the eighth loophole out of the circle of samsara, and it may be used in two very different ways: putting on a mask that is the same as the face may sometimes reveal the secret (that there is no secret), but at other times it may intentionally conceal that very secret. As for revelation, Lacan had this to say: "[W]e rediscover a secret into which truth has always initiated her lovers, and through which they learn that it is in hiding that she offers herself to them *most truly*."[50] As Mary Ann Doane puts it, "Deception, far from distorting truth, operates a double negation by . . . concealing the secret that there is no secret."[51] It is an old Talmudic truism that the hidden meaning may be the most literal. Hiding in plain sight is a particularly good way to reveal something that you secretly want to reveal but must pretend to want to conceal. The repressed that insists on returning, the buried thought that fights to be spoken, often leads people with secrets to blurt them out. Philip Roth remarks of the "passing" (fictional) Coleman Silk, who dropped heavy hints about his "true race": "As it is a human thing to have a secret, it is also a human thing, sooner or later, to reveal it."[52] And Michael Miller remarked of the "passing" (nonfictional) Anatole Broyard, "Freud talked about the repetition compulsion. With Anatole, it's interesting that he was constantly hiding it and in some ways constantly revealing it."[53]

Our discovery of the tautological coincidence of the self is also a transformation into a newly coincided self, as it were, and this deceptively simple statement about deceptive simplicity tells us that, after the masquerade, we discover that the mask was the same as the face all along. Kobo Abe uses a mathematical analogy: "I was dazzled by the double aspect of the mask—was it the negation of my real face or actually a new face? . . . In mathematics there are 'imaginary numbers,' strange numbers which, when squared, become minus. They have points of similarity with masks, for putting one mask over another would be the same as not putting on any at all."[54] Others, too, have capitalized upon this counterintuitive intuition about self-imitation. Groucho Marx, in *Duck Soup*, remarked, "Chicolini may look like an idiot and talk like an idiot, but don't let that fool you: he *is* an idiot." Sir Rudolf Bing (tyrannical director of the Metropolitan Opera for many years) stole this line from Groucho when he remarked of himself, "Don't be misled; behind that cold, austere, severe exterior, there beats a heart of stone."[55]

Hiding in plain sight is also, however, a good way to conceal something that you pretend to be revealing. William Congreve said it in *The Double Dealer* (1694): "No mask like open truth to cover lies, As to go naked is the best disguise." Hamlet conceals his madness by pretending to be mad.[56] Margaret, in the film *Random Harvest*, hides the truth in plain sight in this way when she jokes with Charles that the woman he seeks "might even be me," thus short-circuiting his own misgivings. It's an old literary trick: in the *Mahabharata*, when the Pandava brothers are forced to go into exile in disguise, the gambler Yudhishthira masquerades as a gambler, while the womanizing Arjuna masquerades as a cross-dressing, androgynous dancing master and the gluttonous Bhima as the cook.[57] These masks represent not merely who the Pandavas really are but who they hope they are or fear they are. Yudhishthira, a notorious loser, is now a winning gambler; in the Peter Brook film of the *Mahabharata*, a man who suspects that the gambler is Yudhishthira is put off the trail when he considers, "If he wins at dice, he can't be Yudhishthira."

On one of the many occasions when Tristan, exiled by King Mark, returned to court in disguise, he appeared as a madman with a shaved head, wearing a fisherman's clothes. When King Mark asked him what he sought there, he said:

> "Isolde, whom I love so well; I bring my sister with me, Brunehild, the beautiful. Come, take her, you are weary of the Queen. Take you my sister and give me here Isolde, and I will hold her and serve you for her love." When everyone laughed and asked his name, he replied, "Tristan, that loved the Queen so well, and still till death will love her."[58]

But no one took him seriously. He had invented a sister named, of all things, Brunehild, borrowing her, perhaps, from the neighboring Austrian epic, and the outrageousness of this intertextual fiction then masked the literal truthfulness of his next statement: that he is Tristan, and is in love with the Queen. Framed in the lie about Brunehild, this truth, too, appeared to be a lie. Thus Tristan pretends to be a fool who pretends to be Tristan. He speaks the truth as if it were a lie, and Isolde sees through the double twist and recognizes it, but the king does not. In Béroul's version of this incident, Tristan-as-leper not only imitates himself but includes Isolde and Mark himself in his masquerade when he tells King Mark about his (the leper's) courtly lady: "Good king, her husband was a leper; I made love to her, and I contracted the disease from our union. But there is only one woman more beautiful than she: the beautiful Isolde. She even dresses as the other one did."[59] Has the same name, too.

The locus classicus for this particular form of self-reference is Edgar Allan Poe's story of the letter hidden in plain sight, the letter that masquerades as a letter, "The Purloined Letter." The plot, at least, is simple:

> A certain man had a letter with which he threatened to blackmail the Queen of France. A man named Dupin, who was employed to get it, realized that it was displayed in plain sight on the mantle, where no one would think to look for it. He then took it and replaced it with a facsimile, thinking that the blackmailer, "being unaware that the letter is not in his possession, . . . will proceed with his exactions as if it was. Thus will he inevitably commit himself, at once, to his political destruction."

Dupin explains his logic through the analogy of schoolboys playing a game in which one holds an odd or even number of marbles in his hand, concealed, and the other must guess whether the number is odd or even:

> "Now, with a simpleton a degree above the first, he would have reasoned thus: 'This fellow finds that in the first instance I guessed odd, and, in the second, he will propose to himself, upon the first impulse, a simple variation from even to odd, as did the first simpleton; but then a second thought will suggest that this is too simple a variation, and finally he will decide upon putting it even as before. I will therefore guess even;'— he guesses even, and wins."

And the narrator comments, "It is merely an identification of the reasoner's intellect with that of his opponent."[60]

Dupin drops another hint to the solution of the puzzle through another analogy: a game played with a map, the object of which is "to find a given word—the name of town, river, state or empire—any word, in short, upon the motley and perplexed surface of the chart":

> [T]he adept selects such words as stretch, in large characters, from one end of the chart to the other. These, like the over-largely lettered signs and placards of the street, escape observation by dint of being excessively obvious; and here the physical oversight is precisely analogous with the moral inapprehension by which the intellect suffers to pass unnoticed those considerations which are too obtrusively and too palpably self-evident.[61]

This device was taken up in a film about espionage, *Five Graves to Cairo* (Billy Wilder, 1943), in which the Germans "hide" the marks of the locations of the weapons stores by making them into the most obvious thing: the five letters that stretch across the map of E G Y P T .

Real people, too, do this. We have seen it in the life of Guy Burgess, and it even works with horses. When the public interest in the great racehorse Seabiscuit, in the 1930s, became so fanatic that it interfered with his training, his trainers fooled the newspapermen who wanted to see how fast the horse could run by running in his place on workout gallops a horse named Grog, who looked just like Seabiscuit. Eventually, when this dodge was discovered and the press knew about Grog, the trainers were able to relax and exercise the real Seabiscuit, whom the newsmen mistook for Grog even when he wore the halter with "Seabiscuit" on the brass nameplate. As Laura Hillenbrand tells it: "They found that as easy as it was to convince people that Grog was Seabiscuit, it was even easier to convince them that the real Seabiscuit was not Seabiscuit."[62]

Hide in Plain Sight (James Caan, 1980), a film about the FBI's witness relocation program, also describes a more general device in films. In *Arsenic and Old Lace* (Frank Capra, 1944), everyone but Cary Grant keeps telling the police chief (Jimmy Gleason) that there are thirteen bodies in the cellar (which is true); the policeman laughs, and the cellar is the one place he does *not* search. In *Dark Passage* (Delmer Daves, 1947), Irene (Lauren Bacall), hiding Vincent (Humphrey Bogart) upstairs, puts people off his trail by saying that she is hiding him upstairs; later she explains to him, "People never believe you if you tell them the truth." In Alfred Hitchcock's *Dial M for Murder* (1954), a man named Tony (Ray Milland) hires someone to murder his wife Margot (Grace Kelly), but she kills the assassin and is then charged with murder. Her lover, Mark Halliday (Bob Cummings), who writes murder mysteries for television, makes up a plot he wants Tony to use at the last minute to save Margot ("I've been writing this stuff for years"): pretend he hired someone to kill her, etc., exactly the way it actually happened. Tony says it's so far-fetched no one would believe it, and later, when Mark realizes that his story is true and tells it to the police, Tony laughs and tells the police (truly) that Mark had concocted the story and asked him to tell it as the truth, and the police inspector, too, says no one would believe it as a story. A variant on this theme occurs in *The Man Who Wasn't There* (Joel and Ethan Coen, 2001), when a man kills his wife's lover and then manages to have her put on trial for the murder. He tells her lawyer the truth—"I killed him, because I found out they were having an affair"—but the lawyer assumes that he is just being generous to save his wife and says, "No, we won't let you do that." In *Road to Perdition* (Sam Mendes, 2002), a man and his young son rob a series of banks and stop for a meal at a diner; when the waitress asks them what brings them there, the boy says, "We're bank robbers," and she smiles. Some of these tricksters are mocking people too stupid to see the naked trick right under their noses.

The Edgar Allan Poe story became a canonical text for Lacanian psychoanalysis. Lacan analyzed, at considerable length, the blackmailer's thoughts on choosing a hiding place for the letter and used this sort of self-referential trick as a paradigm for the play of the unconscious: what we expect to be hidden hides by exhibiting itself in the most obvious place.[63] In the course of his larger discussion of the process of mirroring, a hall of mirrors through which two persons formulate their sense of identity in terms of their reflections each in the other in an infinite regress, Lacan called the ego an image of an image. By the logic of the triple cross, Lacan's ego doubles the double, mirroring the mirror image. Derrida, too, spoke of "the infinite play from simulacrum to simulacrum, from double to double."[64] Lacan's remark that "[t]he Truth arises from misrecognition" applies to many of our stories in which masquerade (prompting misrecognition) is the key to the ultimate unmasking (the truth); Zizek applies it, in particular, to the tales of Oedipus[65] and the Appointment in Samarra,[66] but clearly it is directly relevant to "The Purloined Letter."

The Poe story was often analyzed in combination with another parable of self-imitation that was first brought into the analytic literature by Freud himself (who had written a foreword to a book about Poe's life and work[67] but had not discussed "The Purloined Letter"). Freud codified many mythological insights in the form in which they have entered our culture, coloring the minds of people who are often unconscious, if I may use the word, of their debt to Freud (or to the myths on which he drew). These insights include the general hermeneutic of suspicion, the belief that the truth is always concealed, censored—the whole epoch-making concept of an unconscious hidden beneath the conscious mind. Even the simple idea of the Freudian slip, the word (often a double entendre) that escapes what Homer (already) called the barrier of our lips to tell the embarrassing truth instead of the convenient lie that we intend to express, even that is a cliché of ambivalence now built into our culture, carrying with it the double assumption that part of us lies and another part of us wants to tell the truth. This is the particular narrative of self-imitation that Freud told:

> Two Jews met in a railway carriage at a station in Galicia. 'Where are you going?' asked one. 'To Cracow,' was the answer. 'What a liar you are!' broke out the other. 'If you say you're going to Cracow, you want me to believe you're going to Lemberg. But I know that in fact you're going to Cracow. So why are you lying to me?"[68]

Freud calls this a "skeptical" joke and remarks:

This excellent story, which gives an impression of oversubtlety, evidently works by the technique of absurdity. . . . But the more serious substance of the joke is the problem of what determines the truth. . . . Is it the truth if we describe things as they are without troubling to consider how our hearer will understand what we say?

Freud thinks this riddle (or joke, as he calls it) is about what people nowadays call the intersubjectivity of truth, but something else is going on here, too.

The masquerade of the self as the self has the form of a self-referential riddle.[69] We might look upon Freud's joke as an example of primitive industrial espionage: the business rival of the man who is going to Cracow (or, as the case may be, Lemberg) assumes that the man who says he is going to Cracow is a liar.[70] The story demonstrates at least two related corollaries of the doctrine of hiding in plain sight, both based upon the assumption that everyone is lying most of the time. The liar's uncontrollable desire to blurt out the truth may out him, but no one will believe him since no one will expect the liar to be telling the truth. (Indeed, lying may be essential to our sense of identity: psychoanalysts point out that children cannot lie until they realize that they are different from their parents; before that, there no point in lying, since the parent would know all that the child knows. This is one aspect of Lacan's insight that language, more generally, is what allows the child to distinguish himself from someone else. In a new sense, the truth (of identity) arises through misrecognition.

The assumption that everyone lies was built into another riddle, in the form of a logical problem, in the fourth century BCE in what is known as the Liar's Paradox or Epimenides' Paradox. It goes like this:

1: Epimenides is a Cretan.
2: Epimenides states, "All Cretans are liars."

Epimenides must be either a liar or a truth teller, and his statement must be either true or false. But if it's true, then he (being a Cretan) must be a liar, so the statement can't be true. On the other hand, if his statement is false, then he can't be a liar, so the statement must be true. The paradox was devised by Eubulides, a Greek from Miletus, therefore not himself a Cretan, making it an ethnic slur. Various solutions have been proposed,[71] and the paradox has been reformulated in ways that let the Cretans off the hook, such as the statement, "What I am now saying is a lie," or, "This sentence is false." These reformulations retain the element of self-reference, but self-reference is not essential to the paradox; it still remains paradoxical if changed to "the following sentence is true; the preceding sentence is false." It can also be generalized: "All statements on this page are false" (on an otherwise blank page). But the charm of the puzzle inheres not only in its essential logic but also in its nonessential self-referentiality and ethnic slur, so that most people know it as, "All Cretans are liars." The Devil (Peter Cook) in Stanley Donen's Faustian *Bedazzled* (1967) eventually tells his Faust (Dudley Moore), "Everything I've ever told you has been a lie—including that." The woman who pretends to be who she is is saying, "Everything that I am now saying is a lie, especially that."

The logic of Freud's joke is, therefore, one that has plagued the human race for some time, infuriating not only the philosophers but the mythologists. But Freud could also use a self-referential, Möbius strip logic to defend his own theories. Having stated his hypothesis that all dreams are wish fulfillments, he encountered a patient who insisted he was wrong and told him of a dream that clearly expressed what she did *not* wish. Freud countered with another theory, that "the non-fulfillment of one wish meant the fulfillment of another.... It was only necessary to follow the dream's logical consequence in order to arrive at its interpretation. The dream showed that I was wrong. Thus it was her wish that I might be wrong, and her dream showed that wish fulfilled."[72] The memory of a non-wish-fulfilling dream dreamed before we had ever encountered Freud might be taken as counterevidence, but this Freud cannot provide, because anyone telling him a dream is telling it to *him*. Nor can we ever do it now, for now we, too, have read Freud.

Freud's story belongs to a famous genre, as Adam Biro points out: "Two Jews are traveling on a train. All Eastern European Jewish jokes start this way, or almost."[73] Cracow, too, as we have seen, is a buzzword in Jewish stories. Lacan glossed Freud's joke on at least two separate occasions, without crediting Freud for it. In 1956, in his seminar on Poe's "The Purloined Letter," he refers to it merely as "a Jewish joke," never mentions Freud, and slightly alters the ending: "Yes, why do you lie to me saying you're going to Cracow so I should believe you're going to Lemberg, when in reality you *are* going to Cracow?"[74] He cited it again, still without any attribution to Freud, when he told the joke again in 1966, this time in his essay, "The Agency of the Letter in the Unconscious, or Reason since Freud."[75] (When Barbara Johnson quotes this version, she adds the tactful attribution of a "joke quoted by Lacan after Freud."[76]) Lacan's text, Lacanians claim, "may be regarded as a commentary on Freud's statement, an examination of the corrosive effect of the demands of an intersubjective communicative situation on any naïve notion of 'truth.'"[77] So now you know. In other words, what Freud was to sex, Lacan was to gender.

THE RECURSIVE CUNNING OF THE UNCONSCIOUS

Freud's followers went on to develop some of the narrative themes surrounding his basic concept of the hidden and revealed truth, and psychoanalysis continues to wrestle with these issues, returning to the mythology and folklore of self-imitation

for metaphors and offering new interpretations, new commentaries on the narratives. The psychoanalytic explanations are more variants on the old themes, new links in the intertextual chain. In 1921, Ernest Jones, one of Freud's early disciples, wrote an article entitled, "Persons in Dreams Disguised as Themselves," in which he remarked of a particular dream:

> While . . . all the immediate associations led away from the mother who appeared in the dream, and indicated that she was only the substitute for another person, closer consideration shewed that this second person owed much of her significance to the fact that she was an adult substitute for the mother of childhood. In the process in question there are thus three layers: the original person and the infantile thoughts relating to him or her; the secondary person about whom there are similar thoughts also in a state of repression; and the superficial appearance of the original person in a situation that would more naturally apply to the second one. . . . The process illustrates two phenomena with which we are familiar in psycho-analysis: the 'return of the repressed' as Freud terms it; and the significance of free association.[78]

Jones's analysis brings out the triple-cross action in which the surface figure stands for another version of itself that is hidden beneath an intervening second figure. This process offers an insight into the connection between self-imitation and the return of the repressed: imitating someone else is a form of repression, hiding a self that is yours, but going on to imitate a person who is imitating you is the return of the repressed, the reemergence of the hidden self.

Other psychoanalysts branched off in other directions, building on William James's concept of the Divided Self (1902). Most relevant to the mythology of masks and selves is the work of Donald Woods Winnicott (1896–1971), with his concept of the False Self and the relationship between playing and reality. Winnicott, anticipating Lacan, expressed the idea that "[t]he precursor of the mirror is the mother's face,"[79] but unlike Lacan, Winnicott saw this as a "loving gaze." Michel Foucault picked up one of Freud's insights and ran with it in a different direction, challenging our assumptions about what is concealed and what is revealed:

> [W]e also admit that it is in the area of sex that we must search for the most secret and profound truths about the individual, that it is there that we can best discover what he is and what determines him. And if it was believed for centuries that it was necessary to hide sexual matters because they were shameful, we now know that it is sex itself which hides the most secret parts of the individual: the structure of his fantasies, the roots of his ego, the forms of his relationship to reality. At the bottom of sex, there is truth.[80]

Building on these basic concepts in his *History of Sexuality* (1976, 1978 in English), Foucault argued that those Europeans who had most loudly advertised their achievement in removing the mask that had hidden sexuality all this time were masking it more extensively than ever, while those who claimed to conceal it were pruriently exposing it all the time. He showed that we are pretending to be what we are by pretending to talk about sex when we are talking about sex. Thus, for instance, he presented and debunked what he called the "repressive hypothesis," the argument that attitudes toward sex were free and open until the seventeenth century clamped down upon the discourse: "Why do we say, with so much passion and so much resentment against our most recent past, against our present, and against ourselves, that we are repressed? By what spiral did we come to affirm that sex is negated? What led us to show, ostentatiously, that sex is something we hide, to say it is something we silence?" Au contraire, he argued, "Sexuality, far from being repressed in capitalist and bourgeois societies, has on the contrary benefited from a regime of unchanging liberty."[81]

Psychoanalysts speak of "the unconscious cunning,"[82] and Ernest Gellner seized upon this phrase to attack psychoanalysis in a book subtitled *The Cunning of Unreason*. His parody actually brings into clear focus precisely the psychoanalytic insights that concern us here, assumptions that do not seem as silly to me as they seemed to Gellner. Gellner, who in his Popperian moments always felt there was one way of stating a problem so that it had a clear answer and then one way of finding that clear answer, found the Freudian logic of the triple-crossing, double-negative dishonesty infuriating. The kind of argument that Freud made to prove his wish-fulfillment theory disqualified psychoanalysis in Gellner's eyes, banished it from the science club. But for those of us who despair of finding clear answers to the great human questions, as we labor in the messier vineyards of the humanities and social sciences, this sort of infinite regress is a rather satisfying way of admitting defeat.

Lacan and Zizek use sexual metaphors to describe the working of the unconscious mind. Gellner takes this one step further and characterizes the unconscious assumed and excavated by depth psychology as a sexual trickster who tries to anticipate the victim's inversion by producing an inversion of his own. In Gellner's view of the Freudian view, the superego forces the unconscious to disguise itself:

> The Unconscious is like some electronic homing device which can take into account *all* the counter-measures of its intended victim, and which indeed has immediate access to them all. It is, after all, part of the very mind which it deceives. . . . This may be called the Principle of Recursive Cunning. The Unconscious is privy to all the feeble decoy devices attempted by the conscious mind, and can *always* go one further along the regress.[83]

Gellner uses the dishonesty of the two-timing married man (whom we have met on every other page of this book) as the paradigm for his model of the dissembling unconscious: if his wife suspects an affair but doesn't know who the woman is, the husband may go out of his way, when his mistress is present at a gathering with his wife, to treat the mistress coldly; or if *that* makes his wife suspicious, warmly: "Perhaps this game can be played at any level of sophistication and cunning; perhaps the regress simply has no end. The Unconscious is like the erring husband. It aims to deceive." The duplicitous husband, like the unconscious, must double back on his tracks until, half the time, he pretends to be what he is.

THE MÖBIUS STRIP TEASE OF THE SELF

I began this book by suggesting that both the corpus of stories and my analysis of the stories were structured like a Zen diagram: intersecting rings with no single center, not an empty ring in the center, but no central ring. Now I want to conclude by adding my own voice to those stories that visualize the self as such a Zen diagram in which our selves interact with our other selve as stories intersect with stories. The rings of the stories of our lives intersect with other lives for a brief time or a long time—our young children play with their children, they work where we work—and then break away, to play their part in other stories in which we have no role. Just as there is in a narrative text no central ring but groups of rings that make the whole story, so, too, I think, in a life there is no one central self. Polythetic family resemblance reveals a complex subjectivity/objectivity that allows paradox to thrive, the truth that we both love and hate, both know and do not know. And as there is no urtext, so, in a sense, there is no ur-self.

There's a natural human tendency to search for a real self, a center, but I think this is the coward's way out. The temporal aspect of the self, as narrative, is often visualized in a spatial aspect. The multiple selves are stacked like a deck of cards: we discover one by pushing another aside. There is always a self beyond the one we inhabit at any minute, just as (in the *Yogavasishtha*) there is always a life behind and beyond each life in the chain of lives that we first encounter with the monk. The selves nest within one another like so many Chinese boxes or Russian dolls or Indian stories;[84] one by one we peel them off, only to discover that the innermost doll seems to be the same as the doll on the outside, that all the layers and all the masks are real. If we switch to a metaphor of edibility for what is authentic, available to the senses, useful, and, to that degree, real, we might say that the person is not a coconut or a lobster or an oyster, with an outer shell that must be husked to release the delicious heart, nor an avocado or a peach, where the heart alone is inedible. It is, rather, an onion, composed entirely of things we strip off, all edible, but with no center.[85] Onion-soul stories deconstruct the ideal of the central self, demonstrating not only that we can't find it but that it doesn't even exist. This is not to say that both the alternating selves and the masks are simply appearances, that it's appearances all the way down. The layered selves of Chandrashekhara and Taravati, or Udayana and Vasavadatta, suggest a Zen onion consisting of a series of real selves, reality all the way down. This sort of onion is like an artichoke: you can eat (most of) the leaves, and the heart too.[86] These narratives that plumb multiplicity so profoundly, often so playfully, make us experience and understand reality differently but never erase it. We always return to samsara.

In the conventional recognition story, the "real" self at the core is revealed when the many superficial layers are torn away. In C. S. Lewis's book for children *The Voyage of the Dawn Treader*, the boy Eustace commits a series of sins and becomes a dragon, a condition from which he desperately wants to escape. Aslan, the lion who is God, takes him to a cool pool and tells him to undress. Eustace finds he can peel the skin off and is delighted until he sees that he still has another dragon skin under that, and another and another. Then Aslan says, "You will have to let me undress you," and he does it, and it hurts this time, but Eustace gets down to his own skin again.[87] So, too, when Salome strips away the last veil, we see the naked Salome, presumably the real Salome, the erotic body.

But the myths of self-imitation use this metaphor to make the opposite point. As we go deeper and deeper through the alternating layers of masks and faces, we never reach a core. The depilatory process is endless, always shedding a self, as snakes slough their skins (a cross-cultural symbol of rebirth). The Möbius strip tease resonates in world mythology. In the great Sanskrit epic the *Mahabharata*, the villains take the heroine, Draupadi, and drag her into the great assembly hall of the palace, where they attempt to strip her. As they tear away each silk layer, another miraculously appears beneath it until there is a great pile, and they let her go.[88] In contrast with the tale in which Salome strips down to the naked Salome, here, presumably, there are still potentially infinite layers of silk left to go; we will never get to the naked Draupadi, nor would that be the "real" Draupadi. Where lust revealed a single Salome, chastity conceals multiple Draupadis. So, too, when the character known as Thousand-Masks in Mexican wrestling films is finally captured and someone rips his mask off, there is always another mask beneath it.[89] Al-Jahiz's *Book of Misers* (a ninth-century Arabic text) tells of a man from Merv who often went on pilgrimage, where an Iraqi man would entertain him and feed him generously. One day the Iraqi happened to come to Merv and visited his friend, expecting reciprocal hospitality. But the man from Merv did not seem to recognize him, even when he told him his name and patronymic. The Iraqi took off first his turban, then his under cap, but then "the man from Merv now realized that there was nothing left onto which a person making pretence at being unaware and not recognizing, could fasten, so he said: 'If you were to take off your skin I still would not recognize you.'"[90] Here we may recall the husband's willful failure to recognize his wife in many stories.

In this vision of the self, it's "tortoises all the way down"—the fabled retort of the informant replying to a question about the foundation of the world (which, he said, rests on a platform that rests on the back of a tortoise, which rests on the back of another tortoise, ad infinitum).[91] Perhaps this tortoise is being chased by Achilles and cannot escape from Zeno's (and Lewis Carroll's [92]) paradox: every time you take off a mask you get halfway closer to a "true self," and another and another, but you never reach it because it does not exist. In the hall of mirrors, it's selves all the way down. Or as the hard-boiled woman in Graham Greene's *Brighton Rock* put it (speaking of the candy cane with the word "Brighton Rock" built into the pattern), "People don't change; bite it all the way down; you'll still read 'Brighton.'"[93] There is no ground zero for the self. We never get to the final tortoise, the last mirror in the hall of mirrors, the final Morton's salt box within the salt box, or what Russell Hoban (in *The Mouse and His Child*) called "the last visible dog."

The two images of infinite regress are not quite the same: the mirrors facing mirrors begin as equals, while the salt box (or Quaker Oats) image is a container contained or, as Cavell puts it, "a representation of something presenting a representation of itself."[94] (One poster for the film *Memento* [Christopher Nolan, 2000] depicts a Polaroid photo of the face of Leonard looking at a Polaroid of the face of Natalie looking at a Polaroid of Leonard . . . and on as far as we can see.) Yet as Cavell goes on to note, neither of these images adequately represents the play within the play (or, I would add, the self within the self), because both assume that the two entities (mirrors or salt boxes) are the same, whereas the play (or self) within is not the same as the play (or self) outside. There is always that Möbius twist.

Putting on a mask gets us closer to one self and farther from another, and so does taking off the mask. Since every lie covers up a truth, a series of masks passes through a series of lies and truths. Perhaps, then, the best bet is to wear as many as possible, and realize that we are wearing them, and try to find out what each one conceals and reveals. As we strip away masks, or faces, each time we see more in the hall of looking glasses. If we just stand there with our unconscious masks on our faces, like egg in the saying, we never learn anything about the selves. Mary McCarthy once said, "It's absolutely useless to look for [the self], you won't find it, but it's possible in some sense to make. I don't mean . . . making a mask . . . but you finally begin . . . to make and to choose the self you want."[95] This nice distinction between self and mask is hard to call. The stories with the double twist bring us back to the position where we don't seem to have a mask, which is where most people think they are all the time. But the memory of the double journey out and in, unsettling the assumption that we are either masked or unmasked, reminds us that we are never unmasked. Though few of us actually put on masks that replicate our faces, it is not uncommon for us to become unrecognizable travesties of ourselves, particularly as we age and change. For the ultimate mask is the body itself.

Proust, who was well aware of the simultaneous multiple selves, also saw the selves as a series of reincarnations, each self dying after each dying love:

> [F]or then our old self will have changed ... it would be in a real sense the death of the self, a death followed, it is true, by resurrection, but in a different self, to the love of which the elements of the old self that are condemned to die cannot bring themselves to aspire.[96]

And after each death, a new self is born:

> [T]he impression that I now felt [that I no longer loved Albertine was] proof of the death of my former self and of the substitution of a new self ... [O]ne is no more distressed at having become another person, after a lapse of years. ..., than one is at any given moment by ... being, one after another, the incompatible persons, malicious, sensitive, refined, caddish, disinterested, ambitious which one can be ... [T]he caddish self laughs at his caddishness because one is the cad, and the forgetful self does not grieve about his forgetfulness precisely because he has forgotten.[97]

Again we encounter the unfaithful, amnesiac lover as the sign for the protean self.

And so, we look into the mirror and say to the stranger we see there, "Another gray hair; shall I dye it?" "Another five pounds; shall I diet?" But the falling away of the final, unaccented syllable reveals the submerged, suppressed question: "Shall I die?" And then, "Who is this I who will die?" These realizations constantly open up for us the possibility of multiple selves and the infinite regress of self-discovery.

NOTES

Introduction

1. These cultures and many others may very well have mythologies of self-imitation, but I do not know enough about them to include them here.

2. The translations from all languages are my own except where I have cited in the footnote the name of the translator; in citing other translators I have generally paraphrased all but the quotations of words spoken by the characters in the stories, which I have cited verbatim.

3. Henry Louis Gates Jr., "White Like Me," 75.

4. Wendy Doniger, *The Implied Spider*.

5. Hillel Schwartz, *The Culture of the Copy*.

6. Hal Foster, "Nutty Professors." A review of Alexander Star, ed., *Quick Studies: The Best of Lingua Franca*, *London Review of Books*, May 8, 2003, 35–36.

7. Doniger, *The Implied Spider*, 143–151.

8. Ibid., 75–79, 138–145.

9. Sigmund Freud, *Beyond the Pleasure Principle*.

10. Claude Lévi-Strauss, "The Story of Asdiwal," 29–30; *Structural Anthropology*, 229.

11. Terence Cave, *Recognitions*, 489.

12. Mircea Eliade, *The Myth of the Eternal Return*.

13. George Orwell, "Rudyard Kipling," 137.

14. Stanley Cavell, *Pursuits of Happiness*, 51, 19.

15. I owe this delightful epigram to George Kateb, personal communication, Princeton, March 2, 1999.

16. Sometimes they have entirely new titles but sometimes the same titles, so that versions are distinguished only by their dates (as essential to the identity of films as the vintage is to wines) or, like English kings, by "I" or "II."

17. These recycled elements make it extremely difficult to copyright the plot of a film; see Tad Friend, "Copy Cats," *New Yorker*, September 14, 1998, 51–57.

18. Terry Eagleton, "Maybe He Made It Up," 3.

19. Ludwig Wittgenstein, *Philosophical Investigations*.

20. Doniger, *The Implied Spider*, 35, 139, 143; *The Bedtrick*, introduction and chap. 5, "Paternal Insecurity, Family Resemblance, and Male Jealousy."

21. Carlo Ginzburg, *Ecstasies*, 166.

22. It is the fourth in a tetralogy, if you count the book that lays out the comparative method used in the other three: *The Implied Spider*.

23. Doniger, *The Bedtrick*, 22–27.

24. Wendy Doniger O'Flaherty, *Dreams, Illusion, and Other Realities*, 240–244.

25. Wendy Doniger, *Splitting the Difference*, ix.

26. The photo of the author therefore represents her pretending to be who she was almost half a century ago.

Chapter 1

1. The *Oxford English Dictionary* defines *Triple cross* thus: "The act of betraying one party in a transaction by pretending to betray the other, or of betraying a person who has betrayed another." I am paying the word a bit extra, as Humpty-Dumpty would say, to extend its meaning to the act of masquerading as a person who has masqueraded as another person.

2. Let me state here at the start, emphatically, that this is a study of the mythology of amnesia, not of amnesia as it is known to the medical and psychiatric professions—an extremely rare phenomenon that has inspired an entirely disproportionate literary response.

3. Terence Cave, *Recognitions*, 495.

4. Cartoon by Cheney, *New Yorker*, May 5, 2003, 52.

5. This topic occupied most of the first chapter of my last book, *The Bedtrick*, but the focus of that book did not allow me to develop the themes of memory and self-reference that are the subject of this present volume.

6. Oscar Wilde, *The Importance of Being Earnest*, 506. No one who has heard Joan Greenwood say the line (in the 1952 film version directed by Anthony Asquith) can ever hear it in any other voice.

7. Yanagita Kunio, *Japanese Folk Tales*, 108–110.

8. Cartoon by BEK, *New Yorker*, February 2, 2004, 69.

9. Adam Gopnik, "The Naked City"; "On the New Burlesque," 31.

10. Susan Sontag, "Notes on Camp."

11. Alan Dundes, *The Shabbat Elevator and Other Sabbath Subterfuges*. Turning on the refrigerator light poses a problem that is solved by taping it down so that it stays either on or off all the time; the elevator is set to move constantly so that the people getting on and off at each floor are not actually doing the work of running the elevator; and so forth.

12. Eli W. Schlossberg, *The World of Orthodox Judaism*, 75.

13. Edward Said, *Orientalism*, 325

14. James C. Scott, *Domination and the Arts of Resistance*.

15. Christopher Lasch, "The Anti-Intellectualism of the Intellectuals," 336.

16. Stanley Cavell, *Pursuits of Happiness*, 157.

17. Brendan Gill, "Pursuer and Pursued," 87. Sometimes it is cited as "everyone wants to be . . . . Even I want to be." The line surely inspired Richard Gere's laughing remark, in a 2003 British film about Buddhism, "If I could only be like Richard Gere." Someone who met Cary Grant off screen said to him, "You don't look like Cary Grant." "I know," he replied. "Nobody does."

18. The violence of this image may be the tip of a darker side to Cary Grant's wish to be Cary Grant. Much speculation has swirled around the fact that this man, whom women so loved, lived in close friendship for many years with Randolph Scott, who played his rival for the hand of Irene Dunne in *My Favorite Wife*. If there was, indeed, besides the straight Cary Grant on film, at least one other gay or bisexual Cary Grant offstage, which one wished to be the other?

19. Melville Shavelson, cited by Vincent Canby, "Road to Ubiquity," obituary of Bob Hope, *New York Times*, July 29, 2003, A22.

20. Claudia Roth Pierpont, "Born for the Part," 55.

21. Anthony Lane, "Mondo Bond," 82.

22. Annie Dillard, "The Two of Them," 61.

23. Wayne Gretzky, quoted in *Newsweek*, October 7, 1996, 27.

24. Hillary Rodham Clinton's first newspaper column, *New York Times*, July 24, 1995, A10.

25. This story was also told of other notorious womanizers, including Jack Kennedy.

26. Derrida made this point in "Coming into One's Own" in 1977, later revised as "To Speculate: On Freud," in *The Post Card*.

27. Cyril Connolly, *Enemies of Paradise*.

28. Dwight Macdonald, "Ernest Hemingway," 168.

29. Ibid., 178.

30. But Macdonald does not mention that Hemingway also consciously depicted self-imitation in *The Sun Also Rises*, where he describes an aging bull-fighter doing an imitation of his former self, and in

Across the River and Into the Trees, as in this conversation (261): He: "Let's play historic personages." She: "Let's just play that you are you and I am me."

31. Christopher Lasch, "The Anti-Intellectualism of the Intellectuals," 336.

32. Valentine Cunningham, "The Incomparable: A life of the Satirist Max Beerbohm," *New York Times Book Review,* January 19, 2003, 22.

33. Adam Gopnik, "Standup Guys," *New Yorker,* May 12, 2003, 106.

34. Richard F. Shepard with Mel Gussow, obituary of Al Hirschfield, *NewYork Times,* January 21, 2003, A1 and C16.

35. Macdonald, "Ernest Hemingway," 172.

36. Macdonald, *Parodies,* 474.

37. Lasch, "The Anti-Intellectualism of the Intellectuals," 336.

38. Macdonald, "Ernest Hemingway," 178.

39. Lasch, "The Anti-Intellectualism of the Intellectuals," 336.

40. John Shelton Lawrence and Robert Jewett, *The Myth of the American Superhero,* 9.

41. Walter Kaufmann, *Without Guilt and Justice,* 161.

42. Wendy Doniger, *Splitting the Difference,* 73–77; Pliny, *Natural History,* 160.

43. Roland Barthes, *S/Z,* 208.

44. Balzac, *Sarrasine,* 73.

45. Barthes, *S/Z,* 194–197.

46. Ibid., 208. This problem was addressed, in a different way, by Edward Gorey, who depicted a cat standing behind an empty frame (perhaps in imitation of Magritte's famous landscape behind an empty frame), which, therefore, framed the cat as if the cat were a painting. He called it "a cat . . . pretending to be himself."

47. Slavoj Zizek, "From Symptom to *Sinthome,*" 57.

48. In the same way, as soon as the victim of a bedtrick learns the identity of the trickster, the victim is retroactively ashamed of the pleasure he or she had experienced in ignorance of the truth.

49. Robert Osborne, October 12, 2003, broadcast on Turner Classic Movies.

50. *Bhagavata Purana* 10.33.38.

51. Doniger, "Joking with God in a Fragile World"; Anthony Lane, "This Is Not a Movie," 79–80; "American Life Turns into Bad Jerry Bruckheimer Movie," *Onion,* September 27, 2001.

52. A remake of *Men Are Not Gods* (Walter Reisch, 1936), also about an actor who played Othello and lived the part in real life.

53. Colman gloried in double roles, of which perhaps the most famous was his portrayal of the King and the King's British look-alike cousin in *The Prisoner of Zenda* (John Cromwell, 1937).

54. Garbo also made another film of *Anna Karenina,* with Tolstoi's title, a soundtrack, and Frederic March as Vronsky (Clarence Brown, 1935).

55. Internet Movie Data Base, biography of Grace Kelly.

56. The mythic nature of Indian film has long been noted; mythic themes are a major source of plots; filmmakers have been heard to remark, "There are only two stories in the world, the *Ramayana* and the *Mahabharata.*" Rosie Thomas, "Indian Cinema: Pleasures and Popularity," 123.

57. Shashi Tharoor, "A Land Governed by Film Stars," *New York Times,* August 15, 2003, A29. The temples were dedicated to the Tamil star MGR (M.G. Ramachandran) and the Telugu star NTR (N.T. Rama Rao).

58. Alessandra Stanley, "A Nose Job Just Scratches the Surface," *New York Times,* June 18, B1 and B5.

59. Jesse McKinley, "Norman Lear Discovers Soul Mates in 'South Park,'" *New York Times,* April 10, 2003, E1.

60. Alessandra Stanley, "Blurring Reality with Soap Suds," *New York Times,* February 23, A19 and A33.

61. Shashi Tharoor, "A Land Governed by Film Stars."

62. Interview in *Cape Cod Times,* July 13, C2. More precisely, in 2002, Vidal said, "Yes, I turned him down on the ground that he was not right for an Adlai Stevenson–style politician while Melvyn Douglas was. The joke has been refashioned over the years."

63. Personal communication from Mike Macdonald, September 2002.

64. Bob Schieffer and Gary Paul Gates, *The Acting President,* 167.

65. David Thompson, *A Biographical Dictionary of Film*, 617–618.

66. Ronald Reagan, *Where's the Rest of Me?* 137.

67. Lou Cannon, *President Reagan: The Role of a Lifetime*, 485–486.

68. Garry Wills, *Reagan's America*, 164.

69. John Shelton Lawrence and Robert Jewett, *The Myth of the American Superhero*, 338.

70. Frank Rich, "Paar to Leno, J.F.K. to J.F.K," *New York Times*, February 8, 2004, sec. 2, 1, 22.

71. After Reagan's death, Rich referred to Bush as Reagan's "stunt double" (*New York Times*, Sunday, June 13, 2004, section 2, 1).

72. David Thompson, *A Biographical Dictionary of Film*, 617–618.

73. Anthony Lane, "Metal Guru: Terminator 3; Rise of the Machines," 86.

74. Dean E. Murphy, "An Actor, Yes, but No Reagan," *New York Times*, August 10, sec. 4, 1.

75. Patricia Leigh Brown, "Reconciling the Conflicts in a Movie Star's Image," *New York Times*, October 8, 2003, A21.

76. Terry Eagleton, "Maybe He Made It Up," 3.

77. Marcel Proust, *Swann's Way*, 105–106. It is worthy of note that the word Proust uses for his example, *hierarchy*, is one of the buzzwords used most frequently in our day by the scare quoters.

Chapter 2

1. Udayana is King of Vatsa and Kaushambi in North India near the present-day Allahabad, while Vasavadatta is the daughter of the king of Avanti, near the present-day Ujjain. Ratnavali is the daughter of the king of Simhala (Sri Lanka).

2. The characters appear first in *Vasavadatta in a Dream* [*Svapnavasavadatta*], composed by Bhasa, probably in the fourth century CE, and later in several stories in the tenth-century *Ocean of Story* [*Kathasaritsagara*]. See also Wendy Doniger, "The Dreams and Dramas of a Jealous Hindu Queen: Vasavadatta."

3. This Harsha, who is not the Shriharsha who wrote the *Naishadhiyacarita* in the twelfth century, is also known as Harsha-Deva or Harshavardhana. He is best known from a long biographical poem, the *Harsha-Charita* of Bana.

4. David Shulman, "Embracing the Subject," 79.

5. Ibid., 78.

6. Or as Shulman translates it, "I am really Sagarika. For you, my lord, see her everywhere, your heart being entirely in her grip." Shulman, "Embracing the Subject," 79.

7. Ibid., 80.

8. In *Ratnavali*, he says: *kim atah param api priyam asti*; in *Priyadarshika*, he says: *kim atah param priyam*.

9. *-darshika* is derived from the verbal root *drish* that indicates vision, sight, appearance.

10. There were, and are, also other traditions in which men play the parts of women.

11. Shulman, "Embracing the Subject," 81–87.

12. Doniger, *The Bedtrick*, 194.

13. Shulman, "Embracing the Subject," 81–87.

14. The film *The Rules of the Game* (Jean Renoir, 1939) explicitly invokes *The Marriage of Figaro* in various inversions but with a tragic ending: both a man and a woman inadvertently masquerade as their servants, and the man is killed by the maid's jealous husband, who mistakes him for her lover.

15. Mozart, *Marriage of Figaro*, act 3, end of scene 8.

16. Beachmarchais, *The Marriage of Figaro*, 130.

17. Northrop Frye, *A Natural Perspective*, 128.

18. In an extreme example, Bryan Guinness provided false evidence of his own adultery in order to let Diana Mitford divorce him in 1933, even though she had spectacularly and notoriously cuckolded him with Sir Oswald Mosley.

19. Evelyn Waugh, *A Handful of Dust*, 129.

20. John Galsworthy, *In Chancery* (vol. 2 of *The Forsyte Saga*), 227.

21. Martha Grimes, *The Five Bells and Bladebone*, 312.

22. Ibid., 317.

23. Lawrence van Gelder, obituary for Milton Berle, *New York Times*, March 28, 2002, C13. It continues: "Their second marriage also ended in divorce." Several other celebrities, particularly Hollywood stars—most famously, Richard Burton and Elizabeth Taylor, Robert Wagner and Natalie Wood—remarried after they divorced.

24. Gottfried von Strassburg, *Tristan*, 297.

Chapter 3

1. Doniger, *The Bedtrick*, 13–55.

2. In 1848 Wagner published *The Nibelungenmyth: A Scheme for a Drama*. By 1853 he had completed the poetic scenario for the cycle of operas, though the full libretto was first published in 1863 and the full cycle first performed in 1876.

3. Swinburne, "An Interlude" (1866). Thanks to Lorraine Daston for finding this for me.

4. The characters have different names in different texts, but to simplify the analysis, I will call them by the names they have in Wagner: Siegfried (called Sigurd in the *Thidreks Saga, Völsunga Saga*, and Ibsen; Siegfried in the *Nibelungenlied*), Brünnhilde (called Brynhild in the *Thidreks Saga* and *Völsunga Saga*; Brünhild in the *Nibelungenlied*, Hjördis in Ibsen—strangely, since Hjordis is the name of Sigurd's *mother* in the *Völsunga Saga*), Gunther (called Gunnar in the *Thidreks Saga, Völsunga Saga*, and Ibsen; Gunther in the *Nibelungenlied*), and Gutrune (called Grimhild in the *Thidreks Saga*—also strangely, since Grimhild is the name of Gudrun's *mother* in the *Völsunga Saga*; Gudrun in the *Völsunga Saga*; Kriemhild in the *Nibelungenlied*; and Dagny in Ibsen).

5. An Old Norse text written in Norway, the *Thidreks Saga af Bern*, or *Saga of Thidrek of Berne*, was composed during the reign of King Hákon Hákonarson (1217–1263), but scholars hesitate to be much more precise than that. For the dates of the texts, I am indebted to an unpublished essay by Kevin Wanner, "The Virgin and the Valkyrie: A Comparison of Three Medieval Germanic Texts," 1999.

6. Doniger, *The Bedtrick*, 140–150.

7. Ibid., 271–283.

8. This is what happened in the story of Tristan and Isolde, when Brangane slipped into bed with King Mark in Isolde's place and Isolde then returned to finish the night, all in order to supply the missing maidenhead.

9. Freud, "The Taboo of Virginity," 204, 208.

10. Ibid.

11. Stanley Cavell (in *Pursuits of Happiness*, 149) discussed this theme (re *The Philadelphia Story*) in relation not to physical defloration but to a kind of "psychological or spiritual virginity, something for which physical virginity is a trope." But it applies equally well to the actual physical defloration depicted in the old stories.

12. Most scholars regard Aslaug as the result of a superficial attempt to link this saga's story and characters to those of another legendary saga (*Ragnars saga loðbrókar*) that also appears in the only extant medieval manuscript that contains the *Völsunga Saga*. Snorri's *Edda* (Skáldskaparmál 42), which mentions Aslaug, does not identify her mother.

13. Written in German, drawing on Christian and European courtly sources. Byock, "Introduction," *Volsungasaga*, 4.

14. Wilhelm Grimm notes, dryly, that the *Nibelungenlied* assumes "*dass Siegfried schon einmal bei Brünnhilde war*." He gives details from sagas about meetings of Siegfried and Brünnhilde, and he notes (93) that the *Nibelungenlied* assumes that they have met before but does not describe that meeting. (Wilhelm Grimm, *Die Deutsche Heldensage*, 204–205.) Robert W. Gutman remarks that leaving out the prelude "renders the relationship between the hero and Brünnhilde most ambiguous in the German poem" (Gutman, "Introduction," 29).

15. Gutman suggests, "She evidently remembered Hindfell of the *Edda* and *Volsunga Saga*; the old tradition would not die" (Gutman, "Introduction," 40). Hindfell is the mountain where she slept until Siegfried awakened her.

16. An eye for an eye, as it were. Shakespeare, too, often punned on the loss of a woman's maidenhead and the beheading of a man, in *Measure for Measure*, in particular.

17. A. T. Hatto, trans., *The Nibelungenlied*, 332.

18. Ibid., 297.

19. This attitude is well known in other cultures, too, most notoriously among the Dogon, in whose mythology every woman is born with an enormous clitoris, like a penis, that must be removed in order for sexual intercourse to be safe (Marcel Griaule, *Conversations with Ogotemmeli*). In some African cultures, this myth justifies ritual cliterodectomy, as Freud noted in his essay "The Taboo of Virginity."

20. For an argument that this text suppressed the rape of Brünnhilde by Siegfried, see Theodore Andersson, *The Legend of Brünnhilde*, 222–224.

21. Hatto, *Nibelungenlied*, 298–299, 393.

22. Doniger, *The Bedtrick*, 441–443.

23. Wagner was heavily influenced by many factors that other scholars have written a great deal about, including his political views about the Aryan purity of the German race, which fueled the need to purify the character of his great Aryan hero, Siegfried. When Ernst (later Sir Ernst) Gombrich was monitoring German radio for the British during World War II, he telephoned Winston Churchill to tell him that Hitler had just died, which Gombrich knew, despite the fact that no announcement had been made, because German radio was broadcasting Wagner's music for Siegfried's death. This sort of thing cannot be directly blamed on Wagner, but it has done much to blacken his name. Events in his personal life also surely exacerbated his desire to justify Siegfried's betrayal of Brünnhilde: Wagner's son Siegfried was conceived illegitimately in his adulterous relationship with Cosima (herself the illegitimate daughter of Franz Liszt).

24. The theme of the bedtrick had been a very early interest of Wagner's; his first, rather unsuccessful opera, *Das Liebesverbot* (1836), was based on Shakespeare's great bedtrick play, *Measure for Measure*. Artistically, too, Wagner was coming to terms with the growing realization that he might not be able to make Siegfried the hero he wanted him to be. He wrote *Siegfried* first, in a moment of romantic optimism, the pure, high-minded romance with the tragic but noble ending; in fact the opera was originally named *Siegfried's Death*. But as the years went on, he finally wrote the sequel, the sordid and unhappy aftermath of sexual betrayal.

25. From *The Anna Russell Album*, recorded live at Town Hall, New York City, April 23, 1953 (copyright 1972 Sony Music Entertainment), track 9.

26. We know that Wagner derived his knowledge of the Siegfried story from many sources. He read Jakob Grimm's *Deutsche Mythologie*, in which the Norse sources are translated into German, and *Deutsche Heldensagen* by Jakob's brother Wilhelm Grimm, who left the Norse in Norse. Wagner probably could not read this treatment of the sagas, but it influenced him greatly; it contains several sophisticated comparisons between the *Nibelungenlied* and the Norse sagas and Eddas. And Wagner knew other sources, such as Hagen-Simrock's *Das deutsche Heldenbuch*. He read translations of some of the Eddas, as well as the *Völsunga Saga* (which he read in the 1815 translation by H. von der Hagen), *Vilkina*, and Snorri's *Heimskringla*, which were available in German by that time, though he probably did not know the *Thidreks Saga*. He freely adapted the idea of Valhalla from Snorri Sturluson's *Prose Edda* (thirteenth century), developing the character of Hagen and the death of Siegfried out of the *Nibelungenlied* (Jesse Byock, *Volsungasaga*, "Introduction," 2, 27; Robert W. Gutman, "Introduction," *Volsunga Saga*, 62).

27. Wagner also plays at this moment a strangely distorted variation on Gunther's lumbering theme, to suggest the false, not-quite-right form of Gunther assumed by Siegfried. But the leitmotifs can also work against the plot: when Siegmund wonders who his father is, Wagner plays the musical answer—Wotan's theme—but Siegmund never does learn that Wotan is his father.

28. *Er zwang mir Lust und Lieb ab.*

29. In the *Völsunga Saga*, too, there is an earlier episode of actual seduction—and impregnation—and a later one of chastity, though they are never conflated in any actual argument.

30. Siegfried's casual attitude to his various marriage vows comes out even near the end of his life, when he says he would gladly have a casual go at one of the Rhine maidens—if it weren't for the fact that he is true to Gutrune.

31. Wagner manipulates the gendered knowledge of Sieglinde and Siegmund in *Die Walküre*, act 1, in a different direction. In the *Völsunga Saga*, Signy wishes to have a child with her brother Sigmund in order to keep the bloodline pure. Since Sigmund, abhorring incest, refuses to sleep with her, she magically transforms herself into a strange woman and seduces her brother in that form, giving birth to

Sinjfotli. The *Nibelungenlied* does not tell of Siegfried's birth at all but simply says that he is the son of Siegmund and Sieglinde. When Wagner retold this story, he erased the bedtrick: the two fall in love at first sight and realize at the same moment, before they sleep together, that they are brother and sister, so that they are both equally guilty of knowingly committing incest. Yet Sieglinde strongly suspects from the start that Siegmund is her brother, since he tells her the story of their family and childhood, while he does not figure it out for quite a while, since she tells him only of her more recent marriage; and even at his death, Siegmund does not realize that Wotan is his father. Bereft of the exculpating bedtrick, Wagner's Siegmund is punished for his knowing incest, in contrast with Wagner's Siegfried, who is, like his father Siegmund in the Norse sources, the innocent victim of magic.

32. Wanner, "The Virgin and the Valkyrie," 16.

33. *Edda: The Poetic Edda*, translated by Lee M. Hollander, 252.

34. This is one of a number of motifs shared by old English and Germanic sources: the story of Arthur drawing the sword Excalibur out of a stone appears in German transformation as the story of Siegmund drawing his father's sword out of an ash tree, in the *Völsunga Saga* and earlier in Wagner's *Siegfried*.

35. Gram is the name of Siegfried's sword in the *Völsunga Saga*; Wagner changes it to Notung in his opera, perhaps to distinguish it from Grane (or Grani), Brünnhilde's horse, perhaps to make a point about Compulsion (Nötung).

36. Gottfried von Strassburg, *Tristan*, 270–273.

37. Béroul, *Le Roman de Tristran*, 1804–2024.

38. In the Welsh *Mabinogion*, Pwyll and Arawn change places, and Arawn, magically transformed into the shape of Pwyll, in effect his twin, sleeps beside Arawn's wife for a year in chastity, though without a sword between them.

39. "The Two Brothers," in Grimm, *The Complete Grimms' Fairy Tales*, 308–311.

40. William Morris, trans., *Völsunga Saga*, chap. 32.

Chapter 4

1. Gottfried von Strassburg, *Tristan*, 246–248.

2. Béroul, *Le Roman de Tristran*, line 3936: *Yseut la bele chevaucha.*

3. Gottfried von Strassburg, *Tristan*, 236.

4. Béroul, *Le Roman de Tristran*, 20–24.

5. Gottfried von Strassburg, *Tristan*, 248.

6. A. K. Ramanujan, "Towards a Counter-System: Women's Tales," 47–54.

7. Doniger, *Splitting the Difference*, 9–27.

8. Someone else may be playing Sita. The stage manager twice states that his play is staged by women, more precisely by celestial nymphs (apsarases) (4.22, *apsarobhih prayojayishyati*; and again 7.1, *apsarob-hih prayujyamanam*) presumably playing all the parts, including the part of Sita. The character of Sita is called Sita, but so are the characters of Rama and the River Ganga called by their names, and clearly other people are playing them. Yet it may well be, as David Shulman and V. Narayana Rao insist, that Sita herself is playing the part of Sita, and I hope she is.

9. *Idrisho 'smi*. In Harsha's play, the queen accuses the king of being just like himself, using the same term in the same pejorative sense, *sadrisha*.

10. David Shulman, "Bhavabhuti on Cruelty and Compassion," 76–77.

11. *Kim etat* and *katham devi*. And he never speaks to Sita at all for the rest of the play.

12. Stanley Cavell, "Recounting Gains, Showing Losses: Reading *The Winter's Tale*." This reverse oedipal fantasy is what Lowell Edmonds has called the Laius syndrome.

13. Alan Dundes, *Cinderella: A Casebook*.

14. Otto Rank, *The Myth of the Birth of the Hero*.

15. Doniger, *The Bedtrick*, 220–224.

16. Maurizio Bettini, *The Portrait of the Lover*, 187–192, citing Augustine's *Soliloquia*: *mater est falsitatis.*

17. Wendy Doniger and Gregory Spinner, "Misconceptions: Male Fantasies and Female Imaginations in Parental Imprinting"; Wendy Doniger, "The Symbolism of Black and White Babies in the Myth of Maternal Impression."

18. Rosette Willig, *The Changelings*; Doniger, *The Bedtrick*, 357–367.

19. Philip Roth, *The Human Stain*, 137.

20. He then sings to her the Jerome Kern/Oscar Hammerstein love song of self-imitation, "Make Believe," that he had sung to her mother shortly before begetting the daughter.

21. Leslie Halliwell, *Halliwell's Film Guide*, 671.

22. The alternation of comedy and tragedy in texts and films dealing with the story of a woman falsely accused of adultery is in part, but only in part, a function of attitudes to marriage in general and to the double standard in particular, which vary not only between different historical periods but from individual artist to individual artist.

23. Stanley Cavell, *Pursuits of Happiness*, 19.

24. Ibid., 56.

25. The ending of the poem seems to veer into the path of another genre of films, the mother (*Madame X* et al.) who sits there in the dark, watching her child, and in some respects (including Philip the best friend) the Tennyson plot more closely resembles that of *Chances Are* (Emile Ardolino, 1989).

26. McCarey, who worked with Sam and Bella Spewack on the original story, had intended to direct it, too, but an automobile accident forced him to withdraw and to get Garson Kanin to direct it instead.

27. Marilyn Monroe as Ellen, Dean Martin as Nick, Cyd Charisse as Bianca, Wally Cox as the shoe salesman, John McGiver as the judge.

28. The title, slightly modified (*Something's Gotta Give*), was given to a 2003 film by Nancy Meyers with an entirely different plot.

29. Doniger, *The Implied Spider*.

30. Because of the asymmetrical aging of men and women as sexual objects, Cary Grant could have replayed his role of Nick in *Move Over, Darling* in 1963 with Doris Day, with whom he had made a romantic film just one year before (*That Touch of Mink*, Delbert Mann, 1962); Grant was fifty-nine at that time. But Irene Dunne, who was six years older than Grant, made her last film in 1952. She had starred, with Charles Boyer, in the first version of *An Affair to Remember* (*Love Affair*, Leo McCarey, 1939), but when Leo McCarey made the second version in 1957, he cast Cary Grant (now fifty-three) opposite not Irene Dunne (who was now fifty-nine) but Deborah Kerr (who was thirty-six).

31. Irene Dunne (but not Doris Day) had done the same thing (fall into the pool) at a very different moment in the first version, after the awkward poolside confrontation between Nick and Steve.

32. Pauline Kael, *5001 Nights at the Movies*, 41. The theme never dies. In *Laws of Attraction* (Peter Howitt, 2004), two lawyers (Julianne Moore and Pierce Brosnan) get married when they're drunk, immediately begin divorce proceedings when they wake up, and fall in love in the course of getting the divorce.

33. Cavell, *Pursuits of Happiness*, 1, 51.

34. Ibid., 19.

35. Ibid., 58–60.

36. The fox terrier is actually Asta (of *Thin Man* fame) in disguise.

37. Freud, *Three Essays on the Theory of Sexuality*, 88. He was discussing the mother's breast as the prototypical object of love.

38. Cavell, *Pursuits of Happiness*, 70.

39. Freud, "The Taboo of Virginity," 203.

40. Ibid., 206.

41. Ibid., 208.

42. The film was based upon the 1921 Broadway play by Arthur Richman.

43. Cavell, *Pursuits of Happiness*, 244.

44. Bellamy also plays the boring, rich suitor of Ginger Rogers (who rejects him for Fred Astaire in *Carefree* [Mark Sandrich, 1938]) and of Rosalind Russell (who rejects him for Cary Grant in *His Girl Friday* [Howard Hawks, 1940]).

45. As Cavell puts it, her imitation of Dixie Belle manages "to show both her difference from and her solidarity with Dixie Belle and Dixie Bell's performance. You might call this the redemption of vulgarity by commonness." Cavell, *Pursuits of Happiness*, 252–253.

46. Ibid., 260.

47. Ibid., 222.

48. Myrna Loy made another film in the same year (*Libeled Lady*, Jack Conway, 1936) involving faked marriages and divorces that turn into real marriages and divorces; this time she played with and against Spencer Tracy, William Powell, and Jean Harlow.

49. Cavell, *Pursuits of Happiness*, 61.

50. Ibid., 62.

51. Ibid.

Chapter 5

1. I am grateful to Barbara Hall, of the Margaret Herrick Library, Fairbanks Center for Motion Picture Study, in Beverly Hills, California, for looking up the dialogue continuity and Production Code correspondence about *Remember?*

2. The Production Code Administration (better known as the Hays Office) did caution MGM that "[g]reat care will be needed in the shooting of this tag scene. There must be nothing offensive about Linda's announcement that she is going to have a baby, or the reactions thereto, on the part of Jeff and Sky." Personal communication from Barbara Hall, July 7, 2003.

3. A year after Cary Grant and Irene Dunne made their second comic remarriage film, they made a tearjerker, *Penny Serenade* (George Stevens, 1941), about a couple whose marriage is almost destroyed by their poverty, a miscarriage, and the death of their adopted child. The man who unknowingly impregnates his own wife is the staple of comedy ranging from Terence's *The Mother-in-Law* in the second-century BCE through contemporary folk variants of the tale of the clever wife.

4. The dog recognized Tristan when Isolde did not; and in Homer's *Odyssey*, the dog recognized the disguised Odysseus when Penelope did not.

5. Or as Simon and Garfunkle sang it, "After all the changes we are more or less the same."

6. Hitchcock surely had this scene in mind when he filmed Joan Fontaine in *Rebecca* (1940) coming down the stairs wearing the costume, country bonnet and all, from the portrait of Rebecca.

7. See Nathalie Zemon Davis, *The Return of Martin Guerre*; Doniger, *The Bedtrick*, 428–436.

8. Doniger, *Splitting the Difference*, 79–87.

9. Italics are in the original.

10. Cavell, *Contesting Tears*, 14.

11. It is bitterer still in the novel, in which the period of amnesia stretches for four more years.

12. Cavell, *Pursuits of Happiness*, 30.

13. James Hilton, *Random Harvest*, 210. In the film, one of Charles's siblings complains that Charles can remember nothing at all of "his past life," presumably meaning the years between 1917 and 1920.

14. Colman and Garson also made a radio-play version of the story, in the *Lux Presents* series. In that version, the psychiatrist explains it to Paula: "I believe that in that locked chamber of his mind there is a phantom memory of you that will always stand between him and any other woman. But he can't give you reality. You're just the fugitive shadow of a dream."

15. In the radio show, which she narrates, she says, "I wanted to tell him so many times that *I* was Miss Hanson. I went to Dr. Benet, the only one who knew my secret, and pleaded with him to let me tell Charles." Benet, however, warns her: "You must wait, Paula, until he recognizes you." "But that may never happen!" "I know. But if you tell him, and he doesn't remember, there's only disaster for you both. At best, he'd resent you. And a shock could leave him worse than he ever was."

16. In the radio show, she recalls that, when she told him about her son that died, "I couldn't tell him it was his own son. It was too late now to hope that he'd ever remember me. I'd lived on that hope for three years. Oh, I might have told him that I was his wife. He'd have accepted me. He'd have pitied me, then he'd resent me. There was only one thing for me to do." And so she resolves to divorce him.

17. Even today, as Jerome Groopman reports, "More than forty per cent of oncologists withhold a prognosis from a patient if he or she does not ask for it or if the family requests that the patient not be told." Jerome Groopman, "Dying Words," 63.

18. Bette Davis in *Dark Victory* (Edmund Goulding, 1939) and Ronald Colman in *The Light That Failed* (William A. Wellman, 1939) lie about being able to see when they can't, and Robert Taylor (with Irene Dunne) in *Magnificent Obsession* (John M. Stahl, 1935) and Merle Oberon in *Memory of Love* lie to blind people.

19. This attitude persists in our day, in real life; the *New York Times* reported that a man suffering from amnesia as a result of the September 11, 2001, attacks was reunited with his mother, whom doctors told to "proceed slowly in rebuilding a relationship with her son, and act as though they were meeting for the first time. 'I went to see him and I said, "You look so much like my son,"' she recalled." Richard Lezin Jones, "Nearly a Year after Sept. 11, a Missing Man Is Found in a Manhattan Hospital," *New York Times*, August 28, 2002, A17. Hilton wasn't making it all up, you know, unbelievable as it may seem.

20. The novel, like the film, assumes the "don't ask/don't tell" attitude characteristic of its time, which it applies to the relationship between Charles and his father: when Charles returns from the dead, the doctor treating his dying father refuses to inform the old man that Charles is alive because, as the butler reports, "He was rather troubled about the danger of giving the old gentleman a shock" (Hilton, *Random Harvest*, 75). And so Charles never sees his father before he dies, though they are living in the same house, a missed opportunity that foreshadows the missed intimacy that he will have with Mrs. Rainier, also in the same house.

21. Introducing the film on Turner Classic Movies in June 2002.

22. Pauline Kael, *5001 Nights at the Movies*, 616. She much prefers the Carol Burnett–Harvey Korman parody of the film ("Rancid Harvest," episode 158, season 6, of the *Carol Burnett Show*, 24 March 1973).

23. Colman specialized in double parts, such as *Prisoner of Zenda*, *A Double Life*, and this one, his greatest double role. And life had prepared him well to play the wounded Smithy: Colman had been seriously wounded in 1916 in World War I at the battle of Messines.

24. For Margaret is never depicted as Paula-as-Margaret in the novel until the last page, and she is virtually silent until the end; the film gives her many of the lines that belonged, in the novel, to Harrison, Charles's private secretary (and the narrator of the novel), who plays a much smaller part in the film. The film also reduces the voice of the narrator to the one introductory speech, though the character (Harrison, the private secretary) still plays his role inside the frame; by contrast, the radio play made Garson/Paula/Margaret the narrator.

25. The reader of the book is like the virginal operagoer who does not know about the triple cross at the end of *Tosca* and hence is shocked along with Tosca herself; the viewer of the film is like the seasoned operagoer who does know the trick and experiences the poignancy of watching Tosca's mistake.

26. There are a number of trivial changes from the novel to the film: Miss Hansett becomes Miss Hanson, Melbury becomes Melbridge, etc.

27. James Hilton, *Random Harvest*, 184–185.

28. From the somewhat vague references to radio bulletins, this seems to be the day when Hitler invaded Poland (September 1, 1939), though it might be the day, two days later, when England declared war on Germany.

29. Slavoj Zizek, "How Did Marx Invent the Symptom?" 25. Marx had remarked (in *Capital*) that one man is a king only because other men imagine that he is a king.

30. Hilton, *Random Harvest*, 5–6.

31. Thanks to Thalya Gigerenzer for reminding me of this film and its relevance.

32. The film was to be entitled, *O Brother, Where Art Thou?*, a title that the Coen brothers used in 2000 for their film about a chain gang, which was therefore a remake not of a real film but of a film imagined in another film.

Chapter 6

1. Geisel, Theodore [Dr. Seuss], *Dr. Seuss's Sleep Book*.

2. Sir Monier Monier-Williams, *Sanskrit-English Dictionary*, 947, q.v. *vasana*.

3. Kalidasa, *Abhijnanashakuntala*, 5.2.

4. *Raghavabhatta* 9, cited by Robert P. Goldman, "Karma," 423.

5. Plato, *Republic*, Book 10, 613–620.

6. Urwiek, *The Message of Plato*, 213, cited by Paul Shorey, Loeb Classical Library edition of Plato's *Republic*.

7. *Markandeya Purana* 10.1–7, 11.1–21. See Doniger O'Flaherty, *Textual Sources for the Study of Hinduism*, 97–98.

8. *Laws of Manu* 12.74.

9. "*Ach, du warst in abgelebten Zeiten/ Meine Schwester oder meine Frau.*" Freud, *Moses and Monotheism*, 162.

10. Martha McClintock, "Pheromones and Vasanas," 99.

11. Proust, *Swann's Way*, 3.

12. McClintock, "Pheromones and Vasanas."

13. Philip Larkin said it best: "They fuck you up, your mum and dad. They do not mean to, but they do....Man hands on misery to man...Get out as early as you can." ("This Be the Verse," 1974).

14. Sigmund Freud, in *Totem and Taboo*, 14–15, 20–21, discusses sexual overvaluation. See also "A Special Type of Choice of Object Made by Men."

15. I used these stories in an earlier discussion of the Indian philosophy of illusion and the Indian theory of dreams (*Dreams, Illusion, and Other Realities*). But it's a text that one could go on mining forever, and on this occasion I want to look at what it tells us about self-imitation and about gender.

16. *Yogavasishtha* 6.1.62–64; Doniger O'Flaherty, *Dreams, Illusion, and Other Realities*, 207–209.

17. *Yogavasishtha* 6.1.66.22–24, 6.1.62.32, 6.1.63.17.

18. For Indra as performer of horse sacrifices and obstructer of horse sacrifices, see Doniger O'Flaherty, *Origins of Evil*, 102–123. For the identification of the horse with the sacrificer and with Prajapati, see *Shatapatha Brahmana* 13.1.1.1 and 13.2.1.1. For the many variants of the story of Indra's theft of the sacrificial horse of King Sagara, see *Mahabharata* 3.104–108; *Ramayana* 1.38–44; *Visnu Purana* 4.4.1–33. For a discussion of these stories, see Doniger O'Flaherty, *Women, Androgynes, and Other Mythical Beasts*, 220–222.

19. The *Harivamsha*, the appendix to the Sanskrit epic, the *Mahabharata*, was composed a few centuries after the final recension of the *Mahabharata*, perhaps in the sixth century CE.

20. *Harivamsha* 118.11–39.

21. Doniger O'Flaherty, "Dionysos and Siva: Parallel Patterns in Two Pairs of Myths."

22. Doniger O'Flaherty, *Siva*, 128–130; *The Origins of Evil*, 272–277; with Brian K. Smith, "Sacrifice and Substitution."

23. "Siva and Parvati," from Karnataka, no. 48, *Folktales of India*, edited by Brenda E. F. Beck et al., 171–174; Peter Claus, "Playing *Cenne*," 290–293; Shulman, *God Inside Out*, 108; Doniger, *The Bedtrick*, 17–20.

24. Doniger O'Flaherty, *Siva*, 298–299; cf. *Mahabhagavata Purana* 9–11. That husbands less often pray to be reunited with their wives in this way is worthy of note but not surprising.

25. *Kalika Purana* 49.1–58, 50.1–76, 51.1; 52.105–122; Doniger O'Flaherty, *Siva*, 206–207.

26. *Mahabharata* 13, app. 1, no. 5, 69.

27. *Skanda Purana* 1.8.18-19; Doniger, *The Bedtrick*, 397. There are interesting parallels here with Plato's *Symposium*, which tells of a primeval androgyne that split into the ancestors of men and women, who, therefore, always try to get back together again.

28. Doniger, *Siva*; *The Origins of Evil*.

29. This text takes basic themes from the story of Rama: Shiva is cursed to become human, as Vishnu is cursed to take on a human incarnation in the *Ramayana*, and Chandrashekhara is born as Rama is born, out of portions of a god (there Vishnu, here Shiva) distributed to a group of queens. But instead of producing multiple children (as Rama's brothers are produced), the portions here come together to make a single composite child, as Jarasandha, the enemy of Krishna, is created in the *Mahabharata* 2.16–17.

30. Edward Cameron Dimock, "A Theology of the Repulsive."

31. Freud, "The Taboo of Virginity," 204.

32. *Kalika Purana* 52.150–151.

33. Ramanujan, *The Flowering Tree*, no. 59, 163: "Siva Plays Double."

34. Ten is the usual number of avatars, though some texts list eighteen.

35. At one point, for instance, Krishna loses his temper and vows to drink the blood of his enemies; his pal Arjuna appeases him by reminding him of the great deeds that he has accomplished for millennia; that is, Arjuna reminds Krishna that he is god. *Mahabharata* 3.13.

36. Goldman, "Karma," 420.

37. This happens to both his friend Arjuna and his mother, Yashodha. *Bhagavata Purana* 10.8.21–45; Doniger O'Flaherty, *Dreams, Illusion, and Other Realities*, 109–110, *Hindu Myths*, 218–220, *The Implied Spider*, chap. 1.

38. *Bhagavata Purana* 10.22.1–28; Doniger O'Flaherty, *Hindu Myths*, 228–231. This is a well-known theological ruse: When Kleist's Jupiter impersonates Amphitryon with Amphitryon's wife Alcmena, in the course of his double-talk he says, "Pretend that I'm Jupiter." Kleist, *Amphitryon*.

39. *Ramayana* 6.105.8–10.

40. Sheldon Pollock, "Atmanam Manusam Manye," 233. Citing Sanskrit commentary of Tryambaka Makhin (1711–1728).

41. "It was an intentional act on the part of [Rama] that he became for some time ignorant [of his true nature]. Once the task of the gods had been achieved, and he had received instruction [from Brahma] about his true self—which was merely the apparent cause [of his realization]—he abandoned this [ignorance]." Tryambaka, quoting a commentary from 850–900; Pollock, "Atmanam Manusam Manye," 234–235.

42. Pollock, "Atmanam Manusam Manye," 242, citing Govindaraja.

43. Doniger, *Splitting the Difference*, 9–27.

44. *Ramayana* 7.17.1–31, and lines 6–10 excised after 6.48.7. This woman, named Vedavati, sometimes manages to thwart Ravana's attempt to rape her. See Doniger, *Splitting the Difference*.

45. *Sri Venkateca Mahatmiyam* by N. C. Teyvacikamani, chap. 3, 11–12; translated by Norman Cutler. Shiva will become incarnate as the god Venkateshwara and Vedavati as the goddess Padmavati. In the *Brahmavaivarta Purana* (2.14.1–59), Vedavati becomes first the shadow Sita and then Draupadi, heroine of the *Mahabharata*.

46. *Yogavasistha* 3.44–59; Doniger O'Flaherty, *Dreams, Illusion, and Other Realities*, 101–102.

47. What happened in 1988 to spawn all these films at once? But there was also *Freaky Friday*, first in 1976 (Gary Nelson) and then in 2003 (Mark S. Waters).

48. This was the judgment of the Internet Movie Database.

49. The 1943 Ernst Lubitsch version begins the same way but then follows a different script entirely.

50. This theme veers off, in some other films, into the story of a person who dies and is allowed to come back to earth, sometimes for a limited time, sometimes for a full life, to set right some wrong that he or she had committed. (*Cabin in the Sky* [Vincente Minelli, 1943] is the great classic of this genre.) And in *Groundhog Day* (Harold Ramis, 1993), the hero must live the same day over and over again until he gets it right.

51. This is precisely what happens to King Udayana, in a play by Bhasa (*Svapnavasavadatta, The Drama of Vasavadatta in a Dream*), when he speaks, in his dream, to the Vasavadatta of the past and is overheard by the Vasavadatta of the present.

52. Leslie Halliwell, *Halliwell's Film Guide*, 894.

53. Woody Allen in *Sleeper* (1973) and Sylvester Stallone in *Demolition Man* (Marco Brambilla, 1993) also survive cryogenically but without raising the romantic issues that concern us.

54. There may well be some, but I have not been able to find any.

55. See Wendy Doniger O'Flaherty, "The Mythological in Disguise: An Analysis of *Karz*." The same image was used to depict the androgynous Chevalier d'Eon.

56. So called because pizza, born in Sicily, migrated to the United States and only then became more broadly popular in Italy.

57. Doniger O'Flaherty, *Other Peoples' Myths*, 14–15.

Chapter 7

1. Marcel Proust, *Time Regained*, 365–66.

2. Javiar Marias, *Tomorrow in the Battle Think on Me*, 190, 182.

3. For the asymmetry in male and female sexual aging, see Doniger, *The Bedtrick*, 196, 378, 385.

4. Doniger, *The Bedtrick*, 429–430, 445–447, 479–480.

5. Muriel Spark, *Aiding and Abetting*, 64.

6. Angela Carter, *Wise Children*, 208.

7. The use of cosmetic surgery to correct birth defects or mutilations due to trauma is another matter altogether and not a part of this mythology. Yet sometimes the mythology, particularly in films, uses a natural scar or a traumatic mutilation as the occasion not merely for reconstruction but for a

rejuvenating face-lift, and then the tale joins up with the mythology of self-imitation and the attempt to erase the signs of aging.

8. *Padma Purana* 1.46–47; Doniger, *The Bedtrick*, 70–74.

9. Mark Kalluak, *How Kablomat Became*, 18–21.

10. Knud Rasmussen, *Intellectual Culture of the Copper Eskimos*, 289. He spells the name Kivioq.

11. Sir James George Frazer, *Taboo and the Perils of the Soul*, 70.

12. Frazer, *Taboo and the Perils of the Soul*, 74, citing P. Jos. Meier, *Mythe und Erzählungen der Küstenbewohner der Gazelle Halbinsel*, vol. 1, 39.

13. Geza Roheim, "The Garden of Eden," 20.

14. A mother's failure to recognize a transformed son results in incest in the ancient Indian tale of Kutsa in the *Jaiminiya Brahmana*; Doniger O'Flaherty, *Tales of Sex and Violence*, 75–76.

15. Roheim, "The Garden of Eden," 21.

16. Bronislaw Malinowski, *Myth in Primitive Psychology*, 103–105.

17. In some of the older tellings, Red (Riding Hood) eats her grandmother and climbs into bed with the wolf. Mary Douglas, "Children Consumed and Child Cannibals," 43.

18. Carter, *Wise Children*, 155–156, 161.

19. Leslie Kaufman, obituary of Olivia Goldsmith, *New York Times*, January 16, 2004, C10. Olivia Goldsmith also wrote a novel about a man who mistook his wife for his mistress in a bedtrick, *Switcheroo* (1998). See Doniger, *The Bedtrick*, 28–29, 409–410.

20. Kobo Abe, *The Face of Another*, 209.

21. Ibid., 214.

22. Stanley Cavell, *Pursuits of Happiness*, 222

23. This theme of a murderer unwittingly impersonating a murderer was also used in *A Stolen Life* (Curtis Bernhardt, 1946) and *Sommersby* (Jon Amiel, 1993).

24. Leonard Maltin, *Movie and Video Guide*.

25. Leslie Halliwell noted this, too; "Rambling teenage variation on *Random Harvest*, not very well done and about forty years behind its proper times," 920.

26. Richard Neely, *The Plastic Nightmare*, 236.

27. Ibid., 237.

28. Cavell, *Pursuits of Happiness*, 31.

29. A similar sentiment was expressed in Hitchcock's *Spellbound* (1945) by the amnesiac John Ballantine (Gregory Peck), who kisses Dr. Constance Peterson (Ingrid Bergman) and says, "For what it's worth, I don't remember kissing any other woman before."

30. *Bhagavata Purana* 10; Doniger O'Flaherty, *The Origins of Evil*, 298–310.

31. Janet Maslin, "Good and Evil Trade Places, Body and Soul," *New York Times*, June 27, 1997, C1.

32. Ibid., C14.

33. This is also the situation of the folktale figure known as the clever wife, who masquerades sometimes as an actual rival, sometimes as a fantasy woman. This story is best known in English literature from Shakespeare's *All's Well That Ends Well*, based upon a Sanskrit text. See Wendy Doniger, "Jewels of Rejection and Recognition in Ancient India."

34. Kapoor's film ran into trouble with the censors because of this. The display of Zeenat Aman's body in the skimpy outfits, drenched in water, was the major attraction of the film. As Kapoor himself said in an interview, "Let people come to see Zeenat Aman's tits, they'll go out remembering the film." See Rachel Dwyer, "The Erotics of the Wet Sari in Hindi Films."

35. *Encyclopedia of Indian Cinema*.

36. As Debbie Reynolds dubbed for the blonde bimbo in *Singin' in the Rain*.

37. Sherwin Nuland, "Getting in Nature's Way," a review of Sheila M. Rothman and David J. Rothman, *The Pursuit of Perfection: The Promise and Perils of Medical Enhancement* (New York: Pantheon, 2004), in *New York Review of Books*, February 12, 2004, 33.

38. Arlene Judith Klotzko, "About a Face."

39. Marjorie Garber, *Vested Interests*, 117.

40. Max Beerbohm, "The Happy Hypocrite," 37–38.

41. Ibid., 47.

42. Charles Siebert, "The Cuts That Go Deeper," 24.

43. Ibid., 45.

44. Alex Kuczynski, "F.D.A. Plans to Approve a Drug Long Endorsed by the Vainer Set," *New York Times*, February 7, 2002, sec. 1, A18.

45. Saul Bellow, *The Adventures of Augie March*, 540.

46. Heinrich von Kleist, *Amphitryon*, 1.2.

47. Janet Rowling, *Harry Potter and the Prisoner of Azkaban*, 282, 297, 301.

Chapter 8

1. A number of themes from this scene in particular, and *Vertigo* in general, resonate with a Hindi film made in the very same year, making it difficult to determine the direction of influences. In *Madhumati* (Bimal Roy, 1958), as in *Vertigo*, a man follows up to a high roof a woman whom he mistakes for another woman who had previously jumped to her death from that spot; and again there is a fatal leap. In both films, the man first mistakes another woman for his dead lover and then persuades her to masquerade as the dead woman. The Hindi film also has a woman-and-portrait scene that is a strong parallel to that scene in *Vertigo* (as well as to the woman-and-portrait scene in *As You Desire Me*). The differences are significant, too: in the Hindi film, there are four distinct women (all played by the same actress): the lover, the look-alike, the ghost of the lover, and the lover reborn as the wife of the storyteller in the outer frame; and the man, as well as the woman, leaps from the roof at the end.

2. He has also seen it in a self-portrait by his ex-girlfriend Midge, and he has heard (from Gavin) that Madeleine used to wear it.

3. This 360-degree camera shot was reused by Norman Jewison in *The Thomas Crown Affair* (1968), when the trickster Steve McQueen kissed the trickster Faye Dunaway for the first time.

4. J. G. Ballard, "Thirteen for Centaurs," 162.

5. A benevolent example of this mentality is the practice of writing the word AMBULANCE in mirror reversal on the front of ambulances so that they will read correctly in the rearview mirrors of cars the ambulance approaches from the rear.

6. Slavoj Zizek, "How Did Marx Invent the Symptom?" 42.

7. Anthony Lane, "In Love with Fear," 84. Grant indulged in a more lighthearted double back with Bergman in Stanley Donen's *Indiscreet* (1958), where he played an apparently single man who pretended to be married (a trick borrowed from Myrna Loy in *Third Finger, Left Hand* [1936]), hence unable to marry his mistress Bergman. But then he turned out to have been single all along, prompting an outraged Bergman to remark, "How dare he make love to me—And not be a married man!" And in Hitchcock's *To Catch a Thief* (1955), Cary Grant (as John Robie, the cat burglar) used a different kind of triple cross to elude the French police who were watching him at a fancy-dress ball: Robie came costumed as a Moor, in blackface, and spoke with the distinctive Cary Grant accent so the police could hear him; he then went off briefly to do an errand, returned, and danced with Grace Kelly in full sight of the police all night, until we discovered that his accomplice, the British insurance inspector (John Williams III), had taken his place (in costume and blackface) on returning from the errand, while Cary Grant had been doing his thing on the roof.

8. Michael Brunnbauer, in "Epicsnopix" (on the Internet, [www.irc.at/~mib/lib/epicsnopix.pdf], 2002, [1–129, here p. 77]) adds: "Much of the film's action was shot in Spain, which was, at that time, ruled by rigid dictator General Francisco Franco. When movie extras began to sing 'Internationale' during the filming of a protest scene, members of the secret police hid in the crowd in order to see which individuals actually knew the words to the revolutionary ballad. Aware that they were being observed, all the extras stopped singing and refused to resume despite extensive pleading from the film crew."

9. From a documentary, *The Tramp and the Dictator*, written by Christopher Bird and Kevin Brownlow, directed by Kevin Brownlow and Michael Kloft, 2002.

10. Susan Neiman, *Slow Fire: Jewish Notes from Berlin*, 217.

11. Schwarzenegger also mocked the theme of doubles in *The Sixth Day* (Roger Spottiswoode, 2000), in which he plays a pilot who encounters his own clone and isn't sure which is the real person or whether he himself is the clone. At one point he remarks to the scientist who produced the clone: "You should clone yourself now, while you're still alive . . . so you can fuck yourself!"

12. Doniger, *The Implied Spider*, 105. An update of *Invasion of the Body Snatchers* was made in 1978, with Kevin McCarthy, who had played the lead in the first version, now playing a minor role.

13. Eve Sedgwick, *Epistemology of the Closet*.

14. Doniger, *The Bedtrick*, 327.

Chapter 9

1. Elaine K. Ginsberg, *Passing and the Fictions of Identity*.

2. Wendy Doniger, *The Bedtrick*, chap. 7.

3. William Faulkner, *Light in August*, 223.

4. Mary Ann Doane, *Femmes Fatales: Feminism, Film Theory, Psychoanalysis*, 235.

5. Ibid., 237.

6. Philip Roth, *The Human Stain*, 16, 337–338, 243.

7. Henry Louis Gates Jr., "White Like Me," 76–77.

8. Ibid., 68.

9. Ibid., 78.

10. This was inferred by, among others, Sanford Pinsker, *Jewish Journal of Greater Los Angeles*, June 23, 2003; Bob Hoover, *Pittsburgh Post-Gazette*, May 28, 2000; Marion Kilcoyne, *Sunday Business Post*, May 28, 2000.

11. Marjorie Garber, *Vested Interests*, 76.

12. *Yogavasishtha* 6.1.85–108; Doniger O'Flaherty, *Dreams, Illusions, and Other Realities*, 280–281.

13. I am grateful to Mary Douglas for this insight, made when I presented some of these materials at the School of Oriental and African Studies of the University of London in November 2003.

14. *Antony and Cleopatra* 5.2; *Hamlet* 2.2; *A Midsummer Night's Dream* 1.2; epilogue of *As You Like It*; *Twelfth Night* 1.4, 1.5. At the start of *The Taming of the Shrew*, a page is dressed as a woman to trick a man.

15. When Ellen, in *My Favorite Wife*, tells Nick, "I'll be Bianca," her rhetoric owes much to Rosalind's request to Orlando to "Call me Rosalind." The difference is that Orlando is fooled (perhaps), and Nick (whose surname is, in case you did not notice, Arden, as in "Forest of" as well as in "Enoch") is not. A more significant difference between Rosalind and Ellen is that Ellen, unlike Rosalind, is fighting against a real rival: she is taking the place of the woman who is taking her place. The "Call me Rosalind" trope was also used in a *Cyrano de Bergerac* cover, *The Truth about Cats and Dogs* (Michael Lehmann, 1996), in which a man named Brian falls in love with the voice of a radio talk-show hostess named Abby, who sends her gorgeous roommate Donna to their first actual rendezvous, in her place, and then introduces herself to him as Donna, Abby's roommate. When Brian writes a love letter to Abby, he asks Abby-as-Donna to pretend to be Abby so that he can try it out on her first, to get the female perspective, at which point the film segues for a moment into *As You Like It*: "You be Abby," he says; "I'm Abby," she replies cheerfully and truthfully.

16. Doniger, *The Bedtrick*, 427.

17. This was said of Katharine Hepburn in *Sylvia Scarlett* (George Cukor, 1935). Claudia Roth Pierpont, "Born for the Part," 56.

18. This passage is immediately echoed in two other rhetorically parallel passages, in which Rosalind puts herself first, not last. The second dialogue of double entendre (in more senses than one) occurs just two scenes later (5.4), when Rosalind, still as Ganymede and with the same echoing rhetoric, makes her father, taking her place in the rhetorical pattern, promise to give Rosalind to Orlando and then makes Orlando promise to marry Rosalind. (She also makes Phoebe promise to marry Silvius and Silvius to accept Phoebe.) It is after this exchange that the Duke and Orlando comment on the startling resemblance between Ganymede and Rosalind; they are beginning to get the joke but have not quite figured it out. And in the third passage, later in the same scene, Rosalind herself—actually present as herself—gives herself first to her father and then to Orlando, punctuating her actions with yet another echo of the same rhetorical pattern, leaving Phoebe a poor third and Silvius dumbstruck.

19. The audience, as Marjorie Garber points out, is "very much in on the joke," though this "did not mitigate, but rather confirmed, the remanding of women back to their proper places at the end of the play." Marjorie Garber, *Vested Interests*, 72.

20. Stanley Cavell, *Pursuits of Happiness*, 49. The role of Connecticut in *Bringing Up Baby, The Awful Truth, Pillow Talk*, and *Adam's Rib* is played by a more general countryside in *Random Harvest, My Favorite Wife*, and *Satyam Shivam Sundaram*.

21. Angela Carter, *The Passion of New Eve*, 132.

22. Don Shewey, "A Man Plays a Woman, without Any Disguise," *New York Times*, April 13, 2003, sec. 2, 5.

23. Ursula Heise, in "Transvestism and the Stage Controversy in Spain and England," 372–74, summarizes the edition edited by Francisco Ayala (Madrid: Castalia, 1989). I am grateful to Stephen Orgel for telling me about this play.

24. Gary Kates, *Monsieur d'Eon Is a Woman*.

25. Cynthia Cox, *The Enigma of the Age*, cited by John P. Muller and William J. Richardson, "Notes on Lacan," 93. Gary Kates regards this Russian drag as a fantasy.

26. Kates, *Monsieur d'Eon Is a Woman*, 67, 75, 257.

27. He mentions the Chevalier in his seminar on Poe's "The Purloined Letter"; see also John P. Muller and William J. Richardson, "Notes on Lacan," 93.

28. Jacques Lacan, 1986 seminar, "The Ethic of Psychoanalysis," cited by Slavoj Zizek, "How Did Marx Invent the Symptom?" 28–29.

29. Slavoj Zizek, "How Did Marx Invent the Symptom?" 28–29.

30. Kates, *Monsieur d'Eon Is a Woman*, 256, 38, 256.

31. Ibid., 67, 37, 44–45, 220, 223, 257, 4, 221, 47.

32. The same story was told by Shi Peipu and by Richard Strauss and Hugo von Hofmannsthal about their heroine Zdenka/o in *Arabella*; Doniger, *The Bedtrick*, 340–342, 370. It was also told in ancient India about Amba/Shikhandin and Ila; Doniger, *Splitting the Difference*, 271–278, 281–286.

33. Kates, *Monsieur d'Eon Is a Woman*, 47–48.

34. Ibid., 39.

35. "It was clearly a typical case of what Hirschfeld later termed 'transvestism' and what I would call 'sexo-aesthetic inversion', or more simply, 'Eonism.' . . . The Eonist (though sometimes emphatically of the apparent sex) sometimes shows real physical approximations towards the opposite sex." Havelock Ellis, *Studies in the Psychology of Sex*, vol. 7, i, 10, 12.

36. *London Times*, September, 5, 1970, sec. 8, 4. It also called the Chevalier "an a-sexual transvestite."

37. Doniger, *The Bedtrick*, 369–372.

38. Cary Grant, in an earlier age, never came out of the closet, if, indeed, he was ever inside it. But he got into drag in many of his films, notably *Bringing Up Baby* (Howard Hawks, 1938), *My Favorite Wife* (1940), and *I Was a Male War Bride* (Howard Hawks, 1949).

39. Marjorie Garber, *Vice Versa*, 150, 52, citing the journalist George Davis.

40. Parker Tyler, cited by Claudia Roth Pierpont, "The Strong Woman," 108.

41. Garber, *Vice Versa*, 230, 116, 231, 240, 249.

42. Angela Carter, *Wise Children*, 192.

43. Garber, *Vested Interests*, 65, 49.

44. Elaine Showalter, *Sexual Anarchy*, 168.

45. Joan Rivière, "Womanliness as a Masquerade."

46. Jacques Lacan, *Feminine Sexuality*, 85.

47. Slavoj Zizek, "'The Wound is Healed,'" 205.

48. Judith Butler, "Lacan, Rivière," 47.

49. Mary Anne Doane, *Femmes Fatales*, 38.

50. Holly Devor, *Gender Blending*, 128, 130.

51. *Kamasutra* 2.8.6.

52. *Kamasutra* 2.8.39.

Conclusion

1. William Butler Yeats, *The Autobiography of William Butler Yeats*, 340–341.

2. Erving Goffman, *Relations in Public: Microstudies of the Public Order*, ix; *The Presentation of Self in Everyday Life; Behavior in Public Places*.

3. Jacques Lacan, "The Mirror Stage as Formative of the Function of the I."

4. Lacan, "The Agency of the Letter," 171–172. This was a gloss of Freud's "*Wo Es war, soll Ich werden*" ("Where it was, there shall I be," sometimes translated, "Where id was, there shall ego be").

5. Toril Moi, *Sexual/Textual Politics*, 99.

6. This is Wayne Booth's excellent term; personal communication, June 2002.

7. Robert Irwin, *The Arabian Nights*, 195.

8. Slavoj Zizek, "From Symptom to *Sinthome*," 58.

9. Mikhail Bakhtin, *Problems of Dostoyevsky's Poetics*, 233.

10. Heinrich Zimmer, *Myths and Symbols*, 219–221, citing Martin Buber (*Die Chassidischen Bucher* (Hellerau, 1928), 532–533. I must apologize for using Heinrich Zimmer's version of this story here, when I have cited it before, in several other contexts, beginning with a brief citation at the very beginning of my very first book, about Shiva, and continuing through a full telling at the very end of *Other Peoples' Myths*. Apparently it is for me, as the dream of the Christian on the bridge was for the rabbi, a central source of truth to which I cannot help returning; or in other words, it is one of my myths.

11. James Hilton, *Random Harvest*, 53.

12. Paul Ricoeur, *The Symbolism of Evil*, 349.

13. Woody Allen, "Fabulous Tales and Mythical Beasts."

14. Doniger, *The Bedtrick*, chap. 8.

15. Chuang Tsu, "The Equality of Things and Opinions," 2.1.2.22; Doniger O'Flaherty, *Other Peoples' Myths*, 77.

16. Jacques Lacan, "The Split between the Eye and the Gaze," 76.

17. Kobo Abe, *The Face of Another*, 210.

18. Method acting, by contrast, begins with the actor's own emotions. The Method actor, Dustin Hoffman, preparing for the moment in *Marathon Man* (John Schlesinger, 1976) when he runs for hours without stopping, actually ran for several hours and staggered, exhausted, onto the set to do the scene. Sir Laurence Olivier strolled over to him and remarked, "Dustin, ever heard of acting?"

19. Personal communication from Richard Streier, December 2003.

20. *Shrishriramakrishnakathamrita* 1.181, translated by Jeffrey Kripal, personal communication, May 1993; William Buck, *Ramayana* 301. Another example of this Hindu conception appears in the *Kashyapa Samhita*, a Sanskrit medical text from about the sixth or seventh century CE: "As is the face, so is the behavior; as is the eye, so is the mind; as is the voice, so is the vitality; as is the form, so are the qualities."

21. I owe this story to Françoise Meltzer.

22. Zizek, "How Did Marx Invent the Symptom?" 28–29.

23. P. Marivaux, *Télémaque travesti* (Paris, 1972, 772), cited by Sabine Melchior-Bonnet, *The Mirror*, 176.

24. Doniger, *The Implied Spider*, 1–5.

25. Barbara Johnson, "The Frame of Reference," 245–246, here quoting an 1845 edition of Poe's text in Thomas O. Mabbott, *Collected Works of Edgar Allan Poe*, vol. 2, 545 (Cambridge, Mass.: Belknap Press of Harvard University Press, 1978).

26. Peter de Vries, *The Tunnel of Love*, 35, 114.

27. Wilde, *The Picture of Dorian Gray*, chap. 1.

28. Richard Stern, *Other Men's Daughters*, 149.

29. Friedrich Nietzsche, *Beyond Good and Evil*, no. 40.

30. Friedrich Nietzsche, *The Gay Science*, 38.

31. Henry Abramovitch, "Turning Inside Out," 1, 7.

32. Paul Ricoeur, *Hermeneutics and the Human Sciences*.

33. Terry Eagleton, "Maybe He Made It Up," 6, 3.

34. Henry James, "The Real Thing," 21.

35. Doniger, *The Bedtrick*. The same point is made by *Dave* (Ivan Reitman, 1993).

36. Stanley Cavell, *Contesting Tears*, 14.

37. Geoffrey Lloyd, *Polarity and Analogy*; Claude Lévi-Strauss, *Structural Anthropology*.

38. Barbara Johnson, "The Frame of Reference," 223.

39. Marcel Proust, *In a Budding Grove*, 579.

40. Virginia Woolf, *Orlando*, 200–201, 204.

41. Robert J. Lifton, *The Protean Self*, 226, 230.

42. Richard Moskovitz, *Lost in the Mirror: An Inside Look at Borderline Personality Disorder*. Foreword by Chris Costner Sizemore, author of *I'm Eve* (the source of *The Three Faces of Eve* [Nunnally Johnson, 1957]; see Wendy Doniger, *Splitting the Difference*, 79–84).

43. Zizek, "How Did Marx Invent the Symptom?" 46–47.

44. M. M. Bakhtin, "Author and Hero in Aesthetic Activity," 15, 22; "Forms of Time and Chronotope in the Novel," 256. He also says here: "It is just as impossible to forge an identity between myself, my own 'I,' and that 'I' that is the subject of my stories as it is to lift myself up by my own hair."

45. Bakhtin, "Author and Hero in Aesthetic Activity," 22, 25, 38.

46. Shulman, "Embracing the Subject," 87.

47. Shulman, "Bhavabhuti on Cruelty and Compassion," 79.

48. David Shulman, personal communication, June 1996.

49. Zizek, "How Did Marx Invent the Symptom?" 42.

50. Lacan, "Le séminaire sur 'La letter volée,'" translated by Jeffrey Mehlman, 37.

51. Mary Ann Doane, *Femmes Fatales*, 57.

52. Philip Roth, *The Human Stain*, 337–338.

53. Michael Miller, cited by Henry Louis Gates Jr., "White Like Me," 74.

54. Kobo Abe, *The Face of Another*, 93–94

55. Obituary of Rudolf Bing, *New York Times*, September 3, 1997, D25.

56. This is Dr. Jerome Winer's insight.

57. *Mahabharata, Virata Parvan.*

58. Joseph Bédier, *The Romance of Tristan and Iseult*, 135, citing the French poem dealing with this episode alone. In *La folie Tristan d'Oxford*, she thinks him dead and thinks the man before her is a fool pretending to be Tristan.

59. Béroul, *Le roman de Tristran*, 3769–3776.

60. Edgar Allan Poe, "The Purloined Letter," 15.

61. Ibid., 20.

62. Laura Hillenbrand, *Seabiscuit: An American Legend*, 137.

63. Lacan, "Le séminaire sur 'La letter volée,'" 44.

64. Jacques Derrida, "Le facteur de la vérité," *Poétique* 21 (1975): 96–147, cited and translated by Barbara Johnson, "The Frame of Reference," 222.

65. Oedipus learned the truth (that he had killed his father and slept with his mother) from his misrecognition of everything: of the prophecy, of each of his parents, and of the mounting evidence against him

66. Zizek, "From Symptom to *Sinthome*," 57.

67. Marie Bonaparte's *The Life and Works of Edgar Allan Poe: A Psycho-analytic Interpretation*, published in 1949.

68. Freud, *Jokes and Their Relation to the Unconscious*, 137–138.

69. Ilan Amit, "Squaring the Circle."

70. In *The Bedtrick*, I explored the widespread assumption that everyone lies about sex; here I am pursuing the broader assumption that everyone lies, period. T. M. Luhrmann, in *Persuasions of the Witch's Craft* (307), cites Donald Davidson's belief (in *Inquiries into Truth and Meaning*) that you must treat another person's remarks as true, assuming he is like you, which means Davidson assumes you are not a liar. Freud does not share this optimism.

71. John Barwise and John Etchemendy claim to have solved it. See their book, *The Liar: An Essay on Truth and Circularity*. The Liar's Paradox also plays a part in Kurt Gödel's concept of uncertainty.

72. Freud, *Interpretation of Dreams*, 185–186.

73. Adam Biro, *Two Jews on a Train: Stories from the Old Country and the New*, xi, xii.

74. Lacan, "Le séminaire sur 'La letter volée,'" 29–54.

75. Lacan, "The Agency of the Letter in the Unconscious; or, Reason since Freud," 172–173.

76. Barbara Johnson, "The Frame of Reference," 241.

77. Muller and Richardson, "Notes on Lacan," 89, on Lacan, "Le séminaire sur 'La letter volée.'"

78. Ernest Jones, "Persons in Dreams Disguised as Themselves," 422–423.

79. Winnicott, "Mirror-Role of the Mother and Family in Child Development."

80. Michel Foucault, *Herculine Barbin*, x–xi.

81. Michel Foucault, *History of Sexuality*, vol. 1, 8–10.

82. Zizek, "From Symptom to *Sinthome*," 59.

83. Ernest Gellner, *The Psychoanalytic Movement*, 112, 150, 152.

84. Or as often as not, Indian dolls or Russian-American dolls. The sexual doll metaphor was invoked when the *New York Times*, January 18, 1999, reported on a new set of nested dolls: President Clinton, Monica Lewinsky, Paula Jones, Hilary Clinton, and a saxophone. In that order.

85. A program on British television, "Spitting Image," during the Thatcher regime once showed a Nancy Reagan puppet, who pulled off one mask after another until she had no head at all.

86. And there always remains the choke, the inedible parts of the personality that cannot be wedged into any totalizing system. The French say of a person with many lovers, "*Il a un coeur d'artichaut*." I'm grateful to Marina Warner for this fact; personal communication, London, October 10, 2002.

87. C. S. Lewis, *The Voyage of the Dawn Treader*, 96.

88. *Mahabharata* 2.61.

89. An example from my childhood: in Dr. Seuss's *The Five Hundred Hats of Bartholomew Cubbins*, Bartholomew must take off his hat or have his head chopped off, but every time he takes it off, another takes its place.

90. *The Book of Misers: A Translation of al-Bukhala*, by Abu Uthma ibn Bahr al Jahiz, translated by R. B. Serjeant, 18–19 (Garnet Publishing Limited, 1997). Thanks to Philip Kennedy for this reference.

91. This story, which has the alternative punch-line "elephants all the way down," is sometimes told of William James, perhaps because he assumes general knowledge of the elephant-tortoise cosmology in his 1907 work *Pragmatism*. Speaking of the pluralist view of truth, he remarks, "To rationalists this describes a tramp and vagrant world, adrift in space, with neither elephant nor tortoise to plant the sole of its foot upon" (260–61). In the James anecdote, an old lady who attends one of James's lectures has the last word: "It's no use, Mr. James—it's turtles all the way down!" Clifford Geertz tells the story about an anonymous informant in *The Interpretation of Cultures*, 28–29. It has also been told of Bertrand Russell and Isaac Asimov.

92. Lewis Carroll, "What the Tortoise Said to Achilles," 278–280.

93. Graham Greene, *Brighton Rock*, 198.

94. Cavell, *Pursuits of Happiness*, 206.

95. Cited as the frontispiece to Robert J. Lifton's *The Protean Self*.

96. Proust, *In a Budding Grove*, 340.

97. Proust, *The Captive*, 869–70.

BIBLIOGRAPHY

Ancient, Medieval, and Premodern Sources (by title)

Abhijnanasakuntalam. Kalidasa. With the commentary of Raghava. Bombay: Nirnaya Sagara Press, 1958.

Alcestis. Euripides. Edited and translated by Arthur S. Way. Loeb Classical Library. Cambridge, Mass: Harvard University Press, 1912.

Arthashastra. Kautilya. Critical ed., edited by R. P. Kangle. 3 vols. Bombay: Bombay University, 1960.

Bhagavata Purana. With the commentary of Sridhara. Benares: Pandita Pustakalaya, 1972.

Brahmavaivarta Purana. Anandasrama Sanskrit Series, no. 102. Poona: Anandasrama Press, 1935.

Edda: The Poetic Edda. 2d ed. Translated by Lee M. Hollander. Austin: University of Texas Press, 1962.

Edda: The Prose Edda of Snorri Sturluson; Tales from Norse Mythology. Translated by Jean I. Young. Berkeley and Los Angeles: University of California Press, 1954.

Die Geschichte Thidreks von Bern. Sammlung Thule XXII, uebertragen von Fine Erichsen. Duesseldorf: Eugen Diederichs Verlag, 1967.

Harivamsha. Poona: Bhandarkar Oriental Research Institute, 1969.

Jaiminiya Brahmana. Edited by Raghu Vira and Lokesha Chandra. Sarasrati-vihara Series 31. Nagpur: Sarasvati-vihara Press, 1954.

Kalika Purana. Edited by Sri Biswanarayan Sastri. Varanasi: Chowkhamba Sanskrit Series Office, 1972.

Kamasutra. Vatsyayana. With the commentary of Sri Yasodhara. Bombay: Laksmivenkatesvara Steam Press, 1856.

Kamasutra. Vatsyayana. Translated by Wendy Doniger and Sudhir Kakar. Oxford World Classics. London and New York: Oxford University Press, 2002.

Kathasaritsagara [*The ocean of the rivers of story*]. Somadeva. Bombay: Nirnara Sagara Press, 1930.

Kathasaritsagara [*The ocean of story*]. Edited by N. M. Penzer, translated by C. W. Tawney. 10 vols. London: Chas. J. Sawyer, 1924.

The Mabinogion. Translated by Jeffrey Gantz. Harmondsworth, U.K.: Penguin Books, 1976.

Mahabharata. Vyasa. Poona: Bhandarkar Oriental Research Institute, 1933–1969.

Manu: The Laws of Manu [*Manusmrti*]. Edited by Harikrishna Jayantakrishna Dave. Bombay: Bharatiya Vidya Bhavan, 1972–1985.

Manu: The Laws of Manu [*Manusmrti*]. Translated by Wendy Doniger, with Brian K. Smith. Harmondsworth, U.K.: Penguin Books, 1991.

Le morte d'Arthur. Sir Thomas Malory. New Hyde Park, N.Y.: University Books, 1961.

The Nibelungenlied [*Das Ring des Nibelungen*]. Translated by A. T. Hatto. Harmondsworth, U.K.: Penguin Books, 1965.

Odyssey. Homer. Text, with translation by A. T. Murray. Loeb Classical Library. Cambridge, Mass.: Harvard University Press, 1919.

Oedipus Rex. Sophocles. Text, with translation by F. Storr. Loeb Classical Library. Cambridge, Mass.: Harvard University Press, 1913.

Padma Purana. Anandashrama Sanskrit Series, no. 131. Poona: Anandasrama Press, 1893.

Priyadarshika. Harsha. Edited by M. R. Kale. Bombay, Motilal Banarsidass, 1928.

Ramayana. Valmiki. Baroda: Oriental Institute, 1960–1975.

Ratnavali. Harsha. Edited by Ashokanath Bhattacharya and Maheshwar Das. Calcutta: Modern Book Agency, 1967.

Republic. Plato. Text, with translation by Paul Shorey. Loeb Classical Library. Cambridge, Mass.: Harvard University Press, 1982.

Rig Veda. With the commentary of Sayana. 6 vols. London: Oxford University Press, 1890–1892.

Rig Veda. Translated by Wendy Doniger O'Flaherty. *The Rig Veda: An Anthology; 108 Hymns Translated from the Sanskrit*. Harmondsworth, U.K.: Penguin Classics, 1981.

Shatapatha Brahmana. Benares: Chowkhamba Sanskrit Series Office, 1964.

Shiva Purana. Benares: Pandita Pushtakalaya, 1964.

Skanda Purana. Bombay: Shree Venkateshvara [Venkatesvara] Steam Press, 1867.

Svapnavasavadattam: A Sanskrit Drama in Six Acts Attributed to Bhasa. Critically edited with Introduction, Notes, Translation, and Appendices, edited by C. R. Devadhar. Poona: Oriental Book Agency, 1946.

Die Thidrekssaga, oder Dietrich von Bern und die Niflungen. Übersetzt durch Friedrich Heinrich von der Hagen. Mit neuen geographischen Anmerkungen versehen von Heinz Ritter-Schaumburg. St.-Goar: Otto Reichl Verlag, 1989.

Uttararamacarita. Bhavabhuti. Edited by P. V. Kane. Delhi: Motilal Banarasidass, 1971.

Völsunga saga [*The saga of the Volsungs*]. Translated by William Morris, with an introduction by Robert W. Gutman. New York: Collier Books, 1962.

Völsunga saga [*The saga of the Volsungs*]. Translated by George K. Anderson as *The Saga of the Völsungs: Together with Excerpts from the Nornageststhattr and Three Chapters from the Prose Edda*. Newark: University of Delaware Press, 1982.

Völsunga saga [*The saga of the Volsungs*]. Translated by Jesse L. Byock as *The Saga of the Volsungs: The Norse Epic of Sigurd the Dragon Slayer*. Berkeley: University of California Press, 1990; Harmondsworth, U.K.: Penguin, 1999.

Tristan Stories (by author)

Bédier, Joseph. *The Romance of Tristan and Iseult*. Translated by Hilaire Belloc and Paul Rosenfeld. New York: Pantheon, 1945; reprint, New York: Vintage, 1965.

Béroul. *Le roman de Tristran* [The romance of Tristran]. Edited and translated by Norris J. Lacy. Garland Library of Medieval Literature, ser. A, vol. 36. New York and London: Garland Publishing, 1989.

Von Strassburg, Gottfried. *Tristan*. Translated by A. T. Hatto, and supplemented with the surviving fragments of the *Tristan* of Thomas. Harmondsworth, U.K.: Penguin Books, 1960.

Modern Sources (by author)

Abe, Kobo. *The Face of Another*. Translated from the Japanese by E. Dale Saunders. Tokyo, New York, and London: Kodansha International, 1992. Published in Japanese in 1966.

Abramovitch, Henry Hanoch. "Turning Inside Out: Disguise as a Transition to Homecoming." Paper presented at the meetings of the Jung Association, Chicago, August 27, 1992.

Allen, Woody. "Fabulous Tales and Mythical Beasts." In *Without Feathers*. New York: Random House, 1976.

Amit, Ilan. "Squaring the Circle." In *Untying the Knot: On Riddles and Other Enigmatic Modes*, edited by Galit Hasan-Rokem and David Shulman, 284–293. New York: Oxford University Press, 1996.

Anderson, George K., trans. See *Völsunga Saga*.

Andersson, Theodore M. *The Legend of Brynhild*. Ithaca, N.Y.: Cornell University Press, 1980.

Bakhtin, M. Mikhail. "Author and Hero in Aesthetic Activity." In *Art and Answerability: Early Philosophical Essays*, edited by Michael Holquist and Vadim Liapunov, translated by Vadim Liapunov, 4–256. Austin: University of Texas Press, 1990.

———. "Forms of Time and Chronotope in the Novel." In *The Dialogic Imagination: Four Essays*, edited by Michael Holquist, translated by Caryl Emerson and Michael Holquist, 84–258. Austin: University of Texas Press, 1981.

————. *Problems of Dostoyevsky's Poetics*. Edited and translated by Caryl Emerson. Minneapolis: University of Minnesota Press, 1984.

Ballard, J. G. "Thirteen for Centaurus." In *The Best Short Stories of J. G. Ballard*. New York: Picador, 1978.

Balzac, Honoré de. *Sarrasine*. In Barthes, *S/Z*.

Barthes, Roland. *S/Z: An Essay*. Translated by Richard Miller. New York: Farrar, Straus, and Giroux, 1974. Originally published in French as *S/Z* (Paris: Éditions du Seuil, 1970).

Barwise, Joh, and John Etchemendy. *The Liar: An Essay on Truth and Circularity*. New York: Oxford University Press, 1989.

Beaumarchais, Pierre-Auguste Caron de. *The Barber of Seville/The Marriage of Figaro*. Translated by John Wood. Harmondsworth, U.K.: Penguin Books, 1964.

————. *Théatre de Beaumarchais: "Le barbier de Séville," "Le mariage de Figaro," "La mère coupalbe."* Edited by Maurice Rat. Paris: Éditions Garnier Frères, 1956.

Beck, Brenda E. F., et al., eds. *Folktales of India*. Chicago: University of Chicago Press, 1987.

Bédier, Joseph. See *The Romance of Tristan and Iseult*.

Beerbohm, Max. "The Happy Hypocrite." In *Selected Prose*, edited by Lord David Cecil. Boston: Little, Brown, 1970.

Bellow, Saul. *The Adventures of Augie March*. New York: Avon, 1977. First published in 1949.

Béroul. See *Le roman de Tristran* [The romance of Tristran].

Bettini, Maurizio. *The Portrait of the Lover*. Translated from the Italian by Laura Gibbs. Berkeley: University of California Press, 1999.

Bevington, David, ed. *The Complete Works of Shakespeare*. 4th ed. New York: Harper Collins, 1992.

Biro, Adam. *Two Jews on a Train: Stories from the Old Country and the New*. Translated by Catherine Tihanyi. Chicago: University of Chicago Press, 2001. First published in Paris in 1998.

Borgeson, Jess, et al. *The Compleat Works of Wllm Shakspr (Abridged)*. London: Applause Books. 1995.

Buck, William. *The Ramayana*. Berkeley: University of California Press, 1976.

Butler, Judith. "Lacan, Riviere, and the Strategies of Masquerade." In *Gender Trouble: Feminism and the Subversion of Ideas*, 43–56. New York and London: Routledge, 1990.

Byock, Jesse L., trans. See *Völsunga saga*.

Cannon, Lou. *President Reagan: The Role of a Lifetime*. New York: Simon and Schuster, 1991.

Carroll, Lewis. "What the Tortoise Said to Achilles." *Mind* 4, no. 14 (April 1895): 278–280.

Carter, Angela. *The Passion of New Eve*. London: Bloomsbury Publications, 1993.

————. *Wise Children*. New York: Farrar, Straus, and Giroux, 1991.

Cave, Terence. *Recognitions: A Study in Poetics*. London and New York: Oxford University Press, 1988.

Cavell, Stanley. *Contesting Tears: The Hollywood Melodrama of the Unknown Woman*. Chicago: University of Chicago Press, 1996.

————. *Pursuits of Happiness: The Hollywood Comedy of Remarriage*. Cambridge, Mass.: Harvard University Press, 1981.

————. "Recounting Gains, Showing Losses: Reading *The Winter's Tale*." In *Disowning Knowledge: In Seven Plays of Shakespeare*, 193–221. Cambridge, U.K.: Cambridge University Press, 1987.

Claus, Peter. "Playing *Cenne*: The Meanings of a Folk Game." In *Another Harmony: New Essays on the Folklore of India*, edited by Stuart Blackburn and A. K. Ramanujan, 265–293. Berkeley: University of California Press, 1986.

Connolly, Cyril. *Enemies of Paradise*. New York: Macmillan, 1948.

Cox, Cynthia. *The Enigma of the Age: The Strange Story of the Chevalier d'Eon*. London: Longmans, 1961.

Davidson, Donald. *Inquiries into Truth and Meaning*. New York: Oxford University Press, 1984.

Davis, Nathalie Zemon. *The Return of Martin Guerre*. Cambridge, Mass.: Harvard University Press, 1983.

Derrida, Jacques. *The Post Card: From Socrates to Freud and Beyond*. Translated by Alan Bass. Chicago: University of Chicago Press, 1987. First published in Paris in 1980.

Devor, Holly. *Gender Blending: Confronting the Limits of Duality*. Bloomington: Indiana University Press, 1989.

De Vries, Peter. *The Tunnel of Love*. Boston: Little, Brown, and Company, 1949.

Dillard, Annie. "The Two of Them." *Harper's*, November 2003, 61–65.

Dimock, Edward Cameron. "A Theology of the Repulsive: The Myth of the Goddess Sitala." In *The Sound of Silent Guns, and Other Essays*, 130–149. Delhi: Oxford University Press, 1989.

Doane, Mary Ann. *Femmes Fatales: Feminism, Film Theory, Psychoanalysis*. New York and London: Routledge, 1991.

Doniger, Wendy. *The Bedtrick: Tales of Sex and Masquerade*. Chicago: University of Chicago Press, 2000.

———. "The Dreams and Dramas of a Jealous Hindu Queen: Vasavadatta." In *Dream Cultures: Explorations in the Comparative History of Dreaming*, edited by Guy Stroumsa and David Shulman, 74–84. New York: Oxford University Press, 1999.

———. "Enigmas of Sexual Masquerade in Hindu Myths and Tales." In *Untying the Knot: On Riddles and Other Enigmatic Modes*, edited by David Shulman, 208–227. New York: Oxford University Press, 1996.

———. *The Implied Spider: Politics and Theology in Myth*. New York: Columbia University Press, 1998.

———. "Jewels of Rejection and Recognition in Ancient India." *Journal of Indian Philosophy* 26 (1998): 435–453.

———. "Joking with God in a Fragile World." In *Walking with God in a Fragile World*, edited by Jim Langford, 145–162. Lanham, Md.: Rowman and Littlefield, 2003.

———. *Der Mann, der mit seiner eigenen Frau Ehebruch beging. Mit einem Kommentar von Lorraine Daston*. Berlin: Suhrkamp, 1999.

———. "Speaking in Tongues: Deceptive Stories about Sexual Deception." *Journal of Religion* 74, no. 3 (July 1994, ed. Mark Krupnick): 320–337.

———. *Splitting the Difference: Gender and Myth in Ancient Greece and India*. Chicago: University of Chicago Press, 1999.

———. "The Symbolism of Black and White Babies in the Myth of Maternal Impression." *Social Research* 70, no. 1 (Spring 2003): 1–44.

Doniger, Wendy, with Brian K. Smith. "Sacrifice and Substitution: Ritual Mystification and Mythical Demystification." *Numen* 36, no. 2 (December 1989): 190–223.

Doniger, Wendy, with Gregory Spinner. "Misconceptions: Male Fantasies and Female Imaginations in Parental Imprinting." *Daedalus* 127, no. 1 (Winter 1998): 97–130.

Doniger O'Flaherty, Wendy. *Asceticism and Eroticism in the Mythology of Siva*. London: Oxford University Press, 1973. Reprinted as *Siva: The Erotic Ascetic* (New York: Paperback Galaxy, 1981).

———. "Dionysos and Siva: Parallel Patterns in Two Pairs of Myths." *History of Religions* 20, no. 1 (August 1980): 81–111.

———. *Dreams, Illusion, and Other Realities*. Chicago: University of Chicago Press, 1984.

———. *Hindu Myths: A Sourcebook, translated from the Sanskrit*. Harmondsworth, U.K.: Penguin Classics, 1975.

———. "Karma and Rebirth in the Vedas and Puranas." In *Karma and Rebirth in Classical Indian Traditions*, edited by Wendy Doniger O'Flaherty, 1–39. Berkeley: University of California Press; Delhi, Motilal Banarsidass, 1980.

———. "The Mythological in Disguise: An Analysis of *Karz*." *India International Centre Quarterly* 8, no. 1 (January 1981): 23–29. Reprint, *Debonair* (Bombay), January 1982, 30–34.

———. *The Origins of Evil in Hindu Mythology*. Berkeley: University of California Press, 1976.

———. *Other Peoples' Myths: The Cave of Echoes*. New York: Macmillan, 1988; reprint, Chicago, University of Chicago Press, 1995.

———. *Siva: The Erotic Ascetic*. See *Asceticism and Eroticism*.

———. *Tales of Sex and Violence: Folklore, Sacrifice, and Danger in the Jaiminiya Brahmana*. Chicago: University of Chicago Press, 1985.

———. *Textual Sources for the Study of Hinduism*. Chicago: University of Chicago Press, 1990.

———. *Women, Androgynes, and Other Mythical Beasts*. Chicago: University of Chicago Press, 1980.

———. See also *Kamasutra, Manu, Rig Veda*.

Douglas, Mary. "Children Consumed and Child Cannibals." In *Myth and Method*, edited by Laurie Patton and Wendy Doniger, 29–51. Charlottesville: University Press of Virginia, 1996.

Dundes, Alan. *Cinderella: A Casebook*. New York: Wildman Press, 1983.

———. *The Shabbat Elevator and Other Sabbath Subterfuges*. Lanham, Md.: Rowman and Littlefield, 2002.

Dwyer, Rachel. "The Erotics of the Wet Sari in Hindi Films." *South Asia* 23, no. 2 (June 2000): 143–159.

Eagleton, Terry. "Maybe He Made It Up." Review of Nick Groom, *The Forger's Shadow*. *London Review of Books*, 6 June 2002, 3, 6.

Eliade, Mircea. *The Myth of the Eternal Return; or, Cosmos and History*. Translated by Willard Trask. Princeton, N. J. Princeton University Press, 1954.

Ellis, Havelock. *Studies in the Psychology of Sex*. Philadelphia: F. A. Davis, Co., 1903.

Euripides. See *Alcestis*.

Faulkner, William. *Light in August*. New York: Modern Library, 1950.

Ford, Patrick K. See *The Mabinogi and Other Medieval Welsh Tales*.

Foucault, Michel. *History of Sexuality*. 3 vols. Translated by Robert Hurley. New York: Vintage, 1990.

————. "Introduction." In *Herculine Barbin: Being the Recently Discovered Memoirs of a Nineteenth-Century French Hermaphrodite*, translated by Richard McDougall. New York: Pantheon Books, 1980.

Frazer, Sir James George. *Taboo and the Perils of the Soul*. Vol. 3, pt. 2, *The Golden Bough*. New York: Macmillan, 1922; reprint, 1950.

Freud, Sigmund. *Beyond the Pleasure Principle*. Edited and translated by James Strachey. New York: W. W. Norton, 1990.

————. *Collected Papers*. Edited by James Strachey. 5 vols. London: Hogarth Press, 1950.

————. "Family Romances." In *Collected Papers*, vol. 5, 74–78.

————. *The Interpretation of Dreams*. Translated by James Strachey. New York: Basic Books, 1965.

————. *Jokes and Their Relation to the Unconscious*. Translated by James Strachey. New York and London: W. W. Norton, 1960.

————. "Medusa's Head." In *Collected Papers*, vol. 5, 105–106.

————. *Moses and Monotheism*. Translated by Katherine Jones. New York: Vintage Books, 1939.

————. "A Special Type of Choice of Object Made by Men." *SE* 11 (1912), 163–176.

————. *Standard Edition of the Complete Psychological Works*. Edited by James Strachey. London: Hogarth Press, 1958.

————. "The Taboo of Virginity." Contributions to the Psychology of Love III. Translated by Angela Richards. *SE* 11 (1912), 192–208.

————. *Three Essays on the Theory of Sexuality*. Translated by James Strachey. New York: Basic Books, 1962.

————. *Totem and Taboo*. Translated by A. A. Brill. New York: Vintage, 1918.

————. "The Unconscious." *SE* 14 (1915): 161–215.

Frye, Northrop. *A Natural Perspective*. New York: Columbia University Press, 1965.

Galsworthy, John. *In Chancery*. Vol. 2 of *The Forsyte Saga*. New York: Grosset, 1920.

Garber, Marjorie. *Vested Interests: Cross-Dressing and Cultural Anxiety*. New York and London: Routledge, 1992.

————. *Vice Versa: The Bisexuality of Everyday Life*. New York: Simon and Schuster, 1995.

Gates, Henry Louis, Jr. "White Like Me." *New Yorker*, June 17, 1996, 66–81.

Geertz, Clifford. *The Interpretation of Culture*. New York: Basic Books, 1973.

Geisel, Theodore [Dr. Seuss]. *Dr. Seuss's Sleep Book*. New York and Toronto: Random House, 1962.

————. *The Five Hundred Hats of Bartholomew Cubbins*. New York: Random House, 1938.

Gellner, Ernest. *The Psychoanalytic Movement; or, The Cunning of Unreason*. London: Paladin Grafton Books, 1988.

Gill, Brendan. "Pursuer and Pursued." *New Yorker*, June 2, 1997, 84–88.

Ginsberg, Elaine K., ed. *Passing and the Fictions of Identity*. Durham, N.C., and London: Duke University Press, 1996.

Ginzburg, Carlo. *Ecstasies: Deciphering the Witches' Sabbath*. Translated by Raymond Rosenthal. New York: Pantheon Books, 1991.

Goffman, Erving. *Behavior in Public Places*. New York: Free Press, 1963.

————. *The Presentation of Self in Everyday Life*. Garden City, N.Y.: Doubleday, 1959.

————. *Relations in Public: Microstudies of the Public Order*. New York: Basic Books, 1971.

Goldman, Robert P. "Karma, Guilt, and Buried Memories: Public Fantasy and Private Reality in Traditional India." *Journal of the American Oriental Society* 105, no. 3 (1985): 413–425.

Gopnik, Adam. "The Naked City." *New Yorker*, July 23, 2001, 30–34.

———. "Standup Guys." *New Yorker*, May 12, 2003, 104–106.

Greene, Graham. *The End of the Affair*. London: W. Heinemann, 1951.

———. *Our Man in Havana*. London: W. Heinemann, 1958.

Griaule, Marcel. *Conversations with Ogotemmeli: An Introduction to Dogon Religious Ideas*. London: Oxford University Press, 1965.

Grimes, Martha. *The Five Bells and Bladebone*. New York: Onyx, 2002. Originally published in 1987.

Grimm, Jakob. *Deutsche Mythologie*. Translated by Oliver Stallybrass as *Teutonic Mythology*. 4 vols. Gloucester, Mass.: Peter Smith, 1976. The original was published in 1875–1878.

Grimm, Jakob, and Wilhelm Grimm. *The Complete Grimm's Fairy Tales*. Translated by Margaret Hunt and James Stern. New York: Pantheon Books, 1944.

Grimm, Wilhelm. *Die Deutsche Heldensage*. Gütersloh: Bertelsmann, 1899.

Groopman, Jerome. "Dying Words." *New Yorker*, October 28, 2002, 62–70.

Gutman, Robert W. "Introduction to the Volsunga Saga." In *Volsungasaga* [The saga of the Volsungs], translated by William Morris.

Halliwell, Leslie. *Halliwell's Film Guide*. Revised and updated by John Walker. New York: Harper Perennial, 1995.

Harper, Ralph. *On Presence: Variations and Reflections*. Philadelphia: Trinity Press International, 1991.

Hatto, A. T., trans. See *Nibelungenlied*.

Heise, Ursula K. "Transvestism and the Stage Controversy in Spain and England, 1580–1680." *Theatre Journal* 44 (1992), 357–74.

Hemingway, Ernest. *Across the River and into the Trees*. New York: Scribner, 1950.

Hillenbrand, Laura. *Seabisuit: An American Legend*. New York: Random House, 2001.

Hilton, James. *Random Harvest*. New York: Carroll and Graf, 1969. Originally published in 1941.

Hoban, Russell. *The Mouse and His Child*. New York: Harper and Row, 1967.

Hofmannsthal, Hugo von. *Der Rosenkavalier*. Libretto. (1911). New York: Dover, 1987.

Hollander, Lee M., trans. See *Edda: The Poetic Edda*.

Hollis, Christopher. *A Study of George Orwell: The Man and His Works*. London: Hollis and Carter, 1956.

Hwang, David Henry. *M. Butterfly*. New York: Plume [Penguin], 1989.

Ibsen, Henrik. *The Vikings at Helgeland*. Translated by James Walter McFarlane. In *The Oxford Ibsen*, vol. 2, 27–94. London: Oxford University Press, 1962. Originally published in 1858.

Irwin, Robert. *The Arabian Nights: A Companion*. London: Allan Lane, 1994.

James, Henry. "The Real Thing." In *The Real Thing, and Other Tales*, 1–44. New York and London: Macmillan, 1893.

James, William. *Pragmatism: A New Name for Some Old Ways of Thinking*. New York: Longman Green (1907), 1949.

Johnson, Barbara. "The Frame of Reference: Poe, Lacan, Derrida." In Muller and Richardson, *The Purloined Poe*, 213–251.

Jones, Ernest. "Persons in Dreams Disguised as Themselves." *International Journal of Psychoanalysis* 2 (1921): 420–423.

Kael, Pauline. *5001 Nights at the Movies*. New York: Henry Holt, 1982.

Kalluak, Mark, ed. *How Kablomat Became, and Other Legends*. Canada: Program Development, Department of Education, Government of Canada, 1974.

Kates, Gary. *Monsieur d'Eon Is a Woman: A Tale of Political Intrigue and Sexual Masquerade*. New York: Basic Books, 1995.

Kleist, Heinrich von. *Amphitryon*. Translated by Charles E. Passage. In *Plays*, edited by Walter Hinderer, 91–164. New York: Continuum, 1982.

Klotzko, Arlene Judith. "About a Face." *Prospect* 95, February 2004.

Kunio, Yanagita. *Japanese Folk Tales*. 3d ed. Translated by Fanny Hagin Mayer. Tokyo: Tokyo News Service, Ltd., 1961.

Lacan, Jacques. "The Agency of the Letter in the Unconscious; or, Reason since Freud." In Lacan, *Écrits*, 46–78. Originally published in 1966.

———. *Écrits: A Selection*. Translated by Alan Sheridan. New York: W. W. Norton, 1977.

———. *Feminine Sexuality: Jacques Lacan and the École*

Freudienne. Edited by Juliet Mitchell and Jaqueline Rose. Translated by Jacqueline Rose. New York: W. W. Norton, 1982.

———. "The Mirror Stage as Formative of the Function of the I." In Lacan, *Écrits*, 1–7.

———. "Le séminaire sur 'La letter vole.'" *Le Psychanalyse* 2 (1956):1–44. Translated by Jeffrey Mehlman in Muller and Richardson, *The Purloined Poe*, 29–54.

———. "The Split between the Eye and the Gaze." In *The Four Fundamental Concepts of Psychoanalysis*, translated by Alan Sheridan, 67–78. New York: W. W. Norton, 1978.

Lancaster, Evelyn [Chris Costner Sizemore], with James Poling. *The Final Face of Eve*. New York: McGraw-Hill, 1958.

Lane, Anthony. "In Love with Fear." *New Yorker*, August 16, 1999, 80–86.

———. "Metal Guru: Terminator 3; Rise of the Machines." *New Yorker*, July 14 and 21, 2003, 85–86.

———. "Mondo Bond." *New Yorker*, November 4, 2002, 78–82.

———. "This Is Not a Movie." *New Yorker*, September 24, 2001, 79–80.

Lasch, Christopher. "The Anti-Intellectualism of the Intellectuals." In *The New Radicalism in America (1889–1963): The Intellectual as a Social Type*, 286–349. New York: Alfred A. Knopf, 1965.

Lawrence, John Shelton, and Robert Jewett. *The Myth of the American Superhero*. Grand Rapids, Mich.: William B. Eerdmans, 2002.

Lifton, Robert J. *The Protean Self: Human Resilience in an Age of Fragmentation*. New York: Basic Books, 1993.

Lévi-Strauss, Claude. "The Story of Asdiwal." In *The Structural Study of Myth and Totemism*, edited by Edmund Leach, 27–30. London: Tavistock Publications, 1967.

———. *Structural Anthropology*. Translated by Claire Jacobson and Brooke Grundfest Schoepf. Harmondsworth, U.K.: Penguin Books, 1963.

Lewis, C. S. *The Voyage of the Dawn Treader*. London: Puffin Books, 1965.

Lloyd, Geoffrey Ernest Richard. *Polarity and Analogy: Two Types of Argumentation in Early Greek Thought*. Cambridge, U.K.: Cambridge University Press, 1966.

Luhrmann, T. M. *Persuasions of the Witch's Craft: Ritual Magic in Contemporary England*. Cambridge, Mass.: Harvard University Press, 1989.

Macdonald, Dwight. "Ernest Hemingway." In *Encounter*, January 1961. First published in Dwight Macdonald, *Against the American Grain*, 167–184 (New York: Random House, 1962).

———. *Parodies: An Anthology from Chaucer to Beerbohm—and After*. New York: Random House, 1960.

Malinowski, Bronislaw. *Myth in Primitive Psychology*. In *Magic, Science, and Religion, and Other Essays*, edited by Robert Redfield. Glencoe, Ill.: Free Press, 1948. First published in 1926.

Maltin, Leonard. *Leonard Maltin's Movie and Video Guide*. New York: Penguin Books, 1996.

Marcus, Steven. *The Other Victorians: A Study of Sexuality and Pornography in Mid-Nineteenth-Century England*. New York: Basic Books, 1966.

Marias, Javiar. *Tomorrow in the Battle Think on Me*. Translated by Margaret Jull Costa. New York and London: Harcourt Brace and Company, 1996.

Marx, Karl. *Capital*. London, 1974.

Maugham, W. Somerset. *Sheppey: A Play in Three Acts*. London: W. W. Heinemann, 1933.

McClintock, Martha, and Suma Jacob, Bethanne Zelano, and Davinder J. S. Hayreh. "Pheromones and Vasanas: The Functions of Social Chemosignals." In *Evolutionary Psychology and Motivation*, 75–112. Nebraska Symposium on Motivation, edited by Jeffrey A. French, et al., vol. 48. Lincoln: University of Nebraska Press, 2001.

McClintock, M. K. "Pheromones, Odors, and Vasanas: The Neuroendocrinology of Social Chemosignals in Humans and Animals." In *Hormones, Brain, and Behavior*, edited by D. Pfaff, vol. 1, 797–870. San Diego, Calif.: Academic Press, 2002.

Melchior-Bonnet, Sabine. *The Mirror: A History*. Translated by Katherine H. Jewett. New York: Routledge, 2001.

Moi, Toril. *Sexual/Textual Politics: Feminist Literary Theory*. London and New York: Methuen and Co., 1985.

Morris, William, trans. See *Völsunga saga*.

Moskovitz, Richard. *Lost in the Mirror: An Inside Look at Borderline Personality Disorder*. Foreword by Chris Costner Sizemore, author of *I'm Eve*. Lanham, Md., and New York: Taylor Trade Publishing, 1996.

Muller, John P., and William J. Richardson. "Notes on Lacan." In *The Purloined Poe*, 93.

———. *The Purloined Poe: Lacan, Derrida, and Psychoanalytic Reading*. Baltimore, Md., and London: Johns Hopkins University Press, 1988.

Myers, Frederic. *Human Personality and Its Survival of Bodily Death*. New York: Longmans, 1903.

Neely, Carol Thomas. *Broken Nuptials in Shakespeare's Plays*. New Haven, Conn., and London: Yale University Press, 1985.

Neely, Richard. *The Plastic Nightmare*. New York: Ace Publishing Corporation, 1969. Republished, after the movie (1991), as *Shattered* (New York: Vintage Crime, Random House, 1991).

Neiman, Susan. *Slow Fire: Jewish Notes from Berlin*. New York: Schocken Books, 1992.

Nietzsche, Friedrich. *Beyond Good and Evil: Prelude to a Philosophy of the Future*. Translated by Walter Kaufmann. New York: Vintage Books, 1966.

———. *The Gay Science*. Translated by Walter Kaufman. New York: Random House, 1974.

O'Hara, John. *Appointment in Samarra*. New York: Grosset and Dunlap, 1934.

Orwell, George. "Good Bad Books." In *Shooting an Elephant, and Other Essays*. New York: Harcourt Brace, 1950.

———. "Rudyard Kipling." Review of T. S. Eliot's *A Choice of Kipling's Verse*, in *A Collection of Essays*. Garden City, N.Y.: Doubleday, 1954.

Pierpont, Claudia Roth. "Born for the Part: Roles that Katharine Hepburn Played." *New Yorker*, July 14 and 21, 2003, 53–63.

———. "The Strong Woman." In *Passionate Minds: Women Rewriting the World*. New York: Alfred Knopf, 2000.

Pirandello, Luigi. *As You Desire Me: A Drama in Three Acts*. Translated from the Italian by Marta Abba. London and Toronto: Samuel French, 1948.

Poe, Edgar Allan. "The Purloined Letter." In Muller and Richardson, *The Purloined Poe*, 3–27.

Pollock, Sheldon. "'*Atmanam manusam manye*': *Dharmakutam* on the divinity of Rama." *Journal of the Oriental Institute, Baroda* 33, nos. 3–4 (March–June, 1984): 231–243.

———. "The Divine King in the Indian Epic." *Journal of the American Oriental Society* 104, no. 3 (1984): 505–528.

Porter, Andrew, trans. See Wagner, *The Ring of the Nibelung*.

Proust, Marcel. *Remembrance of Things Past*. Vol. 1, *Swann's Way*; Vol. 2: *In a Budding Grove*; Vol. 7: *Time Regained*. The definitive French Pléiade edition, translated by C. K. Scott Moncrieff and Terence Kilmartin. New York: Random House, 1982.

Rajadhyaksha, Ashish, and Paul Willemen. *Encyclopedia of Indian Cinema*. Oxford, U.K.: British Film Institute and Oxford University Press, 1999.

Ramanujan, A. K. *A Flowering Tree, and Other Oral Tales from India*. Berkeley: University of California Press, 1997.

———. "Towards a Counter-System: Women's Tales." In *Gender, Discourse, and Power in South Asia*, edited by Arjun Appadurai et al., 33–55. Philadelphia: University of Pennsylvania Press, 1991.

Rank, Otto. *The Myth of the Birth of the Hero*. New York: R. Brunner, 1914. Republished in *In Quest of the Hero*, by Otto Rank et al. Princeton, N.J.: Princeton University Press, 1990.

Rasmussen, Knud. *Intellectual Culture of the Copper Eskimos*. Translated by W. E. Calvert. Copenhagen: 1932. Reprint, New York, AMS Press, 1976.

Reagan, Ronald, with Richard G. Hubler. *Where's the Rest of Me? The Autobiography of Ronald Reagan*. New York: Karz Publishers, 1981.

Ricoeur, Paul. *Hermeneutics and the Human Sciences*. Edited by John B. Thompson. Cambridge, U.K.: Cambridge University Press, 1981.

———. *The Symbolism of Evil*. Translated by E. Buchanan. New York: Harper and Row, 1967.

Rivière, Joan. "Womanliness as a Masquerade." In *Formations of Fantasy*, edited by Victor Burgin, James Donald, and Cora Kaplan, 35–44. New York: Methuen, 1986.

Roheim, Geza. "The Garden of Eden." *Psychoanalytic Review* 27 (1940): 1–26, 177–199.

Ross, Lillian. *Profile of Hemingway*. New York: Simon and Schuster, 1961.

Roth, Philip. *The Human Stain*. Boston: Houghton Mifflin, 2002.

Rowling, J. K. *Harry Potter and the Prisoner of Azkaban*. London: Bloomsbury Books, 1999.

Russell, Anna. Recorded live at Town Hall. New York City, April 23, 1953.

Said, Edward. *Orientalism*. New York: Vintage Books, 1978.

Schieffer, Bob, and Gary Paul Gates. *The Acting President*. New York: E. P. Dutton, 1989.

Schlossberg, Eli W. *The World of Orthodox Judaism*. Northvale, N.J.: Jason Aronson, 1996.

Schwartz, Hillel. *The Culture of the Copy: Striking Likenesses, Unreasonable Facsimiles*. New York: Zone Books, 1996.

Scott, James C. *Domination and the Arts of Resistance: Hidden Transcripts*. New Haven, Conn., and London: Yale University Press, 1990.

———. *Weapons of the Weak: Everyday Forms of Peasant Resistance*. New Haven, Conn., and London: Yale University Press, 1985.

Sedgwick, Eve Kosofsky. *Epistemology of the Closet*. Berkeley: University of California Press, 1990.

Showalter, Elaine. *Sexual Anarchy: Gender and Culture at the Fin de Siècle*. New York: Penguin Books, 1990.

Shulman, David. *Behind the Mask: Dance, Healing, and Possession in South Indian Ritual*. Edited by David Shulman and Deborah Thiagarajan. Ann Arbor: University of Michigan Press, forthcoming.

———. "Bhavabhuti on Cruelty and Compassion." In *Questioning Ramayanas: A South Asian Tradition*, edited by Paula Richman, 49–82. Berkeley and Los Angeles: University of California Press, 2001.

———. "Embracing the Subject: Harsa's Play within a Play." *Journal of Indian Philosophy* 25 (1997): 69–89.

Shulman, David, with Don Handelman. *God Inside Out: Siva's Game of Dice*. New York: Oxford University Press, 1997.

Siebert, Charles. "The Cuts That Go Deeper." *New York Times Sunday Magazine*, July 7, 1996, sec. 6.

Sontag, Susan. "Notes on Camp." In *Camp: Queer Aesthetics and the Performing Subject: A Reader*. Edited by Fabio Cleto, 53–65. Ann Arbor: University of Michigan Press, 1999. Originally published in 1964.

Spark, Muriel. *Aiding and Abetting*. New York, Anchor Books, 2001.

Stern, Richard. *Other Men's Daughters*. New York: Arbor House, 1986.

Stoppard, Tom. *Rosencrantz and Guildenstern Are Dead*. London: Faber, 1967.

Thomas, Rosie. "Indian Cinema: Pleasures and Popularity." *Screen* 26, nos. 3–4 (1985): 116–132.

Thompson, David. *A Biographical Dictionary of Film*. 3d ed. New York: Alfred Knopf, 1998.

Twain, Mark. *The Prince and the Pauper: A Tale for Young People of All Ages*. New York: Harper and Brothers, 1903.

———. *Pudd'nhead Wilson, and Other Tales*. Edited by R. D. Gooder. London and New York: Oxford University Press, 1992.

Vonnegut, Kurt. *Mother Night*. New York: Harper and Row, 1966.

Von Strassburg, Gottfried. See *Tristan*.

Wagner, Richard. *The Ring of the Nibelung*. Translated by Andrew Porter. New York: W. W. Norton, 1976.

Wanner, Kevin. "The Virgin and the Valkyrie: A Comparison of Three Medieval German Texts." *Ms.*, 2000.

Warner, Marina. "Stolen Shadows, Lost Souls." *Raritan*, Fall 1995, 35–58.

Waugh, Evelyn. *A Handful of Dust*. New York: New Directions, 1945.

Wilde, Oscar. *The Importance of Being Earnest*. In *The Portable Oscar Wilde*, 430–507. New York: Viking/Penguin, 1946, 1974.

———. *The Picture of Dorian Gray*. Edited by Donald L. Lawler. New York: Norton, 1988. Originally published in London (1890, 1891).

Willig, Rosette F. *The Changelings: A Classical Japanese Court Tale* [*Torikaebaya Monogatari*]. Translated, with an introduction and notes. Stanford, Calif.: Stanford University Press, 1983.

Wills, Gary. *Reagan's America*. New York: Penguin Books, 1988.

Winnicott, D. W. "Mirror-Role of the Mother and Family in Child Development." In *The Predicament of the Family*, edited by P. Lomas, 26–33. New York: International Universities Press, 1967.

Wittgenstein, Ludwig. *Philosophical Investigations*. Oxford: Blackwell, 1953.

Woolf, Virginia. *Orlando: A Biography*. New York: Harcourt Brace, 1928.

Yeats, William Butler. *The Autobiography of William Butler Yeats*. New York: Macmillan, 1938.
———. *The Collected Poems of W. B. Yeats*. London: Macmillan and Company, 1965.
———. *W. B. Yeats: Selected Poetry*. Edited by A. Norman Jeffers. London: Pan Books, 1974.
Zizek, Slavoj. "From Symptom to *Sinthome*." In *The Sublime Object of Ideology*, 55–84.
———. "How Did Marx Invent the Symptom?" In *The Sublime Object of Ideology*, 11–54.
———. *The Sublime Object of Ideology*. London: Verso, 1989.

INDEX

Abbott and Costello, 56
Abe, Kobo, 145, 211, 220
Abraham, 119
accent, as disguise, 12, 77, 83–84, 246n.7
Aeschylus, 114
aging, 10, 71, 94, 101, 128–32, 137–45, 147–48, 159–61, 198–99, 205, 240n.30
AIDS, 116
Alice, *Through the Looking-Glass*, 206
alien, 169, 172, 176
Allen, Woody, 209–10, 218, 244n.53
Alzheimer's disease, 94, 151
amnesia, 10, 90–107, 109–11, 118, 123, 134, 141, 149–51, 163, 168, 172–73, 179, 181, 205, 232, 241n.11, 242n.19, 245n.29; double, of Siegfried and Brünnhilde, 40–41, 46, 52, 57, 91–92, 150, 169–70. *See also* drink and drugs; Lethe
androgyny, 16–17, 191, 197–98, 221
android. *See* robot
animal: bear, 51, 70; bee, 117–18; bull, 121; butterfly, 210; cat, 235n.46; crab, 12, 144; doe, 117–18; dog, 21, 80, 82, 94, 129, 231, 240n.36, 241n.4; elephant, 117–18, 129, 251n.91; flying fox, 144; fox, 11, 123; horse, 17–18, 41, 43–45, 54, 65, 119–20, 206, 223, 239n.35, 243n.18; iguana, 144; insect, 144; jackal, 121; lion, 210; lioness, 121; lizard, 144; monkey, 114; serpent, 65, 142–44, 230; sheep, 11; shrimp, 142; snail, 208; stag, 202; tortoise, 231, 251n.91; wolf, 11, 144, 245n.17. *See also* bird
Aristotle, 212
armor, as mask or disguise, 44, 51–53; as maidenhead, 59. *See also* Tarnhelm
Arthashastra, 29
artichoke, as metaphor for self, 230, 251n.86. *See also* onion
Astaire, Fred, 19–20
Auden, W. H., 161

Augustine, *Confessions*, 114

Bakhtin, Mikhail, 207, 211, 219–20, 250n.44
Ballard, J. G., "Thirteen for Centaurus," 168
Balzac, Honoré de, 16, 194, 214
Barbie doll, 157
Barthes, Roland, 16–17, 214
Batman, 12. *See also* superhero
Beatty, Warren, 126–27
Beaumarchais, Pierre-Auguste Caron de, 35–37, 194, 196
bedtrick, 9, 28, 40, 42–43, 46, 51–53, 56, 58, 62, 123, 134, 139, 151, 234n.5, 235n.48, 238n.24, 239n.31, 245n.19
Beerbohm, Max, 14–15, 159, "The Happy Hypocrite," 211–12
Bellow, Saul, 160
Bergman, Ingrid, 13, 174–75, 245n.29, 246n.7
Berle, Milton, 38–39, 81, 126, 164, 237n.24
Béroul, 60–61, 65, 221
Bhagavata Purana, 124, 243n.37. *See also* Hindu deity; *Mahabharata*
Bhavabhuti, 66
Bible, 15, 74
bigamy, 76, 102. *See also* polygyny
bio-queen (female female impersonator), 198, 200
bird, 144; crow, 185; eagle, 114; goose, 117; owl, 21; peacock, 202; swan, 114, 117–18, 199. *See also* animal
bisexuality. *See* queerness
black leather, 21
blindness, 50, 102, 107–8, 128, 241n.18
Bloom, Harold, 7
body double, 21. *See also* double
Bogart, Humphrey, 146, 157, 223
Bollywood, 3, 22, 126, 133, 136, 235nn.56–57. *See also* Filmistan; Hollywood

image (*continued*)
as indexical icon, 38, 98, 109, 164, 233n.26. *See also* statue
incarnation: of Shiva, 244n.45; of Shiva and Parvati, partial, 120–23; of Vishnu (avatar), 123–24. *See also* karma theory; reincarnation
incest, 128–32, 143, 145, 147, 162, 239n.12, 245n.14. *See also* Oedipus
Indian film industry. *See* Bollywood
intertextuality, 6, 7, 47, 58, 61, 80, 120, 139, 221
Inuit, 142, 145, 157, 161
invisibility, 48, 50, 66, 148. *See also* enchantment; transparent body
irony, 26–27, 32, 185
Isolde. *See* Tristan and Isolde
ius primae noctis. See droit du seigneur

Jackson, Michael, 157
Jagger, Mick, 13
James, Henry, 14; "The Real Thing," 215
James, William, 227, 251n.91
Jekyll and Hyde, 93, 168, 212–13, 215–16
jester. *See* clown
Jew, 12, 117, 175–76, 182, 184, 224–26, 246n.2
jewelry, 31, 98, 105, 133, 164–68, 187–88, 192; ring, 70, 72, 161
Jones, Ernest, "Persons in Dreams Disguised as Themselves," 227
journalist, 13, 19, 26, 241n.48
Jung, C. G., 218

Kamasutra, 29, 201
Kanin, Garson, 76, 240n.26. *See also* director
Kapoor, Raj, 153, 245n.34. *See also* director
karma theory, 113, 114–19, 126, 216, 218. *See also* incarnation; reincarnation
Keats, John, 153
Kelly, Grace, 22, 223, 246n.7
Kennedy, John F., 234n.25
key, 98, 100–101, 103–4, 130, 218
king, 105, 117, 119–20, 125–26, 186–90, 215, 219, 235n.53. *See also* Chandrashekhara and Taravati; Harsha; Hindu deity; Louis XVI; Moses; Shakespeare; Siegfried and Brünnhilde; Tristan and Isolde
Kipling, Rudyard, 5, 15
kissing, 41–42, 44, 55, 57, 70, 78–79, 87, 98–100, 164, 166–67, 170, 172, 175, 178–79, 245n.29, 246n.3
kitsch, 12. *See also* camp

Lacan, Jacques, 105, 174, 195–96, 200, 204, 210, 219–20, 224–28, 248n.27
Lasch, Christopher, 14–15
Laws of Manu, The, 115

lawyer, 20, 84–85, 223
le Carré, John, 174
Lee-Thompson, J., 146
leitmotif. *See* musical motif
Lemmon, Jack, 12, 78
LeRoy, Mervyn, 7, 24, 97. *See also* director
lesbian. *See* queerness
Lethe, River of Forgetfulness, 114–15, 130. *See also* amnesia; drink and drugs
Levant, Oscar, 217
Lévi-Strauss, Claude, 4
Lewis, C. S., 210, 230
lip-synch. *See* dubbing
Lifton, Robert Jay, *The Protean Self*, 218
Loathly Lady, 42
Lombard, Carole, 85, 109
Louis XVI, 195–96. *See also* Marie Antoinette
love, as catalyst of self-construction, 204; as purview of this book, 9
Loy, Myrna, 84–85, 92–93, 157, 241n.48, 246n.7
Lugosi, Bela, 19

Macdonald, Dwight, 14–15
madness, 21, 105, 172, 210, 221
Mafia, 21
magical transformation. *See* enchantment
Magritte, René, 217, 235n.46
Mahabharata, 124, 152, 221, 230, 235n.56, 243n.19, 243n.29, 243n.35, 248n.32. *See also* Hindu deity
maid, household, 29–31, 34–36, 47, 73–74, 196
Mailer, Norman, 15
makeup, 193, 199
Malinowski, Bronislaw, 143
Mangeshkar, Lata, "The Nightingale," 156
Marcus, Steven, *The Other Victorians*, 11
Marias, Javier, 138
Marie Antoinette, 37, 138, 193. *See also* Louis XVI
mark, identifying, 129, 138, 157, 160, 171. *See also* scar; tattoo
Marx Brothers, 13, 199, 216, 220
Marx, Karl, 214
mask, 19–20, 119, 145, 152, 157, 159, 170, 203, 205, 211–12, 251n.85; two-sided, of Siegfried, 40–41, 150, 220–21
"maternal impression," 72, 239n.17. *See also* child
Maugham, W. Somerset, 78–79, 206
McCarey, Leo, 11, 78–79, 80, 216, 240n.26, 240n.30. *See also* director
McCarthy, Mary, 231
McCarthyism, 182
McClintock, Martha, 116
McLeod, Norman Z., 92, 150, 169. *See also* director
McLuhan, Marshall, 15
memory wipe. *See* reprogramming

Method acting, 19, 212, 249n.18
mimesis, 214
Minelli, Vincente, 126, 217, 244n.50. *See also* director
mirror, 139, 141, 149, 151, 153, 158, 161, 164, 167–68, 185, 193, 211–12, 216, 224
Möbius strip, 7, 8, 99, 130, 162, 164, 167, 211, 226, 230–32
modernism, 4
Molina, Tirso de, 194
monk, 117–18, 172, 229
Monroe, Marilyn, 20, 79, 157, 215, 240n.27
Moore, Roger, 13
Morris, William, 15, 63
Moses, 74
multiple personality disorder, 218–19
multiplicity of selves, 215–19, 232
musical motif, as metonym, 55, 100, 127, 130, 155
mustache, fake, 175. *See also* wig
mutilation, 153, 158
mythology, Greek. *See* Greek mythology

New Age, 113
Nibelungenlied, 46–51, 53, 57–59, 122, 237n.4, 237nn.13–16, 238n.26, 239n.31
Nietzsche, Friedrich, 5, 213–14
nightclub singer, 82, 94–95
Novak, Kim, as Madeleine, *Vertigo*, 163–68, 246nn.1–2; similar roles, 21, 165
noble birth, 30, 71–72, 109. *See also* genetics
novel, by title: *Across the River and Into the Trees*, 14, 235n.30; *Aiding and Abetting*, 140; *Appointment in Samarra*, 206, 224; *Brighton Rock*, 231; *The Changelings*, 74; *David Copperfield*, 9; *Do Androids Dream of Electric Sheep?*, 196; *Dracula*, 168; *The End of the Affair*, 38; *The Face of Another*, 145, 211; *The First Wives Club*, 145; *The Five Bells and Bladebone*, 38; *The Forsyte Saga*, 38; *Frankenstein*, 168–69; *The Great Gatsby*, 207; *The Great Impersonation*, 174; *A Handful of Dust*, 37; *Harry Potter and the Prisoner of Azkaban*, 162; *The Human Stain*, 74, 184–86, 220; *Imitation of Life*, 184; *Light in August*, 184; *The Little Drummer Girl*, 174; *Mother Night*, 212; *The Mouse and His Child*, 231; *The Old Man and the Sea*, 14–15; *Orlando*, 190, 217–18; *Our Man in Havana*, 16; *The Passion of New Eve*, 193; *The Plastic Nightmare*, 150; *The Portrait of Dorian Gray*, 144, 157, 160, 190, 194, 205, 211, 213–14; *The Prince and the Pauper*, 105; *The Prisoner of Zenda*, 215; *Pudd'nhead Wilson*, 183; *Random Harvest*, 97, 103–7, 192, 209–10, 215, 241n.11, 241n.13, 242n.20, 242nn.24–28; *Sarrasine*, 16–17, 194, 214; *The Sorrows of Young Werther*, 16; *The Strange Case of Dr. Jekyll and Mr. Hyde*, 168; *The Sun Also Rises*, 234n.30; *Switcheroo*, 245n.19; *The Voyage of the Dawn Treader*, 230; *The War of the Worlds*, 16

Oberon, Merle, 107–9, 241n.18
obituary, 38–39
Oedipus, 69, 71, 131, 143, 206, 215, 224, 239n.12, 250n.65. *See also* Freud, incest
O'Hara, John, 206
onion, as metaphor for self, 229–30. *See also* artichoke
opera, by title: *Arabella*, 248n.32; *The Barber of Seville*, 36; *The Ghosts of Versailles*, 36–37, 42, 138–39; *Madama Butterfly*, 197; *The Marriage of Figaro*, 35–37, 42, 80, 138–39, 154, 236n.15; *Pagliacci*, 21; *Der Rosenkavalier*, 139–41, 172, 219; *Tosca*, 18, 242n.25. *See also* plays; Wagner
ordeal: by fire, 66; by iron, 64–65
Orientalism, 12, 198, 206. *See also* ethnic stereotype; parody
Orwell, George, 5
Oscar, 103
Oz, 210; Wizard of, 50

Paradox, Liar's, 225–26, 250nn.70–71; Zeno's, 231
painting. *See* image
Papua New Guinea, 143, 157
parody: racial, 183; self-, 14–15, 25–32, 180, 199
passing: gender, 74, 183–84, 186–202; as parent, 74; of Jews as Poles and of Nazis as Jews, 176; racial, 4, 74, 183–88
perfume, 113, 116, 151, 170
Petersen, Wolfgang, 146. *See also* director
photograph. *See* image
photocopy, 145
Picasso, Pablo, 17
pilgrim, 64–65
Pirandello, Luigi, 95, 97
"pizza effect," 135, 244n.56
plastic surgery, 20, 23, 140–41, 144–49, 151–53, 157–62, 169, 207, 244n.7. *See also* face-lift; transsexual surgery; trans-species surgery
Plato, *Republic*, 114; *Symposium*, 243n.27
play, by title: *Alcestis*, 16, 73; *Amphitryon*, 161, 244n.38; *As You Desire Me*, 95–97; *The Awful Truth*, 240n.42; *The Bacchae*, 120; *The Best Man*, 24, 26, 235n.62; *Cyrano de Bergerac*, 109, 247n.15; *The End of Rama's Story* (*Uttararamacarita*), 66–67, 239n.8, 239n.11; *Home and Beauty*, 78–79; *The Importance of Being Earnest*, 10–11, 72, 199, 234n.6; *M. Butterfly*, 197–99; *The Marriage of Figaro*, 35–37, 42, 80, 138, 154, 196, 236n.15; *The Mother-in-Law*, 241n.3; *Private Lives*, 80;

play, by title (*continued*)
  Rosenkrantz and Guildenstern Are Dead, 8;
  She Stoops to Comedy, 193–94; *Sheppey*, 206; *El
  Vergonzoso en palacio*, 194; *Victor/Victoria*, 186;
  The Vikings at Helgeland, 51–52, 59, 237n.4; *A
  Woman of No Importance*, 199. *See also* Harsha;
  opera; Shakespeare
play-within-a-play, 32–33, 36–37, 66–67, 134, 194,
  231
Poe, Edgar Allan, 14; "The Purloined Letter," 213,
  222, 224, 226, 248n.27
police, 18, 20, 152–53, 174, 223, 246nn.7–8. *See also*
  detective
politician, 23–26, 98, 105–7
polygyny, 29. *See also* bigamy
pornography, 11
possession, 21, 34, 165, 181, 205
postcolonial condition, 4, 12
postmodernism, 4, 214
pregnancy, 66, 69, 72, 80, 130, 154, 241n.2
Powell, William, 92–93, 109, 241n.48
prostitute, 13, 20, 95, 97, 105, 117, 138, 188, 201, 216
Proust, Marcel, 27, 116, 217, 232
psychiatrist, 77, 98–99, 101–2, 106, 130, 149, 173, 213,
  241nn.14–15
pun, revealing, 185–86, 192. *See also* Freudian slip

queen, 119, 125–26, 195, 199, 222. *See also* Chandrashekhara and Taravati; Chudala; Harsha;
  Hindu deity; Marie Antoinette; Shakespeare;
  Siegfried and Brünnhilde; Tristan and Isolde
queerness, 183, 188, 190, 193–94, 198–99, 210, 214

rabbi. *See* Cracow
radio, 16, 238n.23, 241nn.14–16, 242n.24, 242n.28,
  247n.15
Ramayana, of Valmiki, 66–67, 235n.56, 243n.29,
  244n.44. *See also* Hindu deity
rape, 42–43, 45, 49–50, 53–54, 56, 58, 62, 94–95,
  121–23, 190, 212, 244n.44. *See also* droit du
  seigneur; virginity
Reagan, Nancy, 251n.85
Reagan, Ronald, 23–26
Red Riding Hood, 144, 245n.17
reincarnation, 112–19, 124–26, 133–36, 166, 168, 205,
  232; premature, 127–32, 133–35
reprogramming, of memory, 169–73, 177–79
resurrection, 65–71, 73–80, 83, 93, 100, 126, 165, 205,
  232. *See also* feigning death
Reynolds, Debbie, 18–19, 245n.36
Ricoeur, Paul, 214; on "second naïveté," 209
ring. *See* jewelry
Rip van Winkle, 131
Rivière, Joan, "Womanliness as Masquerade," 200

robot, 160, 169–70. *See also* cloning
Rogers, Ginger, 13, 19–20, 205, 216, 240n.44
Roheim, Geza, 143
romance, as genre, 68, 93–94, 100. *See also* Family
  Romance
Roth, Philip, 74, 184, 220
Rousseau, Jean-Jacques, 193
Roy, Bimal, 133, 246n.1. *See also* director
Russell, Anna, 53–54

Sabbath, 12, 234 n.11. *See also* Jew
sacrifice, 119–20, 234n.18
Said, Edward, 12
Salome, 230
samsara (cycle of transmigration), 115, 205, 207,
  209, 220, 230. *See also* incarnation; karma
  theory
Santa Claus, 18, 76–77, 140
scar, 138, 145–47, 151–53, 155–56, 160–61, 170–71. *See
  also* mark; tattoo
Schleiermacher, Friedrich, 214
Schwarzenegger, Arnold, 25–26, 177–80, 246n.11
science, "black" or evil, 163, 168–73, 177–81, 218
Seabiscuit, 223
secretary, 98–99, 101, 104–5, 127, 242n.24
September 11, 2001, 21, 26, 242n.19
shadow, 125, 244n.45
Shakespeare, William, 3, 56, 73, 189–90; and Hollywood, 5, 75–76, 80, 200; *All's Well That Ends
  Well*, 68, 70, 245n.33; *Antony and Cleopatra*,
  247n.14; *As You Like It*, 78, 190–94, 210, 216, 218,
  247nn.14–15, 247n.18; *Cymbeline*, 68–69, 80, 93;
  Hamlet, 15, 70, 247n.14; *King Lear*, 193; *Measure
  for Measure*, 238n.24; *A Midsummer Night's
  Dream*, 247n.14; *Much Ado about Nothing*, 68,
  80; *Othello*, 21, 68; *Pericles*, 70; *The Taming of the
  Shrew*, 247n.14; *Twelfth Night*, 76, 190, 247n.14;
  The Winter's Tale, 16, 68–73, 75, 80, 82, 93, 100,
  154–55; *The Compleat Works of Wllm Shakspr
  (Abridged)*, 68
Shelley, Mary, 168–69
Shepherd, Cybill, 130–31
Short Lay of Siegfried, The, 58
Siegfried and Brünnhilde, 40–59, 62–64, 81,
  87, 90–92, 99, 106, 122, 131, 150, 169–70, 178,
  192, 237n.4, 237n.14, 238n.23, 238nn.26–27,
  238nn.29–30, 238–9n.31
Simpson, O. J., 26
skinning, 142, 145–46. *See also* face-lift
slave woman. *See* maid
Sleeping Beauty, 131
sloughing, 142–44, 161, 230. *See also* face-lift
Snow White, 69
Sontag, Susan, 12

spaceship, 168, 169, 176
Spark, Muriel, 140
special effects, 24
spell. See enchantment
spy. See espionage
Stalin, Josef, 218
Stallone, Sylvester, 25, 244n.53
Stanwyck, Barbara, 74; as Jean, *The Lady Eve*, 86–89, 116, 155
Star Trek, 169, 176
statue, 16–17, 66, 67, 69, 71, 73, 157, 214. *See also* image
Stein, Gertrude, 15, 186
Steinem, Gloria, 200
Stern, Richard, 213
Stevenson, Robert Louis, 168
Stewart, James, for president, 24; as Scottie, *Vertigo*, 163–68, 246nn.1–2
Stoppard, Tom, 8, 189
stripping, 11, 180, 230. *See also* dancing
Sturges, Preston, 18, 85, 109, 206. *See also* director
Sulawesi, 142–43
Sullivan, Ed, 14
superhero, 26, 212. *See also* Batman, Thousand-Masks
Swinburne, Algernon, 15; "An Interlude," 41
sword, in bed (barrier between lovers), 45, 50–51, 55–56, 58–64, 78, 89, 93, 99; as phallic symbol, 59, 62–63; in stone, 239n.34

tail, of Chippendale Mupp (Dr. Seuss character), 112, 178; of Eeyore (Winnie-the-Pooh character), 114
tango, 26–27, 180
Taravati. See Chandrashekhara and Taravati
Tarnhelm (magic helmet of transformation), 54–56
tattoo, 147. *See also* mark; scar
Taylor, Elizabeth, 107, 157, 237n.24; as Barbara, *Ash Wednesday*, 147–48, 159
Taylor, Robert, 92, 97, 241n.2
television, 12, 21, 25, 79, 151, 179, 182, 212, 223, 242nn.21–22, 251n.85; reality television, 22–23, 25, 157; soap opera, 23
Tenn, William, "The Discovery of Morniel Mathaway," 17
Tennyson, Alfred, Lord, "Enoch Arden," 78, 91, 240n.25
terrorism, in films, 152, 163
Thidreks Saga, 41–43, 45–46, 48–50, 53, 58–59, 99, 237nn.4–5, 238n.26
Thousand-Masks, Mexican wrestler-hero, 230
time travel, 37, 115, 129, 162. *See also* cryogenic freezing

transparent body, 134. *See also* invisibility
transsexual surgery, 158–59, 210
trans-species surgery, 158
treasure, buried, 208
tree, of Bishop Berkeley, 103, 204
trichotomy, of mind, body, and soul, 171
triple cross, 10, 21, 28, 31, 38, 72, 81, 139, 169, 175, 177, 180, 186, 189, 219, 224, 227–28, 234n.1, 246n.7
Tristan and Isolde, 59–62, 64–65, 87, 122, 178, 221–22, 237n.8, 241n.4, 250n.58
Trobriand Islands. See Papua New Guinea
Tukaram (Maharashtrian poet-saint), 22
Turner, Lana, 20, 74–75
Twain, Mark, 105, 183
twin, 61, 66, 68, 91, 97, 121–22, 152, 158. *See also* cloning; double

understudy, 32–33
underwear, 20, 83
uniform, 24, 195
Upanishads, 118, 133, 135

vampire, 19, 132
vasana, "perfume" of former life, 113. *See also* déjà vu; karma theory
vaudeville, 104, 107. *See also* dancing
veil, 30, 46, 68–69, 73, 122, 153–56, 165, 200, 206, 230. *See also* costume; curtain
Venn diagram, 7–8. *See also* Zen diagram
vertigo, 163–64, 167, 184
Viagra, 132
Vidal, Gore, 24, 26, 235n.62
Vidor, King, 74. *See also* director
virginity, 42–43, 45, 47, 49–50, 53, 55, 59, 62, 79, 81, 187, 216, 237n.11. *See also* droit du seigneur
Völsunga Saga, 42–47, 49–51, 53–59, 63, 237n.4, 237n.12, 237n.15, 238n.26, 238n.29, 238n.31
Vonnegut, Kurt, 212

Wagner, Richard, 3, 61, 238n.23; and movie music, 53; *Das Liebesverbot*, 238n.24; *The Ring of the Nibelung*, 40–41, 51, 52–58, 237n.2, 237n.4, 238n.26, 238–39n.31; *Siegfried*, 53, 238n.24, 238n.28; *The Twilight of the Gods* (*Götterdämmerung*), 53, 54, 170, 238n.27, 238n.30; *Die Walküre*, 238n.31
war, 26, 49, 117; First World, 94–97, 102, 104, 106, 210, 242n.23; Second World, 24, 104–5, 107, 109, 176, 184, 238n.23, 238n.28; Spanish Civil, 175; Vietnam, 174
Warner, Jack, 24
Waugh, Evelyn, 37
waxwork, 13. *See also* dummy, statue
Welles, Orson, 16, 217. *See also* director